Real Estate Finance

Robert Rico, Carolee Rico, and Chase Milner
Published by US Realty School, LLC

Real Estate Finance

AUTHORS
Robert Rico
Carolee Rico
Chase Milner

CONTENTS

CHAPTER 1
SAFE ACT AND LENDERS

CHAPTER 2
FEDERAL HOUSING ACTS, LAWS AND DISCLOSURES

CHAPTER 3
MORTGAGE LOAN DISCLOSURES: TRID

CHAPTER 4
REAL ESTATE SETTLEMENT PROCEDURES ACT - RESPA

CHAPTER 5
FRAUD, ETHICS, AND PREDATORY LENDING

CHAPTER 6
CALIFORNIA SPECIFIC REAL ESTATE INDUSTRY

CHAPTER 7
LOAN APPLICATION AND TRANSMITTAL SUMMARY

CHAPTER 8
CREDIT

CHAPTER 9
QUALIFYING INCOME

CHAPTER 10
VERIFICATION AND DOCUMENTATION

CHAPTER 11
LOAN PROGRAMS

CHAPTER 12
PURCHASE TRANSACTIONS

CHAPTER 13
APPRAISAL

CHAPTER 14
RATE SHEETS, APPROVAL, AND STORAGE

CHAPTER 15
CLOSING AND TITLE COMPANIES

ACKNOWLEDGEMENTS

US Realty School would like to express its profound gratitude to Deborah Carlisle for her unwavering support and the wealth of expertise she brought to this textbook. Her many years of experience in the real estate industry provided an essential foundation for the concepts and insights presented here. Deborah's notable success in establishing well-regarded real estate education and publishing companies is a testament to her vision and dedication. Above all, her dream of helping students gain their real estate licenses and transform their lives continues to inspire every page of this work, as well as all those who have benefited from her guidance.

We would also like to extend sincere thanks to the following individuals for their invaluable contributions to the development of these materials. Their diligence, creativity, and commitment were instrumental in ensuring the clarity and quality of this textbook:

Michelle C. North
Elias Magers

Together, their efforts have enriched this textbook and helped bring it to fruition. It is with deep appreciation that we acknowledge each of these remarkable contributors, whose efforts have truly made a meaningful difference.

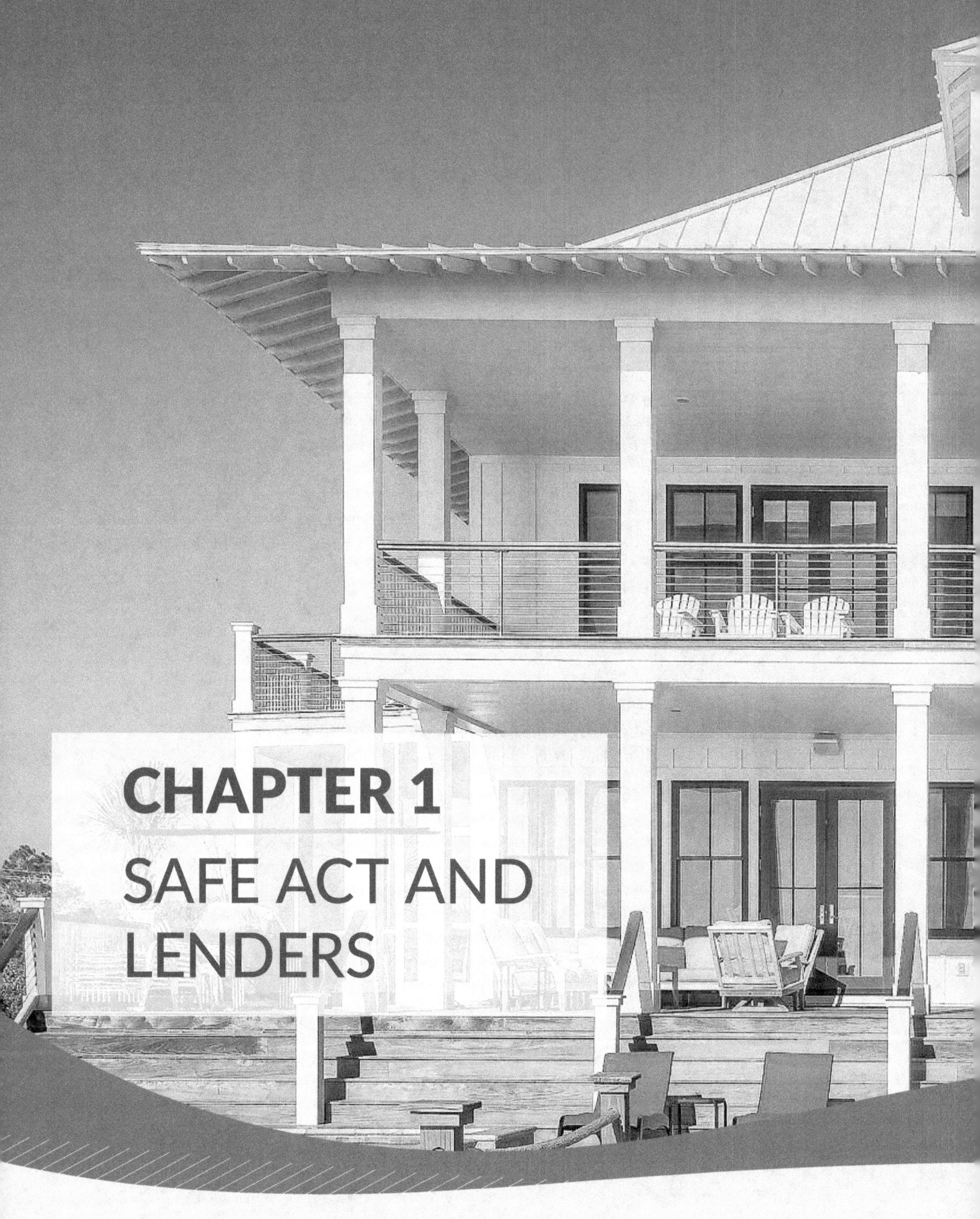

CHAPTER 1
SAFE ACT AND LENDERS

MORTGAGE AND LENDER LICENSING

SAFE ACT SENATE BILL 36

The Secure and Fair Enforcement for Mortgage Licensing (SAFE) Act was implemented as a part of the Housing and Economic Recovery Act of 2008 to place federal controls on the mortgage industry. Through this act, mortgage loan originators (MLOs) have new licensing requirements. Most states have implemented the SAFE Act and those states that do not comply with the federal requirements will only have HUD and government loans. Those loans are available through MLOs or mortgage brokers or lenders not working as a federally insured bank or institution in the future. (As of this writing, only three states have not complied with the SAFE Act: Nevada, Texas, Missouri, and Minnesota.)

The SAFE Act prohibits individuals from doing business as residential mortgage loan originators without annually obtaining the following:

- Registration as registered mortgage loan originators and a unique identifier (federal registration) for individuals who are employees of a covered financial institution.
- For all other individuals, a state license and registration as state-licensed mortgage loan originators, and a unique identifier (state licensing/registration).

The SAFE Act requires that federal registration and state licensing/registration be accomplished through the same online registration system, the Nationwide Mortgage Licensing System and Registry (NMLS&R). The objectives of the SAFE Act include:

- Aggregating and improving the flow of information to and between regulators.
- Providing increased accountability and tracking of MLOs.
- Enhancing consumer protections.
- Supporting anti-fraud measures.
- Providing consumers with easily accessible information at no charge regarding the employment history of and publicly adjudicated disciplinary and enforcement actions against MLOs.

The MLO endorsement will have a Nationwide Identification Number known as a "UNIQUE IDENTIFIER" assigned by the NMLS&R. The term and license number of the original or base real estate license will not change and the licensee will be responsible for the continued filing of the license renewal as required by the DRE. The MLO Designation will remain a separate license from the NMLS&R endorsement.

NATIONWIDE MORTGAGE LICENSING SYSTEM AND REGISTRY (NMLS&R), more commonly known as **NMLS**, is an online database where licensees are required to register. The NMLS contains a single license record for each mortgage lender, broker, branch, and mortgage loan originator (MLO). No fee will be required to create the initial NMLS&R base record for those already working in the industry.

In order to obtain a license, the licensee must satisfy the federal requirements as well as requirements specific to each state in which they plan to work. Requirements include:
- Federal examination.
- State examination(s).
- Background check.
- Credit report.
- Fingerprints.

The NMLS NATIONAL EXAM will only need to be taken once and is valid anywhere in the United States; however, the individual states will provide state-specific requirements and an examination for licensing laws and practices. A separate test for the state-specific NMLS licensing exam will be required. Some states may have reciprocity with other states and the MLO will need to determine the requirements of each state where they plan to work. Eight hours of continuing education is required for an annual renewal of the NMLS registration.

A **"UNIQUE IDENTIFIER"** is a nationwide identification number assigned by the NMLS&R to each person applying and registering for the MLO endorsement. The term and license number of the original or base real estate or mortgage lender's license that was obtained from the individual's state will not change, and the licensee will be responsible for the continued filing of the license renewal as required by the state agency. The state license will remain a separate license from the MLO designation through the NMLS&R endorsement.

The unique identifier is required to be on all loan applications taken by the individual. The purpose is to provide an immediate link between the MLO and any loans that have a problem in the future including the inability to pay or fraud.

SENATE BILL 36 was enacted in October 2009 to identify real estate licensees conducting mortgage activities. It also requires that all states follow the federal *Secure and Fair Enforcement Mortgage License Act (SAFE Act)* of the *Housing and Economic Recovery Act of 2008.*

The Federal SAFE Act for Residential Loan Originators requires all states to adhere to minimum Residential Mortgage Loan Originator License requirements. The Conference of State Bank Supervisors (CSBS) and the American Association of Residential Mortgage Regulators (AARMR) created, and will maintain, the Nationwide Mortgage Licensing System and Registry (NMLS&R) as the basis for state licensing. The NMLS&R will contain a single license record for each mortgage loan lender, broker, branch, and mortgage loan originator that can be used to apply for, amend, and renew a license in any state. For further information, see the NMLS&R Resource Center at www.dre.ca.gov or www.mortgage.nationwidelicensingsystem.org.

The **SAFE ACT PROHIBITS** an **MLO** License if an applicant has:
- **Felony conviction** involving an act of:
  - Fraud.
  - Dishonesty.
  - Breach of trust.
  - Money laundering.
  - Any felony within the seven years before filing an application for the endorsement.
- **Revoked loan originator license** in any governmental jurisdiction.
- **Demonstrated a lack of financial responsibility** by showing disregard in management of their finances.

REQUIREMENTS for all licensees who conduct Residential Mortgage Loan Originator (MLO) activities to qualify for the MLO real estate license endorsement are as follows:
- Obtain a unique identifier number from NMLS&R.
- Pass the national written exam (100 questions).
- Pass the California state-specific components of the SAFE written exam.

- Complete 20-hours of pre-license education. (Some licensees may have met the requirements through their state licensing education).
- File an online MLO License Endorsement Application (MU4) and pay the fee on the NMLS&R website.
- Submit a new set of fingerprints using an NMLS&R live scan vendor. Vendor information is available in the application process.
- Provide authorization to run a credit report.

DEROGATORY CREDIT EXPLANATIONS may be acceptable. Bankruptcy or foreclosure activity within the previous three years may not be acceptable. If disqualified, the MLO may reapply after the 3-year period has passed.

Loan processors and underwriters are also required to be licensed under the NMLS&R if they are working as independent contractors. If direct employees or W2 employees of the broker or lender, they will not be required to become licensed.

CALIFORNIA SPECIFIC SAFE ACT

Through this act, mortgage loan originators in California have new licensing requirements as of January 1, 2010.

The licensee must also register on the *Nationwide Mortgage Licensing System and Registry (NMLS&R)*. The NMLS&R will contain a single license record for each mortgage lender, broker, branch, and mortgage loan originator (MLO). No fee will be required to create the initial NMLS&R base record for those already working in the industry.

The licensee must satisfy the federal requirements to obtain an MLO License. Requirements include new qualification assessments:
- Federal examinations.
- State examinations.
- Background checks.

California licensees are required to notify the DRE to obtain a licensing designation as an MLO. This designation is required to be on the license of anyone engaged in the mortgage industry who make, arrange, or service loans secured by real property both residential and commercial.

Licensees currently active in the mortgage industry must complete a report to the DRE at *www.dre.ca.gov* using **Form 866, Mortgage Loan Activity Notification.**

Initial MLO endorsements for those already working as mortgage loan originators are required to obtain the required endorsements as follows:

- The federal MLO license endorsement is required to be renewed and issued annually.
- Future licensees will proceed with the DRE or CFL licensing requirements, meet the NMLS 20-hour education requirements, and take both the federal and the state-specific examination prior to becoming an MLO.

Failure by those actively working as a mortgage loan originators to submit Form 866 may result in the assessment and penalty fees of:

- Fifty dollars ($50) per day for the first 30 days
- One hundred dollars ($100) per day for every day thereafter up to a maximum of $10,000.

These fines will apply in the future to any person acting as an MLO without the appropriate licensing and endorsement.

MORTGAGE LENDER OR MORTGAGE BANKER

A MORTGAGE LENDER OR MORTGAGE BANKER is a company that lends its own money or lends directly to the borrower. Mortgage lenders and bankers may become licensed as one or more of a variety of legal entities, but usually work under the same type of licensing as the mortgage broker with whom they work. It is advisable to obtain licensing as a bank if operating as a mortgage lender/banker. *There are many considerations when choosing licensure, and legal advice is recommended prior to entering into this area of the mortgage industry.*

Once a mortgage broker lends their own money or money that they control ten times or more within a 12-month period, they become a mortgage lender or banker. Most mortgage brokers do not close loans in their own name or loan their own money.

NOTE

When a broker lends their own funds or are in control of the funds being lent, they must disclose this fact to the borrower.

Brokers may choose to put together a group of private investors in order to control the funds being lent. This is often done to provide funds or loans to borrowers with credit issues or properties that may not meet conventional lending standards such as sub-prime or construction loans. Private investor funds are commonly used in the sub-prime lending market and in economically difficult times.

PORTFOLIO LENDERS are lenders who retain the loans that they fund for servicing. Portfolio lenders underwrite, fund using their own money, close, and maintain the loans in-house. Loans from portfolio lenders are typically not sold on the secondary mortgage market.

SERVICING is the process of maintaining the loan transaction from the point of closing forward, which includes collecting payments, providing late notices, paying funds from escrow accounts, adding fees to the balance, implementing foreclosure proceedings, and any other duties involved in maintaining loan records.

WHOLESALE LENDERS are the lenders with whom mortgage brokers typically work. The broker is the contact with the public, making them "retail" lenders, while wholesale lenders lend money to retail lenders and are generally not available to the public.

There are lenders that are both wholesale and retail such as Bank of America or Wells Fargo Bank. This places them in a situation of being a competitor to the mortgage broker who is also their client. When a broker has submitted a loan to a lender who works both ways, the lender will not accept a loan from that same borrower while the broker's loan is open and will not accept a loan from another broker for the same borrower during that time period.

SECONDARY MORTGAGE MARKET

SECONDARY MORTGAGE MARKET is a term used to describe the buying and selling of mortgages between lenders and investors. This typically involves banks or other lenders selling mortgages to investors in order to get their money back, and the investors, in turn, earn higher returns than they would with other kinds of investments. Lenders on the secondary mortgage market are not available to the public and may, in fact, be largely unknown to the public. The secondary mortgage market lender is generally made up of investors or groups of people investing their money. *Wall Street or the stock market is an example of an entity that sells bonds or interest in real estate paper for the public.*

The secondary mortgage market lenders generally provide funds to wholesale lenders by buying closed loans then hiring the lenders to service the loans after they have been purchased.

An analogy that helps explain these relationships is a grocery store. The public goes to the retail grocery store to purchase their food. The grocery store purchases the food from the wholesale supplier. The wholesale supplier goes to the farmer or food producer to obtain the food for distribution the same as the wholesale lender goes to the secondary mortgage market or the investor for money to lend.

Lenders have contractual agreements with the secondary mortgage market investors, such as the Federal National Mortgage Association (FNMA) or Fannie Mae, and the Federal Home Loan Mortgage Corporation (FHLMC) or Freddie Mac, to sell large blocks of loans at a certain interest rate by a pre-determined date. *For example, on the day the loan is locked, the lender makes a commitment to the investor to ship a specified dollar value of loans by a certain date. From the date of closing, the lender has a short period of time, usually about ten days, to put the package together in the Secondary mortgage market's stacking order and prepare the package for shipping and delivery for sale to the Secondary mortgage market on the secondary mortgage market.* It is very important that the wholesale lender's shipper follows through with any post-funding documentation required, *such as the *HUD-1,* to accommodate the sale of the loan to the investor within the allotted time frame.

* **The HUD-1 settlement statement is a document that lists all charges and credits to the buyer and to the seller in a real estate settlement, or all the charges in a mortgage refinance. If you applied for a mortgage on or before October 3, 2015, or if you are applying for a reverse mortgage, you receive a HUD-1. In transactions that do not include a seller, such as a refinance loan, the settlement agent may use the shortened HUD-1A form. If you applied for a mortgage after October 3, 2015, for most kinds of mortgage loans you receive a form called the Closing Disclosure instead of a HUD-1 (*Consumer Financial Protection Bureau*).**

The lender ships a block of loans to the investor who, in turn, has their underwriters perform a cursory review of the loan packages. A block of loans is a predetermined or contractual amount of loans to be delivered by a set date. The block is usually set in a dollar amount of the loans such as a package of loans totaling $50,000,000. They perform what is called due-diligence underwriting, which is a cursory review and will verify the documentation that is in the file.

If the package is unacceptable or does not meet their guidelines, they will require the lender to repurchase the loan package or provide additional documentation to make the loan acceptable. Occasionally the lender will need to find a different investor to buy the loan and may lose money by selling the loan for less than face value.

CORRESPONDENT LENDING

CORRESPONDENT LENDING allows the broker to fund loans in their own name yet remain a broker. The name of the lender is the one that appears on the loan documents, but by being a correspondent lender, the broker's name will appear on the loan documents as the lender. This is a way of instilling confidence in the borrower, as borrowers often prefer dealing directly with the lender. Additionally, this program also offers several laws and advertising benefits that are available to bankers and not brokers.

Brokers may also choose to be a correspondent lender for a number of other reasons, including having someone in-house who can perform the following functions:

- **Underwriter** to approve and sign-off on the loans.
- **Document Drawer** to prepare the loan documents.
- **Funder** to fund and close the loan.
- **Escrow** to provide the services of escrow.

These in-house services expedite the loan process considerably. It is conceivable that a loan can be closed in a few days' time when the entire process is overseen by a correspondent lender. This method of doing business has incredible advantages, **but bear in mind that with that comes increased liability.** It is not advisable for an inexperienced broker to work as a correspondent broker since the broker of record is ultimately responsible for the actions of everyone in their employ.

To become a correspondent lender, it is necessary for a lender to arrange a line of credit for the broker. The broker then funds loans in their own name. The broker is borrowing the funds from the lender in order to make a loan to the borrower. As soon as the loan is closed through escrow, the broker forwards the loan file and transfers or sells the loan to the actual lender, who then credits the broker's line of credit making the funds available to fund additional loans.

Correspondent lending is a contractual agreement and can be revoked at any time. Brokers are usually only allowed to work as a correspondent lender with one

> **NOTE**
>
> *Lending law prohibits the closing of a loan in less than seven days from the signing of the loan application.*

lender at a time; however, they may be allowed to work with more than one lender, which would enable them to widen their capabilities and loan products available.

Correspondent lenders will usually operate their business as a retail lender which allows them more flexibility in the service they provide to the borrower. They may also operate as a wholesale lender, meaning that they are acting as a mortgage lender offering their services to other brokers.

Caution should be used when operating as a wholesale lender. The correspondent lender must avoid competing with their broker clients for borrower clients. The broker must also be aware that the correspondent lender may need to charge higher fees than a mortgage banker in order to make a profit.

MORTGAGE BROKER

MORTGAGE BROKER is a person or company acting as an agent for a consumer with the purpose of obtaining for them a mortgage or a loan secured by real property. Each state has its own licensing requirements for the operation of a mortgage broker. A mortgage broker, like a **mortgage loan originator,** takes a loan application with a consumer/borrower and compiles a package for submission to a lender or mortgage bank for approval. The mortgage broker works with the lender to obtain all pertinent documentation for the completion and closing of the loan on behalf of the borrower.

A MORTGAGE LOAN ORIGINATOR (MLO) is an individual who works to obtain a loan secured by real property with the expectation of monetary compensation or gain. The MLO has the ultimate responsibility for the loan transaction.

BORROWER is the party in a mortgage loan transaction who receives money or a loan instrument that acts as security against their property. In exchange for the money or mortgage loan, the borrower promises to repay the debt under specified terms that are spelled out in the note.

*The borrower may also be referred to as the **customer, client,** or **consumer** depending on the local customs. They are also the buyers in a real estate purchase transaction.*

Borrowers must be a United States citizen or have proof as a resident alien and must be of legal age to sign documents. Legal age is 18 years old unless any of the following apply:

- Married.
- Active duty in the US Military.
- Emancipated by a court of law.

An **EMPLOYMENT CONTRACT** is required between the broker of record and each MLO/licensee in their employ if the licensee is to be considered self-employed. If there is no contract, the licensee is considered an employee and must be paid accordingly, with taxes withheld and a W2 provided at the end of the tax year for income tax reporting purposes.

The Employment Contract should clearly state:
- Terms of employment.
- Terms and method of payment.
- Commission- (1099).
- Wages- (W2).
- Use of the broker's office space and equipment.
- Membership requirements such as the Multiple Listing Service (MLS) or The California Association of Realtors (CAR).

Technically, contract employees are not employees of the broker, but rather are "self- employed" and working under the authority of the broker of record. Most loan officers are contract employees and receive a 1099 at the end of the tax year from the broker showing the amount of pay received for income tax purposes. A self- employed loan officer is responsible for paying their own taxes, and it is advisable to file IRS quarterly tax withholding to avoid large payments and fines to the IRS when filing annual tax returns.

BORROWER PAID FEES require payment of the mortgage broker fees/ commission through close of escrow (COE). Federal regulations require that the mortgage loan originator must be paid as a W2 or salaried employee. Rebate pricing may be used to pay the borrower's fees when the borrower is paying the broker commission fees directly. All costs of the loan may also be paid from the rebate, such as appraisal, escrow, title, etc. when the costs are borrower-paid.

LENDER PAID FEES are paid by the lender and the MLO may be paid as a commission employee or 1099. Lender-paid fees are accomplished by increasing the interest rate to pay the broker fees through rebate pricing which creates a *yield spread premium (YSP)*. Once the broker has determined that they will use the "lender paid fees" option, they must set the amount they will charge, and that amount is set for all loans that are paid by the lender or as YSP.

"Lender paid fees" may only be used to pay the lender, the mortgage broker, and the direct non-recurring-closing-costs (NRCCS) involved in financing. Brokers should always check for compliance with TRID when utilizing YSP.

A CONTRACT EMPLOYEE will file their income on IRS Schedule C (Profit and Loss for Self-Employed) unless they are paid W2 income. W2 employees may deduct their business expenses on Schedule A under "non-reimbursed employee expenses." It is important to retain accurate expense and mileage records for the allowable income tax deductions.

It is crucial to consult a tax professional when starting a business in order to be aware of the expenses and to maintain the most accurate records possible. An appointment book or "Day-Timer" is recommended to help in verify and justify records such as mileage. Noting the miles driven to any business appointment in the appointment book is acceptable proof of mileage deductions for the IRS. An electronic device may not be advisable as the information may be lost with equipment failure. A hardcopy version is less likely to be lost or destroyed.

CLERICAL OR OFFICE EMPLOYEES are generally employees of the company and are paid either salary or wages earned. Processors or underwriters doing work for a mortgage company must be W2 employees or have an NMLS unique identifier number as a registered MLO. Unlicensed contract employees of a mortgage broker, as well as anyone in the mortgage industry who is required to be licensed and registered, are not allowed to represent themselves or work independently.

Loan Processors and underwriters are individuals who perform clerical support by obtaining information and documentation to create a complete, saleable loan file. It is the underwriter, specifically, who reviews loan application files and approves loans on behalf of the lender.

An individual working solely as a loan processor or underwriter may not represent themselves to the public as one who is licensed or capable of engaging in loan origination activities in either written or oral communication.

LOAN OPERATING SYSTEMS (LOS)

LOAN OPERATING SYSTEMS (LOS) are available in a variety of either Apple or Windows driven programs. Some of the more commonly used programs are **GENESIS, CONTOUR, and CALYX POINT.** There are also several available websites for use, such as **Encompass.** Once you are familiar with one program, it is easy to adapt to the others. The computer will generate the forms that will be required by the lender, including the all disclosures, verifications, and the 1003. All LOS program providers will provide necessary updates, as laws and required forms change periodically. The broker must update the program in order to maintain compliance.

When emailing or faxing files or forms on behalf of the client, the broker must verify security and confidentiality. Emailed information must always be password protected. *It has been customary practice to include the password in the email to which the confidential information is attached. This is a violation of the federal E-sign Act. The client's personal information is not protected when the password to open the confidential file is in the same email. Sending a separate email or even a phone call to provide the secure password is a better practice.* All activities using computers for client information must be e-sign compliant, according to standards of the Federal Reserve Board.

NOTE

The LOS must be managed with confidentiality in mind. Computers containing personal information must always be password protected, and loan application files must be locked in a secure area or filing cabinet within the broker's office. Firewalls and security programs are essential on all computers used for loan processing.

CHAPTER 2

FEDERAL HOUSING ACTS, LAWS AND DISCLOSURES

HISTORY OF FINANCE

Financing has a history as old as mankind with the roots of our modern financial system first appearing in the Roman Empire. The word **"fiduciary"** is commonly used in the modern real estate and finance industries. Meaning "a relationship of trust, the word fiduciary originated from the Latin word "fides," which means faith or trust. Money also originated from the Roman use of government-authorized coins. This now includes coins and paper money. The word money comes from the Latin word "moneta," which described the accepted form of exchange which, in that era, was coins.

IN THE MIDDLE AGES, the system known as feudalism developed. Under feudalism, all land belonged to the king. Land was owned as a life estate, which means that ownership lasted only for the duration of their life. Ownership reverted to the king upon the death of the property owner. The king gave land to people known as lords as a reward for loyalty or service to the king, especially in war. **Fee simple estates** was the type of ownership given by the king as a means of providing maximum property ownership. The term "fee simple" is still used to describe the maximum ownership available. These gifts of land created earls, dukes, and other titles distinguishing the landowner.

Serfs were at the bottom of society and were the majority of the population. Serfs were considered chattel, or property, of the landowner. They held no rights and existed in a state similar to slavery. Loans for purchasing real estate did not exist during the medieval period; however, borrowing money using real estate as security was a widespread practice. This was called **"pledging"** property or using the property as a "pawn." As is the practice today, the property would be taken in exchange for repayment of the debt in case of default.

USURY is defined as an excessive charge of interest rates. During the Middle Ages, usury was defined as the use of interest rates. The Catholic Church exercised tremendous influence in Europe at the time, and did not allow the use of interest, therefore charging interest was considered usury. Other religions did not have the same prohibition and charged interest on loans. The lenders were often viewed as unscrupulous because of this, but the practice nevertheless formed the basis for the banking system.

NOTE

Usury does not exist in mortgage lending.

THE KNIGHTS TEMPLAR, a religious order of knights during the Crusades, provided a number of financial services that are often seen as the foundation for modern banking. This took place in the latter half of the Middle Ages, a time when travel and trade were expanding to other kingdoms and countries, necessitating a greater variety of financial services. The Crusades, as well as increased travel, created a need for notes that could be carried with less fear of theft, much like today's checks, travelers' checks, and credit cards. A person could deposit their money with a party at the onset of their trip and obtain a note documenting the amount of funds available to cover their expenses as they travelled.

Kings in the Middle Ages were frequently engaged in war, which was costly. As a means to finance the wars, they would often borrow from the Knights Templar. The loans were generally secured by real estate within the king's realm. The Knights Templar created a system of underwriting the loans to determine any risk that might be incurred in making the loans.

THE RENAISSANCE brought the financing of European expeditions to far-flung parts of the world. Several wealthy and powerful families of the period made a business of lending money and financing merchant ventures for trade. The de Medici, Roth, and Fugger are a few of the family names that made banking a common and respectable business.

GOLDSMITH ACCOUNTS were created in London by using paper money in the form of **bearer notes**. The customers, usually merchants, would put their cash on deposit with the Goldsmiths and in exchange, they were given receipts of an equal amount. The receipts themselves were used to pay debts rather than withdrawing the cash from the Goldsmiths. Because they were used to pay debts, they were named bearer notes, allowing the holder of the note to collect the funds or use it to pay a debt or purchase goods.

The account holders left much of their money on deposit with the Goldsmiths, allowing the Goldsmiths to use the money held in accounts to lend to others. They were able to charge interest on the loans and share the profits with the depositors by paying interest on the deposit accounts, basically the same way banks pay on savings accounts today.

STOCK SUBSCRIPTION was a creation of the large trading companies such as the East India Company and the Hudson Bay Company. By purchasing a stock or investing in a company, an individual was able to own a portion of a business and its profits. Once the stocks were sold and the company collected the investors' money, the company would occasionally need additional funds to operate the business. To generate additional funds, a company would issue bonds.

BONDS are debt instruments that guarantee to pay the bearer the original amount borrowed plus a specified amount if cashed-in at a specified date. The additional funds represent interest to be paid for the loan or investment. If a bond was sold prior to the specified date, it was sold for less than the principal amount. The reduced amount is the discount based on a percentage of the principal and is therefore called the **discount points**.

During the **AMERICAN REVOLUTION**, the new government needed to fund the war effort and issued paper money called "**fiat money**," which was issued by decree. Fiat money is always inflationary because it is issued without the purpose of raising or creating money in spite of the economic climate and without solid backing of gold or other value. Paper money was not trusted after the war, causing the U.S Constitution to state that any printed money must be "**legal tender**" for gold or silver. In other words, paper money must have equal value in gold or silver similar to the Goldsmith Notes that were created many years earlier in England.

During the EARLY YEARS OF THE UNITED STATES, banking was not regulated and the early to mid-1800s witnessed what was often referred to as "**wildcat banking**." The term expressed the lack of controls and regulations on the banking industry, as well as the chartering of banks in remote, sparsely settled frontier areas that were more accessible to wildcats than to people. Banks were unaccountable for their actions and about one-third of them were fraudulent. After many years of unstable banking, the **National Banking Act of 1863** set a minimum amount of reserves and capital for all banks applying for a National Bank Charter.

Nationally chartered banks were restricted from mortgage lending or making loans using real property as security. Most borrowers obtained balloon loans that were due and payable in five (5) years.

THE FEDERAL RESERVE ACT OF 1913 was enacted to resolve banking issues and created a central bank for the United States. The *Federal Reserve System*, also known as the **Fed**, is responsible for controlling the flow of money, therefore managing the economy by controlling the monetary policy. The Federal Reserve Bank is also responsible for regulating the cost of money and credit. Some of the main duties of the Fed are to perform and otherwise oversee the following:

- **Establish the interest rate**, which is also called the discount rate that member banks must pay when they borrow money from the Fed.
- **Control the reserve rate** that a bank is required to maintain.
- **Buy and sell government securities** to generate cash flow or available funds.

The Fed establishes INTEREST RATES that are charged to member banks when they borrow money from the FED. The member bank in turn may lend money to other member banks within their district by adding a small profit to the rate that they paid, thus creating income or profit for the bank. The bank also determines their **prime rate,** an amount based on what they pay for their money plus the amount added on for profit or income for the bank.

> *Example: ABC Bank will be funding a number of mortgage loans by the end of the month and needs to increase their cash reserves, so they borrow money from the Fed. The Fed charges ABC Bank 3.5% interest for the loan.*
>
> *XYZ Bank, another member bank in their District, also needs to borrow funds to increase their reserves so they get a loan from ABC Bank who charges them 4.0%. ABC Bank makes .50% profit on the money they have loaned XYZ Bank over the 3.5% they originally paid the FED for the money.*
>
> *Mr. Smith wants to buy a new car and approaches ABC Bank for a car loan. He is a good customer with a good credit rating. The bank makes the loan to Mr. Smith at their prime interest rate of 6.5%.*
>
> *ABC Bank is now making an additional 3.0% profit on the money loaned to Mr. Smith from the money they borrowed from the Fed at 3.5%. The bank will also make money by loaning funds that are on deposit with either certificate of deposits or savings accounts. If the bank pays Mr. Jones 4.5% on his savings account, they can loan the same funds to another bank customer for 7.5%, making a profit of 3.0%.*

When the Fed Chairman makes an announcement that they are changing the interest rate, it affects everyone in a variety of ways, from the interest they pay on loans to the money they earn on investments.

RESERVE RATE is the percentage of deposits held by the bank that must be available for customer withdrawal at any time. Many bank failures during the Depression of the 1930s occurred because the individual banks did not hold enough of their cash reserves to cover customer withdrawals from their savings accounts. When customers became scared that their bank was going to close, they made what was called a "**run on the bank**." That, then, caused more customers to panic and rush to withdraw their money. The banks had not anticipated so many withdrawals and therefore did not have sufficient funds or reserves, with the result being that thousands of banks across the country had to close their doors.

The Fed now regulates the amount of cash that banks must hold in reserve. This control not only protects customer money, but it also helps control the cash flow into the economy. When the Fed decides the economy needs a boost, they will reduce the percentage of cash that banks are required to have in reserve.

> *Example:* ABC Bank has $1,000,000 in customer savings account deposits. The Fed notifies ABC Bank that that the deposit reserve needs to be no less than 65% of the funds in deposits. This means that ABC Bank can loan $350,000 of the $1,000,000 in savings accounts and keep $650,000 available for their customers who may choose to withdraw their money.
>
> Several months later, the Fed contacts ABC Bank and informs them that they need to increase their deposit reserve to a reserve rate of 75%. The Fed has made this decision as a way to slow spending and help prevent inflation. This means that now ABC Bank can loan only $250,000 of available cash deposits and must retain $750,000 in Reserve to have available to its depositors.

The reserve rate is a direct percentage of the funds on deposit.

GOVERNMENT SECURITIES The government can help generate cash flow by selling securities and can slow spending or cash flow by withdrawing the sale of securities. This works in much the same as increasing or decreasing the reserve rate.

Fed banks are divided into twelve regional Federal Reserve Banks governed by the **Board of Governors**. The Board consists of seven members who are appointed by the President of the United States and confirmed by the US Senate for a term of 14 years. The 12th Federal Reserve District is in San Francisco and includes California, Nevada, Arizona, Idaho, Washington, and Oregon. Most banks are members of the Federal Reserve and as of 1980, even non-member banks must adhere to the regulations set forth by the **Federal Reserve Board and Bank**.

The **FEDERAL HOME LOAN BANK SYSTEM OR THE FHL BANK SYSTEM** was established by Congress in 1932. The FHL Bank System established banking districts similar to the regions established by the Fed. California, Nevada, and Arizona are in the FHL Bank System's 11th District. The FHL's organization and purpose are much the same as that of the Fed. In 1989, Congress opened membership in the FHL to all commercial banks and federally insured credit unions.

THE 11TH DISTRICT COST OF FUNDS, or Cofi or Cost of Funds Index, is the index of monthly interest expenses of savings institutions in the 11th District. The index is used to establish the interest rate for variable-rate loans, such as Option ARMs or NegAm (negative amortization) loans.

FEDERAL DEPOSIT INSURANCE CORPORATION (FDIC) was also a result of the Great Depression. It was established in 1933 by Congress to protect bank depositors from losing their money as a result of a bank failure. The FDIC insures consumer bank deposits up to $250,000 per account.

THE FINANCIAL INSTITUTIONS REFORM, RECOVERY, AND ENFORCEMENT ACT (FIRREA) was put in place in 1989 as a way to prevent the fraud and abuses that occurred in the 1980s as a result of the **Depository Institutions Deregulation and Monetary Control Act of 1980**. The purpose of the deregulation was to give thrifts and savings and loans the same benefits as commercial banks. The FDIC assumed the insuring of savings and loans and thrifts, and the Federal Savings and Loan Insurance Corporation (FSLIC) ceased to exist.

NATIONAL HOUSING ACT OF 1934

THE NATIONAL HOUSING ACT OF 1934 was established by President Franklin Roosevelt as part of the New Deal, far-reaching programs and agencies meant to improve the country's economy during the Great Depression. The following organizations were established through the Act:

FEDERAL HOUSING ADMINISTRATION (FHA)
- Provided for fully amortized loans by requiring **monthly Principal and Interest payments.**
- Required the borrowers to provide **mortgage insurance** to protect the lender from loss due to default.
- Required taxes and insurance to be collected with the monthly **principal** and interest payments. This created an **impound account** to guarantee payment for those items.
- Established the **secondary mortgage market**.

FEDERAL DEPOSIT INSURANCE CORPORATION (FDIC)
- Provided **insurance** for the funds deposited into banks which encouraged people to begin using banks without fear of losing their savings account funds.
- Created **more funds** available to lend to the public.
- Encouraged home ownership by creating **practical terms** for the consumer.

FEDERAL SAVINGS AND LOAN INSURANCE CORPORATION (FSLIC)
- Provided **insurance** for the funds deposited into a savings and loan, which encouraged people to begin using banks and savings and loans without fear of losing their savings account funds.
- Created a **mortgage market** for the public.

FEDERAL NATIONAL MORTGAGE ASSOCIATION (FNMA OR FANNIE MAE) was created by Congress in 1938 as a government entity to buy and sell FHA loans on the secondary mortgage market.

Local banks use depositor funds to make loans, but they are only allowed to loan a percentage of funds on deposit. The purpose of retaining a percentage of deposited funds is to ensure that depositors will be able to withdraw funds as needed.

As a means to generate additional funds to lend, a bank will sell mortgages, or "paper," to the secondary mortgage market, or to provide FHA loans which are sold immediately to FHA to reimburse the bank's funds. When the FHA needs to free up money to provide additional loans, they sell mortgage paper to FNMA. In this manner, a lender can generate funds to create new loans.

Congress expanded FNMA in 1944 to include **Veteran's Administration (VA) loans** to accommodate servicemen returning from World War II as part of the **Readjustment Act**. In 1954 FNMA became partly owned by private shareholders along with the federal government.

FNMA was divided into two separate agencies in 1968. These agencies are now overseen by the OFHEO and FHFA:

- **FANNIE MAE** became a federally chartered, stockholder-owned corporation.
- GOVERNMENT NATIONAL MORTGAGE CORPORATION (GINNIE MAE) is a government-owned corporation within the **Department of Housing and Urban Development (HUD) and** was created for special programs that required government subsidies or funding. Today, Ginnie Mae provides funding through **mortgage-backed securities** guaranteed by the federal government against investor loss due to default of the performance of loans.

The **SECONDARY MORTGAGE MARKET** and the mortgage industry evolved further in 1970 when Congress authorized FNMA to buy and sell conventional mortgage loans.

FEDERAL HOME LOAN MORTGAGE CORPORATION (FHLMC OR FREDDIE MAC) was also created at this time for the purpose of creating a secondary mortgage market for savings and loans. Freddie Mac has since expanded to provide a securitized secondary mortgage market for the conventional lending market. In 1971, Freddie Mac created the first pass-through securities, which were called **participant securities**. Fannie Mae then introduced mortgage-backed securities in the early 1980s.

In the late 1970s and early 1980s, the country experienced what is often termed **run- away inflation,** when the prices of goods and services increase at a rapid and uncontrollable rate. The country's economy was negatively affected by high interest rates, which grew to 18.50% for an A-paper mortgage.

Banks were not allowed to pay more than 5.25% interest to their savings account depositors, which caused investors to put their funds into money market accounts that were paying an average of 18% to 25% interest.

Banks that were holding investments in mortgage loans with lower interest rates were unable to sell the paper, as investors could make higher profits elsewhere. Unable to sell the paper, banks were also unable to generate additional funds to make loans without taking losses on the investments they already had.

Fannie Mae and Freddie Mac developed standards in the form of **guidelines** that are the basis of mortgage underwriting throughout the industry today. Freddie Mac now deals in the secondary mortgage market with the handling of securitized investments. These agencies are now controlled by the **Federal Housing & Finance Agency (FHFA)** and the Office of **Federal Housing Enterprise Oversight (OFHEO)**.

LENDERS

LENDERS in the primary mortgage lending market include:
- COMMERCIAL BANKS
- SAVINGS AND LOANS
- CREDIT UNIONS

RETAIL LENDERS are the most frequently used sources for real estate financing. These sources, referred to as retail because they work directly with the public or the consumer, are banks, savings and loans, and other lenders that loan mortgage money directly to the consumer using their own money. Many of these lenders will retain the mortgages, or "**paper,**" and generate income from the collection of interest and fees charged for servicing loans. Servicing a loan involves the various duties performed in collecting payments and managing accounts. When a lender funds a loan with their own funds and keeps the paper, retains the servicing, the lender is called a **portfolio lender**.

The SECONDARY MORTGAGE MARKET is an arena of funds for mortgages and loans using real property as security. Deregulations allowed many of these new sources to create investments such as **mortgage-backed securities.**

When a lender chooses to generate more cash in order to fund more mortgages, they sell some of the mortgages, or paper, that they hold on the secondary mortgage market. The secondary mortgage market is not available to the consumer but only to retail lenders, which are the banks or other entities funding mortgage loans.

MAIN SOURCES or entities in the secondary mortgage market are:

- **WALL STREET MORTGAGE-BACKED SECURITIES:** These are pools of securities sold on Wall Street to investors. The pools generate a steady stream of income from the interest earned on the paper. The pools also generate large pools of funds to be used to buy paper.

- **MORTGAGE BANKERS:** These are institutions licensed under the **California Residential Mortgage Lending Act**, typically regulated by the **Department of Financial Protection and Innovation (DFPI)**. They perform functions similar to a mortgage department within a traditional bank, such as originating, funding, and servicing loans secured by real estate.

- **FEDERAL NATIONAL MORTGAGE ASSOCIATION (FNMA) FANNIE MAE:** A privately-owned corporation that purchases loans on the secondary mortgage market and is backed by and works closely with the Federal Reserve Bank. The Fed assumed control of FNMA in 2008 as a result of failed mortgages and excessive losses due to foreclosures. *www.fanniemae.com*

- **FEDERAL HOME LOAN MORTGAGE CORPORATION (FHLMC) FREDDIE MAC:** A federally backed Private Corporation created by Congress in 1970 and supervised by the Federal Government. Freddie Mac serves the same purpose as Fannie Mae. *www.freddiemac.com*

- **INSURANCE COMPANIES:** Investment funds from insurance companies are used as funds for funding mortgages. It has become a frequent practice for large companies to invest funds, such as retirement funds, in real estate, especially financing mortgages.

GUIDELINES ESTABLISHED BY FANNIEMAE (FNMA) AND FREDDIEMAC (FHLMC) set the guidelines used for conventional loans throughout the industry. Conventional loans are any first trust deeds or mortgages on 1- to- 4-unit residential properties. Conventional loans that meet FNMA/FHLMC guidelines are called **conforming loans** as they conform to FNMA/FHLMC guidelines.

FNMA has established **uniform underwriting,** which will determine such things as **loan-to-value (LTV) and** provides for standard documentation to be provided by the borrower to verify their credit-worthiness.

Loans that do not fall under the conforming loan limits are funded by a variety of other investors and are called **jumbo loans**. Most lenders, including those outside of the FNMA guidelines use many of the guidelines established even when not selling to FNMA.

CONFORMING LOAN LIMITS, as established by FNMA on January 1, 2019, are subject to change as determined by state and county, and should be verified by the broker, lender and the available rate sheets prior to quoting rates and programs to a borrower/ client:

Number of Units	Contiguous States, District of Columbia, and *Puerto Rico		Alaska, Guam, Hawaii, and U.S. Virgin Islands	
	General	High-Cost	General	High-Cost*
1/SFR	$766,550	$1,149,825	$1,149,825	Not Applicable
2/Duplex	$981,500	$1,472,250	$1,472,250	Not Applicable
3/Triplex	$1,186,350	$1,779,525	$1,779,525	Not Applicable
4/Fourplex	$1,474,400	$2,211,600	$2,211,600	Not Applicable

A number of states (including Alaska and Hawaii), Guam, Puerto Rico, and the U.S. Virgin Islands do not have any high-cost areas in 2024.

*Go to https://www.fanniemae.com/singlefamily/loan-limits click on **Loan Limit Look-Up Table 2024 for the most current information.***

GOVERNMENT LOANS

GOVERNMENT LOANS, or government-backed loans, are either through the Veteran's Administration (VA) or through the Federal Housing Administration (FHA). California also offers a VA loan Through the Cal Vet Program.

VA LOANS are loans guaranteed by the federal government for the benefit of all veterans of the United States military. The maximum loan amount has historically been 75% of the FNMA/FHLMC maximum loan amount. The maximum amount changed on January 1, 2002, to be equal to the FNMA/FHLMC guidelines for maximum loan amount. These amounts also now apply to FHA loans.

> ### NOTE
> *Conventional Loans are any 1-to-4-unit residential properties which are not to be confused with conforming loans that refers to loans that conform to FNMA/ FHLMC guidelines.*

- A VA loan is obtained through the usual banking entities with which the broker is approved. The Veteran's Administration then guarantees the loan to the bank. This means that if the veteran defaults on the loan, the VA will assume the loan and oversee the servicing of the loan.

- The Veteran's Administration was created following World War II to help re-introduce returning veterans into civilian life by offering education, loans, and other compensation for their service.

- VA loans allow 100% financing plus closing costs up to 104% of the purchase price or appraised value, whichever is less. VA loans must be fully documented and verify all income and all assets.

MORTGAGE LENDING DISCLOSURES

Both state and federal laws require DISCLOSURES to be provided to the borrower within three business days of signing the loan application. The original loan application is also known as the 1003, or the **Uniform Residential Loan Application (URLA)**. Once the borrower completes and signs the loan application, the following disclosures must be delivered to the borrower within three (3) business days of signing the loan application, if not at the time of taking or receiving the signed application:

LOAN ESTIMATE (LE), formerly GOOD FAITH ESTIMATE (GFE), the federal form required to provide the estimated interest rate, monthly payment, and closing costs that will be required to be paid in order to obtain the loan. This form will be discussed in detail in the following chapter.

CLOSING DISCLOSURE (CD), formerly HUD-1/SETTLEMENT STATEMENT, another federal form that provides final details about the mortgage loan the borrower has selected. It includes the loan terms, projected monthly payments, and the closing costs. This form is further discussed in the following chapter.

SETTLEMENT SERVICE PROVIDER LIST is part of the LE and provides the borrower with the choices that they have in selecting service providers involved in obtaining a residential loan, such as escrow and title companies. If the borrower is not allowed to select the service provider, the form must still be provided and left blank. Some services, such as the credit reporting agency, will be pre-determined because the broker is generally approved to work with only one such agency.

EQUAL CREDIT OPPORTUNITY ACT (ECOA), also known as REGULATION B, explains the consumer's legal rights as required by the federal government. This disclosure explains the federal law prohibiting discriminatory lending and includes the address for the borrower to write if they have a complaint or feel that their civil rights have been violated. *See Figure 1: Equal Credit Opportunity Act (ECOA)*

ECOA prohibits creditors from discriminating against any applicant for a credit transaction for any of the following reasons or categories:
- Race
- Color
- National origin
- Marital status
- Religion
- Age
- Sex
- Receipt of public assistance

ECOA prohibits lenders or creditors from making any discriminatory statements that will prevent or cause a person to not apply for credit based on those statements whether made orally, written, or in any form of advertisement.

A signed copy must be retained in the file as required by law and verifies that the borrower has been given a copy of each and notified of the various rights and laws designed to protect them on a mortgage loan transaction.

Creditors may not inquire whether the borrower is receiving income from child support or alimony. If the borrower chooses to disclose it or if they choose to declare under that section on the loan application, it may be discussed and verification requested, but the person taking the application cannot ask until or unless the borrower declares the source of the income.

Creditors may not request information from a borrower's spouse unless that spouse will be directly involved in the transaction by being obligated to the resulting contract.

The exceptions to this would be if the Borrower is reliant on the spouse's income for qualifying such as if they are receiving child support or separate maintenance, or if the property is in a community property state in which the spouse may be able to claim a right to the property.

When determining a borrower's creditworthiness, the lender must base the decision on the pertinent information provided in the loan file without prejudice. The lender cannot determine that one type of income is more dependable than another without providing evidence to that effect. The lender must use standard, accepted methods of income qualifying. On a stated income loan, the lender must evaluate the stated income based on the probable continuance of that income and treat the statements as true and correct.

INCOME FROM PUBLIC ASSISTANCE must be included for qualifying if the borrower discloses it as qualifying income.

A spouse cannot be excluded from the application because they do not qualify and likewise, the lender cannot require that a spouse be added to the application even though the applicant qualifies on their own. These decisions cannot be influenced by any discrimination against the applicant for any reason, such as sex or familial status.

The lender cannot require that a spouse be added to a loan if the applying spouse does not qualify, but the non-qualifying spouse may choose to add the spouse in order to qualify.

ECOA not only prohibits discrimination in lending, it also does not allow the lender to make unfair demands on an applicant for credit.

ECOA/Regulation B requires that a borrower must receive a response to a loan application within 30 days of receipt of the application. If the application is incomplete, the lender will provide a list of missing items or additional items that are required in order for the lender to be able to make a decision regarding the borrower's creditworthiness. This may be called a **conditional approval** or a **Request for Additional Information**. The borrower then has fifteen business days from the receipt of the request to respond by providing the required information/documentation. If the borrower does not respond within that period, the loan may be cancelled at the lender's discretion.

EQUAL CREDIT OPPORTUNITY ACT

APPLICATION NO:

PROPERTY ADDRESS:

The Federal Equal Credit Opportunity Act prohibits creditors from discriminating against credit applicants on the basis of race, color, religion, national origin, sex, marital status, age (provided the applicant has the capacity to enter into a binding contract); because all or part of the applicant's income derives from any public assistance program; or because the applicant has in good faith exercised any right under the Consumer Credit Protection Act. The Federal Agency that administers compliance with this law concerning this company is the Office of the Comptroller of the Currency, Customer Assistance Group, 1301 McKinney Street, Suite 3710, Houston, Texas 77010

We are required to disclose to you that you need not disclose income from alimony, child support or separate maintenance payment if you choose not to do so.

Having made this disclosure to you, we are permitted to inquire if any of the income shown on your application is derived from such a source and to consider the likelihood of consistent payment as we do with any income on which you are relying to qualify for the loan for which you are applying.

_____		_____	
(Applicant)	(Date)	(Applicant)	(Date)
_____		_____	
(Applicant)	(Date)	(Applicant)	(Date)

4/95

Figure 1: Equal Credit Opportunity Act/ECOA

ADVERSE ACTION NOTICES OR THE STATEMENT OF CREDIT DENIAL is required by ECOA/Regulation B to be delivered to an applicant in writing if the loan application is declined for any reason. The form has a list of possible reasons for the decline, such as unacceptable property, insufficient income, and "withdrawn by applicant," among others. If the reason for the decline of an application is due to unacceptable credit or any credit-related issues, the lender must provide the information that influenced the decision. The name and contact information for the credit repositories is required and there is a space available for that information on the form. This information satisfies both the ECOA requirements and that of the Fair Credit reporting Act.

ECOA requires that the Adverse Action Notice only needs to be delivered to the primary borrower; however, if the reason for decline was based on credit, all co- borrowers must also be provided with a copy of the notice.

BORROWERS SIGNATURE AUTHORIZATION gives the broker authorization to acquire a credit report and other necessary documentation such as the verification of assets. A copy will accompany each request for verification and will also be required before talking to any necessary parties such as the borrower's tax preparer. *See Figure 2, Borrower Signature Authorization* 4506-T authorizes the lender to obtain a copy of the borrower's tax transcripts from the IRS. The purpose is to verify authenticity of the tax returns provided for loan qualification. *See Figure 3, 4506-T*

CREDIT SCORE INFORMATION DISCLOSURE is a disclosure that is required in all loan packages dated July 1, 2001, or later. In the past, the information on a borrower's credit report was not disclosed. As of July 1, 2001, the information must be disclosed in a form that explains the way the credit score works, the borrower's credit score, and the information that has affected their credit score. Also included are the addresses of the credit agency for the borrower to contact to correct any errors in the report. *See Figure 4, Credit Score Information Disclosure*

> **NOTE**
>
> *ECOA/ Regulation B requires that all files for the purpose of obtaining a consumer loan must be retained for a period of 60 months or 5 years.*

Borrower Signature Authorization

Privacy Act Notice: This information is to be used by the agency collecting it or its assignees in determining whether you qualify as a prospective mortgagor under its program. It will not be disclosed outside the agency except as required and permitted by law. You do not have to provide this information, but if you do not your application for approval as a prospective mortgagor or borrower may be delayed or rejected. The information requested in this form is authorized by Title 38, USC, Chapter 37 (if VA); by 12 USC, Section 1701 et. seq. (if HUD/FHA); by 42 USC, Section 1452b (if HUD/CPD); and Title 42 USC, 1471 et. seq., or 7 USC, 1921 et. seq. (if USDA/FmHA).

Part I - General Information

1. Borrower	2. Name and address of Lender/Broker
3. Date 4. Loan Number	

Part II - Borrower Authorization

I hereby authorize the Lender/Broker to verify my past and present employment earnings records, bank accounts, stock holdings, and any other asset balances that are needed to process my mortgage loan application. I further authorize the Lender/Broker to order a consumer credit report and verify other credit information, including past and present mortgage and landlord references. It is understood that a copy of this form will also serve as authorization.

The information the Lender/Broker obtains is only to be used in the processing of my application for a mortgage loan.

_____   _____

Borrower   Date

(10/98)

Figure 2: Borrower's Signature Authorization

Form 4506-T
(September 2024)
Department of the Treasury
Internal Revenue Service

Request for Transcript of Tax Return

► **Do not sign this form unless all applicable lines have been completed.**

► **Request may be rejected if the form is incomplete or illegible.**

► **For more information about Form 4506-T, visit** *www.irs.gov/form4506t.*

OMB No. 1545-1872

Tip: Get faster service: Online at www.irs.gov, **Get Your Tax Record** (Get Transcript) or by calling **1-800-908-9946** for specialized assistance. We have teams available to assist. **Note:** Taxpayers may register to use Get Transcript to view, print, or download the following transcript types: **Tax Return Transcript** (shows most line items including Adjusted Gross Income (AGI) from your original Form 1040-series tax return as filed, along with any forms and schedules), **Tax Account Transcript** (shows basic data such as return type, marital status, AGI, taxable income and all payment types), **Record of Account Transcript** (combines the tax return and tax account transcripts into one complete transcript), **Wage and Income Transcript** (shows data from information returns we receive such as Forms W-2, 1099, 1098 and Form 5498), and **Verification of Non-filing Letter** (provides proof that the IRS has no record of a filed Form 1040-series tax return for the year you request).

1a Name shown on tax return. If a joint return, enter the name shown first.	**1b** First social security number on tax return, individual taxpayer identification number, or employer identification number (see instructions)
2a If a joint return, enter spouse's name shown on tax return.	**2b** Second social security number or individual taxpayer identification number if joint tax return

3 Current name, address (including apt., room, or suite no.), city, state, and ZIP code (see instructions)

4 Previous address shown on the last return filed if different from line 3 (see instructions)

5 Customer file number (if applicable) (see instructions)

Note: Effective July 2019, the IRS will mail tax transcript requests only to your address of record. See **What's New** under **Future Developments** on Page 2 for additional information.

6 **Transcript requested.** Enter the tax form number here (1040, 1065, 1120, etc.) and check the appropriate box below. Enter only one tax form number per request. ► _____

a **Return Transcript,** which includes most of the line items of a tax return as filed with the IRS. A tax return transcript does not reflect changes made to the account after the return is processed. Transcripts are only available for the following returns: Form 1040 series, Form 1065, Form 1120, Form 1120-A, Form 1120-H, Form 1120-L, and Form 1120S. Return transcripts are available for the current year and returns processed during the prior 3 processing years. Most requests will be processed within 10 business days . . . . . . ☐

b **Account Transcript,** which contains information on the financial status of the account, such as payments made on the account, penalty assessments, and adjustments made by you or the IRS after the return was filed. Return information is limited to items such as tax liability and estimated tax payments. Account transcripts are available for most returns. Most requests will be processed within 10 business days . ☐

c **Record of Account,** which provides the most detailed information as it is a combination of the Return Transcript and the Account Transcript. Available for current year and 3 prior tax years. Most requests will be processed within 10 business days . . . . . . ☐

7 **Verification of Nonfiling,** which is proof from the IRS that you **did not** file a return for the year. Current year requests are only available after June 15th. There are no availability restrictions on prior year requests. Most requests will be processed within 10 business days . . ☐

8 **Form W-2, Form 1099 series, Form 1098 series, or Form 5498 series transcript.** The IRS can provide a transcript that includes data from these information returns. State or local information is not included with the Form W-2 information. The IRS may be able to provide this transcript information for up to 10 years. Information for the current year is generally not available until the year after it is filed with the IRS. For example, W-2 information for 2016, filed in 2017, will likely not be available from the IRS until 2018. If you need W-2 information for retirement purposes, you should contact the Social Security Administration at 1-800-772-1213. Most requests will be processed within 10 business days . ☐

Caution: If you need a copy of Form W-2 or Form 1099, you should first contact the payer. To get a copy of the Form W-2 or Form 1099 filed with your return, you must use Form 4506 and request a copy of your return, which includes all attachments.

9 **Year or period requested.** Enter the end date of the tax year or period requested in mm/dd/yyyy format. This may be a calendar year, fiscal year or quarter. Enter each quarter requested for quarterly returns. Example: Enter 12/31/2018 for a calendar year 2018 Form 1040 transcript.

/ /	/ /	/ /	/ /

Caution: Do not sign this form unless all applicable lines have been completed.

Signature of taxpayer(s). I declare that I am either the taxpayer whose name is shown on line 1a or 2a, or a person authorized to obtain the tax information requested. If the request applies to a joint return, at least one spouse must sign. If signed by a corporate officer, 1 percent or more shareholder, partner, managing member, guardian, tax matters partner, executor, receiver, administrator, trustee, or party other than the taxpayer, I certify that I have the authority to execute Form 4506-T on behalf of the taxpayer. **Note:** This form must be received by IRS within 120 days of the signature date.

☐ Signatory attests that he/she has read the attestation clause and upon so reading declares that he/she **has the authority to sign the Form 4506-T.** See instructions.

Phone number of taxpayer on line 1a or 2a

Sign Here

► Signature (see instructions)   Date

► Title (if line 1a above is a corporation, partnership, estate, or trust)

► Spouse's signature   Date

For Privacy Act and Paperwork Reduction Act Notice, see page 2.   Cat. No. 37667N   Form **4506-T** (Rev. 9-2024)

Figure 3: 4506-T Request for Transcript of Tax Return

NOTICE TO THE HOME LOAN APPLICANT
CREDIT SCORE INFORMATION DISCLOSURE

APPLICANT(S) NAME AND ADDRESS	LENDER NAME AND ADDRESS (ORIGINATOR):

In connection with your application for a home loan, the lender must disclose to you the score that a consumer reporting agency distributed to users and the lender used in connection with your home loan, and the key factors affecting your credit scores.

The credit score is a computer-generated summary calculated at the time of the request and based on information a consumer reporting agency or lender has on file. The scores are based on data about your credit history and payment patterns. Credit scores are important because they are used to assist the lender in determining whether you will obtain a loan. They may also be used to determine what interest rate you may be offered on the mortgage. Credit scores can change over time, depending on your conduct, how your credit history and payment patterns change, and how credit-scoring technologies change.

Because the score is based on information in your credit history, it is very important that you review the credit related information that is being furnished to make sure it is accurate. Credit records may vary from one company to another.

If you have questions about your credit score or the credit information that is furnished to you, contact the consumer reporting agency at the address and telephone number provided with this notice, or contact the lender, if the lender developed or generated the credit score. The consumer reporting agency plays no part in the decision to take any action on the loan application and is unable to provide you with specific reasons for the decision on a loan application.

If you have questions concerning the terms of the loan, contact the lender.

The consumer reporting agencies listed below provided a credit score that was used in connection with your home loan application.

Consumer Reporting Agency	Borrower:		Co-Brw:	
Experian P.O. Box 2002 Allen, TX 75013 (P)888-397-3742	Score:	Created:	Score:	Created:
	Factors		Factors	
Model Used: _____				
Range of Possible Scores _____ to _____				

page 1 of 2

(11/07)

Figure 4: Credit Score Information Disclosure - Page 1 of 2

Consumer Reporting Agency	Borrower:		Co-Brw:	
TransUnion P.O. Box 1000 Chester, PA 19022 (P)800-888-4213 Model Used: _____ Range of Possible Scores _____ to _____	Score: Created: Factors		Score: Created: Factors	
Equifax P.O. Box 740241 Atlanta, GA 30374 (P)800-685-1111 Model Used: _____ Range of Possible Scores _____ to _____	Score: Created: Factors		Score: Created: Factors	

I/We have received a copy of this disclosure.

_____   _____   _____   _____
Applicant   Date   Applicant   Date

(11/07)

page 2 of 2

Figure 4: Credit Score Information Disclosure Page 2 of 2

Request for Appraisal

Part I - Request	
To (Name & Address of Appraiser):	From (Name & Address):
Applicant (Name & Address):	Lender (Name & Address):

Authorized by (Signature):	Title:	Date:

Part II - Property and Mortgage Information

Property Type:	Occupancy Status:	Type of Loan:	Lien Position:	Loan Purpose:
☑ Detached	☑ Primary Residence	☑ Conventional	☑ First Mortgage	☑ Purchase
☐ Attached	☐ Second Home	☐ FHA	☐ Second Mortgage	☐ Cash-Out Refi
☐ Condo	☐ Investment Property	☐ VA		☐ No Cash-Out Refi
☐ PUD		☐ USDA/Rural Housing		☐ Construction
☐ CO-OP				☐ Construction-Perm
	No. of Units ____	☐ Other _____		☐ Other _____

Sales Price: $	Estimated Value: $	Loan Amount: $

Property Address:	Estate Will Be Held In: ☑ Fee Simple ☐ Leasehold expiration date: _____

Legal Description:

Escrow Company:	Title Company:
Listing Agent:	Selling Agent:

Part III - Appraisal Information

Appraisal Type: ☐ Interior/Exterior(Full) ☐ Exterior Only ☐ Market Rent analysis ☐ Land Appraisal	Due Date:	Appraisal Order Number:
		Appraisal Type(s) Ordered:

Estimate of Value Should Be: ☐ As is ☐ As Completed	Appraisal Cost: $	

Payment Method: ☐ C.O.D ☐ Credit Card ☐ Invoice Client ☐ Bill _____ ☐ Other _____	E-mail Appraisal To:
	Contact for Entry: (if not the same as borrower)

Comments:

(01/07)

Figure 5: Request for Appraisal

RIGHT TO RECEIVE A COPY OF THE APPRAISAL REPORT informs the borrower that they have the right to obtain a copy of the appraisal of their property.

REQUEST FOR APPRAISAL provides the borrower with a form to send to the broker/lender formally requesting a copy of the appraisal. The form *Notice of Right to Receive Appraisal* notifies the borrower that, based on the premise that they paid for the appraisal, they have a right to receive a copy of the appraisal on completion of the loan.

The borrower must submit a written request whether using this form or a written request in any form within 90 days of the loan closing, or upon notification of a decline. The loan agent is not required to automatically provide a copy of the appraisal. The creditor must immediately furnish a copy of the appraisal to the borrower upon receipt of a written request received within a reasonable period of time after submission of the loan application. *This requirement falls under ECOA/Regulation B.*

Borrowers typically were not provided with a copy until the late 1990s, when the law made it clear that the borrower has a right to this information. The notice is longer available because the disclosure is now included in the 1003. *See Figure 5, Request for Appraisal.*

DISCLOSURE NOTICES is a form that combines the Affidavit of Occupancy, Anti- Coercion Statement, Fair Credit reporting Act, and FHA/Government Loans only. *See Figure 6, Disclosure Notices.*
- Occupancy Affidavit, in which the borrower confirms the intended occupancy, whether owner-occupied or non-owner occupied.
- Anti-Coercion Statement, which discloses to the borrower that insurance laws prohibit the lender from requiring the borrower to use a particular insurance provider.
- Fair Credit reporting Act, notifying the borrower that a credit report will be run, and the results will be provided to them.
- FHA and government loans only provide pre-payment information regarding interest charges and the Right to Financial Privacy Act of 1978.

FLOOD DISASTER ACT OF 1973 notifies the borrower of the act and the availability of flood insurance for properties located in a designated flood hazard area. *See Figure 7, Flood Disaster Protection Act of 1973.*

DISCLOSURE NOTICES

Date:

Applicant(s):	Property Address:

AFFIDAVIT OF OCCUPANCY

Applicant(s) hereby certify and acknowledge that, upon taking title to the real property described above, their occupancy status will be as follows:

[✓] Primary Residence - Occupied by Applicant(s) within 30 days of closing.

[ ] Secondary Residence - To be occupied by Applicant(s) at least 15 days yearly, as second home (vacation, etc.), while maintaining principal residence elsewhere. [Please check this box if you plan to establish it as your primary residence at a future date (e.g., retirement)].

[ ] Investment Property - Not owner occupied. Purchased as an investment to be held or rented.

The Applicant(s) acknowledge it is a federal crime punishable by fine or imprisonment, or both, to knowingly make any false statement concerning this loan application as applicable under the provisions of Title 18, United States Code, Section 1014.

_____ _____
APPLICANT SIGNATURE   CO-APPLICANT SIGNATURE

ANTI-COERCION STATEMENT

The insurance laws of this state provide that the lender may not require the applicant to take insurance through any particular insurance agent or company to protect the mortgaged property. The applicant, subjected to the rules adopted by the Insurance Commissioner, has the right to have the insurance placed with an insurance agent or company of his choice, provided the company meets the requirement of the lender. The lender has the right to designate reasonable financial requirements as to the company and the adequacy of the coverage.
I have read the foregoing statement, or the rules of the Insurance Commissioner relative hereto, and understand my rights and privileges and those of the lender relative to the placing of such insurance.
I have selected the following agencies to write the insurance covering the property described above:

_____ _____
Insurance Company Name   Agent

_____ _____
Agent's Address   Agent's Telephone Number

_____ _____
APPLICANT SIGNATURE   CO-APPLICANT SIGNATURE

FAIR CREDIT REPORTING ACT

An investigation will be made as to the credit standing of all individuals seeking credit in this application. The nature and scope of any investigation will be furnished to you upon written request made within a reasonable period of time. In the event of credit denial due to an unfavorable consumer report, you will be advised of the identity of the Consumer Reporting Agency making such report and of your right to request within sixty (60) days the reason for the adverse action, pursuant to provisions of section 615(b) of the Fair Credit Reporting Act.

_____ _____
APPLICANT SIGNATURE   CO-APPLICANT SIGNATURE

FHA LOANS ONLY

IF YOU PREPAY YOUR LOAN ON OTHER THAN THE REGULAR INSTALLMENT DATE, YOU MAY BE ASSESSED INTEREST CHARGES UNTIL THE END OF THAT MONTH.

GOVERNMENT LOANS ONLY

RIGHT TO FINANCIAL PRIVACY ACT OF 1978 - This is a notice to you as required by the Right to Financial Privacy Act of 1978 that the Department of Housing and Urban Development or Department of Veterans Affairs has a right of access to financial records held by a financial institution in connection with the consideration of administration of assistance to you. Financial records involving your transaction will be available to the Department of Housing and Urban Development or Department of Veterans Affairs without further notice or authorization but will not be disclosed or released to another Government agency or Department without your consent except as required or permitted by law.

_____ _____
APPLICANT SIGNATURE   CO-APPLICANT SIGNATURE

Figure 6: Disclosure Notices

**FLOOD DISASTER
PROTECTION ACT OF 1973**

DATE:

APPLICATION NO:

PROPERTY ADDRESS:

I/We hereby acknowledge that we have been advised of the Flood Disaster Protection Act of 1973 and the requirements that I/We provide such insurance coverage on any property located within an area designated as a Flood Hazard Area. Should the subject property fall within a flood hazard area as defined in the Act, then I/We authorize
its successors and/or assigns to purchase such insurance and I/We further agree to pay promptly the cost thereof.

_____   _____
(Applicant)   (Date)   (Applicant)   (Date)

_____   _____
(Applicant)   (Date)   (Applicant)   (Date)

Calyx Form fdact.frm 12/96

Figure 7: Flood Disaster Protection Act of 1973

Notice of Intent to Proceed with Loan Application

Date of Change: _____

Name of Originator: _____

Company Name: _____

Borrower Name(s): _____

Property Address: _____

NOTE: DO NOT SIGN THIS FORM UNLESS YOU WISH TO PROCEED WITH THE LOAN APPLICATION COVERED BY THE GFE. IF YOU DO WISH TO PROCEED, PLEASE RETURN A SIGNED AND DATED COPY OF THIS NOTICE OF INTENT TO PROCEED TO THE LOAN ORIGINATOR.

Each of the undersigned Borrower(s), having received a copy of a Good Faith Estimate ("GFE") dated _____, hereby expresses his or her intention to continue with the loan application covered by the GFE.

_____   _____
Borrower   Date

_____   _____
Borrower   Date

I hereby certify that this form was executed by the borrowers.

_____   _____
Originator or Representative of the Originator   Date

Figure 8: Intent to Proceed

PATRIOT ACT
INFORMATION DISCLOSURE

Applicant Name _____

Co-Applicant Name _____

Present Address _____

Mailing Address _____

To help the government fight the funding of terrorism and money laundering activities, Federal law requires all financial institutions to obtain, verify, and record information that identifies each person who opens an account.

What this means for you: When you open an account, we will ask for your name, address, date of birth, and other information that will allow us to identify you. We may also ask to see your driver's license or other identifying documents.

I/we acknowledge that I/we received a copy of this disclosure.

_____   _____
Applicant   Date

_____   _____
Applicant   Date

Figure 9: Patriot Act Information
Page 1 of 2

Customer Identification Documentation
Patriot Act

The USA Patriot Act requires all financial institutions to obtain, verify and record information that identifies every customer. Completion of this documentation is required in order to comply with the USA Patriot Act. A completed copy of this information must be retained with the loan file.

Application Number _____   Date _____ 12/09/2009 _____

Name of Applicant _____

Social Security # _____   Date of Birth _____

Present Address _____

Mailing Address _____

Primary Identification Documentation

Document Type _____   Other Document Type _____

Document Number _____

Issue Date _____   Expiration Date _____

Issued by _____

Secondary Identification Documentation

Document Type _____   Other Document Type _____

Document Number _____

Issue Date _____   Expiration Date _____

Issued by _____

Discrepancies and Resolution

Completed by _____

Figure 9: Patriot Act/ Customer Identification Page 2 of 2

NOTICE OF INTENT TO PROCEED WITH THE LOAN is provided to the borrower to state that they do intend to proceed with the loan application based on the information provided in the GFE, now LE. *See Figure 8: Notice of Intent to Proceed*

PATRIOT ACT is a requirement of the federal government as a way of tracking any potential terrorist and any questionable activities by obtaining identification of borrowers. The purpose of the forms is to verify the borrower's identification. There are three pages to the form.

Page 1 requires the mortgage broker or lender to complete the information obtained from the borrower's two required forms of identification, which are usually the driver's license and the Social Security card. Pages 2 and 3 are for completion by the borrower and co-borrower. *See Figure 9, Patriot Act.*

PRIVACY POLICY DISCLOSURE is required to notify the borrower that, per Title V of the **Gramm-Leach-Bliley Act**, financial institutions and their affiliates are generally prohibited from sharing non-public personal information concerning their clients. A client has the right to "opt out" if they choose. There are businesses that sell lists of their clients to other businesses for the purpose of advertising. Brokers must disclose to borrowers whether they share any client contact information with other businesses.

SERVICING DISCLOSURE STATEMENT informs the borrower that the servicing of their loan may be sold or transferred. The statement also discloses what percentage of loans the lender or broker sells as a normal course of business. Page 4 of the 1003 now states that the lender may sell the loan. The disclosure declares the lender's intentions and history of loan transfers.

RESPA requires that this form be provided to the borrower by lenders and brokers that perform table findings. Brokers that do not fund using their own funds are not required to provide the disclosure; however, many lenders will require that the form be provided by the broker. *See Figure 10, Servicing Disclosure Statement.*

A MORTGAGE LOAN ORIGINATION AGREEMENT is a federal form notifying the client of the relationship with the broker. The **Mortgage Loan Origination Agreement** is required by the federal government to explain to the borrower the relationship between the consumer and the mortgage broker/agent. The **Mortgage Loan Origination Agreement states that the mortgage originator is not an agent per federal definition.** *See Figure 11, Mortgage Loan Origination Agreement.*

REQUEST FOR TITLE COMMITMENT provides the information that will be needed by the escrow and title companies to open escrow and provide title insurance. RESPA requires that the borrower choose the title company, and this form acts as documentation of that choice. *See Figure 12, Request for Title Commitment.*

PMI DISCLOSURES are available for adjustable rate, fixed rate, and high-risk loans. The disclosures explain to the consumer the reason for primary mortgage insurance (PMI), how it works, and the benefits. The potential problems that may occur as a result of adjusting interest rates are also disclosed. *See Figures 13 and 14, PMI Disclosures.*

PMI ARM Disclosure provides the borrower with information about adjustable-rate mortgages and how they work. Since 2008, the TIL disclosure includes Page 3, which provides additional information on the potential changes that may occur to the interest rate sand payment. *See Figure 15, PMI ARM Disclosure.*

- **Regulation Z, THE FEDERAL TRUTH-IN-LENDING DISCLOSURE ACT (TIL/TILA)** requires that Regulation Z, which is now part of the loan estimate (LE), be provided within three (3) business days. The MDIA now requires the disclosure to be provided on the Regulation Z, so it has now become a requirement for California licensees to provide the form. This form will be discussed in detail in a later chapter.

LOCK-IN CONFIRMATION notifies the borrower in writing of the terms of the loan, the locked interest rate, and period to complete the loan under the stated terms. This is to be provided to the borrower once the loan is locked. This document will allow the borrower to have written confirmation of the terms of the loan that they are obtaining. This can eliminate misunderstandings when documents are signed. If the loan is not locked at the time that the borrower signs the loan application, the MLO should provide this once it is locked. There is no actual form, but the MLO may provide the information either in letter form or a form created by the broker's office.

SERVICING DISCLOSURE STATEMENT

Lender: Date:

NOTICE TO FIRST LIEN MORTGAGE LOAN APPLICANTS: THE RIGHT TO COLLECT YOUR MORTGAGE LOAN PAYMENTS MAY BE TRANSFERRED.

You are applying for a mortgage loan covered by the Real Estate Settlement Procedures Act (RESPA) (12 U.S.C. 2601 et seq.). RESPA gives you certain rights under Federal law. This statement describes whether the servicing for this loan may be transferred to a different loan servicer.

"Servicing" refers to collecting your principal, interest, and escrow payments, if any, as well as sending any monthly or annual statements, tracking account balances, and handling other aspects of your loan. You will be given advance notice before a transfer occurs.

☐ We may assign, sell or transfer the servicing of your loan while the loan is outstanding.

☐ We do not service mortgage loans of the type for which you applied. We intend to assign, sell, or transfer the servicing of your mortgage loan before the first payment is due.

☐ The loan for which you have applied will be serviced at this financial institution and we do not intend to sell, transfer, or assign the servicing of the loan.

Acknowledgment of Mortgage Loan Applicant(s)

I/We have read and understood the disclosure, and understand that the disclosure is a required part of the mortgage application as evidenced by my/our signature(s) below;

_____   _____
Applicant   Date   Applicant   Date

_____   _____
Applicant   Date   Applicant   Date

Figure 10: Servicing Disclosure Statement

MORTGAGE LOAN ORIGINATION AGREEMENT
(Warning to Broker: The content of this form may vary depending upon the state in which it is used.)

You _____ agree to enter into this Mortgage Loan Origination Agreement with _____ as an independent contractor to apply for a residential mortgage loan from a participating lender with which we from time to time contract upon such terms and conditions as you may request or a lender may require. You inquired into mortgage financing with _____ on _____ We are licensed as a "Mortgage Broker" under _____

SECTION 1. NATURE OF RELATIONSHIP. In connection with this mortgage loan:

* We are acting as an independent contractor and not as your agent.

* We will enter into separate independent contractor agreements with various lenders.

* While we seek to assist you in meeting your financial needs, we do not distribute the products of all lenders or investors in the market and cannot guarantee the lowest price or best terms available in the market.

SECTION 2. OUR COMPENSATION. The lenders whose loan products we distribute generally provide their loan products to us at a wholesale rate.

* The retail price we offer you - your interest rate, total points and fees - will include our compensation.

* In some cases, we may be paid all of our compensation by either you or the lender.

* Alternatively, we may be paid a portion of our compensation by both you and the lender. For example, in some cases, if you would rather pay a lower interest rate, you may pay higher up-front points and fees.

* Also, in some cases, if you would rather pay less up front, you may be able to pay some or all of our compensation indirectly through a higher interest rate in which case we will be paid directly by the lender.

We also may be paid by the lender based on (i) the value of the Mortgage Loan or related servicing rights in the market place or (ii) other services, goods or facilities performed or provided by us to the lender.

By signing below, the mortgage loan originator and mortgage loan applicant(s) acknowledge receipt of a copy of this signed Agreement.

MORTGAGE LOAN ORIGINATOR	APPLICANT(S)	
Company Name	Applicant Name(s)	
Address	Address	
City, State, Zip	City, State, Zip	
Phone/Fax	Borrower Signature	Date
Broker or Authorized Agent Signature Date	Co-Borrower Signature	Date

Figure 11: Mortgage Loan Origination Agreement

Request for Title Commitment

Part I - Request			
1 To (Name and address of title company)		2 From (name and address)	
3. Signature of Lender	4 Title	5 Date	6 Lender's No.
7 Name and address of applicant			

Part II - Property and Mortgage Information

8. Occupancy Status
- Primary Residence
- Second Home
- Investment Property

9. Loan Purpose
- Purchase
- Cash-Out Refi
- No Cash-Out Refi

10. Sales Price
$

11. Loan Amount
$

12. Property Address

13. Legal Description

14. Home Owner's Name and Phone Number

15. Property Type
- Detached
- Attached
- Condo
- PUD
- CO-OP

16. Seller

17. Mortgagee   Lender Case #

Part III - Request for Title Commitment

18. Attachment
- Prior Title Policy
- Warranty Deed
- Title Insurance Requirements
- Survey
- Contract

19. Type of Policy

20. Estimated Closing Date

21. Mail Away
- Yes
- No

Part IV - Special Instruction

Figure 12: Request for Title Commitment

Private Mortgage Insurance Disclosure - Fixed Rate Mortgages

Borrower(s) : _____   Date : _____

_____   Property
Address : _____

Loan Number : _____

You are obtaining a mortgage loan that requires private mortgage insurance ("PMI"). PMI protects lenders and others against financial loss when borrowers default. Charges for the insurance are added to your loan payments.

Under certain circumstances, federal law gives you the right to cancel PMI or requires that PMI automatically terminate. This disclosure describes when cancellation and termination may occur. Please note that PMI is not the same as property/casualty insurance -- such as homeowner's or flood insurance - which protects you against damage to the property. Cancellation or termination of PMI does not affect any obligation you may have to maintain other types of insurance. In this disclosure, "loan" means the mortgage loan you are obtaining; "you" means the original borrower (or his or her successors or assigns); and "property" means the property securing the mortgage loan.

Initial Amortization Schedule
An amortization schedule showing the principal and interest due on your loan, along with the balance remaining after each scheduled payment, is attached for your reference.

Borrower Requested Cancellation of PMI
You have the right to request that PMI be canceled on or after the following dates:

(1) The date the principal balance of your loan is first **scheduled** to reach 80% of the original value of the property. This date is _____ . **For balloon loans with a fixed interest rate and no conditional right to refinance, if applicable, this date will not be reached before the loan matures.**

(2) The date the principal balance **actually** reaches 80% of the original value of the property.

"Original value" means the lesser of the contract sales price of the property or the appraised value of the property at the time the loan was closed. **If this loan refinances an existing loan secured by the property, "original value" means the appraised value relied on by the lender to approve this loan.**

PMI will only be canceled if all the following conditions are satisfied:

(1) you submit a written request for cancellation;

(2) you have a good payment history;

(3) you are current on the payments required by your loan; and

(4) we receive, if requested and at your expense, evidence satisfactory to the holder of your loan that the value of the property has not declined below its original value, and certification that there are no subordinate liens on the property.

A "good payment history" means no payments 60 or more days past due within two years and no payments 30 or more days past due within one year of the later of (a) the cancellation date, or (b) the date you submit a request for cancellation.

Automatic Termination of PMI
If you are current on your loan payments, PMI will automatically terminate on the date the principal balance of your loan is first **scheduled** to reach 78% of the original value of the property. This date is _____ .
For balloon loans with a fixed interest rate and no conditional right to refinance, if applicable, this date will not be reached before the loan matures. If you are **not** current on your loan payments as of that date, PMI will automatically terminate on the first day of the month immediately following the date you thereafter become current on your payments.

Exceptions to Cancellation and Automatic Termination
The cancellation and automatic termination requirements described above do not apply to certain loans that may present a higher risk of default. Your loan, however, does not fall into this category. Accordingly, the cancellation and automatic termination provisions described above apply to your loan.

I/we have received a copy of this disclosure.

_____   _____
Borrower   Date

_____   _____
Borrower   Date

Figure 13: Private Mortgage Insurance- Fixed rate

Private Mortgage Insurance - Initial Disclosure - High Risk Loans

Borrower(s) : _____   Date : _____

_____   Property Address :

_____

Loan Number : _____   _____

You are obtaining a mortgage loan that requires private mortgage insurance ("PMI"). PMI protects lenders and others against financial loss when borrowers default, and charges for the insurance are added to your loan payments.

Lender-Defined High Risk Loans. PMI will not be required on your mortgage loan beyond the date the principal balance of your loan is first **scheduled** to reach 77% of the original value of the property. If PMI is not sooner terminated in accordance with the foregoing sentence, PMI will not be required on your mortgage loan beyond the date that is the midpoint of the amortization period for the loan, if you are current on your loan payments on that date. "Original value" means the lesser of (a) the contract sales price of the property or (b) the appraised value of the property at the time the loan was closed.

Fannie Mae / Freddie Mac. PMI will not be required on your mortgage loan beyond the date that is the midpoint of the amortization period for the loan, provided you are current on your loan payments on that date.

Please note that PMI is **not** the same as property/casualty insurance -- such as homeowner's or flood insurance -- which protects you against damage to the property. Termination of PMI does **not** affect any obligation you may have to maintain other types of insurance.

I/we have received a copy of this disclosure.

_____   _____
Borrower   Date

_____   _____
Borrower   Date

Figure 14: Private Mortgage Insurance- High Risk Loans

Private Mortgage Insurance Disclosure - Adjustable Rate Mortgages

Borrower(s) : _____   Date : _____

_____   Property
Address : _____

Loan Number : _____

You are obtaining a mortgage loan that requires private mortgage insurance ("PMI"). PMI protects lenders and others against financial loss when borrowers default. Charges for the insurance are added to your loan payments.

Under certain circumstances, federal law gives you the right to cancel PMI or requires that PMI automatically terminate. This disclosure describes when cancellation and termination may occur. Please note that PMI is not the same as property/casualty insurance -- such as homeowner's or flood insurance - which protects you against damage to the property. Cancellation or termination of PMI does not affect any obligation you may have to maintain other types of insurance. In this disclosure, "loan" means the mortgage loan you are obtaining; "you" means the original borrower (or his or her successors or assigns); and "property" means the property securing the mortgage loan.

Borrower Requested Cancellation of PMI

You have the right to request that PMI be canceled on or after the following dates:

(1) The date the principal balance of your loan is first **scheduled** to reach 80% of the original value of the property. **For balloon loans with either an adjustable interest rate or a conditional right to refinance, if applicable, this date will not be reached before the loan matures.**

(2) The date the principal balance **actually** reaches 80% of the original value of the property.

"Original value" means the lesser of the contract sales price of the property or the appraised value of the property at the time the loan was closed. **If this loan refinances an existing loan secured by the property, "original value" means the appraised value relied on by the lender to approve this loan.**

You will be notified when these dates are reached.

PMI will only be canceled if all the following conditions are satisfied:

(1) you submit a written request for cancellation;

(2) you have a good payment history;

(3) you are current on the payments required by your loan; and

(4) we receive, if requested and at your expense, evidence that the value of the property has not declined below its original value, and certification that there are no subordinate liens on the property.

For purposes of PMI Cancellation, a good payment history means no payments 60 or more days past due within two years and nopayments 30 or more days past due within one year of the later of (a) the cancellation date, or (b) the date you submit a request for cancellation.

Automatic Termination of PMI

If you are current on your loan payments, PMI will automatically terminate on the date the principal balance of your loan is first **scheduled** to reach 78% of the original value of the property. **For balloon loans with either an adjustable interest rate or a conditional right to refinance, if applicable, this date will not be reached before the loan matures.** This date is called the "termination date." If you are **not** current on your loan payments as of the termination date, PMI will automatically terminate on the first day of the month immediately following the date you thereafter become current on your payments. On or about the termination date, you will be notified that the PMI has been terminated or will be terminated when you become current on on your loan payments.

Exceptions to Cancellation and Automatic Termination

The cancellation and automatic termination requirements described above do not apply to certain loans that may present a higher risk of default. Your loan, however, does not fall into this category. Accordingly, the cancellation and automatic termination provisions described above apply to your loan.

I/we have received a copy of this disclosure.

_____   _____
Borrower   Date

_____   _____
Borrower   Date

Figure 15: Private Mortgage Insurance- Adjustable Rate

The **ANTI-STEERING LOAN OPTIONS DISCLOSURE** must be provided when the mortgage broker origination will be lender-paid or paid through a YSP, the broker must provide the Anti-Steering Disclosure. The disclosure provides detailed information regarding interest rates and costs associated with the loan. The purpose of the disclosure is to make the financing options clear to the borrower.

HUD BOOKLETS are manuals which provide borrowers with information on their rights as consumers, as well as to help protect them against unscrupulous lending practices. They are categorized according to whether the loan is a purchase, refinance, ARM, or home equity line of credit (HELOC). HUD booklets must be provided on all loan programs.

HUD provides the booklets to explain the borrowers' rights, costs, and laws in relation to real estate transactions. Providing the appropriate pamphlet is a federal law. These pamphlets may be purchased from a variety of companies that sell real estate-related forms and documents, or they may be printed from the HUD website at *www.hud.gov*. See Figure 16, HUD Booklet.

HUD Booklets:

1. **SETTLEMENT COSTS AND YOU** is to be given with **all** loan applications and real estate sales transactions. The disclosure provides information regarding potential costs.

2. **WHEN YOUR HOUSE IS ON THE LINE** is to be given with applications for Home Equity Lines of Credit. The disclosure provides information regarding the way an Equity Line of Credit works, including rate and payment changes and the potential problems that may arise from the unusual terms of this loan type.

3. **ADJUSTABLE-RATE MORTGAGES** is to be given when an adjustable-rate loan is to be obtained for the borrower to explain the information about the intricacies of the workings of adjustable-rate mortgages.

> **NOTE**
>
> *The booklets can be copied or re-typed; however, it is against federal law to change the wording in any way, although a broker or lender is allowed to add their business name and address.*

U.S. DEPARTMENT OF HOUSING AND URBAN DEVELOPMENT

Shopping for Your Home Loan

HUD's Settlement
Cost Booklet

Figure 16: HUD Booklet
Page 1 of 2

I. Introduction

The *Real Estate Settlement Procedures Act (RESPA)* requires lenders and mortgage brokers to give you this booklet within three days of applying for a mortgage loan. RESPA is a federal law that helps protect consumers from unfair practices by settlement service providers during the home-buying and loan process.

Buying a home is an important financial decision that should be considered carefully. This booklet will help you become familiar with the various stages of the home-buying process, including deciding whether you are ready to buy a home, and providing factors to consider in determining how much you can afford to spend. You will learn about the sales agreement, how to use a *Good Faith Estimate* to shop for the best loan for you, required settlement services to close your loan, and the *HUD-1 Settlement Statement* that you will receive at closing.

This booklet will help you become familiar with how interest rates, points, balloon payments, and prepayment penalties can affect your monthly mortgage payments. In addition, there is important information about your loan after settlement, including how to resolve loan servicing problems with your lender, and steps you can take to avoid foreclosure. After you have purchased your home, this booklet will help you indentify issues to consider before getting a home equity loan or refinancing your mortgage. Finally, contact information is provided to answer any questions you may have after reading this booklet. There is also a Glossary of Terms in the booklet's Appendix.

Using this booklet as your guide will help you avoid the pitfalls and help you achieve the joys of home ownership.

3

Figure 16: HUD Booklet- Buying Your Home
Page 2 of 2

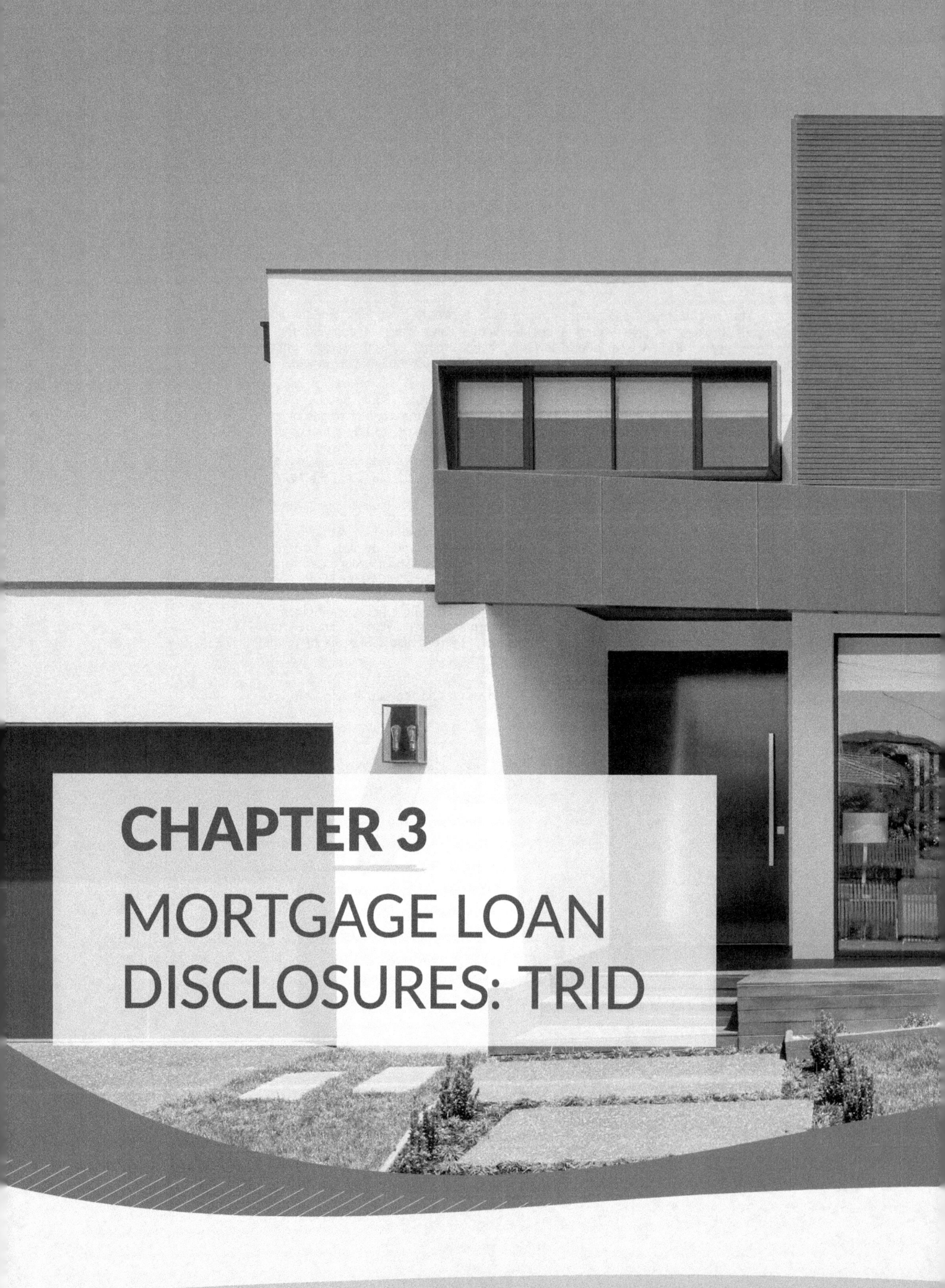

CHAPTER 3
MORTGAGE LOAN DISCLOSURES: TRID

MORTGAGE LOAN DISCLOSURES: TRID

Mortgage Loan Disclosures are a result and requirement of several different state and federal laws. For more than three decades, federal law required lenders to provide two different *disclosure forms* to consumers applying for a home loan.

Additionally, the law required two different forms at or before closing on the loan. These were the Truth in Lending Act (TILA) and the Real Estate Settlement Procedures Act (RESPA). Unfortunately, the information on these forms overlapped and their language was inconsistent. As a result, consumers often found the forms confusing, while lenders and settlement agents found the forms burdensome to explain.

The Dodd-Frank Wall Street Reform and Consumer Protection Act (Dodd- Frank Act) created the Consumer Financial Protection Bureau (CFPB) whose main objective is to protect consumers by enforcing federal consumer financial laws. Arguably the most noteworthy result of the legislation was the establishment of TRID, or the TILA-RESPA Integrated Disclosure Rule, which consolidated and streamlined required loan disclosures. The new rule was designed to help mortgage loan applicants understand the terms of their home financing transaction. The TRID rule became effective on October 3, 2015.

This new rule applies to most closed-end consumer mortgage loans; it does not apply to home-equity lines of credit, reverse mortgage loans, mortgage loans secured by a mobile home, or to creditors that write five or fewer mortgages a year.

The **TRID rule** aims to simplify the mortgage process by streamlining and encapsulating certain loan disclosures and changing the timing of certain mortgage processes. First, applicants will see consumer disclosures that are easy to read – the new TRID documents have the most vital information located in more prominent places. The *loan estimate* (which replaced the good faith estimate) forms will clearly set forth the terms of the proposed transaction to help the applicant determine whether they would like to proceed with the transaction. Next, applicants are to be given their *closing disclosure* forms early in the process (the *closing disclosure* replaced the HUD-1 statement). Applicants should receive a copy of their closing disclosure at least three business days before closing, so that if they have questions, their lenders can provide them with additional information. The format of the closing disclosure will also mirror the loan estimate to make comparison easy.

Specific benefits of the new forms and rules include:
- **Combining several forms** and additional statutory disclosure requirements into two forms. This will reduce paperwork and consumer confusion.
- **Use of clear language** will help consumers understand complicated mortgage loan and real estate transactions.
- **Highlighting the information** that has proven to be most important to consumers. On the new forms, the interest rate, monthly payments, and the total closing costs will be clearly presented on the first page. This will make it easier for consumers to compare mortgage loans and choose the one that is right for them.
- **Providing more information** about the costs of taxes and insurance and how the interest rate and payments may change in the future. This information will help consumers decide whether they can afford the mortgage loan.
- **Warning consumers about features** they may want to avoid, like penalties for paying off the loan early or increases to the mortgage loan balance even if payments are made on time.
- **Making the cost estimates consumers receive** for services required to close a mortgage loan (such as appraisals or pest inspections) more accurate. The rule prohibits increases in charges from lenders, their affiliates, and for services for which the lender does not permit the consumer to shop, unless a specific exception applies.

  Examples of the specific exceptions include when information provided by a consumer at application was inaccurate or becomes inaccurate, or when the consumer asks for a change in the services.

- **Requiring that consumers receive** the closing disclosure at least three business days before closing on the mortgage loan. Currently, consumers often receive this information at closing or shortly before closing.

This additional time will allow consumers to compare the final terms and costs to the terms and costs they received in the estimate. That will better equip them to raise any questions before they go to the closing table.
Source: Consumer Financial Protection Bureau (CFPB)

WHAT HAS AND HAS NOT CHANGED ABOUT THE MORTGAGE LOAN PROCESS

- *Preapprovals* and *Prequalifications* are unchanged by the new rule.
- **The application process starts with a *loan estimate*.** The application process generally starts after the applicant has identified a property. A lender must provide a *Loan estimate* within three business days after the applicant has provided such lender with:
  - their name
  - their income
  - their Social Security number
  - the property's address
  - the property's estimated value
  - the desired mortgage loan amount

In the past, comparing multiple loans could be burdensome because each lender may have different requirements. Now, while lenders may accept and consider income verification documents and other information provided voluntarily, they cannot require this documentation as a condition of providing a *loan estimate*.

As a result, applicants should have a much easier time getting and comparing loan estimate from various lenders; and by comparing the same type of loan among various lenders, applicants are more likely to find their best deal.

NOTE

The lender must provide the loan estimate within three business days, but there is no set time limit for the applicant to receive it. If the lender mails the loan estimate, the applicant may receive it more than three days after their application.

- **Applicants must indicate their intent to proceed.** After applicants have compared loan estimates and determined which loan best meets their needs, they must let the lender know; if the applicant is silent, the lender must not assume an intent to proceed. In general, lenders will not move forward with an application without a strong indication from the applicant that they intend to proceed. However, after 10 business days without such indication, the lender is no longer obligated to honor the terms initially offered in the loan estimate.

- **After an applicant indicates their intent to proceed, lenders can start charging fees.** Until applicants indicate their intent to proceed, lenders cannot charge any fees related to a mortgage application, including the mortgage application or appraisal fee. The *only exception* is a reasonable fee for the credit report. In the past, lenders may have requested credit card information or a post-dated check to be charged or deposited later, after a required estimate was sent, but this is no longer allowed. Payment information can only be obtained after the lender provides the *loan estimate* and the applicant has expressed their intent to proceed.

- **Since lenders cannot collect payment information in advance**, lenders may require the applicants to provide payment for an appraisal, mortgage application, or other loan processing fee immediately after, or, as part of confirming the intent to proceed with the application. Lenders may require payment before beginning the processing, verification, appraisal, or underwriting processes.

- **A *changed circumstance* may necessitate a revised *loan estimate* or a revised *closing disclosure*.** The lender is responsible for providing accurate information about the loan requested based on the data available to the lender when the disclosure is provided.

- **But if the information about the applicant, the proposed mortgage loan, or the property was incorrect or *changes*,** a revised loan estimate may be issued. This is referred to as a *changed circumstance*.

> **NOTE**
>
> *Issuing a loan estimate does not mean the lender approved or denied the loan. By issuing the loan estimate, the lender has pledged to honor the fees described in the loan estimate - as long as the loan is approved later without any changes in circumstance affecting the loan application.*

> **NOTE**
>
> *If the lender closes an application because it is incomplete, the applicant will most likely have to start the process again.*

A new *loan estimate* may indicate changed rates and terms affected by the added information. However, not all changes require the lender to issue a revised loan estimate. Minor changes do not require the lender to issue a revised loan estimate, but significant changes will most likely require a new estimate.

The common reasons a loan estimate may be revised include:
- The applicant decided to change loan programs or the amount of the down payment.
- The property's appraisal came in higher or lower than expected.
- The applicant's credit status changed.
- The lender could not verify the applicant's overtime, bonus, or other income provided on the application.

• **The applicant must receive the *closing disclosure* at least three business days before closing.** A lender needs to make sure that the applicant receives the closing disclosure at least three business days before closing. This gives the applicant time to go over the summary of the final loan terms. Applicants should no longer face significant changes from the lender and be pressured to sign on the same day. Flexibility has been built into the rule in order to accommodate small, last-minute changes common to purchase transactions. However, when such transaction changes are significant, a *new* three-business-day review period is required. Because substantial, last-minute changes would be unusual, an additional review period would be unusual, as well.

In providing a closing disclosure three business days before closing that confirms all the terms of the transaction, settlement agents and creditors need as much information as possible from all parties as far in advance of closing as possible.

• **Additional three-day reviews are unlikely.** Applicants should not encounter major changes to their loan terms on the day of closing and thus be required to make a major decision under duress. Although most changes that come up in the last few days before settlement typically would not delay a closing, there are three crucial changes to loan terms that would require the lender to issue a revised closing disclosure and would cause a new three-business-day review period.

> **NOTE**
>
> *The closing disclosure must contain the names, addresses, license ID numbers, email addresses, and phone numbers for both the buyer's and seller's brokers and agents. If this information is not established, the form cannot be completed.*

Primary changes that would cause a new three-business-day review period are:

- The Annual Percentage Rate (APR) increases by more than 1/8 of a percent for regular loans (fixed-rate loans), or 1/4 of a percent for irregular loans (adjustable loans). A decrease in APR will not require a new three-day review if it is based on changes to the interest rate or other fees.
- A prepayment penalty is added, making it expensive to refinance or sell.
- The basic loan product changes, such as a switch from fixed rate to adjustable interest rate, or to a loan with interest-only payments.

ENFORCEMENT OF THE TILA-RESPA FINAL RULE/TRID

The CFPB can impose sizable penalties, so it is crucial that lenders be vigilant.

- Up to $5,000 per day for any violation of a law, rule, or final order or condition imposed in writing by the CFPB.
- Up to $25,000 per day for any person who recklessly engages in a violation of a federal consumer financial law.
- Up to $1,000,000 per day for any person who knowingly violates a federal consumer financial law.

THE LOAN ESTIMATE FORM EXPLAINED

The *loan estimate (LE)* is a three-page form, which includes a list of all costs and fees that will arise during processing of the loan.

It provides the applicant with important details about their loan, including the estimated interest rate, monthly payment, total closing costs, estimated costs of taxes and insurance, and how the interest rates and payments may change in the future; these estimates are not legally binding, but the final costs of the loan can have no more than 10 percent difference from any third-party fees associated with the loan.

NOTE

In general, applicants may not waive their right to this new three-business-day review period.

NOTE

Lenders have been required to provide a three-day review for such changes in APR since 2009.

NOTE

Resources to help consumers understand and comply with the Dodd-Frank Act mortgage reforms and the CFPB regulations, including downloadable guides, are available through the CFPB's website at consumerfinance. gov/policy- compliance/ guidance/ implementation- guidance.

The LE is expounded more below - this according to the CFPB:

- "Either a mortgage broker or creditor is required to provide the loan estimate form upon receipt of an application by a mortgage broker. However, even if the mortgage broker provides the loan estimate, the creditor remains responsible for complying with the all requirements concerning provision of the form."

- "The creditor or mortgage broker must provide the form to the consumer no later than three business days after the consumer applies for a mortgage loan. The final rule contains a definition of what constitutes an "application" for these purposes, which consists of the consumer's name, income, social security number to obtain a credit report, the property address, an estimate of the value of the property, and the mortgage loan amount sought."

- "Consistent with current law, the creditor generally cannot charge consumers any fees until after the consumers have been given the loan estimate form and the consumers have communicated their intent to proceed with the transaction. There is an exception that allows creditors to charge fees to obtain consumers' credit reports."

- "Creditors and other persons may provide consumers with written estimates prior to application. The rule requires that any such written estimates contain a disclaimer to prevent confusion with the loan estimate form. This disclaimer is required for advertisements."

THE CONSUMER FINANCIAL PROTECTION BUREAU'S GUIDE TO PAGE 1 OF THE LOAN ESTIMATE FORM

DATE
The *date issued* is the date the loan estimate is placed in the mail or delivered to the consumer (not the date the form is actually printed).

APPLICANTS
Applicants include the name and mailing address of the consumer(s) applying for the loan. Use each applicant's name and mailing address if there are multiple applicants. The mailing address disclosed must be the U.S. postal mailing address of the consumer applying for credit. The mailing address cannot be any other type of address, such as an applicant's email address. An additional page may be added to the loan estimate if the space provided is insufficient to list all of the applicants.

If credit is extended to a trust established for tax or estate planning purposes, the loan estimate may be provided to the trustee on behalf of the trust. If the loan estimate is delivered to the trustee on behalf of the trust (and to no other consumer), a creditor may opt to disclose the name and mailing address of the trust only, although nothing in the TILA-RESPA rule prohibits the creditor from additionally disclosing the names of the trustee or other consumers applying for the credit.

PROPERTY

Property is the address of the property (which must include the zip code) that will secure the transaction. If the address of the property is unavailable, use a description of the location of the property, such as a lot number. Always use a zip code. Personal property, such as furniture or appliances that also secure the credit transaction, may be but is not required to be included as property. An additional page may not be appended to the loan estimate to disclose a description of personal property.

SALE PRICE

Sale price or appraised value or estimated value. If the loan is for a purchase money mortgage, the contract sale price should be used and labeled "Sale Price." If personal property is included in the sale price of the property, that price should be used without any reduction for the appraised or estimated value of the personal property. If the sale price is not yet known, disclose the estimated value of the property, using the label "sale price." For a transaction without a seller, disclose an appraised value or an estimated value, as applicable, and use the label "prop. value."

The disclosed value must be based on the best information available to the creditor at the time the loan estimate is provided to the consumer. If the creditor has obtained an appraisal of the property at the time the loan estimate is provided to the consumer, disclose the appraised value stated in the appraisal that the creditor will use during the underwriting of the loan.

> If the creditor does not know which appraisal it will use to underwrite the loan at the time the loan estimate is provided, the value set forth in any appraisal that the creditor reasonably believes will be used in the underwriting should be disclosed.

> If the creditor has not obtained an appraisal but has prepared its own estimate of value, the creditor's estimate of value should be used.

If the creditor has not obtained an appraisal or prepared its own estimate of value, it may disclose an estimate of value provided by a consumer. When disclosing an appraised value or an estimated value for a construction loan without a seller, the creditor has the option to include the estimated value of improvements to be made on the property. Alternatively, the creditor may disclose a value that does not include the estimated value of the improvements.

Loan Term is the term of the debt obligation. Describe the loan term as "years" when the loan term is in whole years. For a loan term that is more than 24 months but is not whole years, describe using years and months with the abbreviations "yr." and "mo.," respectively. For a loan term that is less than 24 months and not whole years, use months only with the abbreviation "mo."

For a construction-permanent loan disclosed as a single transaction, the loan term is the total combined term of both phases. If the construction-permanent loan is disclosed as two separate transactions, the loan term for the permanent phase is counted from the date interest for the permanent phase's periodic payment begins to accrue.

LOAN TERM

PURPOSE

Describe the consumer's intended use for the loan. Purpose is disclosed using one of four descriptions:

- *Purchase* is disclosed if the loan will be used to finance the property's acquisition. The purpose of a simultaneous subordinate lien loan is disclosed as "purchase" if the loan will be used to finance the property's acquisition and will be secured by the property.
- *Refinance is* disclosed if the loan will be used for the refinance of an existing obligation that is secured by the property (even if the creditor is not the holder or servicer of the original obligation).
- *Construction* is disclosed if the loan will be used to finance the initial construction of a dwelling on the property.
- *Home Equity Loan* is disclosed if the loan will be used for any other purpose.

FICUS BANK

4321 Random Boulevard · Somecity, ST 12340

Save this Loan Estimate to compare with your Closing Disclosure.

Loan Estimate

Date disclosure mailed/delivered to Borrower

DATE ISSUED 2/15/2013
APPLICANTS Michael Jones and Mary Stone
123 Anywhere Street
Anytown, ST 12345
PROPERTY 456 Somewhere Avenue
Anytown, ST 12345
SALE PRICE $180,000

LOAN TERM 30 years
PURPOSE Purchase *Transaction Type: Purchase, Refinance, Construction, or Home Equity Loan*
PRODUCT Fixed Rate
LOAN TYPE ☒ Conventional ☐ FHA ☐ VA ☐ _____
LOAN ID # 123456789
RATE LOCK ☐ NO ☒ YES, until 4/16/2013 at 5:00 p.m. EDT
Before closing, your interest rate, points, and lender credits can change unless you lock the interest rate. All other estimated closing costs expire on 3/4/2013 at 5:00 p.m. EDT

Loan Terms

Not rounded but truncated at decimal point when loan is an even dollar amount

Loan Terms		Can this amount increase after closing?
Loan Amount	$162,000	**NO** *If YES, the loan has a negative amortization feature*
Interest Rate	3.875%	**NO**
Monthly Principal & Interest *See Projected Payments below for your Estimated Total Monthly Payment*	$761.78	**NO**
		Does the loan have these features?
Prepayment Penalty		**YES** · As high as $3,240 if you pay off the loan during the first 2 years *A YES shows information specific to loan program*
Balloon Payment		**NO**

Projected Payments

Loans with adjustable payments may show up to four projected payment columns

Payment Calculation	Years 1-7	Years 8-30
Principal & Interest	$761.78	$761.78
Mortgage Insurance	+ 82	+ —
Estimated Escrow *Amount can increase over time*	+ 206	+ 206
Estimated Total Monthly Payment	$1,050	$968

Estimated Taxes, Insurance & Assessments *Amount can increase over time*	$206 a month	This estimate includes ☒ Property Taxes ☒ Homeowner's Insurance ☐ Other: *See Section G on page 2 for escrowed property costs. You must pay for other property costs separately.*	In escrow? YES YES *If NO, this item is not included in the Estimated Total Monthly Payment*

Costs at Closing

Includes items paid at and before closing

Estimated Closing Costs	$8,054	Includes $5,672 in Loan Costs + $2,382 in Other Costs – $0 in Lender Credits. *See page 2 for details.*
Estimated Cash to Close	$16,054	Includes Closing Costs. *See Calculating Cash to Close on page 2 for details.*

Visit **www.consumerfinance.gov/mortgage-estimate** for general information and tools.

Figure 17: LOAN ESTIMATE - Page 1 of 3 (with some item detailing)

PRODUCT

Provide a description of the loan. You are required to include two pieces of information in this disclosure.

The first piece of information is any payment feature that may change the periodic payment, which includes:

- *Negative amortization* is when the principal balance of the loan may increase due to the addition of accrued interest to the principal balance.

- *Interest only* is when one or more regular periodic payments may be applied only to interest accrued and not to the principal of the loan.

- *Step payment* is when the scheduled variations in regular periodic payment amounts occur that are not caused by changes to the interest rate during the loan term.

- *Balloon payment* is when the terms of the legal obligation include a payment that is more than two times that of a regular periodic payment.

- *Seasonal payment* is when the terms of the legal obligation expressly provide that regular periodic payments are not scheduled between specified unit/periods on a regular basis.

The second piece of information disclosed is whether the loan uses an adjustable rate, step rate, or fixed rate to determine the interest rate applied to the principal balance.

- An interest rate is an adjustable rate if the rate may increase after consummation, but the rates that will apply or the periods for which they will apply are not known at consummation.
  - Each description must be preceded by the duration of any introductory rate or payment period, and the first adjustment period, as applicable.
  - When there is no introductory period for an adjustable rate, disclose "0"
- An interest rate is a step rate if the interest rate changes after consummation, and the rates that will apply and the periods for which they apply are known at consummation.
  - Each description must be preceded by the duration of any introductory rate or payment period, and the first adjustment period, as applicable.
  - When there is no introductory rate for a step rate, disclose "0" and then the applicable time period until the first adjustment.

- An interest rate is a fixed rate if the interest rate is not an adjustable rate or step rate.
- If the loan product consists of a combination of product types, only one product type is used.
  - If a loan has a step rate for a set period of time followed by an adjustable rate for the remaining term, only the adjustable rate is disclosed. Here, there will be periods of the loan where the rate is not known at consummation, and as a result, the product cannot be disclosed as step rate.
  - If a loan has a fixed rate for a set period of time followed by an adjustable rate for the remaining term, only the adjustable rate is disclosed. Here, there will be periods where an adjustable rate applies, and as a result, it would not meet the requirements of a fixed rate disclosure.

The following are examples of product with both pieces of information included:
- Year 7 balloon payment, 3/1 step rate: a step rate with an introductory interest rate that lasts for three years and adjusts each year thereafter until a balloon payment is due in the seventh year of the loan term.
- 2 Year negative amortization, fixed rate: a fixed rate product with a step-payment feature for the first two years of the legal obligation that may negatively amortize.

When the time periods disclosed in product are not in whole years, for time periods of 24 months or more, disclose the applicable fraction of a year by use of decimals rounded to two places. For time periods of 24 months or less, disclose the number of months with the abbreviation "mo."
- An adjustable-rate product with an introductory interest rate for 31 months that adjusts every year thereafter is a 2.58/1 adjustable rate.
- An adjustable-rate product with an introductory interest rate for 18 months that adjusts every 18 months thereafter is an 18 mo./18 mo. adjustable rate.

LOAN TYPE

Loan type is the type of the loan, such as conventional or FHA. For loan type, disclose:
- Conventional if the loan is not guaranteed or insured by a federal or state government agency.
- FHA if the loan is insured by the Federal Housing Administration.
- VA if the U.S. Department of Veterans Affairs guarantee the loan.
- Other with a brief description, if the loan is insured or guaranteed by another federal or a state agency.

LOAN ID

The loan ID # is the creditor's loan identification number that may be used by a creditor, consumer, and other parties to identify the transaction.

The loan ID # may contain alphanumeric characters and must be unique to the particular transaction. The same loan ID # may not be used for different, but related, loan transactions. When a revised loan estimate is issued, the loan ID # must be sufficient for the purpose of identifying the transaction associated with the initial loan estimate.

When a mortgage broker completes the Loan estimate:
- If the creditor is known, the loan ID # must be completed. The creditor can outsource the generation and assignment of the loan ID # to the mortgage broker, or the creditor can provide the loan ID # in advance of the disclosures for inclusion.
- If the creditor is unknown and the Loan ID # is not available, the mortgage broker may leave that disclosure blank.

RATE LOCK

Indicate the rate is locked with Yes; indicate the rate is not locked with No. When the interest rate is locked at the time of the loan estimate's delivery, the date and time when the lock period ends must be disclosed. The date and time at which the estimated closing costs expire are disclosed on the loan estimate. However, the date and time are left blank on any revised loan estimate provided after a consumer has indicated an intent to proceed with the transaction.

LOAN AMOUNT

Use the total amount the consumer will borrow as set forth on the face of the note. If the amount is in whole dollars, do not disclose cents.

INTEREST RATE AND MONTHLY PRINCIPAL & INTEREST

The interest rate disclosed is the initial rate at consummation. If the initial interest rate is not known at consummation, the fully indexed rate is disclosed; a fully- indexed rate is the interest rate calculated using the index value and margin at the time of consummation. The initial principal and interest payment amount would also be calculated using the same fully indexed rate if the initial interest rate is not known at consummation.

PREPAYMENT PENALTY

A prepayment penalty is a charge imposed for paying all or part of a transaction's principal before the date on which the principal is due. It does not include a waived third-party charge that the creditor imposes if the consumer prepays the loan's entire principal sooner than 36 months after closing.

BALLOON PAYMENT

A balloon payment is a payment that is more than two times a regular periodic payment.

Under the subheading "Does the loan have these features," if the loan has a prepayment penalty or a balloon payment, the lender should answer "yes." When the answer is "yes" to either, the following should also be disclosed:

- The maximum amount of the prepayment penalty and the date when the penalty period will end.
- The maximum amount of the balloon payment and the due date of such payment.

PAYMENT CALCULATION

Payment calculation column headings. To the right of the payment calculation label, as column headings, use the years of the loan during the payments, or ranges of payments shown in that column will apply.

- Use a sequence of whole years, counting from the due date of the initial periodic payment.
- For periodic payments that may increase based on an adjustment of the interest rate, use the maximum loan term possible under the terms of the legal obligation. To calculate the maximum loan term, assume that the interest rate rises as rapidly as is possible under the terms of the legal obligation, considering any applicable interest rate caps.
- For a balloon payment scheduled as a final payment, use final payment as the column heading.

PRINCIPAL & INTEREST

Use the amount due for principal & interest for the period shown in the column heading. If the payment or range of payments includes any payments of interest only, use the phrase "Only Interest" under the amount of the payment or range of payments.

MORTGAGE INSURANCE

Disclose the maximum amount payable as mortgage insurance that corresponds to the principal & interest payment shown in the same column. This amount should be disclosed as a rounded number. Mortgage insurance includes any mortgage guarantee that provides coverage similar to mortgage insurance, even if not technically considered insurance under state or other applicable law.

Mortgage insurance premiums should be calculated based on the principal balance that will exist after changes to the interest rate and payment amounts pursuant to the legal obligation. The calculations should consider any initial discounted or premium interest rate. If
Mortgage Insurance is not required, disclose "0."

Disclose the mortgage insurance amount that corresponds with the principal & interest amount shown in the same column, even if mortgage insurance is paid on a different schedule than principal & interest.

ESTIMATED ESCROW

Disclose the amount the consumer will pay into an escrow account each month under the terms of the legal obligation. Use a rounded number. If an escrow account will not be established, disclose "0." Disclose "—" if there will be an escrow account, but the escrow account will be closed during the period attributable to the applicable periodic payment.

ESTIMATED TOTAL MONTHLY PAYMENT

For each column, disclose the sum of the principal & interest, mortgage insurance, and estimated escrow as estimated total monthly payment. The amount is rounded if any of the component amounts are rounded.

ESTIMATED TAXES, INSURANCE & ASSESSMENTS

For estimated taxes, insurance & assessments, the total monthly amount due for property taxes, homeowner's insurance, cooperative charges, condominium or HOA fees, and any other fees should be disclosed. This figure should be disclosed as a rounded number.

ESTIMATED CLOSING COSTS

Estimated closing costs are calculated in the same manner as the total closing costs disclosed on Page 2 of the loan estimate. The estimated closing costs are also itemized to show the following:
- The total of the loan costs table.
- The total of the other costs table.
- Lender credits in the total closing costs subheading.

ESTIMATED CASH TO CLOSE

The estimated amount of cash the consumer will be expected to pay at closing is also shown as estimated cash to close. This amount is the same as the estimated cash to close found on the "calculating cash to close" table on page 2 of the loan estimate.

Loan estimate--Page 1 Definition of Terms

- **Monthly Principal & Interest.** Principal (the amount the borrower borrows), and interest (the lender's charge for lending money to the borrower) usually make up the main components of the borrower's monthly mortgage payment. The borrower's total monthly payment will typically be more than this amount due to taxes and insurance.
- **Prepayment Penalty.** A prepayment penalty means that the lender can charge the borrower a fee if the borrower pays off their mortgage early.
- **Balloon Payment.** A balloon payment means that the final mortgage payment is a lump sum much larger than the regular monthly payments.
- **Principal & Interest.** Principal is the amount the borrower will borrow; interest is the lender's charge for lending money to the borrower.
- **Mortgage Insurance.** Mortgage insurance is typically required if the borrower's down payment is less than 20 percent of the price of the home.
- **Estimated Escrow.** Escrow refers to additional charges related to homeownership, such as property taxes and homeowners' insurance, which are bundled in the borrower's monthly payment.
- **Estimated Total Monthly Payment.** The total payment the borrower will make each month, including mortgage insurance and escrow, if applicable.
- **Estimated Closing Costs.** Closing costs are the upfront costs the borrower will be charged to get their loan and transfer ownership of the property. Closing costs are also sometimes referred to as "settlement costs."
- **Estimated Cash to Close.** The total amount the borrower will have to pay at closing, in addition to any money they have already paid.

THE CONSUMER FINANCIAL PROTECTION BUREAU'S GUIDE TO PAGE 2 OF THE LOAN ESTIMATE FORM

ORIGINATION CHARGES

Origination charges are items the consumer will pay to each creditor and loan originator for originating and extending credit. These will include the amount paid, if any, by the consumer to the creditor to reduce the interest rate (sometimes referred to as "points") as both a percentage of the loan amount and a dollar amount. If no points are charged, the percentage of points and the dollar amount should be left blank. Any other items—up to thirteen-- that the consumer will pay to the creditor and loan originator may also be disclosed. If there are more than thirteen origination charges, the total amount of the items exceeding twelve should be disclosed as additional charges. Describe the items, other than for points paid, using terminology that clearly and conspicuously describes the service that is disclosed.

The following items should be itemized separately in the origination charges subheading:
- Compensation paid directly by a consumer to a loan originator that is not also the creditor.
- Any charge imposed to pay for a *loan level pricing adjustment* (LLPA) assessed on the creditor that is passed on to the consumer as a cost at consummation and not as an adjustment to the interest rate.

Only items paid directly by the consumer to compensate a loan originator are origination charges. Compensation paid to an originator by a creditor through the interest rate on the loan estimate should not be disclosed. Also, if the LLPA is accounted for through the rate but not charged as a direct up-front fee, do not disclose the LLPA as a separately itemized origination charge.

SERVICES YOU CANNOT SHOP FOR

Services You Cannot Shop For are items provided by persons other than the creditor or mortgage broker that the consumer cannot shop for and that will be paid for at settlement. Items listed as Services You Cannot Shop For must use terminology that describes each item and disclose them in alphabetical order.

Closing Cost Details

Loan Costs

A. Origination Charges		$1,802
.25 % of Loan Amount (Points)	*All charges are listed*	$405
Application Fee	*alphabetically with the*	$300
Underwriting Fee	*exception of the % of*	$1,097
	Loan Amount (Points)	

B. Services You Cannot Shop For	$672
Appraisal Fee	$405
Credit Report Fee	$30
Flood Determination Fee	$20
Flood Monitoring Fee	$32
Tax Monitoring Fee	$75
Tax Status Research Fee	$110

C. Services You Can Shop For	$3,198
Pest Inspection Fee	$135
Survey Fee	$65
Title – Insurance Binder	$700
Title – Lender's Title Policy	$535
Title – Settlement Agent Fee	$502
Title – Title Search	$1,261

D. TOTAL LOAN COSTS (A + B + C)	$5,672

Other Costs

E. Taxes and Other Government Fees		$85
Recording Fees and Other Taxes	*These are in the 10% variation/*	
Transfer Taxes	*tolerance category*	$85
	These are in the zero variation/tolerance category	

F. Prepaids		$867
Homeowner's Insurance Premium (6 months)		$605
Mortgage Insurance Premium (months)		
Prepaid Interest ($17.44 per day for 15 days @ 3.875%)		$262
Property Taxes (months)		

G. Initial Escrow Payment at Closing		$413
Homeowner's Insurance	$100.83 per month for 2 mo.	$202
Mortgage Insurance	per month for mo.	
Property Taxes	$105.30 per month for 2 mo.	$211

These totals are rounded and truncated at the decimal

H. Other	$1,017
Title – Owner's Title Policy (optional)	$1,017

"Optional" indicates premium not required by Lender and purchased by Borrower

I. TOTAL OTHER COSTS (E + F + G + H)	$2,382

J. TOTAL CLOSING COSTS	$8,054
D + I	$8,054
Lender Credits	

Calculating Cash to Close

Total Closing Costs (J)	$8,054
Closing Costs Financed (Paid from your Loan Amount)	$0
Down Payment/Funds from Borrower	$18,000
Deposit	– $10,000
Funds for Borrower	$0
Seller Credits	$0
Adjustments and Other Credits	$0
Estimated Cash to Close	$16,054

Additional Tables appear here if loan program includes Adjustable Payment (AP) or Adjustable Interest Rate (AIR) features

Figure 17: LOAN ESTIMATE - Page 2 of 3 (with some item detailing)

Services You Cannot Shop For might include:
- Appraisal fee.
- Appraisal management company fee.
- Credit report fee.
- Flood determination fee.
- Government funding fee (such as a VA or USDA guarantee fee, or any other fee paid to a government entity as part of a governmental loan program).
- Homeowner's association certification fee.
- Lender's attorney fee.
- Tax status search fee.
- Third party subordination fee.
- Title – closing protection letter fee.
- Title – lender's title insurance policy.
- An upfront mortgage insurance fee (unless the fee is a prepayment of future premiums or a payment into an escrow account).

Items describing services related to the issuance of title insurance policies should begin with the word "title." Items that are required for the issuance of title insurance policies may include:
- Examination and evaluation of title evidence to determine the insurability of the title being examined and what items to include or exclude in any title commitment and policy to be issued.
- Preparation and issuance of the title commitment or other document that discloses the status of title, identifies the conditions that must be met before the policy will be issued, and obligates the insurer to issue a policy of title insurance if such conditions are met.
- Resolution of title underwriting issues and the steps needed to satisfy any conditions for the issuance of title insurance policies.
- Preparation and issuance of the title insurance policies.
- Payment of premiums for any lender's title insurance coverage.

The amount of the premium for the lender's title insurance coverage must be disclosed without any adjustment to the premium that might be made for the simultaneous purchase of an owner's title insurance policy.

SERVICES YOU CAN SHOP FOR

Services You Can Shop For are services that the creditor requires but that are provided by people other than the creditor or mortgage broker. They are services that the consumer can shop for and will pay for at settlement. Items listed as Services You Can Shop For must use terminology that describes each item and disclose them in alphabetical order. Whether a creditor permits a consumer to shop is determined by the relevant facts and circumstances.

Services You Can Shop For might include:
- Pest inspection fee.
- Survey fee.
- Title – closing agent fee.
- Title – closing protection letter fee.

When disclosing services related to the issuance of title insurance policies, use the word "Title" at the beginning of the item. Items that are related to the issuance of title insurance policies may include:
- Examination and evaluation of title evidence to determine the insurability of the title being examined and what items to include or exclude in any title commitment and policy to be issued.
- Preparation and issuance of the title commitment or other document that discloses the status of title, identifies the conditions that must be met before the policy will be issued, and obligates the insurer to issue a policy of title insurance if such conditions are met.
- Resolution of title underwriting issues as well as steps needed to satisfy any conditions for the issuance of title insurance policies.
- Preparation and issuance of the title insurance policies.
- Payment of premiums for any lender's title insurance coverage.

The creditor must disclose the amount of the premium for the lender's title insurance coverage without any adjustment to the premium that might be made for the simultaneous purchase of an owner's title insurance policy.

Disclose no more than 14 Services You Can Shop For. If there are more than 14 Services You Can Shop For, disclose the total amount of the items that exceed thirteen with the label "Additional Charges." An addendum to the loan estimate can be used to disclose the additional items.

TOTAL LOAN COSTS

Total loan costs is the sum of the subtotals listed as origination charges, services you cannot shop for, and services you can shop for.

TAXES AND OTHER GOVERNMENT FEES

Under *Taxes and Other Government Fees*, recording fees and other taxes should be disclosed first, followed by transfer taxes.

RECORDING FEES AND OTHER TAXES

Recording Fees and Other Taxes are fees assessed by a government authority to record and index the loan and title documents as required under state or local law, together with any charges or fees imposed by a state or local government that are not transfer taxes. Recording fees and other taxes do not include fees that are based on the sale price of the property or loan amount.

TRANSFER TAXES

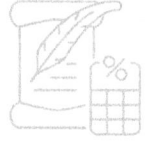

Transfer Taxes are state and local government fees on mortgages and home sales that are based on the loan amount or sale price of the property. The name that is used under state or local law to refer to these amounts is not determinative of whether or not they are disclosed as transfer taxes on the loan estimate.

> Disclose only transfer taxes paid by the consumer on the loan estimate. Whether the consumer pays the transfer tax is based on applicable state or local law. Transfer taxes to be paid by the seller are not disclosed on the loan estimate as transfer taxes.

The amount of transfer taxes disclosed could be modified to the extent that the creditor has knowledge of the apportionment of transfer taxes in the contract for sale between the consumer and a seller when it issues the loan estimate. When a creditor does not have the contract of sale when it issues the loan estimate, the creditor must use the apportionment of transfer taxes provided for by state or local law, or common practice when state or local law is unclear.

> Disclose the sum of all transfer taxes paid by the consumer as transfer taxes. No additional items may be listed or deleted in the taxes and other government fees category.

PREPAIDS

Pre-paid are items to be paid by the consumer in advance of the first scheduled payment of the loan.

Pre-paids are:
- Homeowner's insurance premium.
- Mortgage insurance premium.
- Prepaid interest.
- Property taxes.
- A maximum of three additional items.

Each item must include the applicable time period covered by the payment amount, as well as the total amount to be paid.

INITIAL ESCROW PAYMENT AT CLOSING

Initial Escrow Payment at Closing includes items that the consumer will be expected to place into a reserve or escrow account at consummation, which will then be applied to recurring periodic payments.

Initial escrow payment at closing includes:
- Homeowner's insurance.
- Mortgage insurance.
- Property taxes.
- A maximum of five other items.

The monthly escrow amount for each item and the number of months collected at consummation should also be disclosed.

OTHER

"Other" includes items in connection with the transaction that the consumer is likely to pay or has contracted with a person other than the creditor or loan originator to pay at closing and of which the creditor is aware at the time of issuing the loan estimate.

Separate insurance, warranty, guarantee, or event coverage products may include:
- Owner's title insurance.
- Credit life insurance.
- Debt suspension coverage.
- Debt cancellation coverage.
- Warranties of home appliances and systems.
- Similar products.

These items are disclosed when coverage is written in connection with the mortgage loan. These examples would not include additional coverage and endorsements on insurance otherwise required by the creditor.

Items that disclose any premiums paid for separate insurance, warranty, guarantee, or event coverage products not required by the creditor must include the parenthetical description "optional" at the end of the label. A maximum of five items can be disclosed as 'Other.'

Services related to the issuance of title insurance policies should be described with the word "title." When the owner's title insurance premium includes a simultaneous issuance premium, the premium is calculated by taking the full owner's title insurance premium, adding the simultaneous issuance premium for the lender's coverage (if any), and then deducting the full premium for lender's coverage.

When the creditor is aware of those items, "other" may include the following:

- Commissions of real estate brokers or agents.

- Additional payments to the seller to purchase personal property pursuant to the contract of sale.

- Homeowner's association and condominium charges associated with the transfer of ownership.

- Fees for inspections not required by the creditor but paid by the consumer pursuant to the contract of sale.

Other does not include construction costs, payoffs of existing liens, or payoffs of other secured debt or unsecured debt.

TOTAL CLOSING COSTS
Total Closing Costs is the sum of *total loan costs*, *total other costs*, and *lender credits*.

LENDER CREDITS
A Lender Credit is the amount of any payments from the creditor to the consumer that do not pay for a particular fee on the loan estimate and is disclosed as a negative number.

Lender credits include specific lender credits (if any) that pay for a particular fee disclosed on the loan estimate, as well as general or non-specific lender credits (if any) that do not pay for a particular fee on the Loan estimate.

For loans where all or a portion of closing costs are offset by a credit or rebate provided by the creditor (sometimes referred to as "no cost" loans), such credits or rebates should be disclosed as lender credits.

The creditor should ensure that lender credits are sufficient to cover the estimated items disclosed to the consumer as being unpaid at consummation, regardless of whether such representations pertained to specific items.

TOTAL CLOSING COSTS

Total Closing Costs is the same amount disclosed as total closing costs in the other costs table.

CLOSING COSTS FINANCED
(PAID FROM YOUR LOAN AMOUNT)

Closing Costs Financed (Paid from your Loan Amount) is calculated by subtracting the estimated total amount of payments to third parties not otherwise disclosed in the loan costs and other costs tables from the loan amount disclosed on Page 1 of the loan estimate.

For a purchase loan other than a simultaneous subordinate lien loan, the sale price is included in the closing costs financed calculation as a payment to a third party. The sale price is not included in the closing costs financed disclosure for a simultaneous subordinate lien loan, even if it is a purchase transaction.

Other examples of payments to third parties not otherwise disclosed in the loan costs or other costs tables include the amount of construction costs for transactions that involve improvements to be made on the property and payoffs of secured or unsecured debt.

- If the result of the calculation is a positive number, closing costs financed (paid from the loan amount) is that amount disclosed as a negative number. However, only disclose the amount to the extent that it (as a positive number) does not exceed the amount of total closing costs.

- If the result of the calculation is zero or negative, then closing costs financed (paid from the loan amount) is $0.

DOWN PAYMENT/FUNDS FROM BORROWER

- In a purchase loan other than a simultaneous subordinate lien loan or a loan that involves improvements to be made on the property, subtract the sum of:
  - The loan amount.
  - Any existing loans the borrower will assume.
  - Any loans subject to which the borrower will take title to the property, from the sale price. The calculation is sale price less loan amount less the amount that will be disclosed as existing loans assumed or taken subject to on the closing disclosure's summaries of transactions table. If the result is $0 or a positive number, disclose that result as down payment/ funds from borrower. However, when the sum of the loan amount and the amount to be disclosed as existing loans assumed or taken subject to exceed the sale price, the result will be negative. In such cases, the creditor must perform another calculation, (discussed below), to determine what number to disclose as down payment/ funds from borrower.

- For a purchase loan that is a simultaneous subordinate lien loan, a purchase loan that involves improvements to be made on the property, or a purchase loan where the sum of the loan amount and the amount to be disclosed as existing loans assumed or taken subject to exceeds the sale price, subtract the sum of the loan amount and the amount that will be disclosed as existing loans assumed or taken subject to (excluding any amount disclosed as closing costs financed (paid from the loan amount)) from the total amount of all existing debt being satisfied in the transaction.
  - If this calculation yields an amount that is positive, that amount should be disclosed as the down payment/funds from borrower.
  - If this calculation yields a negative amount or $0, $0 should be disclosed as the down payment/funds from borrower.

For purposes of calculating the down payment/funds from borrower, "the total amount of all existing debt being satisfied in the transaction" is the sum of amounts that will be disclosed on the closing disclosure in the summaries of transactions, as applicable. Generally, this includes the sale price of property, the sale price of any personal property included in the sale as well as the adjustments and the other consumer charges that may be disclosed on line K.04.

- In all other transactions, subtract the sum of the loan amount and the amount that will be disclosed as existing loans assumed or taken subject to (excluding any amount disclosed as closing costs financed (paid from your loan amount) from the total amount of all existing debt being satisfied in the transaction.
  - If this calculation yields an amount that is positive, that amount should be disclosed as the down payment/funds from borrower.
  - If this calculation yields a negative amount or $0, $0 should be disclosed as the down payment/funds from borrower.

DEPOSIT

- In a purchase transaction, deposit is the amount disclosed as a negative number, which is paid to the seller or held in trust or escrow by an attorney or other party under the terms of the contract for sale of the property.
- In all other transactions, the deposit is $0.

FUNDS FOR BORROWER

- In a purchase loan (other than a simultaneous subordinate lien loan, a purchase loan that involves improvements to be made on the property, or a loan where the sum of the loan amount and the amount to be disclosed as existing loans assumed or taken subject to exceeds the sale price), disclose $0 as funds for borrower.

- In all other transactions, subtract the sum of the loan amount and the amount to be disclosed as existing loans assumed or taken subject to (excluding any amount disclosed as closing costs financed (paid from your loan amount) from the total amount of all existing debt being satisfied in the transaction.
  - If this calculation yields a negative amount, the amount should be disclosed as funds for the borrower.
  - If the calculation yields a positive amount or $0, $0 should be disclosed as funds for borrower.

For purposes of calculating the funds for borrower, "the total amount of all existing debt being satisfied in the transaction" is the sum of amounts that will be disclosed on the closing disclosure in the summaries of transactions, as applicable. Generally, this includes the sale price of property, the sale price of any personal property Included in the sale as well as the adjustments and the other consumer charges that may be disclosed on line k.04.

SELLER CREDITS

Seller Credits is the sum of the amounts that the seller will pay for items included in the loan costs and other costs table, to the extent known.

The amount disclosed as seller credits in the calculating cash to close table includes non- specific or general seller credits and any specific seller credits not disclosed in the loan costs or other costs table. Non-specific, or general seller credits, are payments from the seller to the consumer that do not pay for a particular fee, whereas specific seller credits are payments from the seller that are applied to a specific fee. The seller credit amount in the calculating cash to close table is disclosed as a negative number.

ADJUSTMENTS AND OTHER CREDITS

Adjustments and Other Credits is the sum of adjustments requiring additional funds from the consumer, calculated as a positive amount, and other credits for certain items expected to be paid at closing by persons other than the loan originator, creditor, consumer, or seller, calculated as negative amounts.

The calculation includes:

- The total of all items in the loan costs and other costs tables that are expected to be paid at closing by persons other than the loan originator, creditor, consumer, or seller. A creditor is not required to include such amounts if they are expected to be paid in advance of closing. Examples of items that are paid by persons other than the loan originator, creditor, consumer, or seller include:
  - Gifts from family members expected to be paid at closing. Gifts expected to be paid in advance of closing are not included.
  - Credits from a developer or home builder to be applied to items in the loan costs and other cost tables.

- Funds provided to the consumer from the proceeds of subordinate financing, local or state housing assistance grants, or other similar sources. For a purchase transaction that involves both a first lien loan and a simultaneous subordinate lien loan, these amounts should be included only in the loan estimate for the first lien loan.

- Any other amounts that are required to be paid by the consumer at closing or pursuant to the contract of sale (if any) as long as they are not already included in the calculation for down payment/funds from borrower or funds for borrower as debt that is being satisfied in the transaction. Examples of amounts to be paid by the consumer at closing pursuant to the contract of sale include:
  - Charges for personal property to be acquired by the consumer.
  - Proration for property taxes.
  - Proration for homeowner's association dues.

ESTIMATED CASH TO CLOSE

Estimated Cash to Close is calculated as the sum of the seven other amounts disclosed in the loan estimate's calculating cash to close table.

Loan estimate Page 2 Definition of Terms

- **Origination Charges.** Upfront charges from the borrower's lender for making the loan.
- **Points.** An upfront fee that the borrower pays the lender in exchange for a lower interest rate than the borrower would have paid otherwise.
- **Closing Services.** Third-party services required by the lender in order to get a loan. These services are also sometimes referred to as "settlement services." The borrower can shop separately for services listed in section C.
- **Other Costs.** Costs associated with transferring the property to the borrower, as well as costs associated with owning the home.
- **Lender Credits**. A rebate from the lender that offsets some of the borrower's closing costs. Lender credits are typically provided in exchange for the borrower's agreeing to pay a higher interest rate.

THE CONSUMER FINANCIAL PROTECTION BUREAU'S GUIDE TO PAGE 3 OF THE LOAN ESTIMATE FORM

CONTACT INFORMATION

Provide the Name and NMLS/____License ID number for the creditor and mortgage broker, if any, and the individual loan officer of both. The NMLS/____ License ID number should be the same as that identified on the note and other documents. The email and phone number of the loan officer should also be provided, as the individual loan officer will be the primary contact for the consumer.

COMPARISONS IN 5 YEARS

In 5 Years **includes the following information:**

- The total amount the consumer will have paid in principal, interest, mortgage insurance, and loan costs paid through the end of the 60th month after the due date of the first periodic payment.

- The amount of principal paid through the end of the 60th month after the due date of the first periodic payment.

Additional Information About This Loan

LENDER	Ficus Bank	
NMLS/__ LICENSE ID		
LOAN OFFICER	Joe Smith	
NMLS/__ LICENSE ID	12345	
EMAIL	joesmith@ficusbank.com	
PHONE	123-456-7890	

MORTGAGE BROKER
NMLS/__ LICENSE ID
LOAN OFFICER
NMLS/__ LICENSE ID
EMAIL
PHONE

Comparisons
Use these measures to compare this loan with other loans.

In 5 Years	$56,582	Total you will have paid in principal, interest, mortgage insurance, and loan costs.
	$15,773	Principal you will have paid off.
Annual Percentage Rate (APR)	4.274%	Your costs over the loan term expressed as a rate. This is not your interest rate.
Total Interest Percentage (TIP)	69.45%	The total amount of interest that you will pay over the loan term as a percentage of your loan amount.

Other Considerations

Appraisal	We may order an appraisal to determine the property's value and charge you for this appraisal. We will promptly give you a copy of any appraisal, even if your loan does not close. You can pay for an additional appraisal for your own use at your own cost.
Assumption	If you sell or transfer this property to another person, we ☐ will allow, under certain conditions, this person to assume this loan on the original terms. ☒ will not allow assumption of this loan on the original terms.
Homeowner's Insurance	This loan requires homeowner's insurance on the property, which you may obtain from a company of your choice that we find acceptable.
Late Payment	If your payment is more than 15 days late, we will charge a late fee of 5% of the monthly principal and interest payment.
Refinance	Refinancing this loan will depend on your future financial situation, the property value, and market conditions. You may not be able to refinance this loan.
Servicing	We intend ☐ to service your loan. If so, you will make your payments to us. ☒ to transfer servicing of your loan.

Confirm Receipt

Consumer is not required to sign; signature is acknowledgement of receipt, NOT acceptance of the loan

By signing, you are only confirming that you have received this form. You do not have to accept this loan because you have signed or received this form.

_____ _____ _____ _____
Applicant Signature   Date   Co-Applicant Signature   Date

LOAN ESTIMATE

Figure 17: LOAN ESTIMATE - Page 3 of 3 (with some item detailing)

ANNUAL PERCENTAGE RATE (APR)

Disclose the APR, together with a brief descriptive statement, in the comparisons table on Page 3.

TOTAL INTEREST PERCENTAGE (TIP)

The TIP is the total amount of interest that the consumer will pay over the loan term, expressed as a percentage of the loan amount. The TIP includes prepaid interest that the consumer will pay but does not include prepaid interest paid by someone other than the consumer. If prepaid interest is disclosed as a negative number, the negative value of the prepaid interest must be included in the calculation of the TIP.

OTHER CONSIDERATIONS

Other Considerations includes the following information:

- **Appraisal**- Once the appraisal is complete, the appraiser will create an appraisal report which documents their findings of value, comparables used to determine value, and market trend pertaining to the subject property.

- As to an **assumption**, whether the subsequent purchaser of the property can assume the loan on its original terms.

- At the option of the creditor, a statement that **homeowner's insurance** is required and that the consumer may choose the provider.

- A statement detailing any amount that may be imposed for a **late payment.**

- A statement about the nature of a **refinance** of the loan in the future.

- A statement regarding whether the creditor intends to **service** the loan or transfer it to another servicer.

- For **refinance** transactions, a statement regarding legal protections against liability after foreclosure.

- At the option of the creditor, for transactions involving new construction, where the creditor reasonably expects that settlement will occur 60 days or more after the provision of the loan estimate, a clear and conspicuous statement that the creditor may issue a revised disclosure any time prior to 60 days before consummation.

CONFIRM RECEIPT

The consumer is not required to sign the loan estimate. The creditor may add a signature statement and have the consumer sign page 3 of the loan estimate in order to confirm receipt of the loan estimate by the consumer. If used by the creditor, the signature statement must contain the exact language from the model form. If the confirm receipt table is not used by a creditor, a statement about loan acceptance must be included at the end of the other consideration table that states, "You do not have to accept this loan because you have received this form or signed a loan application."

Loan estimate Page 3 Definition of Terms

- **Annual Percentage Rate (APR)** - The APR is one measure of the borrower's cost of the loan.

- **Total Interest Percentage (TIP)** - This number helps the borrower understand how much interest they will pay over the life of the loan and lets them make comparisons between loans.

- **Appraisal** - The lender uses an appraisal by an independent, professional appraiser, to decide how much the borrower's home is worth. The borrower has a right to receive a copy.

- **Assumption** – Some loans allow assumption, which means that if the borrower sells the home, the new buyer may be allowed to take over the borrower's loan on the same terms, instead of taking out a new loan. If the borrower's loan does not allow assumptions, the buyer will not be allowed to take over the borrower's loan. Most loans do not allow assumptions.

- **Servicing** - Servicing means managing the loan on a day-to-day basis (such as accepting payments) once the loan is made. The lender can choose to service the loan itself or transfer that responsibility to a different company.

> **NOTE**
>
> *Revised loan estimate - When there is a changed circumstance after the loan estimate has been provided, the creditor can revise the loan estimate within three business days of receiving notification of the changed circumstance. Revised loan estimates can generally be provided no later than four business days before consummation.*

THE CLOSING DISCLOSURE FORM EXPLAINED

On October 3, 2015, after the Consumer Financial Protection Bureau (CFPB) took over the Real Estate Settlement Procedures Act (RESPA), homebuyers began receiving *closing disclosures*, in lieu of the previously used HUD-1 Settlement Statement (used while RESPA was under HUD administration). Of the numerous documents that a homebuyer will encounter during the mortgage process, the closing disclosure is arguably the most important.

The *Closing Disclosure (CD)* is a five-page form that summarizes the final details of the borrower's home loan once a final offer is made. This standard form, which the CFPB requires lenders to provide to borrowers three business days before closing, lets the borrower compare their final loan offer to the *loan estimate* provided to them when the loan application was submitted. The three-day period also gives the borrower time to ask the lender any questions before closing.

The CD includes the loan terms, the borrower's projected monthly payments, and how much they will pay in fees and other costs to get their mortgage. Aside from comparing the costs, there is other information on the CD that the borrower needs to validate. Borrowers can determine whether the loan has a prepayment penalty or a balloon payment. Are there items that are not in the borrower's escrow account? It is vital that the borrower take the three days before closing to go over the information on the CD with the loan officer.

The Closing Disclosure At-A-Glance:
- This new form consists of five pages.

- This new form replaces the TILA and HUD-1.

- One closing disclosure is required for each loan.

- Charge descriptions used on both the loan estimate and closing disclosure must be similar.

Closing Disclosure

This form is a statement of final loan terms and closing costs. Compare this document with your Loan Estimate.

Closing Information		Transaction Information		Loan Information	
Date Issued	4/15/2013	Borrower	Michael Jones and Mary Stone	Loan Term	30 years
Closing Date	4/15/2013		123 Anywhere Street	Purpose	Purchase
Disbursement Date	4/15/2013		Anytown, ST 12345	Product	Fixed Rate
Settlement Agent	Epsilon Title Co.	Seller	Steve Cole and Amy Doe		
File #	12-3456		321 Somewhere Drive	Loan Type	☒ Conventional ☐ FHA
Property	456 Somewhere Ave		Anytown, ST 12345		☐ VA ☐ _____
	Anytown, ST 12345	Lender	Ficus Bank	Loan ID #	123456789
Sale Price	$180,000			MIC #	000654321

Borrower & Seller names/ addresses are required
Date mailed/delivered to Borrower
Consummation Date; often the signing date, but is determined by Lender
Transaction type: Purchase, etc.

Loan Terms

Not rounded but truncated at decimal point when loan is an even dollar amount

Loan Terms		Can this amount increase after closing?
Loan Amount	$162,000	NO *If YES, the loan has a negative amortization feature*
Interest Rate	3.875%	NO
Monthly Principal & Interest *See Projected Payments below for your Estimated Total Monthly Payment*	$761.78	NO
		Does the loan have these features?
Prepayment Penalty		YES • As high as $3,240 if you pay off the loan during the first 2 years *A YES shows information specific to loan program*
Balloon Payment		NO

Projected Payments

Loans with adjustable payments may show up to four projected payment columns

Payment Calculation	Years 1-7	Years 8-30
Principal & Interest	$761.78	$761.78
Mortgage Insurance	+ 82.35	+ —
Estimated Escrow *Amount can increase over time*	+ 206.13	+ 206.13
Estimated Total Monthly Payment	$1,050.26	$967.91

"Estimated" is used because the Escrow amount can change over time

Estimated Taxes, Insurance & Assessments *Amount can increase over time* *See page 4 for details*	$356.13 a month	This estimate includes ☒ Property Taxes ☒ Homeowner's Insurance ☒ Other: Homeowner's Association Dues *See Escrow Account on page 4 for details. You must pay for other property costs separately.*	In escrow? YES YES NO *If NO, this item is not included in the Estimated Total Monthly Payment*

Costs at Closing

Includes items paid at and before closing

Closing Costs	$9,712.10	Includes $4,694.05 in Loan Costs + $5,018.05 in Other Costs – $0 in Lender Credits. *See page 2 for details.*
Cash to Close	$14,147.26	Includes Closing Costs. *See Calculating Cash to Close on page 3 for details.*

The actual amount required for closing may differ from this Cash to Close amount if the Lender does not allow a title premium adjustment on Page 3, Sections L and N

Figure 18: CLOSING DISCLOSURE – PAGE 1 of 5

THE CONSUMER FINANCIAL PROTECTION BUREAU'S GUIDE TO PAGE 1 OF THE CLOSING DISCLOSURE FORM

CLOSING INFORMATION

For *closing information*, the following information should be provided:

- The date issued, which is the date the closing disclosure is delivered or placed in the mail to the consumer (not the date the form is actually printed).

- The closing date, which is the date of consummation.

- The disbursement date, which is the date funds are disbursed.
  - In a purchase other than a simultaneous subordinate lien transaction, the disbursement date is the date that the cash to close amount is expected to be paid to the consumer or seller, as applicable.
  - In a simultaneous subordinate lien transaction or a non-purchase transaction, the disbursement date is the date that some or all of the loan amount is expected to be paid to the consumer or a third party other than the settlement agent.

- The name of the settlement agent, which is the name of the entity, not the individual agent conducting the closing.

- The file #, which is assigned to the transaction by the settlement agent (the TILA-RESPA Rule does not prescribe how the settlement agent creates the file number; the file number, for example, may be alphanumeric)

- The property address or location

- For the property:
  - Sale price
  - Appraised prop. value
  - Estimated prop. value

The appraised prop. value is disclosed for transactions without a seller if a creditor has obtained an appraisal of the property. If a creditor has obtained more than one appraisal, the creditor discloses the value stated in the appraisal that the creditor used to approve the loan. The estimated prop. value is disclosed if the creditor has not obtained an appraisal for a transaction without a seller. If the creditor has prepared its own estimate of value, it must use that value when disclosing the estimated prop. value, rather than an estimate provided by the consumer.

If the creditor has prepared more than one estimate of value, it discloses the value in the estimate it used to approve the transaction. If a creditor considers the value of improvements to the property when approving a construction loan where there is no seller, it must include the value of the improvements when disclosing the appraised prop. value or estimated prop. value.

TRANSACTION INFORMATION

For *transaction information*, disclose the name of the seller (if any) as seller, and the name of the creditor as lender. Disclose the name(s) and address of the person(s) to whom credit is extended as borrower. Names and addresses of other consumers should not be provided. The name and address of each person who is a seller or borrower in the transaction must be disclosed. However, the name and address of seller may be left blank on the closing disclosure for a simultaneous subordinate lien loan if the closing disclosure for the first lien loan will disclose the entirety of the seller's transaction. The name and address of the seller is also left blank for transactions without a seller. If there is not enough space to show the name and address of all parties, an additional page may be appended to the end of the closing disclosure.

LOAN INFORMATION

For *loan information,* disclose the loan term, purpose, product, loan type, the creditor's loan identification number as loan ID #, and mortgage insurance case number, if required by the creditor, as MIC # under the loan information subheading. The information disclosed for loan term, purpose, product, loan type, and loan ID # will be the same as that provided for those items on the loan estimate. These items should be updated to reflect the terms of the legal obligation at consummation.

LOAN TERMS

The *loan terms* table on the closing disclosure provides the same information required to be given on the loan estimate but updated to reflect the terms of the legal obligation at consummation.

PROJECTED PAYMENTS

The *projected payments* table on the closing disclosure provides the same information given on the projected payments table on the Loan estimate and is updated to reflect the terms of the legal obligation at consummation.

However, there are two differences in the closing disclosure:

- For loans subject to RESPA, the amounts disclosed under the estimated escrow and estimated taxes, insurance, and assessments sections on the closing disclosure must be determined under the escrow account analysis described in Regulation X. Loans not subject to RESPA also have this option on the closing disclosure.

- The closing disclosure refers the consumer to page 4 of the closing disclosure, unlike the loan estimate, which refers the consumer to page 2.

COSTS AT CLOSING

The *costs at closing* table discloses:

- The total amount disclosed as total closing costs in the other costs table on Page 2 of the closing disclosure. Total closing costs are also itemized to show the total loan costs, the total other costs, and lender credits from the total closing costs subheading provided on page 2 of the closing disclosure.

- The estimated amount of cash the consumer will pay or receive at closing as cash to close. This amount is the same as the cash to close calculated in the calculating cash to close table on page 3 of the closing disclosure.

Closing Cost Details

Unlike the HUD-1, Borrower subtotals are shown at the TOP of each section

Loan Costs		Borrower-Paid		Seller-Paid		Paid by Others
		At Closing	Before Closing	At Closing	Before Closing	
A. Origination Charges *All items in this section are zero variation/*		**$1,802.00**				*Payor not specified*
01 0.25 % of Loan Amount (Points) *tolerance charges*		$405.00				*in this column*
02 Application Fee		$300.00				
03 Underwriting Fee		$1,097.00				
04						
05 *Except for Line A.01, all charges are listed alphabetically*						
06 *in each section*						
07						
08						
B. Services Borrower Did Not Shop For		**$236.55**				
01 Appraisal Fee	to John Smith Appraisers Inc.					$405.00
02 Credit Report Fee	to Information Inc.		$29.80			
03 Flood Determination Fee	to Info Co.	$20.00				
04 Flood Monitoring Fee	to Info Co.	$31.75				
05 Tax Monitoring Fee	to Info Co.	$75.00				
06 Tax Status Research Fee	to Info Co.	$80.00				
07						
08 *Items in this section are zero or 10% variation/tolerance*						
09 *charges, as determined by the Lender*						
10						
C. Services Borrower Did Shop For *All items in this section are unlimited*		**$2,655.50**				
01 Pest Inspection Fee	to Pests Co. *variation/tolerance charges*	$120.50				
02 Survey Fee	to Surveys Co.	$85.00				
03 Title – Insurance Binder	to Epsilon Title Co.	$650.00				
04 Title – Lender's Title Insurance	to Epsilon Title Co.	$500.00				
05 Title – Settlement Agent Fee	to Epsilon Title Co.	$500.00				
06 Title – Title Search	to Epsilon Title Co.	$800.00				
07 *Any item that is a component of/related to title insurance or*						
08 *settlement must contain description that begins with the word "Title"*						
D. TOTAL LOAN COSTS (Borrower-Paid)		**$4,694.05**				
Loan Costs Subtotals (A + B + C)		$4,664.25	$29.80			

Recording Fees: 10% variation/tolerance category if paid by Borrower
Transfer Tax: Zero variation/tolerance category, if paid by Borrower

Other Costs						
E. Taxes and Other Government Fees		**$85.00**				
01 Recording Fees	Deed: $40.00 Mortgage: $45.00	$85.00				
02 Transfer Tax	to Any State			$950.00		
F. Prepaids		**$2,120.80**				
01 Homeowner's Insurance Premium (12 mo.) to Insurance Co.		$1,209.96				
02 Mortgage Insurance Premium (mo.)						
03 Prepaid Interest ($17.44 per day from 4/15/13 to 5/1/13)		$279.04				
04 Property Taxes (6 mo.) to Any County USA		$631.80				
05						
G. Initial Escrow Payment at Closing		**$412.25**				
01 Homeowner's Insurance $100.83 per month for 2 mo.		$201.66				
02 Mortgage Insurance per month for mo.						
03 Property Taxes $105.30 per month for 2 mo.		$210.60				
04						
05						
06						
07						
08 Aggregate Adjustment		– 0.01				
H. Other		**$2,400.00**				
01 HOA Capital Contribution	to HOA Acre Inc. *If paid by Borrower, it*	$500.00				
02 HOA Processing Fee	to HOA Acre Inc. *must include 'Optional'*	$150.00				
03 Home Inspection Fee	to Engineers Inc. *at end of description*	$750.00				$750.00
04 Home Warranty Fee	to XYZ Warranty Inc.			$450.00		
05 Real Estate Commission	to Alpha Real Estate Broker *Full commission is shown regardless of*			$5,700.00		
06 Real Estate Commission	to Omega Real Estate Broker *who holds the earnest money deposit*			$5,700.00		
07 Title – Owner's Title Insurance (optional) to Epsilon Title Co.		$1,000.00				

Charges in sections F, G, and H are in the unlimited variation/tolerance category

However, if paid by Seller, 'Optional' may be indicated but is not required

Additional charges for services provided are itemized separately

If Lender allows title premium adjustment between Borrower & Seller, it will show on Page 3, Sections L & N; if Lender does not

I. TOTAL OTHER COSTS (Borrower-Paid)		**$5,018.05**				
Other Costs Subtotals (E + F + G + H)		$5,018.05				

allow title premium adjustment,
Cash To/From Borrower & Seller will not be accurate

J. TOTAL CLOSING COSTS (Borrower-Paid)		**$9,712.10**				
Closing Costs Subtotals (D + I)		$9,682.30	$29.80	$12,800.00	$750.00	$405.00
Lender Credits						

Figure 18: CLOSING DISCLOSURE – PAGE 2 of 5 (with some item detailing)

THE CONSUMER FINANCIAL PROTECTION BUREAU'S GUIDE TO PAGE 2 OF THE CLOSING DISCLOSURE FORM

ORIGINATION CHARGES

Origination Charges - Loan originator compensation is disclosed as origination charges, even though loan originator compensation is not disclosed on the loan estimate. Compensation from the consumer to a third-party loan originator is designated as borrower-paid at closing or before closing on the closing disclosure. Compensation from the creditor to a third-party loan originator is designated as paid by others on the closing disclosure. A designation of (L) can be listed with the amount to indicate that the creditor pays at consummation. The amount of compensation from the creditor to the third-party loan originator is the dollar value of salaries, commissions, and any financial or similar compensation provided by the creditor and considered to be points and fees. Compensation to individual loan originators is neither calculated nor disclosed on the closing disclosure.

SERVICES THE CONSUMER (BORROWER) DID AND DID NOT SHOP FOR

Services the Consumer (Borrower) Did and Did Not Shop For. Items that the consumer could have shopped for, but did not, are disclosed in the services borrower did not shop for subheading, regardless of where the item was disclosed on the loan estimate. When a consumer chooses a provider that was on the written list of providers for a service, that service is listed as services borrower did not shop for in the closing disclosure loan costs table. For example, if the consumer could have shopped for the flood determination fee on the loan estimate but chose a provider from the creditor's list of providers, that charge is listed as services borrower did not shop for even though the creditor did not require that particular provider. Items disclosed as services borrower did shop for and services borrower did not shop for are re-alphabetized when an item is added to or removed from the closing disclosure.

TOTAL LOAN COSTS (BORROWER-PAID)

Total Loan Costs. The amounts that are designated as borrower-paid at or before closing are subtotaled as total loan costs (borrower-paid). The amounts that are designated seller-paid at or before closing and paid by others are not subtotaled as total loan costs (borrower-paid).

TAXES AND OTHER GOVERNMENT FEES

In the shaded column of the line with the subheading *Taxes and Other Government Fees,* disclose the total amount expected to be paid by the consumer for recording fees and transfer taxes at or before closing. In the appropriate columns of the next line, disclose the total amount expected to be paid to state or local governments for recording the deed, security instruments, and any other instrument or document recorded to preserve marketable title or to perfect the creditor's security interest in the property. The total fees expected to be paid for recording deeds should also be stated on this line, following the word "Deed." On the same line, but separate, the total fees expected to be paid for recording security instruments should be stated, following the word "mortgage." An itemization of transfer taxes paid by the consumer and the seller is disclosed under the heading "taxes and other government fees," instead of the sum total of transfer taxes to be paid by the consumer. This itemization is given after the disclosure of the recording fees.

The name of the government entity assessing the fee (which may not necessarily be the payee of the check cut by the settlement agent) is provided on the closing disclosure. Each transfer tax and government entity should be itemized, as multiple taxes may be assessed by each government entity.

PREPAIDS

Prepaids are items to be paid by the consumer in advance of the first scheduled payment of the loan. Prepaids include:
- Homeowner's insurance premium
- Mortgage insurance premium.
- Prepaid interest.
- Property taxes.
- A maximum of three additional items.

Each item must include the total amount to be paid, as well as the period to which the amount applies. If homeowner's insurance premiums, mortgage insurance premiums, prepaid interest, or property taxes are not applicable to the loan, the inapplicable lines should not be deleted.

Instead:
- If there are no prepaid homeowner's insurance premiums, mortgage insurance premiums, or property taxes associated with the loan, the time period, daily amount, and percentage used in the labels should be left blank.

If no Prepaid Interest will be collected at consummation, the amount should be disclosed as "$0.00."

INITIAL ESCROW PAYMENT AT CLOSING

Property taxes paid during different time periods can be disclosed as separate items. For example, general property taxes assessed for January 1 to December 31 and property taxes to fund schools for November 1 to October 31 can be disclosed as separate items. The last item disclosed in the *Initial Escrow Payment at Closing* is the aggregate adjustment, which is calculated under Regulation X.

OTHER

In some instances, a consumer or seller may incur costs that are not required to be disclosed on the loan estimate. These are recorded as *Other* and may include the following:
- Real estate brokerage fees.
- Homeowner or condominium association fees paid at consummation.
- Home warranties.
- Inspection fees.
- Other fees paid at closing that are not required to be stated elsewhere on the closing disclosure.

The amount of an earnest money deposit does not affect the amount of real estate commissions paid by the consumer or seller on the closing disclosure, even if the earnest money deposit is held by the real estate brokerage.

TOTAL OTHER COSTS (BORROWER-PAID) AND TOTAL CLOSING COSTS (BORROWER- PAID)

Total Other Costs and Total Closing Costs. The total of all closing costs paid by the consumer, minus the lender credit, is stated as total closing costs (borrower- paid). The total of items designated as borrower-paid at or before closing, seller-paid at or before closing, and paid by others are disclosed as closing cost subtotals. Lastly, the total amount of lender credits, if any, are disclosed and designated as borrower-paid at closing.

Amounts shown in LE column are rounded; amounts shown in Final column are not rounded; Final column may appear larger due to rounding

Calculating Cash to Close

Use this table to see what has changed from your Loan Estimate.

	Loan Estimate	Final	Did this change?
Total Closing Costs (J)	$8,054.00	$9,712.10	YES · See Total Loan Costs (D) and Total Other Costs (I)
Closing Costs Paid Before Closing	$0	– $29.80	YES · You paid these Closing Costs before closing
Closing Costs Financed (Paid from your Loan Amount)	$0	$0	NO
Down Payment/Funds from Borrower	$18,000.00	$18,000.00	NO
Deposit	– $10,000.00	– $10,000.00	NO
Funds for Borrower	$0	$0	NO
Seller Credits	$0	– $2,500.00	YES · See Seller Credits in Section L
Adjustments and Other Credits	$0	– $1,035.04	YES · See details in Sections K and L *This figure is an aggregate of debits and credits shown in Sections K and L; it may also include subordinate financing, gift funds, prorations & generalized credits*
Cash to Close	$16,054.00	$14,147.26	

Summaries of Transactions

Use this table to see a summary of your transaction.

BORROWER'S TRANSACTION

K. Due from Borrower at Closing	$189,762.30
01 Sale Price of Property	$180,000.00
02 Sale Price of Any Personal Property Included in Sale	
03 Closing Costs Paid at Closing (J)	$9,682.30
04	

Adjustments
05
06
07

Adjustments for Items Paid by Seller in Advance

08 City/Town Taxes	to	
09 County Taxes	to	
10 Assessments	to	
11 HOA Dues	4/15/13 to 4/30/13	$80.00
12		
13		
14		
15		

L. Paid Already by or on Behalf of Borrower at Closing	$175,615.04
01 Deposit	$10,000.00
02 Loan Amount	$162,000.00
03 Existing Loan(s) Assumed or Taken Subject to	
04	
05 Seller Credit	$2,500.00
Other Credits	
06 Rebate from Epsilon Title Co.	$750.00
07	

Adjustments
08 *If Lender allows title premium adjustment between Borrower &*
09 *Seller, it will show on Page 3, Sections L & N; if Lender does*
10 *not allow title premium adjustment, Cash To/From Borrower &*
11 *Seller will not be accurate*

Adjustments for Items Unpaid by Seller

12 City/Town Taxes 1/1/13 to 4/14/13	$365.04
13 County Taxes to	
14 Assessments to	
15	
16	
17	

SELLER'S TRANSACTION

M. Due to Seller at Closing	$180,080.00
01 Sale Price of Property	$180,000.00
02 Sale Price of Any Personal Property Included in Sale	
03	
04	
05	
06	
07	
08	

Adjustments for Items Paid by Seller in Advance

09 City/Town Taxes	to	
10 County Taxes	to	
11 Assessments	to	
12 HOA Dues	4/15/13 to 4/30/13	$80.00
13		
14		
15		
16		

N. Due from Seller at Closing	$115,665.04
01 Excess Deposit	
02 Closing Costs Paid at Closing (J)	$12,800.00
03 Existing Loan(s) Assumed or Taken Subject to	
04 Payoff of First Mortgage Loan	$100,000.00
05 Payoff of Second Mortgage Loan	
06	
07	
08 Seller Credit	$2,500.00
09 *If Lender allows title premium adjustment between Borrower*
10 *& Seller, it will show on Page 3, Sections L & N; if Lender does*
11 *not allow title premium adjustment, Cash To/From Borrower*
12 *& Seller will not be accurate*
13

Adjustments for Items Unpaid by Seller

14 City/Town Taxes 1/1/13 to 4/14/13	$365.04
15 County Taxes to	
16 Assessments to	
17	
18	
19	

CALCULATION

Total Due from Borrower at Closing (K)	$189,762.30
Total Paid Already by or on Behalf of Borrower at Closing (L)	– $175,615.04
Cash to Close ☒ From ☐ To Borrower	**$14,147.26**

CALCULATION

Total Due to Seller at Closing (M)	$180,080.00
Total Due from Seller at Closing (N)	– $115,665.04
Cash ☐ From ☒ To Seller	**$64,414.96**

CLOSING DISCLOSURE *If Lender does not allow title premium adjustment, Cash To/From Borrower & Seller will not be accurate on the CD; Borrowers & Sellers must refer to the Settlement Statement for the final figures* PAGE 3 OF 5 · LOAN ID # 123456789

Figure 18: CLOSING DISCLOSURE – PAGE 3 of 5 (with some item detailing)

Closing Disclosure Page 2 Definition of Terms

- **Borrower-Paid** -This column lists the costs that are charged to the borrower.

- **Taxes and Other Government Fees** - Costs associated with transferring the property to the borrower and registering the borrower's mortgage with the county records office.

- **Prepaids** - This category includes interest on the borrower's loan between the time of closing and the end of that month. It is also common to pay the borrower's first year's homeowner's insurance premium in advance at closing.

- **Initial Escrow Payment at Closing** - This payment will establish an initial balance in the borrower's escrow account.

- **Total Closing Costs** - Total upfront costs associated with the borrower's loan and real estate transaction, excluding the borrower's down payment. This is different from the actual amount of money the borrower had to bring to closing, which is called "cash to close" on Page 3.

THE CONSUMER FINANCIAL PROTECTION BUREAU'S GUIDE TO PAGE 3 OF THE CLOSING DISCLOSURE FORM

CALCULATING CASH TO CLOSE

The *Calculating Cash to Close* table has nine items listed in the table:
- Total closing costs.
- Closing costs paid before closing.
- Closing costs financed (paid from your loan amount).
- Down payment/funds from borrower.
- Deposit.
- Funds for borrower.
- Seller credits.
- Adjustments and other credits.
- Cash to close.

The table has three columns to disclose the amount for each item as it was stated on the loan estimate, the final amount for the item, and an answer to the question:

Did this change? The amounts disclosed in the loan estimate column are the same as the amounts disclosed in the most recent loan estimate provided to the consumer. The amounts disclosed in the loan estimate column are rounded to the nearest dollar in order to match the corresponding amount on the loan estimate's calculating cash to close table. Generally, the amounts in the final column are calculated using the same methods that were used for the calculating cash to close table on the loan estimate and must be based on the best information available to the creditor at the time that the closing disclosure is provided to the consumer.

When the answer to the question *Did this change?* is Yes, the amounts that changed on the loan estimate should be clearly indicated to the consumer. If the seller credit amount changed and the change is attributable only to general seller credits, the creditor may disclose "See Seller Credits in Section L." Examples of language for disclosing changes to other items are found in example form H-25(B) in appendix H of Regulation Z.

BORROWER'S TRANSACTION

A creditor can work with a settlement agent, and the settlement agent can disclose the *Borrower's Transaction* column of the summaries of transactions table. In such instances, any references to the creditor would apply to the settlement agent.

DUE FROM BORROWER AT CLOSING

Generally, in a purchase transaction the amount *Due from Borrower at Closing* includes:
- *Sale price of property.*
- *Sale price of any personal property included in sale.*
- *Closing costs paid at closing.*
- *Adjustments.*
- *Adjustments for items paid by the seller in advance*, pursuant to the terms of the real estate sale contract.
- *Other consumer charges* disclosed in Section K, such as those that may be disclosed on line K.04

It should be noted that the sale price is not disclosed in the summaries of transactions table for a simultaneous subordinate lien loan in a purchase transaction. For the purposes of disclosing the sale price of any personal property included in sale, personal property is defined by state law, but could include such items as carpets, drapes, and appliances. Manufactured homes are not considered personal property for the closing disclosure. Closing costs paid at closing is the amount of closing costs designated as borrower-paid at closing minus any lender credits on Page 2 of the closing disclosures.

Under the heading *Adjustments,* a description and amount for each of the following should be disclosed:
- Items not otherwise disclosed in Section K of the closing disclosure that the seller has paid prior to the real estate closing but that will be reimbursed by the consumer at closing.
- Items not otherwise disclosed in Section K of the closing disclosure are owed to the seller but payable to the consumer after the closing.

Examples of items that are disclosed as adjustments include:
- A balance in a seller's reserve account transferred to the consumer in connection with an assumed loan.
- Rent that the consumer will collect after closing for a period of time prior to the closing.
- A tenant security deposit.

Under *Adjustments for Items Paid by the Seller in Advance,* disclose the prorated amounts for prepaid city/town taxes, county taxes, and other assessments due from the consumer to reimburse the seller and the time period corresponding to that amount. A description and amount for any item paid by the seller prior to closing that is due from the consumer at closing should also be disclosed.

Examples of these items include:
- Taxes (other than county or city/town taxes) paid in advance for an entire year when the closing occurs prior to the expiration of the year.
- Flood or hazard insurance premiums when the consumer is being substituted as an insured under the same policy.
- Mortgage insurance in connection with an assumed loan.
- Planned unit development or condominium association assessments paid for in advance.
- Fuel or other supplies purchased by the seller which the consumer will use once the property is transferred.
- Ground rent paid in advance by the seller.

Disclose other charges owed by the consumer in the real estate closing that are not otherwise stated in the loan costs table, other costs table, or Section K of the closing disclosure. Generally, these amounts may be disclosed on line K.04.

Examples include:
- Amounts paid to any existing holders of liens on the property in a refinance transaction.
- Payoffs of other secured or unsecured debt.
- Any outstanding real estate property taxes.
- Construction costs that the consumer will be obligated to pay in connection with the transaction.
- Principal reductions.
- For a simultaneous subordinate lien loan, the proceeds of the loan are applied to the first-lien loan.

These amounts are disclosed without a corresponding credit in the seller's transaction column.

PAID ALREADY BY OR ON BEHALF OF BORROWER AT CLOSING

The amount *Paid Already by or on Behalf of Borrower at Closing* is the sum of:
- Deposit
- Loan amount
- Existing loan(s) assumed or taken subject to
- Seller credits
- Other credits
- Adjustments for items unpaid by seller pursuant to the terms of the real estate sale contract

A Deposit is the amount paid into a trust account by the consumer pursuant to a contract of sale. If the deposit has been applied toward a closing cost paid by the consumer, the amount so applied should be deducted from the amount of the deposit. No deduction in the amount of the deposit is to be made for the payment of any real estate commission disclosed on Page 2 of the closing disclosure.

Existing Loan(s) Assumed or Taken Subject to is the total amount of all loans that the consumer is assuming in the transaction, even if more than one loan is being assumed, and all loans to which the consumer is taking title.

Seller Credits include any general or non-specific seller credits. However, if the seller credit is attributable to a charge listed on *Closing Disclosure* Page 2, then the amount should be listed with the item and designated as *seller paid at closing or seller paid before closing* on closing disclosure page 2. *Seller credits* include any seller credits for issues identified at a walk-through of the property.

Other Credits include a general credit from any party other than the seller or creditor. One example is a credit a consumer receives from a real estate agent. A description of the credit and the name of the party giving the credit must also be included. However, if the credit or rebate is attributable to a charge listed on Page 2 of the *closing disclosure*, then the amount should be listed with the item and designated as *paid by others on closing disclosure* Page 2. *Other credits* include any transferred escrow balance in a refinance transaction. *Other credits* also include a credit for any money or other payments made at closing by third parties (including gifts from family members) not otherwise associated with the transaction, along with a description of the nature of the funds. Amounts provided in advance of the closing to consumers by third parties (including gifts from family members) but not otherwise associated with the transaction are not required to be disclosed.

Any financing arrangements or other new loans not otherwise disclosed in the *borrower's transaction* column table as part of the *loan amount or existing loans assumed or taken subject to* must be disclosed under the subheading *other credits* (or on line L.04) for the first lien loan. If the net proceeds of the subordinate lien loan are less than its principal amount, the net proceeds must also be disclosed. The net proceeds may be disclosed on the same line as the principal amount of the subordinate lien loan. Disclosure of any amount paid with funds other than closing funds by a consumer in connection with the payoff of an existing subordinate loan are disclosed with a statement that such amounts were paid outside of closing.

Under *adjustments for items unpaid by seller*, disclose the prorated amounts for any unpaid city/town taxes, county taxes and other assessments due from the seller to reimburse the consumer at the real estate closing and the time period corresponding to that amount. Also, disclose a description and amount for any additional items which have not been paid for and which the consumer is expected to pay for after the closing but are attributable to a period of time prior to the closing.

Examples of these items include:
- Utilities used but not paid for by the seller.
- Interest on loan assumptions.

CASH TO CLOSE FROM OR TO BORROWER

Under a subheading of calculation:

- Disclose total due from the borrower at closing as a positive number.
- Disclose total paid already by or on behalf of the borrower at closing as a negative number.
- Disclose the sum of total due from the borrower at closing and total paid already by or on behalf of the borrower at closing as cash to close from borrower when the sum is a positive number, or as cash to close to borrower when the sum is a negative number. The sum is disclosed as a positive number in either event.

SELLER'S TRANSACTIONS

The settlement agent completes and discloses the *Seller's Transaction* column of the summaries of transactions table.

The requirement to complete the seller's transaction column of the summaries of transactions table does not apply to a simultaneous subordinate lien loan if the closing disclosure for the first lien loan discloses the entirety of the seller's transaction. If the requirement to complete the seller's transaction column applies to a simultaneous subordinate lien loan, complete the disclosures based only on the terms and conditions of the subordinate lien loan and do not include sale price.

DUE TO SELLER AT CLOSING

Generally, the amount *due to seller at closing* includes:

- The sale price of the property.
- Sale price of any personal property included in sale.
- Adjustments for items paid by seller in advance due to the seller pursuant to the terms of the real estate sales contract.
- Other items owed by the consumer and disclosed in Section M of the closing disclosure.

For purposes of disclosing the sale price of any personal property included in sale, personal property is defined by state law, but could include such items as carpets, drapes, and appliances. Manufactured homes are not considered personal property for the closing disclosure. Under adjustments for items paid by the seller in advance, disclose the prorated amounts for prepaid city/town taxes, county taxes, and other assessments due from the consumer to reimburse the seller, as well as the time period corresponding to that amount.

Also, disclose a description and amount for any additional items paid by the seller prior to the real estate closing that are due from the consumer at the closing.

Examples of these items include:
- Taxes paid in advance for an entire year when the closing occurs prior to the expiration of the year.
- Flood or hazard insurance premiums when the consumer is being substituted as an insured under the same policy.
- Mortgage insurance in connection with an assumed loan.
- Planned unit development or condominium association assessments paid in advance.
- Fuel or other supplies purchased by the seller which the consumer will use when the property is transferred.
- Ground rent paid in advance by the seller.

Also, disclose in Section M, such as on lines M.03 to M.08, a description and amount for any other items paid to the seller by the consumer pursuant to the contract of sale or other agreement.

Examples of these amounts include:
- A balance in a seller's reserve account transferred to the consumer in connection with an assumed loan.
- Rent that the consumer will collect after closing for a period of time prior to the closing.
- The treatment of any tenant security deposit.

DUE FROM SELLER AT CLOSING
Disclose the amount *Due from Seller at Closing* as the sum of:
- Any excess deposit.
- Closing costs paid at closing by the seller.
- Existing loan(s) assumed or taken subject to by the consumer.
- Payoff of first mortgage loan.
- Payoff of second mortgage loan.
- Seller credit.
- Payment of other seller obligations.
- Adjustments for items unpaid by seller due to the consumer pursuant to the terms of the real estate sale contract.

If a simultaneous subordinate lien loan is disclosed using the alternative tables, the *closing disclosure* for the first lien loan must include any contributions from the seller that are disclosed in the *payoffs and payments* table as amounts contributed to the simultaneous subordinate lien loan.

Excess deposit is the amount of any deposit made by the consumer that has been disbursed to the seller prior to closing. Note that the calculation of the excess deposit does not include any deposits held by the real estate brokerage.

Seller credit is an amount the seller is giving as a general credit not tied to a specific charge on Page 2 or as an allowance to the consumer for items to purchase separately. The amount of seller credit would include any credits to the consumer as the result of a walk-through of the property prior to the closing.

However, if the amount of a credit is attributable to a charge listed on Page 2, then the amount should be listed with the applicable item on Page 2 and designated as *seller-paid at closing or seller-paid before closing*, as appropriate.

Disclose the *payoff of the first mortgage loan*, if any, and then the *payoff of the second mortgage loan*, if any. The payoff or satisfaction amounts for any additional seller obligations should be disclosed as separately itemized amounts.

Examples of these seller obligations include, but are not limited to:
- Satisfaction of outstanding liens imposed due to federal, state, or local income taxes, real estate property tax liens.
- Judgments against the seller reduced to a lien upon the property.
- Other obligations the seller wishes the *settlement agent* to pay from the seller's proceeds at closing.
- Funds to be held by the *settlement agent* for repairs or the payment of water, fuel, or other utility bills that cannot be prorated between the parties at closing because the amounts used by the seller prior to closing are not yet known. Subsequent disclosure of a corrected *closing disclosure* after the repairs are made or the utility bill is received is optional.

Disclose any amount paid with funds other than closing funds as part of a subordinate loan payoff by stating that such amounts were paid from outside of closing funds.

Adjustments for Items Unpaid by Seller due to the consumer to be paid by the seller pursuant to the real estate sales contract has two components:

- First, disclose amounts owed by the seller with the time period associated with the adjustments. Examples include:
  - Taxes paid in arrears for an entire year when the closing occurs prior to the start of the year.
  - Flood or hazard insurance premiums when the consumer is being substituted as an assured under the same policy.
  - Mortgage insurance in connection with an assumed loan.
  - Planned unit development or condominium assessments not yet paid.
  - Ground rent not yet paid by the seller.

- Second, disclose amounts owed by the seller that are neither disclosed on Page 2 nor specifically disclosed as *Due from Seller at Closing*. Examples of these amounts include:
  - Utilities used but not paid for by the seller.
  - Rent collected in advance by the seller from a tenant for a period extending beyond the closing date.
  - Interest on loan assumptions.

CASH TO CLOSE DUE TO OR FROM SELLER

Under a subheading of Calculation:

- Disclose *total due to the seller at closing*, as a positive number.
- Disclose *total due from seller at closing*, as a negative number.
- Disclose the sum of *total due to the seller at closing* and *total due from seller at closing* as a positive number. When the result is a positive number, disclose the amount as *cash to seller*. When the result is a negative number, disclose the amount as *cash from seller*. The sum is disclosed as a positive number in either event.

Closing Disclosure Page 3 Definition of Terms

- **Due from borrower at closing.** Total amount charged to the borrower at closing.
- It includes the borrower's house price and closing costs. It does not include any credits or rebates that lower the borrower's closing costs. (Those are below in Section L).
- **Adjustments for items paid by seller in advance.** Costs that have been prepaid by the seller that the borrower are now reimbursing the seller for.

- **Paid already by or on behalf of borrower at closing.** This section details how the borrower will pay for the items in Section K. It includes the amount they are borrowing, the amount of their deposit, and any rebates or credits paid by the seller or third-party service providers. It does not include the amount the borrower had to bring to closing - that is below in "cash to close."
- **Adjustments for items unpaid by seller.** This includes prior taxes and other fees owed by the seller that the borrower will pay in the future. The seller is reimbursing the borrower now to cover these expenses.
- **Cash to close.** This is the actual amount the borrower will have to pay at closing, and this will typically need to be done with a cashier's check or wire transfer. Ask the closing agent how the payment should be made. Depending on the borrower's location, this person may be known as a settlement agent, escrow agent, or closing attorney.

THE CONSUMER FINANCIAL PROTECTION BUREAU'S GUIDE TO PAGE 4 OF THE CLOSING DISCLOSURE FORM

LOAN DISCLOSURES - In the loan disclosures table, the following should be disclosed:

- Information concerning future **assumption** of the loan by a subsequent purchaser.

- Whether the legal obligation contains a **demand feature** that can require early payment of the loan.

- The terms of the legal obligation that impose a fee for a **late payment** including the amount of time that passes before a fee is imposed and the amount of such fee or how it is calculated.

- Whether the regular periodic payments can cause the principal balance of the loan to increase, creating **negative amortization.**

- The creditor's policy in relation to **partial payments** by the consumer.

- A statement that the consumer is granting a **security interest** in the property (along with an identification of the property).

- Information related to any **escrow account** held by the servicer (or a statement that an escrow account has not been established with a description of estimated property costs during the first year)

Additional Information About This Loan

Loan Disclosures

Assumption

If you sell or transfer this property to another person, your lender

☐ will allow, under certain conditions, this person to assume this loan on the original terms.

☒ will not allow assumption of this loan on the original terms.

Demand Feature

Your loan

☐ has a demand feature, which permits your lender to require early repayment of the loan. You should review your note for details.

☒ does not have a demand feature.

Late Payment

If your payment is more than 15 days late, your lender will charge a late fee of 5% of the monthly principal and interest payment.

Negative Amortization (Increase in Loan Amount) *These are new disclosures*

Under your loan terms, you

☐ are scheduled to make monthly payments that do not pay all of the interest due that month. As a result, your loan amount will increase (negatively amortize), and your loan amount will likely become larger than your original loan amount. Increases in your loan amount lower the equity you have in this property.

☐ may have monthly payments that do not pay all of the interest due that month. If you do, your loan amount will increase (negatively amortize), and, as a result, your loan amount may become larger than your original loan amount. Increases in your loan amount lower the equity you have in this property.

☒ do not have a negative amortization feature.

Partial Payments *These are new disclosures*

Your lender

☒ may accept payments that are less than the full amount due (partial payments) and apply them to your loan.

☐ may hold them in a separate account until you pay the rest of the payment, and then apply the full payment to your loan.

☐ does not accept any partial payments.

If this loan is sold, your new lender may have a different policy.

Security Interest

You are granting a security interest in

456 Somewhere Ave., Anytown, ST 12345

You may lose this property if you do not make your payments or satisfy other obligations for this loan.

Escrow Account

For now, your loan

☒ will have an escrow account (also called an "impound" or "trust" account) to pay the property costs listed below. Without an escrow account, you would pay them directly, possibly in one or two large payments a year. Your lender may be liable for penalties and interest for failing to make a payment.

Escrow		
Escrowed Property Costs over Year 1	$2,473.56	Estimated total amount over year 1 for your escrowed property costs: *Homeowner's Insurance Property Taxes*
Non-Escrowed Property Costs over Year 1	$1,800.00 *These are new disclosures*	Estimated total amount over year 1 for your non-escrowed property costs: *Homeowner's Association Dues* You may have other property costs.
Initial Escrow Payment	$412.25	A cushion for the escrow account you pay at closing. See Section G on page 2.
Monthly Escrow Payment	$206.13	The amount included in your total monthly payment.

☐ will not have an escrow account because ☐ you declined it ☐ your lender does not offer one. You must directly pay your property costs, such as taxes and homeowner's insurance. Contact your lender to ask if your loan can have an escrow account.

No Escrow		
Estimated Property Costs over Year 1		Estimated total amount over year 1. You must pay these costs directly, possibly in one or two large payments a year.
Escrow Waiver Fee		

In the future,

Your property costs may change and, as a result, your escrow payment may change. You may be able to cancel your escrow account, but if you do, you must pay your property costs directly. If you fail to pay your property taxes, your state or local government may (1) impose fines and penalties or (2) place a tax lien on this property. If you fail to pay any of your property costs, your lender may (1) add the amounts to your loan balance, (2) add an escrow account to your loan, or (3) require you to pay for property insurance that the lender buys on your behalf, which likely would cost more and provide fewer benefits than what you could buy on your own.

Additional Tables appear here if loan program includes Adjustable Payment (AP) or Adjustable Interest Rate (AIR) features

Figure 18: CLOSING DISCLOSURE - PAGE 4 of 5 (with some item detailing)

Closing Disclosure Page 4 Definition of Terms

- **Demand feature**. A demand feature allows the lender to demand immediate payment of the entire loan at any time.

- **Negative amortization**. Negative amortization means the borrower's loan balance can increase even if they make their payments on time and in full. Most loans do not have negative amortization.

- **Security interest**. The security interest allows the lender to foreclose on the borrower's home if the borrower does not pay back the money they borrowed.

- **Escrow account**. An escrow account lets you pay your homeowner's insurance and property taxes monthly as part of your mortgage payment, instead of in a large lump sum.

THE CONSUMER FINANCIAL PROTECTION BUREAU'S GUIDE TO PAGE 5 OF THE CLOSING DISCLOSURE FORM

LOAN CALCULATIONS

Disclose *loan calculations, other disclosures, questions, contact Information,* and, if desired by the creditor, *confirm receipt* tables on Page 5 of the closing disclosure.

Disclose the *total of payments,* the *finance charge,* the *amount financed,* the *APR,* and the *total interest percentage (TIP)* in the loan calculations table.

The **total of payments** is the amount a consumer will have paid after making all payments of principal, interest, mortgage insurance, and loan costs, as scheduled. The amount disclosed as the total of payments excludes any portion of the principal, interest, mortgage insurance, or loan costs that is offset by a specific credit from another party. However, non- specific or general credits do not pay for a specific fee or amount. Therefore, they do not offset amounts used to calculate the total of payments.

The **APR** and **TIP** amounts should be updated from the amounts disclosed on the loan estimate to reflect the terms of the legal obligation at consummation.

Loan Calculations

Total of Payments. Total you will have paid after you make all payments of principal, interest, mortgage insurance, and loan costs, as scheduled.	$285,803.36
Finance Charge. The dollar amount the loan will cost you.	$118,830.27
Amount Financed. The loan amount available after paying your upfront finance charge.	$162,000.00
Annual Percentage Rate (APR). Your costs over the loan term expressed as a rate. This is not your interest rate.	4.174%
Total Interest Percentage (TIP). The total amount of interest that you will pay over the loan term as a percentage of your loan amount.	69.46%

Questions? If you have questions about the loan terms or costs on this form, use the contact information below. To get more information or make a complaint, contact the Consumer Financial Protection Bureau at **www.consumerfinance.gov/mortgage-closing**

Other Disclosures

Contains required disclosure language

Appraisal
If the property was appraised for your loan, your lender is required to give you a copy at no additional cost at least 3 days before closing. If you have not yet received it, please contact your lender at the information listed below.

Contract Details
See your note and security instrument for information about
- what happens if you fail to make your payments,
- what is a default on the loan,
- situations in which your lender can require early repayment of the loan, and
- the rules for making payments before they are due.

Liability after Foreclosure
If your lender forecloses on this property and the foreclosure does not cover the amount of unpaid balance on this loan,

[X] state law may protect you from liability for the unpaid balance. If you refinance or take on any additional debt on this property, you may lose this protection and have to pay any debt remaining even after foreclosure. You may want to consult a lawyer for more information.

[ ] state law does not protect you from liability for the unpaid balance.

Refinance
Refinancing this loan will depend on your future financial situation, the property value, and market conditions. You may not be able to refinance this loan.

Tax Deductions
If you borrow more than this property is worth, the interest on the loan amount above this property's fair market value is not deductible from your federal income taxes. You should consult a tax advisor for more information.

Contact Information

	Lender	Mortgage Broker	Real Estate Broker (B)	Real Estate Broker (S)	Settlement Agent
Name	Ficus Bank		Omega Real Estate Broker Inc.	Alpha Real Estate Broker Co.	Epsilon Title Co.
Address	4321 Random Blvd. Somecity, ST 12340		789 Local Lane Sometown, ST 12345	987 Suburb Ct. Someplace, ST 12340	123 Commerce Pl. Somecity, ST 12344
NMLS ID	*Nationwide Mortgage Licensing System ID*				
ST License ID			Z765416	Z61456	Z61616
Contact	Joe Smith		Samuel Green	Joseph Cain	Sarah Arnold
Contact NMLS ID	12345				
Contact ST License ID			P16415	P51461	PT1234
Email	joesmith@ ficusbank.com		sam@omegare.biz	joe@alphare.biz	sarah@ epsilontitle.com
Phone	123-456-7890		123-555-1717	321-555-7171	987-555-4321

Confirm Receipt

By signing, you are only confirming that you have received this form. You do not have to accept this loan because you have signed or received this form.

Consumer is not required to sign; signature is acknowledgment of receipt, NOT acceptance of the loan

Applicant Signature	Date	Co-Applicant Signature	Date

CLOSING DISCLOSURE

PAGE 5 OF 5 • LOAN ID # 123456789

Figure 18: CLOSING DISCLOSURE - PAGE 5 of 5 (with some item detailing)

OTHER DISCLOSURES

In the *other disclosures* table, the creditor will disclose the following:

- A statement regarding the consumer's rights in relation to any **appraisal** conducted for the property.
- A statement informing the consumer of consequences of nonpayment, what constitutes default, when a creditor can accelerate maturity, and prepayment rebates and penalties pursuant to **contract details.**
- A statement regarding whether state law provides for continued consumer responsibility for any **liability after foreclosure.**
- A statement concerning the consumer's ability to **refinance** the loan.
- A statement concerning the extent to which interest on the loan can be used as a **tax deduction** by the consumer.

CONTACT INFORMATION

In the *contact information* table, disclose the following information for the *lender*, the *mortgage broker*, the consumer's *real estate brokerage*, the seller's *real estate brokerage*, and the *settlement agent* in a columnar format:

- Name
- Address
- The NMLS or State license ID, as applicable
- The Contact name of an individual (and the NMLS or State license ID)
- Email
- Phone number

Unused columns may be removed, and columns may be added for additional parties. For example:

- If there are two real estate brokers representing the seller, a column may be added to identify that party and a column for a party not involved in the transaction may be deleted.

CONFIRM RECEIPT

The creditor, at its option, may include a line for the signatures of the consumers to *confirm receipt*. Although the creditor only lists persons to whom credit is extended as *borrowers* on the first page of the *closing disclosure*, in rescindable transactions, the creditor may add signature lines for other consumers who have the right to rescind. If the creditor includes a signature line to *confirm receipt*, the creditor must also include a statement that the signature only signifies receipt of the *closing disclosure*.

If the creditor includes neither a statement line nor the consumer's signature, the following statement should be added to the *Other Disclosures* concerning *Loan Acceptance*: "You do not have to accept this loan because you have received this form or signed a loan application."

Closing Disclosure Page 5 Definition of Terms

Total of payments. The total of payments tells the borrower the total amount of money they will pay over the life of their loan if they make all payments as scheduled.

Finance charge. The finance charge tells the borrower the total amount of interest and loan fees they will pay over the life of their loan if they make all payments as scheduled.

Amount financed. The amount financed is the net amount of money that is borrowed from the lender, minus most of the upfront fees the lender is charging the borrower.

> **NOTE**
>
> *Corrected Closing Disclosure - Prior to consummation, an additional three-business-day waiting period applies when there are changes to the closing disclosure that result in an increase to the APR that becomes inaccurate, the addition of a prepayment penalty, or the change of a loan product. For other changes prior to consummation, provide the consumer the updated information in a corrected closing disclosure no later than consummation. Upon the consumer's request, by the business day before consummation, a creditor must permit the consumer to inspect the closing disclosure, although the creditor may omit items related only to the seller's transaction. In addition, provide a corrected closing disclosure if an event related to the settlement occurs during the 30-calendar-day period after consummation that causes the closing disclosure to become inaccurate and results in a change to an amount paid by the consumer from what was previously disclosed. Deliver or place in the mail the corrected closing disclosure no later than 30 calendar days after receiving information sufficient to establish changes to the amount paid by the consumer.*

CHAPTER 4
REAL ESTATE SETTLEMENT PROCEDURES ACT - RESPA

REAL ESTATE SETTLEMENT PROCEDURES ACT - RESPA

RESPA and Regulation X are the result of the focus by Congress on settlement costs beginning in the 1950s. HUD and the VA adopted standards for settlement costs in the 1970s through a provision of the Emergency Home Finance Act. On December 22, 1974, the Real Estate Settlement Procedures Act was enacted.

REGULATION X was RESPA's initial regulation which was adopted in 1976. Regulation X created provisions addressing escrow accounting, controlled business arrangements (CBAs), and mortgage servicing transfer. RESPA has been amended a number of times since then including the 1990 amendments which addressed servicing transfer and escrow accounting. In 1992, the amendments expanded RESPA coverage to apply to refinance loans, subordinate liens, and purchase money loans. Amendments added in 1996 addressed payments by employers to their employees for referral of settlement services, computerized loan systems (CLOs), or loan operating systems (LOSs), and disclosure requirements when affiliated business fees are involved. The 1996 amendments were not actually implemented until 1998 when there was a final decision on the escrow accounting procedures.

Congress created and amended the law under the Federal Reserve, and the Department of Housing and Urban Development (HUD) is the agency responsible for adopting regulations regarding the implementation of RESPA.

More policies issued in 2002 address CLO or LOS fees and the payment of yield spread premiums or premium pricing offered to brokers as compensation. Changes to the format of the good faith estimate, now known as the loan estimate, facilitated comparison shopping by the borrower and limited the variation between the amounts disclosed on the GFE and the amount showing as settlement costs on the HUD-1, which is now the closing disclosure.

According to the Predatory Lending Laws, the original GFE cannot vary more than .125% from the original disclosure without re-disclosing to the borrower.

> ## NOTE
>
> *After 2011, however, HUD's responsibilities regarding RESPA were assumed by the Consumer Financial Protection Bureau (CFPB) due to the Dodd-Frank Wall Street Reform and Consumer Protection legislation.*

This amendment also removes barriers to the packaging of settlement services which has not yet been adopted due to a great deal of objection to the proposed amendment. HUD is proposing that by requiring brokers to disclose one flat fee that will be charged to the borrower, it will eliminate the "bait and switch" problem that arises when unscrupulous lenders do not disclose all costs that will be included in the procuring of a mortgage loan.

THE "FLAT FEE" CONCEPT requires brokers to disclose all of the broker fees including processing and administration as a single figure. The broker would give a set dollar amount that would include all fees to be paid directly to the broker at close of escrow. The proposal recommended a flat fee that cannot be changed from the time of initial disclosure to the final closing statement, no matter what changes. In other words, if there is an increase in fees for any reason--including an increase in the loan amount--the broker cannot increase the fees being charged and will instead absorb the increased costs, which may reduce the broker's profit.

GFE LAWS AS OF JANUARY 1, 2010, requires that a mortgage broker disclose their total income, including a rebate or yield spread premium on Line 1 of the GFE, and that it cannot be increased or decreased. The broker will be paid the amount disclosed to the borrower on the original GFE.

YIELD SPREAD PREMIUM (YSP) is a premium or rebate paid directly to the mortgage broker by the lender. These are commonly called "lender paid" fees. In 2011, a law was passed which required a broker to disclose to the borrower whether the loan fees were "borrower paid" or "lender paid."

LENDER PAID YSP may only be used to pay the non-recurring closing costs (NRCCs) including the broker's origination. The broker origination fee must be bundled to include any costs such as processing and administration fees. Any excess amount must be applied to the loan balance. The borrower must pay taxes and insurance. Generally, a lender paid rate and term (R&T) refinance will be for the amount of the existing loan with the costs to be paid by the YSP and the taxes and insurances by the borrower. The benefit to the borrower is to reduce the interest rate or the payment by changing the terms.

THE METHOD OF PASSING BILLS AND AMENDMENTS TO LAWS allows for a "**comment period,**" which allows for arguments and suggestions to refine the proposed law so that it might better serve its purpose. Because of this, many laws and amendments, such as the RESPA amendment addressing settlement costs and the "bundling of fees," remain in a state of revision and have not been put into effect. The "comment period" allows for input from the public and the industry affected by the new bill or amendment. Professional associations have legislative committees which actively follow the proposals and will often call on membership to contact their government officials regarding proposed legislation. Therefore, it is important that real estate professionals consider joining their professional associations, as they often play a crucial part in shaping relevant legislation.

HUD is authorized through RESPA to provide unofficial interpretations of the laws to the mortgage industry and the consumer. Guidance and interpretations are available in the form of "RESPA Statements of Policy" and "RESPA Interpretive Rules." These are available online at *www.hud.gov.*

RESPA is a federal law that requires disclosures by mortgage brokers and lenders for all federal mortgages involving the sale or refinance of a 1- to-4-unit residential dwelling. A federal mortgage meets the following guidelines:
- Funded by a lender that is insured by FDIC or any other federal agency.
- Financed by any federal agency such as HUD, FHA, or VA.
- Sold on the secondary mortgage market to FNMA, FHLMC, or GNMA.
- Refinance transactions.
- Purchase of property for resale.
- Purchase of property of twenty-five acres or more.
- Purchase of a vacant lot.
- Transfer of property ownership subject to the assumption of an existing loan.

Every applicant of federal mortgage must be provided with the following items within three business days of signing a loan.

APPLICATION:
- Loan estimate of closing costs *(See Chapter 3).*
- HUD Special Information Booklet.

FEDERAL COMPLIANCE AND THE PURPOSE OF RESPA is spelled out in RESPA's Chapter 27. The following is an excerpt from that portion of RESPA. In the following sections, the wording that is italicized is directly from RESPA and is not an interpretation by the author. The document is worded plainly and has been provided here for clarification and knowledge of those in the mortgage lending industry. The entire document is not included; only the main points needed to operate a mortgage brokerage within the law and provide an understanding of the basics of the industry. RESPA was recently updated and could be updated in the future; the prudent mortgage broker should be aware of changes to the law in order to perform their job effectively, ethically, and legally. RESPA information can be obtained by contacting HUD at the previously named website and *https://www.federalreserve.gov/boarddocs/supmanual/cch/respa.pdf*. The websites allow questions to be submitted to the agencies.

The **PURPOSE OF RESPA** is to:
- Provide for an advance disclosure of all estimated costs involved in closing a loan.
- Eliminate kickbacks and referral fees.
- Reduce or control the amount of funds required to be placed/held in an escrow or impound account.

> *Federal Compliance/Real Estate Settlement Procedures Act (12 USC2601)/Chapter 27: REAL ESTATE SETTLEMENT PROCEDURES*
> *(01/06/03)2601: Congressional Findings and Purpose (01/06/03)*

2601: CONGRESSIONAL FINDINGS AND PURPOSE

(a) *The Congress finds that significant reforms in real estate settlement process are needed to insure that consumers throughout the Nation are provided with greater and more timely information on the nature and costs of the settlement process and are protected from unnecessarily high settlement charges caused by certain abusive practices that have developed in some areas of the country.*

....

b. *It is the purpose of this Act to effect certain changes in the settlement process for residential real estate that will result—*
    1.) *In more effective advance disclosure to homebuyers and sellers of settlement costs;*
    2) *In the elimination of kickbacks or referral fees that tend to increase unnecessarily the costs of certain settlement services;*

> *3.) In a reduction in the amounts homebuyers are required to place in escrow accounts established to insure the payment of real estate Taxes and insurance; and*
> *4.) In significant reform and modernization of local recordkeeping of land title information.*

2602: Definitions: This section provides definitions as used by the HUD and the Federal Reserve Board throughout RESPA. The mortgage broker should be familiar with and use the terms as defined herein.

A federally related mortgage loan fits the guidelines of most mortgages that are obtained through a mortgage broker. Any first trust deed that will be financed and/or owned by any lender that is insured by a federal agency or has any connections with federal agencies is a federally related mortgage loan.

FEDERALLY RELATED MORTGAGE LOAN includes any loan which is secured by a first or subordinate lien on residential properties that are designed for the occupancy of one- to- four families. This definition includes individual units of condominiums and cooperatives. A federally related mortgage includes any secured loan for which the proceeds are used to pre-pay or pay off an existing loan secured by the same property. This does not include temporary financing such as a construction loan.

A **THING OF VALUE** refers to forms of payment for any services associated with obtaining a mortgage loan.

> *(2) the term "thing of value" includes any payment, advance, funds, loan, service, or other consideration:*

SETTLEMENT SERVICES refers to any charges that a consumer may/or will pay in order to obtain a mortgage loan. Closing costs is used synonymously with the term settlement services and includes all costs involved in closing a loan transaction whether recurring, such as insurance and taxes, or non-recurring.

> *(3) ..."Settlement Services" includes any service provided in connection with a real estate settlement including, but not limited to, the following: title searches, title examinations, the provisions of title certificates, title insurance, services rendered*

by an attorney, the preparation of documents, property surveys, the rendering of credit reports or appraisals, pest and fungus inspections, services rendered by real estate agent or broker, the origination of a federally related mortgage loan (including , but not limited to, the taking of loan applications, loan processing, and the underwriting and funding of loans), and the handling of the processing, and closing or settlement;

(4) ..."**title company**" *means any institution which is qualified to issue title insurance, directly or through its agents, ...*

PERSON refers to a legal entity that is legally capable of owning property and obtaining a mortgage loan.

(5) ..."**person**" *includes individuals, corporations, associations, partnerships, and trusts;*

AFFILIATED BUSINESS ARRANGEMENT is a legal entity that is allowed by law to make a profit from another business entity by providing referral business.

*(7) ... "**affiliated business arrangement**" means an arrangement in which*
(A) a person who is in a position to refer business incident to or a part of a real estate settlement service involving a federally related mortgage loan, or an associate of such person, has either an affiliate relationship with or direct or beneficial ownership interest of more than 1 percent in a provider of settlement services; and
(B) either of such persons directly or indirectly refers such business to that provider or affirmatively influences the selection of that provider, and

ASSOCIATE refers to a person who is in a position or has a relationship with a business which allows for payment for either referral business or payment by commission. This may include any of the following with a relationship to such person:

* Spouse, parent, or child.
* Corporation or business entity that controls, is controlled by, or is under common control.
* Employer, officer, director, partner, franchisor, or franchisee.
* Any party that has an agreement, arrangement, or understanding with the purpose to refer business for the financial benefit from the referrals of such business such as a salesperson.

Section 3500.2 (b) addresses Regulation X providing the definitions of:
- Application
- Business day
- Dealer
- Good faith estimate
- Lender
- Mortgage broker
- Required use
- Settlement service
- Table funding

§3500.2: Definitions

Statutory terms are terms that are created, regulated, and used according to the laws to which they apply.

(a) *Statutory terms. All terms defined in RESPA (121 USC 2602) are used in accordance with their statutory meaning unless otherwise defined in paragraph (b) of this section or elsewhere in this part.*

(b) *Other terms. As used in this part:*

APPLICATION refers to the standard loan application that is commonly used. The form provided on the various LOSs and on the various real estate form's websites (for those that are not computerized) meet the FNMA/FHLMC guidelines, which meet the Federal RESPA requirements. The form is also known as the:
- Uniform Residential Loan Application
- URLA
- 1003

APPLICATION is the submission of a borrower's financial information for the purpose of obtaining credit approval. The application may be written or computer- generated in relation to a federally related mortgage loan. If the submission does not identify a specific property, the submission is an application for a prequalification and is not considered an application for a federally related mortgage. The addition of a property to the application changes the pre-qualification status to an application for a federally related mortgage.

BUSINESS DAY is often used in the mortgage industry when counting days in conjunction with such things as the right of rescission on an owner-occupied refinance. It refers to a day that business is normally conducted or may be expected to be conducted. Generally, Sundays and holidays are not considered to be a "business day."

"Business day" means a day on which the offices of the business entity are open to the public for carrying on substantially all of the entity's business functions.

DEALER means, in the case of property improvement loans, a seller, contractor, or supplier of goods or services. In case of manufactured home loans, "dealer" means one who engages in the business of manufactured home retail sales.

FEDERALLY RELATED MORTGAGE LOAN fits the guidelines of most mortgages that are obtained through a mortgage broker. Any first trust deed that will be financed and/or owned by any lender that is insured by a federal agency or has any connections with federal agencies is a federally related mortgage loan.

Construction loans are temporary loans and are therefore not a federally related mortgage loan.

"Federally related mortgage loan" means as follows:
(1) Any loan (other than temporary financing, such as a construction loan)
  (i.) That is secured by a first or subordinate lien on residential real property, including a refinancing of any secured loan on residential real property upon which there is either:
    (A) Located or, following settlement, will be constructed using proceeds of the loan, a structure or structures designed principally for occupancy of from one to four families (including individual units of condominiums and cooperatives and including any related interests, such as a share in the cooperative or right to occupancy of the unit); or
    (B) Located or following settlement, will be placed using proceeds of the loan, a manufactured home; and
  (ii.) For which one of the following paragraphs applies. The loan:
    (C) Is made in whole or in part by any lender that is either regulated by or shoes deposits or accounts are insured by an agency of the Federal Government; ...

The **LOAN ESTIMATE,** which replaced the old mortgage loan disclosure statement/good faith estimate, is required in all States. *See Chapter 3 for information on preparing this form designed to provide details of all costs the borrower will be required to pay to obtain a mortgage loan.*

HUD-1, or HUD-1A SETTLEMENT STATEMENT is the form that escrow prepares to disclose all closing costs required to obtain a mortgage loan to the parties involved in a real estate transaction. This may include a borrower in a finance transaction or a buyer and seller in a purchase transaction. The MLDS and the GFE are both fashioned after the HUD-1 and the lines are numbered the same on the GFE, MLDS, HUD-1, and HUD-1A. The HUD-1 and HUD-1A are often referred to as the "Settlement Statement". The terms are used synonymously.

> **HUD-1 or HUD-1A "settlement statement"** (also HUD-1 or HUD-1A) refers to the statement that states all the settlement charges in connection with either the purchase or refinancing (or other subordinate lien transaction) of 1-to4- family residential property.
>
> **"LENDER"** means, generally, the secured creditor or creditors named in the debt obligation and document creating the lien. For loans originated by the mortgage broker that closes a federally related mortgage loan in its own name in a table funding transaction, the lender is the person to whom the obligation is initially assigned at or after settlement. …
>
> **"MANAGERIAL EMPLOYEE"** means an employee of a settlement service provider who does not routinely deal directly with consumers, and who either hires, directs, assigns, promotes, or rewards other employees or independent contractors, or is in a position to formulate, determine, or influence the policies of the employer. Neither the term "managerial employee" nor the term "employee" includes independent contractors, but a managerial employee may hold a real estate brokerage or agency license.
>
> **"MORTGAGE BROKER"** means a person (not an employee or exclusive agent of a lender) who brings borrower and lender together to obtain a federally related mortgage loan, and who renders services as described in the definition of "settlement services" in this section. A loan correspondent approved under §202.8 of this title for Federal Housing Administration programs is a mortgage broker for the purposes of this part.

"MORTGAGED PROPERTY" means the real property that is security for the federally related mortgage loan.

"PERSON" is defined in section 3(5) of RESPA (12USC 2602(5).

"REFINANCING" means a transaction in which an existing obligation that was subject to a secured lien on residential real property is satisfied and replaced by a new obligation undertaken by the same borrower and with the same or a new lender. **The following shall not be treated as a refinancing,** even when the existing obligation is satisfied and replaced by a new obligation with the same lender (this definition of "refinancing" as to transactions with the same lender is similar to Regulation Z, 12 CFR 226.20(a)).

A note which is to be paid at the end of the term with one single payment is renewed without changing the other terms of the note other than the due date.

(1) *A renewal of a single payment obligation with no charge in the original terms.*

An adjustable-rate mortgage may allow for changes in the interest rate to increase or decrease according to the Index per the terms of the original note as indicated on the Truth in Lending Reg Z form.

(2) *A reduction in the annual percentage rate as computed under the Truth in Lending Act with a corresponding change in the payment schedule.*

A bankruptcy court may establish a temporary or alternative payment arrangement to satisfy the terms of the bankruptcy; a reorganization of debt is one such possibility.

(3) *An agreement involving a court proceeding.*

A Loan Modification is an example of an agreement between the lender and the borrower to alleviate the financial hardship of the borrower.

(4) *A workout agreement, in which a change in the payment schedule or change in collateral requirements is agreed to as a result of the consumer's default or delinquency, unless the rate is increased or the new amount financed is*

NOTE

The following items are not considered a refinance transaction as stated above:

increased or the new amount financed exceeds the unpaid balance plus earned finance charges and premiums for continuation of allowable insurance; and

If a borrower has failed to pay their insurance or property taxes, the lender has the right to require that the borrower establish an impound account to assure payment of those obligations.

(5) The renewal of optional insurance purchased by the consumer that is added to an existing transaction, if disclosures relating to the initial purchase were provided.

REGULATION Z is most often used to refer to the form Truth in Lending which provides disclosure information to the borrower. The complete information on the form is available in Chapter 3. This disclosure is also known as:

- Reg Z
- TIL
- TILA

"Regulation Z" means the regulation is issued by the Board of Governors of the Federal Reserve System (12CFR part 226) to implement the Federal Truth in Lending Act (15 USC 1601 et seq.), and includes the Commentary on Regulation Z.

REQUIRED USE refers to the practice of requiring a consumer to use a specific service provider. All services and service providers must be the consumer's choice. It is good practice for real estate professionals to provide consumers with a list of no less than five service providers, such as appraisers, escrow companies, et cetera.

If the services are being provided as a package with discounts or rebates, the package must truly be discounted, or include the discounts and rebates as stated. The reduced price or discount cannot be compensated for by increasing other fees.

"Required use" means a situation in which a person must use a particular provider of a settlement service in order to have access to some distinct service or property, and the person will pay for the settlement service of the particular provider or will pay a charge attributable, in whole or in part to the settlement service.

However, the offering of a package (or combination of settlement services) or the offering of discounts or rebates to consumers for the purchase of multiple settlement services does not constitute a required use. Any package or discount must be optional to the purchaser. The discount must be a true discount below prices that are otherwise generally available and must not be made up by higher costs elsewhere in the settlement process.

"RESPA" means the Real estate Settlement Procedures Act of 1974, 12 USC 2601 et seq.

The SERVICER receives payments from the borrower, logs payments; makes impound account payments and manages the impound accounts; notifies parties of delinquencies and the need for filing foreclosure; manages late payments and additional fees per the terms of the note.

"Servicer" means the person responsible for the servicing of a mortgage loan (including the person who makes or holds a mortgage loan if such a person also services the loan). The term does not include:

(1) The Federal Deposit Insurance Corporation (FDIC) or the Resolution Trust Corporation (RTC), in connection with assets acquired, assigned, sold, or transferred pursuant to section 13© of the Federal Deposit Insurance Act or as receiver or conservator of an insured depository institution; and

(2) The Federal National Mortgage Corporation (FNMA);the Federal Home Loan Mortgage Corporation (Freddie Mac); the RTC; the FDIC; HUD, including the Government National Mortgage Association (NMA) and the Federal Housing Administration (FHA) (including cases in which a mortgage insured under the National Housing Act (12 USC 1701 et seq.) is assigned to HUD); the National Credit Union Administration (NCUA); the Farmers Home Administration or its successor agency under Public Law 103-354 (FmHA); and the U. S. Department of Veterans Affairs (VA), in any case in which the assignment, sale, or transfer of the servicing of the mortgage loan is preceded by termination of the contract for servicing the loan for cause, commencement of proceedings for bankruptcy or the servicer, or commencement of proceedings by the FDIC or RTC for conservatorship or receivership of the servicer (or an entity by which the servicer is owned or controlled).

"Servicing" means receiving any scheduled periodic payments from a borrower pursuant to the terms of any mortgage loan, including amounts for escrow accounts under section 10 of RESPA (12 USC 2609), and making payments to the owner of the loan or other third parties of principal and interest and such other payments with respect to the amounts received from the borrower as may be required pursuant to the terms of the mortgage servicing loan documents or servicing contract. In the case of a home equity conversion mortgage or reverse mortgage as referenced in this section, servicing includes making payments to the borrower.

SETTLEMENT is the final step of a real estate transfer when final documents are signed. Escrow oversees the terms of the agreement, prepares deeds for proper transfer of interest in real property, manages the signing of loan documents, records documents, and delivers documents as required for proper transfer of rights in Real Property.

"Settlement" means the process of executing legally binding documents regarding a lien on property that is subject to a federally related mortgage loan. This process may also be called "closing" or "escrow" in different jurisdictions.

"Settlement service" means any service provided in connection with a prospective or actual settlement, including, but not limited to, any one or more of the following:

MORTGAGE BROKER/LOAN AGENT provides the service of originating the mortgage loan. The mortgage broker also provides the services involved with the processing of the loan application, including ordering such services as the credit report and the appraisal.

(1) *Origination of a federally related mortgage loan (including, but not limited to, the taking of loan applications, loan processing, and the underwriting and funding of such loans);*

(2) *Rendering of services by a mortgage broker (including counseling, taking of applications, obtaining verifications and appraisals, and other loan processing and originations services, and communicating with the borrower and lender);*

(3) *Provision of any services related to the origination, processing or funding of a federally related mortgage loan.*

TITLE SERVICES provide the title insurance and the research and compilation of the preliminary title report and the final report. This would include any search or verification that may be needed in regard to the items recorded against the property that may be questionable, such as an unreleased lien.

(4) *Provision of title services ...*

(5) *...services of an attorney;*

ESCROW SERVICES provide the preparation, delivery and recording of documents.

(6) *Preparation of documents, including notarization delivery, and recordation.*

(7) *...credit reports and appraisals.*

INSPECTION SERVICES are provided by private companies that specialize in a particular kind of inspection that may be required, such as a termite inspection or home inspection.

(8) *...inspections ...*

(9) *Conducting of settlement by settlement agent ...*

(10) *...services involving mortgage insurance;*

(11) *...services involving hazard, flood, or other insurance or homeowner's warranties;*

(12) *...mortgage life, disability, or similar insurance designed to pay a mortgage upon disability or death of a borrower, but only if such insurance is required by the lender as a condition of the loan;*

(13) *...services involving real property taxes or any other assessments or charges on real property;*

(14) *...services by a real estate agent or a real estate broker; and*

(15) *...other services for which a settlement service provider requires a borrower or seller to pay.*

SPECIAL INFORMATION BOOKLETS are to be provided to all consumers according to the type and purpose of the mortgage loan they are obtaining. See Chapter 3 for information about the booklets that are available.

"Special information booklet" means the booklet prepared by the Secretary pursuant to section 5 of RESPA (12 USC 2604) to help persons understand the nature and costs of settlement services. ...

STATES are liable for their actions under federal laws. The states also establish their individual licensing laws and requirements for mortgage lending transactions. Because of the Supremacy Clause of the Constitution, federal law takes precedence over state law, including on issues relating to real estate.

"State" means any State of the United States, the District of Columbia, the Commonwealth of Puerto Rico, and any territory or possession of the United States.

TABLE FUNDING is a practice in which a mortgage broker funds loans in their own name by using a temporary transfer of funds and ownership of the loan. The funds are actually those of the lender that have been advanced to the broker for use of the funding. The broker benefits in several ways, primarily by being able to advertise the business as a direct lender. A table funding transaction is not a secondary mortgage market transaction (see §3500.5(b)(7)).

A TITLE COMPANY is any institution, or its duly authorized agent, which is qualified to issue title insurance.

Transaction Covered under RESPA is found in Section 3(1)(A) Federally related mortgage loans. The following loans and property types are covered in this section:
- *Mortgage Loan types*
  - First and subordinate liens
  - Permanent construction loans
  - Purchase loans
  - Refinance loans
- *Property types*
  - Individual units of a condominium complex
  - Cooperatives (Co-ops)
  - Manufactured homes
  - 1-to-4 residential properties

Federally related mortgage loan or mortgage loan means as follows:
  (1) *Any loan (other than temporary financing, such as a construction loan).*
  - *That is secured by a first subordinate lien on residential real property, including a refinancing of any secured loan on a residential property upon which there is either:*
  (A) *Located or, following settlement, will be constructed using proceeds of the loan, a structure or structures designed principally for occupancy of from one to four families (including individual units of condominiums and cooperatives and including any related interests, such as a share in the cooperative or right to occupancy of the units); or*
  (B) *Located or, following settlement, will be placed using proceeds of the loan, a manufactured home; and*

- *For which one of the following paragraphs applies. The loan:*
  - *(A) Is made on whole or in part by any lender that is either regulated by or whose deposits or accounts are insured by any agency of the Federal Government.*
  - *(B) Is made in whole or in part, or is insured, guaranteed, supplemented, or assigned in any way:*
    - *1) By the Secretary or any officer or agency of the Federal Government; or*
    - *2) Under or in connection with a housing or urban development program administered by the Secretary or a housing or related program administered by any other officer or agency of the Federal Government;*
  - *(C) Is intended to be sold by the originating lender to the Federal National Mortgage Association, the Government National Mortgage Association, the Federal Home Loan Mortgage Corporation (or its successors), or a financing institution from which the loan is to be purchased by the Federal Home Loan Mortgage Corporation (or its successors);*
  - *(D) Is made in whole or in part by a "creditor" as defined in section 103(f)of the Consumer Credit Protection Act (15 USC 1602(f), that makes or invests in residential real estate loans aggregating more than $1,000,000 per year. ...*
  - *(E) Is originated by either a dealer or, if the obligation is to be assigned to any maker of mortgage loans specified in paragraphs (1) (ii) (A) through (D) of this definition, by a mortgage broker; or*
  - *(F) Is the subject of a home equity conversion mortgage, also frequently called a "reverse mortgage" issued by any maker of mortgage loans?*

    ...
- *2) Any installment sales contract, land contract, or contract for deed on otherwise qualifying residential property ...*
- *3) If the residential real property securing a mortgage loan is not located in a State, the loan is not a federally related mortgage loan.*

§3500.5: Coverage of RESPA. RESPA applies to all federally related mortgage loans except for those provided for in paragraph (b) of this section.

Exempt Mortgage Loan transactions according to Regulation X, Section 3500.5 must meet specific guidelines. RESPA applies to all federally related mortgage loans with the following exemptions:

- **Loan transactions** on properties of twenty-five acres or more are exempt from the applicable RESPA laws.
- **Business loans** that are used primarily for business, commercial, or agricultural purposes, and the loan transactions do not fall under RESPA regulations.
- **Temporary financing,** such as construction loans, are exempt from RESPA. The exemption does not apply to construction loans that have a clause which converts the loan to a permanent mortgage loan when construction is complete. The original loan will fall under RESPA laws; however, the conversion will not require new disclosure as long as a new note is not required, and the terms were provided in the original note.
- **Vacant land loan transactions** that are secured by vacant or unimproved property unless a structure will be built in two years or less from the date of settlement or close of escrow.

The placement of a residential structure, including manufactured homes, on the property that will be secured by a new mortgage loan will qualify the mortgage loan transaction for the RESPA laws under this section.

- **Loan assumption transactions** that **do not require** the lender's express approval for a subsequent owner/borrower to assume the responsibility of an existing mortgage loan is exempt from RESPA for the assumption transaction only.

Any federally related mortgage loan transaction that requires the approval of the new owner/borrower by the lender prior to assuming the responsibilities of the existing mortgage loan does fall under RESPA laws.

- **LOAN CONVERSION TRANSACTIONS** are exempt from RESPA, provided that the new terms are consistent with the provisions of the original mortgage and a new note is not required even if the lender charges an additional fee for the conversion. This may also apply to loan modifications.
- **SECONDARY MORTGAGE MARKET TRANSACTIONS** that are true transactions on the secondary mortgage market are exempt from RESPA. HUD considers the real source of the funds and the owner or actual funding lender. Who did the funds actually belong to? A table funding by a mortgage broker is not a true secondary mortgage market transaction.

The sale of one mortgage lender to another of the real estate paper of a closed mortgage loan is a true or bona fide secondary mortgage market transaction and is exempt from RESPA.

SECONDARY MORTGAGE MARKET is the part of the industry that funds loans and buys and sells loans that have already closed. This is also considered a part of wholesale lending. The consumer has minimal contact with the secondary mortgage market. Loans being transferred on the secondary mortgage market are exempt from RESPA because consumers are not involved and there is no change to the terms of the note or the original agreement.

RESPA §2608 Title Companies; Liabilities of Seller

Section 9- *Title Companies states that the Seller may not require that Title Insurance be purchased from a particular Company. If the Seller requires that the Buyer use a Title Company specified by the Seller, the Seller may be liable for three (3) times the Buyer's cost of Title Insurance.*

No seller of property that will be purchased with the use of a federally related mortgage may require, directly or indirectly, as a condition of selling the property, that title insurance covering the property be purchased by the buyer from a particular title company. Any seller who violates the provisions will be liable to the buyer for an amount equal to three times all charges made for title insurance.

> **NOTE**
> *The validity of a Purchase Contract, Loan Agreement, or Mortgage is NOT affected by the fact that the transaction is non-compliant with RESPA 12 USC 2615*

SPECIAL INFORMATION BOOKLETS

Information booklets must be provided, and Section 3500.6 establishes the parties that are responsible for the distribution of the booklets to the borrower. The special information booklets were defined in Section 3500.2(b). HUD designed the booklets to provide information for the consumer regarding closing costs as well as additional booklets for the various types of loans available to the borrower.

Additional booklets contain important information regarding the refinancing of one's home, adjustable-rate loans, primary mortgage insurance (PMI), and equity lines of credit. The booklets are available in a variety of places, primarily office supply businesses that specialize in mortgage lending supplies.

These suppliers are best found online such as *www.greatland.com*.

The mortgage broker can copy the information exactly as provided by HUD. No changes can be made to the information, but the broker may add their personal business information to include name, address, phone, email, etc.

The special information booklets must be provided to any consumer who has applied for a mortgage loan with the lender unless the loan is being obtained through a mortgage broker. In this case, the mortgage broker must provide the special information booklet, and the lender must verify that the booklet was delivered to the borrower. The mortgage broker should create a statement to this effect to be signed by the borrower along with the other required disclosures.

The following verbiage may be used on the broker's company letterhead:

> I, hereby, confirm that I have received a copy of the following booklet(s):
> _____ Buying Your Home: Settlement Costs and Helpful Information
> _____ What You Should Know About Home Equity Lines of Credit/ When Your Home is on the Line
> _____ Consumer Handbook on Adjustable-Rate Mortgages
> _____ Primary Mortgage Insurance

_____

Borrowers Signature   Date

The appropriate booklets must be delivered to the borrower within three (3) business days of the borrower signing the application for a federally related mortgage loan. If the loan application is withdrawn, cancelled, or declined within the three-day period, the booklet does not need to be delivered. The booklet may be delivered in person or mailed no later than three business days following the signing of the loan application. Only one booklet needs to be delivered to one of the borrowers when there is more than one borrower.

The mortgage broker is required to provide booklets under RESPA for the following loan transactions under this section. Other booklets regarding these transactions may be provided as required.
- Closed-End Subordinate Liens
- Reverse Mortgages
- Refinancing Your Home

- Purchases for 1-to-4 Unit Residential Dwellings

REPRODUCTION OF THE INFORMATION BOOKLETS may be in any form, provided there are no changes made to the content of the booklets. The booklets cannot be made a part of a larger text but must remain as a separate document. Any color, size and quality of paper, type of print, and method of reproduction may be used so long as the booklet is clearly legible. Changes to the pamphlets are generally not allowed; however, the mortgage broker, real estate agency, and lender may put their name and contact information on the cover, and the booklets may be translated into languages other than English.

LOAN ESTIMATE (LE) applies to both the lender and the mortgage broker. The lender is responsible for providing the GFE for dealer loans (**the loan estimate replaced the good faith estimate**). The mortgage broker is responsible for providing the GFE to the borrower unless they are an exclusive agent of the lender.

RESPA requires that the loan estimate be provided to the borrower within three (3) business days of the borrower signing the mortgage loan application. It may be delivered in person or by mail. The loan estimate is not required if the loan application is withdrawn, cancelled, or declined within three business days of the borrower signing the loan application.

> *The lender shall provide to all applicants for a federally related mortgage loan with a Loan estimate of the amount or range of charges for the specific settlement services the borrower is likely to incur in connection with the settlement.*

All costs that may be incurred for the purpose of obtaining the mortgage loan should include all costs and failure to include known costs, whether intended or not, is a clear violation of RESPA.

NOTE

It is often a practice by Lenders and their Agents to omit items from the LE to obtain a client by demonstrating reduced closing costs over their competitor. This is a blatant violation of RESPA and an act of fraud. Such acts must never be practiced.

NO COST LOANS should always be processed with care because the term itself is precarious and may leave the broker subject to lawsuits through misinterpretation of the term.

All loans do in fact have costs involved, and the broker must clearly disclose these to the borrower. The borrower does not pay the closing costs directly; a broker generally pays the closing costs with either a rebate or a yield spread premium received from the lender in exchange for giving the borrower a higher interest rate. Technically, the borrower pays the closing cost by paying a higher interest rate. This fact must be clearly disclosed to the borrower.

> *(a) (2) For "No Cost" or "No Point" loans, the charges to be shown on the good faith estimate include payment to be made to affiliated or independent settlement service providers. These payments should be shown as POC (Paid Outside Closing) on the Good Faith Estimate and the HUD-1 or HUD-1A*

The content of the good faith estimate consists of items normally listed on the HUD-1 or HUD-1A. It must contain items that are normally included in the closing costs as a typical for the area.

> *(b) (2) ... As to each charge with respect to which the lender requires a particular settlement service provider to be used, the lender shall make their estimate based upon the lender's knowledge of the amounts charged by such providers.*

The FORM OF GOOD FAITH ESTIMATE is set forth in Appendix C of RESPA. The California Department of Real Estate (DRE) developed their own version of the good faith estimate using all of the information required under RESPA and HUD as well as additional information that the DRE has deemed necessary for the consumer. The DRE form is called the Mortgage Loan Disclosure Statement/Good Faith Estimate of Closing Costs (GFE). The federal form was revised, and the new form must be used with all federally related mortgage loans made after January 1, 2010.

The Federal Reserve Board and HUD have been reviewing and revising the Good Faith Estimate (GFE) for a number of years in an effort to make it as easy to read and understand as it can be. The form may change again in the future. Whenever the required disclosures are changed, the LOS systems will provide the updated form.

*GFE is a three-page government-mandated form that includes the breakdown of estimated costs due upon the closing of a mortgage loan. Mortgage brokers and lenders are required to provide prospective borrowers with this document within three days of a loan application.

On October 2015, a new document called the Loan Estimate (LE) replaced the GFE and TILA (Truth in Lending Act) statement.

Borrowers who applied for a mortgage on or after October 3, 2015, will receive a form, called the Loan Estimate, instead of a GFE for most kinds of mortgage loans. Borrowers applying for a reverse mortgage, a home equity line of credit, a manufactured housing loan that is not secured by real estate, or a loan through certain types of homebuyer assistance programs, will not receive a GFE or a loan estimate, but will receive a disclosure. Furthermore, they will not receive a loan estimate if they are applying for a reverse mortgage. For those loans, there will be two forms - a GFE and an initial Truth-in-Lending disclosure instead of a Loan estimate. (*Consumer Financial Protection Bureau*)

Providers of services that are required by the lender as classified as "required use" for settlement services, other than the lender's own employees, and the borrower is required to pay for any portion of the service, the good faith estimate must:

- Clearly state the use or need such as: "credit report"
- Estimate must be based on the charges of the designated provider meaning that the Lender cannot charge more than the actual cost of the service.
- Provide name, address, and phone number for each provider.
- Describe the nature of any relationship that may exist between the provider and the lender.

Part 3500, Appendix C provides a sample form of the good faith estimate. The form provided on the broker's LOS meets all guidelines required by the federal and state Laws. California brokers are required to provide the MLDS/GFE provided by DRE.

§3500.8 and §3500.9 address the use and reproduction of the HUD-1 or HUD- 1A settlement statements is directed and applies mainly to escrow companies. Any mortgage brokers or lenders that also operate an escrow as a part of their business should research this section to ensure that the actions meet the legal requirements.

The **HUD-1 and HUD-1A** are similar to the GFE and the numbers used on the GFE are the same designations on the HUD-1 and HUD-1A. The mortgage broker and lender must be familiar with the settlement statement.

§3500.10 One Day Advance Inspection of HUD-1 or HUD-1A Settlement Statement; Delivery; Recordkeeping.

This section provides for the delivery of the settlement statement to and inspection by the borrower no less than twenty-four (24) hours prior to funding the loan. This allows the borrower sufficient time to review the document, approve the charges, or cancel the loan if the terms and charges are not satisfactory.

"WET FUNDING" is a method of funding a loan that is practiced is many states which allows for the closing on the same day that loan documents are signed. "Wet funding" is a term that means the ink is still wet on the docs when the loan closes. Generally, a wet funding is performed when all parties to the transactions meet, loan documents are signed, and checks are distributed. The transaction is completed and closes once the signing and distribution of funds have been completed.

This type of closing does not allow the borrower time to review the HUD-1 or HUD-1A with the RESPA required 24-hour review. The HUD-1 or HUD-1A must be delivered to the borrower at least 24 hours prior to the meeting to close the transaction. In the states that practice "wet funding," escrow or the attorney is required to provide the HUD-1 or HUD-1A to the borrower (and seller for a purchase transaction) 24 hours before close of escrow. Although this is part of RESPA, this section is mainly applicable to "wet funding" states.

"DRY FUNDING" is the practice of closing a loan after the lender has had time to review the loan documents prior to funding the loan. "Dry funding" means that the ink has time to dry on the docs before the loan funds. The loan docs are sent to the escrow or attorney and the borrower (and seller for a purchase transaction) is given the HUD-1 or HUD-1A and sign the loan docs. Once signed by the borrower, the docs are returned to the lender, who verifies to verify the paperwork and signatures were properly completed. This process usually takes at least 24 to 48 hours before the lender clears the loan to fund. Most counties in California will fund the loan one day and record it the next, at which time the transaction is closed.

Using this method of funding and closing a transaction allows for several days from the time the borrower receives the HUD-1 or HUD-1A which meets the requirements of RESPA. California is a "dry funding" state, which means that the ink has had time to dry on the loan documents before close of escrow, which also means that the borrower was given a copy of the HUD-1 or HUD-1A Settlement Statement at the time that they signed the loan documents several days before close of escrow. This more than meets the RESPA requirement of allowing the borrower 24 hours to review the settlement statement.

The **HUD-1 OR HUD-1A SETTLEMENT STATEMENT** delivered to the borrower one day prior to close of escrow will be the accurate and final statement in a dry funding state. The HUD-1 is the standard form used for a purchase transaction and the HUD-1A is used for refinance transactions.

The HUD-1 or HUD-1A settlement statement delivered to the borrower at the signing prior to the close of escrow will be the accurate and estimated statement. The final statement will be delivered to the borrower when escrow closes.

RECORDKEEPING REQUIREMENTS for the lender by RESPA state that the lender shall retain a copy of the HUD-1 or HUD-1A and related documents for a period of five years after settlement. This rule does not apply in the event that the lender disposes of their interest in the mortgage, such as by selling the loan, and they no longer service the mortgage.

Part 3500, Appendix A: Provides i**nstructions for completing HUD-1 and HUD-1A Settlement Statements.** The HUD-1 and HUD-1A are prepared by the escrow officer for delivery to the borrower. The mortgage broker should become familiar with the forms for their own knowledge and the ability to assist the borrower with any questions. Most issues should be referred to the escrow officer.

> **NOTE**
>
> *The borrower is the party referred to in this section because the primary topic is mortgages. The requirements also apply to buyers and sellers.*

> **NOTE**
>
> *RESPA requires that all documentation/ files be retained for five (5) years. Fair Lending requires that all documentation/files be retained for seven (7) years. The State of California requires three (3) years.*

CHARGES TO BE PAID OUTSIDE of settlement, including situations whereby non-settlement agents such as attorneys, title companies, escrow agents, real estate agents or brokers hold the borrower's deposit as earnest money against the sales price and apply the entire deposit towards the fee for the settlement service rendered must be included on the HUD-1. Such fees are to be marked "POC" for "paid outside closing" (settlement) and should not be included in computing totals due at closing. POC items should not be placed in the borrower or seller columns, which will appear as due, but rather on the appropriate line next to the columns.

Blank lines are provided for any additional settlement charges. The names of the recipients of settlement charges should always be included on the lines.

The mortgage broker will follow these guidelines and requirements for the completion of the MLDS/GFE as appropriate. Any broker who also owns/operates an escrow company should obtain a complete copy if this Appendix as it provides line-by-line instructions for completion of the HUD-1 and HUD-1A.

§3500.14: Prohibition Against Kickbacks and Unearned Fees
   a) Section 8 violation
   b) No referral fees

SECTION 8 of RESPA clearly states that no person may give or accept any fee, kickback, or any other thing of value as a referral based on an agreement for a service provided for a federally related mortgage. Referral of a settlement service does not constitute or warrant a service deserving of compensation except as stated in §3500.14(g) (1). A business entity also may not pay any other business entity or the employees of any other business entity for the referral of settlement service business whether or not that business is an affiliate. Likewise, fees and charges may not be split or shared unless actual services have been performed by all parties being paid.

THING OF VALUE is defined by RESPA as:

> "discounts, salaries, commissions, fees, duplicate payments of charge, stock, dividends, distributions of partnership profits, franchise royalties, credits representing money that may be paid at a future date, the opportunity to participate in a money-making program, retained or increased earnings, increased equity in a parent or subsidiary entity, special bank deposits or accounts, special or unusual banking terms, services of all types at special or free rates, sales or rentals at special prices or rates, lease or rental payments

based in whole or in part on the amount of business referred, trips and payment of another person's expenses, or reproduction in credit against an existing obligation."

PAYMENT is considered as the giving or receiving of anything of value and does not necessarily include the transfer of money or cash.

AGREEMENT OR UNDERSTANDING regarding the referral of business as part of a service provided in conjunction with obtaining a federally related mortgage does not to be in writing or verbalized. An agreement may be established by a practice or conduct of action. When a thing of value is received repeatedly in conjunction with the value of the business referred, receiving the thing of value is evidence of referral of business.

REFERRAL includes any action that affirmatively influences the selection of a provider of a service or a business for which a borrower will pay a fee or a charge for the service or business. A referral also occurs when a person that is paying for the service or business is required to use a particular provider of a service or business.

FEES, SALARIES, COMPENSATION, or any other type of payment for services rendered are regulated and restricted under RESPA. Section 8 of RESPA permits payment to the following:
- Attorney at law for services actually rendered.
- Title company
- Lender's duly appointed agent or contractor for services actually performed in the origination, processing, or funding of a loan.
- Any person of a bona fide salary within the appointed duties.
- Co-operative brokerage and referral arrangements or agreements between real estate agents and brokers. Exemption refers only to fee divisions within real estate brokerage agreements when the parties are acting in that capacity. This is not applicable to fee arrangements between real estate brokers and mortgage brokers or between mortgage brokers.
- Normal promotional and educational activities that are not subject to the referral of business and do not defray expenses that would normally be incurred by persons in a position to refer services or business.
- Employer's payment to its own employees for ordinary business such as in normal sales activities

HUD may investigate high prices to see if they are the result of a referral fee or a split of a fee.

MULTIPLE SERVICES occur when a person in a position to refer settlement service business, such as an attorney, mortgage lender, real estate broker or agent, or developer or builder, receives a payment for providing additional settlement services as part of a real estate transaction. Payment must be for services that are actual, necessary, and distinct from the primary services provided by that person. For example, for an attorney for the buyer or seller to receive compensation as a title agent, the attorney must perform necessary core title services that are separate from normal attorney services.

2607: Prohibitions Against Kickbacks and Unearned Fees

provides that any persons or person who violate the provisions of this section shall be fined not more than $10,000 or imprisoned for not more than one year, or both. Any person or persons who violate restrictions detailed in this section may be jointly and severally liable to the person or persons charged for the service(s) involved in the violation in an amount equal to three times the amount of any charge paid for such settlement service. The courts may award to the prevailing party the costs of any private actions taken pursuant to this section plus reasonable attorney's fees.

2602: Definitions

For the purpose of this chapter:

AFFILIATED BUSINESS ARRANGEMENT is an arrangement in which a person who is in a position to refer business as a part of a real estate settlement service involving a federally related mortgage, or an associate, has an affiliate relationship with or a direct or beneficial ownership interest of more than 1 percent in a company or a provider of settlement services.

3500.15: Affiliated Business Arrangements

An affiliated business arrangement is not a violation of Section 8 of RESPA (12 USC 2607) and of §3500.14 if the following conditions are satisfied:

- The person making the referral has provided to each person whose business is referred a written disclosure stating the nature of the relationship.
- The person making a referral has not required any person to use any particular provider of settlement services or business.

- Exception is if such person is a lender requiring a buyer, borrower, or seller to pay for the services of an attorney, credit reporting agency, or real estate appraiser chosen by the lender to represent the lender's interest in a real estate transaction, or except if such person is an attorney or law firm for arranging issuance of a title insurance policy for a client *See Figure 19, Appendix D*

§3500.21: Mortgage Servicing Transfers

(a) Definitions. As used in this section:

MASTER SERVICER is the owner of the right to perform servicing, which may actually perform the servicing itself or may do so through a sub-servicer.

MORTGAGE SERVICING LOAN refers to a federally related mortgage loan that is secured by a first lien, as that term is defined in §3500.2, subject to the exemptions in §3500.5. The definition does not include subordinate lien loans or open-end lines of credit (home equity plans) covered by the Truth in Lending Act and Regulation Z, including open-end lines of credit secured by a first lien.

A QUALIFIED WRITTEN REQUEST is a written correspondence from the borrower to the servicer.

SUBSERVICER is a party that does not own the right to perform servicing, but who does so, on behalf of the master servicer.

TRANSFEREE SERVICER is a servicer who obtains or who will obtain the right to perform servicing functions based on an agreement or understanding.

TRANSFEROR SERVICER is a servicer, including a table funding mortgage broker or dealer on a first lien who transfers, or will transfer, the right to perform servicing functions based on an agreement or understanding.

§3500.21: Mortgage Servicing Transfers

(b) Servicing Disclosure Statement and Applicant Acknowledgement; Requirements.

According to RESPA, a mortgage broker does not need to provide a Servicing Disclosure Statement to the borrower because mortgage brokers rarely fund a loan using their own money or by table funding. Lenders, however, do require that the mortgage broker provides the form. This can be disputed with the lender if the broker does not want the added liability associated with providing the disclosure.

**PART 3500, APPENDIX D: AFFILIATED BUSINESS ARRANGEMENT
DISCLOSURE STATEMENT FORMAT
NOTICE**

To: _____   Property: _____

From: _____   Date: _____
[Entity Making Statement]

This is to give you notice that [referring party] has a business relationship with
[settlement services provider(s)] . [*Describe the nature of the relationship between the
referring party and the provider(s), including percentage of ownership interest, if
applicable.*] Because of this relationship, this referral may provide [referring party] a
financial or other benefit.

[A.] Set forth below is the estimated charge or range of charges for the settlement
services listed. You are NOT required to use the listed provider(s) as a condition
for [settlement of your loan on] [or] [purchase, sale, or refinance of] the subject
property. THERE ARE FREQUENTLY OTHER SETTLEMENT SERVICE
PROVIDERS AVAILABLE WITH SIMILAR SERVICES. YOU ARE FREE TO
SHOP AROUND TO DETERMINE THAT YOU ARE RECEIVING THE BEST
SERVICES AND THE BEST RATE FOR THESE SERVICES.

[provider and settlement service]   [charge or range of charges]

_____   _____

_____   _____

[B.] Set forth below is the estimated charge or range of charges for the settlement
services of an attorney, credit reporting agency, or real estate appraiser that we, as
your lender, will require you to use, as a condition of your loan on this property,
to represent our interests in the transaction.

[provider and settlement service]   [charge or range of charges]

_____   _____

_____   _____

Figure 19: RESPA 3500, Appendix D:
Affiliated Business Arrangement Disclosure Format Notice
Page 1 of 2

ACKNOWLEDGMENT

I/we have read this disclosure form, and understand that [referring party] is referring me/us to purchase the above-described settlement service(s) and may receive a financial or other benefit as the result of this referral.

_____
Signature

[INSTRUCTIONS TO PREPARER:] [Use paragraph A for referrals other than those by a lender to an attorney, a credit reporting agency, or a real estate appraiser that a lender is requiring a borrower to use to represent the lender's interests in the transaction. Use paragraph B for those referrals to an attorney, credit reporting agency, or real estate appraiser that a lender is requiring a borrower to use to represent the lender's interests in the transaction. When applicable, use both paragraphs. Specific timing rules for delivery of the affiliated business disclosure statement are set forth in 24 CFR 3500.15(b)(1) of Regulation X. These INSTRUCTIONS TO PREPARER should not appear on the statement.]

Figure 19: RESPA 3500, Appendix D:
Affiliated Business Arrangement Disclosure Statement Format
Page 2 of 2

(1) *At the time of the application for a mortgage servicing loan is submitted, or within 3 business days after submission of the application, the lender, mortgage broker who anticipates using table funding, or dealer who anticipates a first lien dealer loan shall provide to each person who applies for such loan a Servicing Disclosure Statement.*

(2) *The Applicant's Acknowledgement portion of the Servicing Disclosure Statement in the format stated as mandatory. Additional lines may be added to accommodate more than two applicants.*

(3) *The Servicing Disclosure Statement must contain the following information, except as provided in paragraph (b)(3)(ii) of this section:*

    (i.) *Whether the servicing of the loan may be assigned, sold or transferred to any other person at any time while the loan is outstanding. If the lender, table funding mortgage broker, or dealer in a first lien dealer loan does not engage in the servicing of any mortgage servicing loans, the disclosure may consist of a statement to the effect that there is a current intention to assign, sell, or transfer servicing of the loan. (IV)... (V) A written acknowledgement that the applicant (and any co-applicant) has/have read and understood the disclosure and understand that the disclosure is a required part of the mortgage application. This acknowledgement shall be evidenced by the signature of the applicant and any co-applicant. ...*

(c) ***Servicing Disclosure Statement and Applicant Acknowledgement; delivery.*** *The lender, table funding mortgage broker, or dealer that anticipates a first lien dealer loan shall deliver a Servicing Disclosure Statement to each applicant for mortgage servicing loans. Each applicant must sign and Acknowledgement of receipt of the Servicing Disclosure Statement before settlement.*

    (1) *In the case of **a face-to-face interview** with one or more applicants, the Servicing Disclosure Statement shall be delivered **at the time of application**. ...*

    (2) *If there is no **face-to-face interview**, the Servicing Disclosure Statement shall be delivered by placing it in the mail, with prepaid first-class postage, **within 3 business days from receipt of the application**. ...*

    (3) *The signed Applicant Acknowledgement(s) shall be retained for a period of 5 years after the date of settlement as part of the loan file for every settled loan....*

(d) *Notices of Transfer; loan servicing—*

    (1) ***Requirement for notice.***

        (i.) *Except as provided in this paragraph ... The following transfers are not considered an assignment, sale, or transfer of the mortgage loan servicing for the purpose of this requirement if there is no change in the payee, address to which the payment must be delivered, account number, or amount of payment due:*

(A) Transfers between affiliates.

(B) Transfers resulting from mergers or acquisitions of servicers or sub-servicers; and

(C) Transfers between master servicers, where the sub-servicers remains the same.

*(2) **Time of notice.** ....*

This section applies to lenders in the secondary mortgage market. Any Brokers engaging in this arena of the Mortgage Lending industry should obtain this RESPA information from FRB or HUD.

§3500.17: Escrow Accounts

Definitions. A used in this section:

ACCEPTABLE ACCOUNTING METHOD is an accounting that a servicer uses to maintain accurate records in the conduct of an account analysis for an escrow account.

AGGREGATE ANALYSIS is an accounting method a servicer uses in analyzing an escrow account by computing the required escrow account funds by analyzing the account as a whole.

ANNUAL ESCROW ACCOUNT STATEMENT is a statement containing all of the information to the borrower within 30-calendar days of the end of the fiscal year for the escrow account.

CUSHION is the amount of reserve funds that a servicer may require a borrower to pay into an escrow account to cover unanticipated disbursements or disbursements made before the borrowers' payments are available in the amount. The maximum is to be no more than equal to two (2) months of the monthly figure or one-sixth of the annual figure. Any excess of that amount plus $50 dollars must be refunded to the borrower within fifteen (15) calendar days.

DEFICIENCY Is the amount of a negative balance in an escrow account. The servicer may require the borrower to correct the deficiency by increasing the monthly payment until sufficient funds are available in the escrow account.

DELIVERY is the placing of a document in the United States mail, first- class postage paid, addressed to the last known address of the recipient. Hand delivery also constitutes delivery.

DISBURSEMENT DATE is the date on which the servicer actually pays an Escrow Item such as property taxes or hazard insurance from the escrow account.

ESCROW ACCOUNT is an account that a servicer establishes or controls on behalf of a borrower to pay taxes, insurance premiums including flood insurance, or any other charges required in regard to the servicing requirements of a mortgage. Generally, the charges have been agreed upon by the borrower and servicer or lender for collection and payment. To make such payments, a portion of the amounts owed for taxes and insurance is added to the principal payment each month. The definition encompasses any account established for this purpose including a trust account, reserve account, impound account, or other term that may be customary in different areas.

CHARGES AT SETTLEMENT or upon creation of an escrow account may be an amount sufficient to pay the charges on behalf of the mortgaged property, such as taxes and insurance, which are calculated from the last payment date until the initial payment date. The amount sufficient to pay is computed so that the lowest month-end target balance projected for the escrow account computation year is zero ($0). The servicer may charge the borrower a cushion that shall be no greater than one- sixth (1/6) of the estimated total annual payments from the escrow account.

This section applies primarily to lenders who calculate impound accounts when preparing loan documents. The loan officer and mortgage broker should understand the requirements of an impound account in order to properly explain the accounts to a Borrower and also to calculate the borrower's potential closing costs. Brokers that also operate as a lender or table funder and draw their own loan docs should obtain the remainder of this section for reference.

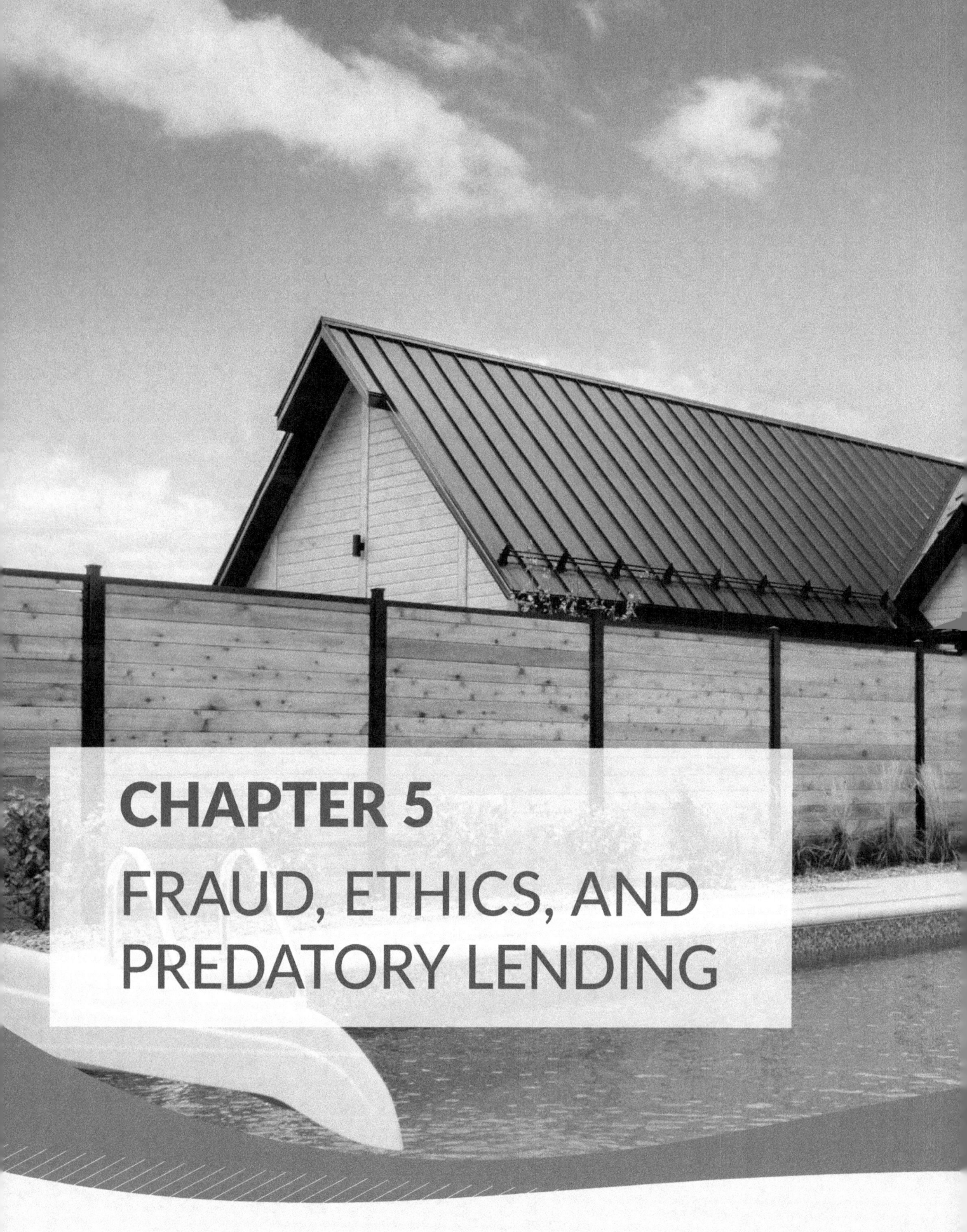

CHAPTER 5
FRAUD, ETHICS, AND PREDATORY LENDING

DISCRIMINATION IN HOUSING

Discrimination in Housing is illegal and there are laws protecting the public from various types of discrimination. Owners of real property are prohibited from discrimination in the sale, rental, or leasing of their property. Real estate professionals should not accept a listing or any other type of real property contract from an owner who attempts to discriminate in any way, including making the discriminatory act a condition of the contract. Property owners, real estate professionals, salespeople, lenders, and hotel management are all prohibited from exercising any acts of discrimination in regard to housing accommodations.

Federal Laws that address discrimination are as follow:

The Civil Rights Act of 1866 prohibits racial discrimination and the Thirteenth Amendment abolishes slavery, however, little was done to uphold the Civil Rights Act for nearly one hundred years. Many county records and preliminary title reports still contain covenants, conditions, and restrictions (CC&Rs) from the early 1900s that allow discrimination in the establishment of housing development and subdivisions. Such CC&Rs are illegal, and the title insurance companies clearly state that, although they remain a part of recorded documents with the county recorder's offices.

The Federal Fair Housing Act of 1968 was created to control discrimination in the housing market. The *Federal Fair Housing Act* applies to all residential property transactions including sale, lease, lending, advertising, and any other acts relating to housing. This Act became a part of *Title VIII* of the *Civil Rights Act of 1968*.

The Act prohibits discrimination in housing on the basis of any of the following:
- Race
- Color
- Religion
- Sex
- National Origin
- Ancestry
- Handicap
- Familial Status

NOTE

There are no exemptions to the Civil Rights Act of 1866.

The following are exempt from the compliance with this Act:

- Families with minor children may prohibit based on familial status.
- Adult communities may discriminate based on age if all residents are 62 or older.

-or-

- Eighty percent of the complex is occupied by residents fifty-five and older and special services for the elderly are offered.
- Religious organizations, societies, or affiliated non-profit organizations dealing with their privately owned property may limit transactions to their members. Membership may not be restricted based on race, color, or national origin.
- Private clubs limited to members only for lodgings that are not open to the public in a commercial capacity.
- Rental by a property owner of a single-family residence (SFR) if they own three SFR rentals or less.
- Room rental in an owner-occupied dwelling of up to four units.

Exemption from the *Federal Fair Housing Act* does not provide exemption from the *Civil Rights Act of 1866* and does not override any state laws prohibiting discrimination.

Department of Housing and Urban Development (HUD) and the US Attorney General are responsible for hearing complaints of discrimination in housing by the public. A party that has been discriminated against has one year to file a complaint of discrimination with *HUD's Office of Equal Housing Opportunity (OEO)* or two years to file a lawsuit in either state or federal court.

STATE LAWS against discrimination are, in some instances, broader than the federal laws, and California's laws against housing discrimination are among the strictest in the country.

Fair Employment and Housing Act (FEHA) was formerly known as the ***Rumford Act.*** The *Rumford Act* was named for and influenced by Robert Rumford, who was a prominent African American business man and politician. Mr. Rumford was instrumental in establishing rights for minorities in the early 1900s.

The FEHA prohibits discrimination in housing (including sales, leases, and financing) in all types of housing accommodations based on:

- Race
- Color
- Religion
- Sex
- Gender identity
- Sexual orientation
- Marital status
- National origin
- Ancestry
- Disability- either physical or mental
- Medical condition
- Familial status
- Source of income

Blockbusting is the discriminatory act of attempting to cause panic selling in a neighborhood. This is typically done by instilling fear among property owners that people of a different race, ethnic group, or religion are beginning to buy property in the area and that this could lower property values. The intent is to cause owners to sell their property quickly and at a loss; real estate agents could then buy them and resell them at a higher price. This is an illegal act under the *FEHA* and is punishable by loss of real estate license, fines, and/ or imprisonment.

Steering is the practice of showing clients properties that are located in similarly ethnic neighborhoods.

Civil Rights Housing Act of 2006 became effective January 1, 2007. The Act allows for automatic updates as additional areas of discrimination in housing and housing related areas become apparent and a need is proven. This Act extends the *FEHA* to prohibit discrimination in housing and housing related areas which include:

- Real estate licensing.
- Mortgage lending.
- Club membership established by condo associations.
- Housing developments.
- Mobile home parks.
- Community redevelopment.

The Unruh Civil Rights Act prohibits discrimination in accommodations and business establishments such as hotels. This Act includes all of the prohibitions in the *FEHA*. Discrimination on the basis of any of the categories covered by the FEHA is also prohibited in all aspects of housing accommodation.

DISCRIMINATION IN LENDING

Discrimination in Lending is addressed under several laws. Federal banking laws prohibit discrimination in lending by banks, savings & loans, and federal credit unions.

REDLINING has been illegal under anti-discrimination regulation since 1976. Redlining is the practice of denying loans on properties that are located in low income and otherwise unfavorable areas. California prohibits the practice of redlining on all loans secured by 1-to-4-unit residential dwellings. This prohibition applies to loans that are conventional, insured by FHA, or guaranteed by VA.

Housing Financial Discrimination Act of 1977/ Fair Lending Notice also known as the **Holden Act**, which went into effect January 1, 1978, prohibits discrimination by all financial institutions based on the geographic location, neighborhood, or other related characteristics of the property. This prohibition does not apply to negative decisions based on sound business practice such as changing neighborhood, zoning changes, or condition of property. See Figure 36, the *Housing Discrimination Act/Fair Lending Notice*

This law applies to all loans on owner-occupied residential properties of 1-to-4 units for purchase, refinance, construction, or remodeling. The law also applies to home improvement loans from a financial institution for owner-occupied and non- owner-occupied properties. All categories covered under the *FEHA* are covered under the *Holden Act*.

The following categories may not be discriminated against:
- Race
- Color
- Religion
- Sex
- Sexual orientation
- Marital status
- National origin

- Ancestry
- Disability: either physical or mental
- Medical condition
- Familial status
- Source of income
- Geographic area of subject property
- Condition of the neighborhood
- Characteristics of the neighborhood

COMPLAINTS OF DISCRIMINATION under this Act should be filed with the *Secretary for Business, Transportation, and Housing.* The secretary has 30 days from the date of receiving any complaint to initiate an investigation. When incidences of discrimination are discovered or proven, the following remedies are available, depending on the extent of the discriminatory act and the damages resulting from the acts:

- Provide the requested loan.
- Offer better loan terms.
- Monetary damages up to $1,000.

APPEALS may be presented to the *Office of Administrative Hearings* and then to a court for a decision to overturn the secretary's decision.

Lenders are required to provide borrowers with notification that this law exists, and that they have rights under the law. They must also provide the necessary information to file a complaint.

FRAUD

Fraud is defined as the intentional deception or material misrepresentation, misstatement, or an omission of facts pertinent to the responsible decision-making process of determining the quality of the loan package as a whole. This applies whether the information provided or excluded is intentional or unintentional if the information and facts are known or should be known. The failure to ask certain important and relevant questions is equivalent to intentional fraud.

Examples of fraudulent information include false or inaccurate documentation, such as original papers that have been tampered with or created from scratch to meet the qualifying requirements, including:

- **Identification:** Driver's license, resident alien card, Social Security card and number.
- **Employment:** Paystubs, verification of employment, W2s, tax returns
- **Assets:** Bank statements, verification of deposit.
- **Appraisals**

When fraud is found in a file by the investor, they will require that the lender buy the loan back and they will, in turn, go back to the broker and the borrower for resolution.

The borrower of a **fraudulent loan** is usually given a certain amount of time, typically 60 or 90 days, to refinance and pay off the existing, fraudulent loan.

The broker of record may be required to purchase the loan from the lender. The lender has the option of not accepting any additional loans from the broker. The lender will generally file a complaint with the California Department of Real estate (DRE) or Department of Financial Protection and Innovation (DFPI) as appropriate per the broker's licensing. Criminal charges may be filed against the broker, which may result in loss of license, fines, and imprisonment.

TYPES OF FRAUD that are common practice in today's mortgage market may include any of the following acts:

1. **MORTGAGE FRAUD** is an act of material misrepresentation, misstatement, or omission of pertinent facts that a mortgage lender, or a financial institution would normally rely on to determine the creditworthiness of a borrower. This applies to all mortgage loans that are being considered for the purpose of extending a loan or funding, or for the purchase of already funded mortgages including those associated with a mortgage-backed security or a similar type of instrument that is guaranteed by a financial institution under the auspices of the Office of the Federal Housing Enterprise Oversight (OFHEO) or the Federal Housing finance Agency (FHFA).

> **NOTE**
>
> *Caution and care should always be exercised to avoid committing fraud, either intentionally or unintentionally, as doing so puts the borrower, broker, business, and licenses in jeopardy.*

2. **PROFESSIONAL FRAUD** is an act of intentionally deceiving consumers or other entities, such as lenders, by misrepresentation as a licensed professional or one in the business of providing a professional service, or misrepresenting the services being provided.

> *Example 1: Sam is not licensed as an MLO but presents himself as a mortgage broker to Mr. and Mrs. Jones. He takes a loan application and charges them an upfront application fee.*
>
> *Sam is intentionally misrepresenting himself as a mortgage professional, which is illegal, and collects an upfront or unearned fee, which is also illegal.*
>
> *Example 2: Joe is a licensed MLO; however, during the processing of the mortgage for Mary, he intentionally tells her that the loan she is receiving is a 30-year fixed-rate loan at 4.00% APR, when in fact the loan is a 30-year loan that is only fixed for the first 5 years of the term.*

3. **CONSUMER FRAUD** is the act of intentionally deceiving a business or institution for the purpose of gaining money or something of value. Consumer fraud includes the misstatement, misrepresentation, or the omission of facts that are material or pertinent to a decision to extend business services or product.

> *Example: John creates fake income documentation including paystubs, W2s and 1040s in order to obtain a mortgage that he could not actually afford. He would not have qualified for the loan if he had used his real documentation.*

4. **FRAUD FOR PROPERTY** is a form of consumer fraud when a consumer blatantly misrepresents themselves through falsified or fraudulent documentation for the purpose of obtaining/purchasing property. Forms of documentation that may be falsified include and may not be limited to the following:
   - Occupancy: stating they will occupy the property when they will not. **This is the most common form of consumer fraud.**
   - Income: paystubs, W2s, 1099s, tax returns.
   - Assets: bank statements, VODs, cash, gift funds and letters, liquid, and non-liquid assets.

5. **FRAUD FOR PROFIT** is a form of fraud that is generally perpetrated as an organized method of stealing large amounts of funds through repeated transactions. Fraud for profit will generally involve elaborate schemes involving many parties including MLOs, real estate agents, appraisers, closers and title, and developers.

    Example: A loan application is packaged and submitted to the lender. The lender performs their due diligence by calling the employer to perform a verbal verification of employment. The phone number provided for the employer is actually a direct line to one of the parties involved in the fraudulent transaction.

    The parties perpetrating the fraud may have a set of telephones each with a different number and each will be answered according to the designation such as the proper name of the employer: "ABC Industries, may I help you." One phone may be assigned as the appraiser and another as the closer or title company.

    The appraisal may be completed on a non-existent property. A photograph of any property with the correct house number may be inserted as the subject property.

    A preliminary title report may be assembled using a plat map and legal description that have been tampered with.

The following are examples of a variety of schemes:
*   **Property flipping** involves a buyer purchasing a property at an inflated value based on a falsified appraisal. The buyer re-sells or "flips" the property in a short period of time at the inflated price making a profit. Most lenders now require that a property not re-sell in less than 90 days.

*   Quite often the original buyer has falsified documentation and does not qualify for the loan and will probably not make many payments, if any, before the property is resold.

*   **Backward application** is a method of creating documentation to make the borrower fit the loan. In other words, the borrower's income and asset documentation will be created according to the amount of income required to qualify for the loan required.

- **Straw buyer** refers to the practice of obtaining a mortgage using created documentation for a person that does not exist. The term "straw" comes from a scarecrow, or a creation stuffed to look like a real person.

- **A nominee loan** means that a person other than the actual buyer is nominated to apply for the loan. Usually someone with good credit and sufficient assets will be asked to obtain a loan for a person who does not qualify. Once the loan is in place, the real buyer takes possession of the property and maintains the payments and all other responsibilities. It is agreed that at some time in the future, the actual buyer will obtain a loan in their own name and the nominee will be released from the liability.
  Unfortunately, this can result in damage to the nominee's credit, as they are the person responsible for the loan and because it is fraud since the lender approved the nominee and is unaware of the actual buyer.

- **Equity skimming** is similar to the nominee scheme as it involves a person other than the actual buyer making the loan application. Before or at the time the transaction closes, the actual buyer signs their ownership rights over to another by using a grant deed, quitclaim deed, or an instrument of property transfer according to the local customs. Once the transaction is completed, the actual owner of the property will collect rents until the foreclosure process re-claims the property on behalf of the lender. The buyer has pocketed the rent, the nominee buyer has ruined credit, and the lender has suffered losses in time, money, and legal fees.

- **An air loan** is a scheme involving a loan application on a non- existent property. A borrower in this type of scheme may often maintain the payments on the loans even though there is no collateral, or they may just walk away with the acquired cash.

- **Silent seconds** are often used in a purchase transaction when the buyer does not have sufficient funds to close, and the seller agrees to carry a second to cover the funds. If the lender is not made aware of the second, they cannot make an informed assessment as to borrower's credit- worthiness.

Often a sales price will be inflated so it appears that the buyer/borrower has paid the required amount down by hiding it in the price.

> *Example: Seller Miller shows a property with an increased sales price from $240,000 to $260,000. Buyer Clark applies for a 90% LTV mortgage or $234,000 with $26,000 down. If he had shown a purchase price of $240,000, a 90% LTV would require a down payment of $24,000.*
>
> *Showing a purchase price of $260,000 and a loan amount of $234,000, Buyer Clark actually only uses $6,000 of his own money which is the difference between the actual purchase price of $240,000 and the loan amount. Buyer Clark then owes Seller Miller $20,000 on a second mortgage. The lender believes that Buyer Clark has actually paid $26,000 down and that Seller Miller received a total of $260,000, which is not true.*

Failure to disclose or obscuring the fact that there is a second or subordinate lien is fraudulent. It is also fraudulent to verify non-existent funds for the purpose of obtaining a loan.

- **Selling for more than the list price** is used in a variety of schemes to obtain cash by inflating the sales price. This method is used by both buyers and sellers in an attempt to gain excessive profit.
- **Foreclosure schemes** are used in a number of ways that prey on financially troubled homeowners who are fearful of losing their homes. Once the Public Notice of Foreclosure has been printed in the local newspaper, the homeowner will be contacted with a variety of ways to "help" them.
- **Refinancing** into a new loan is possible; however, the MLO may collect an upfront fee, which is illegal. Then, if the homeowner cannot obtain a new loan, the MLO can retain the fee, and the borrower still loses their home. Upfront fees may have benign-sounding names, such as "consulting fee" to minimize the possibility of legal ramifications.
- **Loan modifications** are similar to refinancing and rely on the existing lender working with the borrower to reduce the interest rate and/or payment and loan amount to one that the borrower can afford. The borrower must have a legitimate reason for not being able to afford the current payment, such as loss of employment. Lenders will not accept a loan modification for a borrower who could not afford the payment initially and obtained the loan through deceptive practices, such as getting a low variable rate loan, when they would not qualify for the loan once it increased.

An Attorney at Law must manage Loan Modifications, not an NMLS licensee. An attorney can legally charge an upfront fee for their services.

There is no guarantee that a lender will agree to a loan modification and a borrower cannot apply for one until their loan is seriously delinquent. A borrower should not stop making their payments and become delinquent for the sole purpose of justifying a loan modification. A lender will expect a borrower to have saved a sufficient amount of money to pay towards the loan balance as part of the loan modification process. If a borrower has not been making payments, the lender will likely expect them to have saved those funds to put towards the mortgage.

- **Cash to transfer ownership** is a common practice in which a homeowner facing foreclosure is offered a lump sum of cash to forfeit the property and sign it over to a new owner. The new owner will bring the payments current and obtain a new mortgage, then give the homeowner cash to move. The amount of cash will vary depending on the area and the property value, but it will often be in the range of $5,000 to $10,000. The desperate homeowner salvages their credit to some extent and has cash to relocate and reestablish themselves. The buyer will have the advantage of purchasing a home below value.

- **Appraisal fraud** is perpetrated by an appraiser. An appraiser may be drawn into a fraudulent transaction with the promise of increased fees and/or additional payment beyond the fee that would be charged.

The most obvious fraudulent practice is the lack of checking the proper sources for comparable properties. The MLS or local Board of Realtors' Multiple Listing Service is the most accurate source for an appraiser to establish the recent sales of comparable properties (comps). An appraiser may choose to use comps provided by the realtor or MLO or may search only comps that are within a specified value. Neither one of these practices will provide an accurate and complete picture of the true values in an area and is construed as fraud.

An astute appraiser should always check the listing and sales history of a property which can be done through MLS and the prelim. The appraiser should also notice if the same names continue to appear in real estate transactions as it may indicate a scheme, such as property flipping or the use of a nominee or straw buyer.

An appraiser working outside of his/her normal area may be an indication of fraud because a local appraiser would likely recognize irregularities in transactions. An appraiser should always familiarize themselves with an area before completing an appraisal and contact local appraisers for information.

CONSUMERS SHOULD NEVER BE ASKED, encouraged, or told to:
- Provide false information or omit pertinent information on loan applications.
- Sign blank documentation in relation to a loan application.
- Allow a broker to change information to fit the loan applied for
- Refinance with no benefit to them. If the balance, payment, and interest are increasing with no benefit, such as cash out to remodel, pay debt, invest, or education, the refinance may not be in their best interest.
- Sign loan documents with costs and payments higher than initially disclosed.

Consumers may contact the following agencies with complaints regarding illegal or predatory loan transactions:
- District attorney's office in the county where the transaction occurred.
- Federal Bureau of Investigation (FBI) *www.fbi.gov* or *www.fbi.gov/whitecollarcrime.htm*
- National Association of Mortgage Brokers (NAMB) *www.namb.org*
- Federal Trade Commission (FTC) *www.ftc.gov*

Phone numbers can be obtained for all of these agencies and the FBI will have a local office for most areas.

PENALTIES FOR FRAUD

A perpetrator of a crime in a real estate-related transaction may be indicted under several statutes including, but not limited to, bank fraud, mail fraud, wire fraud, and making false statements. There does not need to be actual loss to any party involved for the crime of mortgage fraud to have occurred. Willfully committing any type of fraud in the obtaining or selling of a mortgage transaction constitutes a crime.

The FBI will actively investigate valid complaints of fraud, especially when a consumer files the complaint. The FBI will confiscate all files and computer systems in the suspected office to complete their investigation. The related and licensing agencies will be notified, including HUD for NMLS licensees, the state real estate and corporation licensing agencies, and the local district attorney.

Depending on the crime and the statute that is violated, the penalty may be $10,000 per incident, with a potential fine of up to $1,000,000, up to 30 years in jail, or both.

ETHICS

ETHICS ARE THE VALUE SYSTEM of moral principles that one uses to make choices and live by distinguishing right from wrong. An ethical code that one lives by is determined by their environmental training and the cultural and societal influences in which one lives.

Mortgage Loan Originators must always maintain the highest ethical standards when working with the consumer in a mortgage transaction. The following guidelines should be exercised at all times by the practicing MLO:
- Know, understand, and work within the guidelines set forth by the laws of state and federal governing agencies.
- Conduct business in a professional manner by being knowledgeable and compliant with ethical industry practices.
- Ensure that employees are knowledgeable and capable of providing quality service.
- Never discriminate. Conduct business without regard to race, color, creed, religion, national origin, ancestry, age, marital or familial status, or handicap.
- Never breach a contract, a confidence, or an agreement whether oral or written.
- Make all reasonable efforts to provide the best service possible as requested by the consumer.
- Provide all services in as timely a manner as possible. Do not delay providing the consumer with information whether good or bad as this affects their life and important decisions.
- Provide full disclosure to both the consumer and the lender.
- Protect the consumer privacy and rights. Do not allow disclosure of confidential information.
- Be prudent with any money being managed on behalf of the consumer by depositing in the appropriate escrow account at the earliest opportunity.
- Maintain accurate and appropriate records.
- Provide the best terms available to the consumer within their needs, desires, and qualifications.
- Do not provide a consumer with a loan they cannot afford.

- Encourage healthy and honest competition within the industry by encouraging the consumer's right to "shop" and by not discrediting competitors.
- Always conduct business with the utmost integrity, honesty, and ethics towards all involved in any given transaction. Make every effort possible to fulfill the obligations entrusted to them in the service of obtaining a mortgage loan for a consumer.
- Cooperate fully with any investigations by any agency in the event of a violation of the Code of Ethics and laws.

FEDERAL ACTS AND RULES have been created for the purpose of managing ethical lending practices and providing lending opportunities for the public. Some of these agencies and acts are as follows.

OFFICE OF FEDERAL HOUSING ENTERPRISE AND OVERSIGHT (OFHEO) was created as an agency within the Department of Housing and Urban Development (HUD). The purpose was to ensure sufficient capital and financial safety of the government sponsored enterprises (GSEs) Federal National Mortgage Association (FNMA) and Federal Home Loan Mortgage Corporation (FHLMC).

OFHEO was combined with the **Federal Housing Finance Board (FHFB)** under the Housing and Economic Recovery Act of 2008 to form the **Federal Housing Finance Agency (FHFA).**

FEDERAL HOUSING FINANCE AGENCY (FHFA) created an empowered regulator with the authority to oversee the secondary mortgage market, specifically FNMA, or Fannie Mae, and FHLMC, or Freddie Mac. The formation of the new agency in June 2008, promotes a more secure housing market through better management of the GSEs.

FEDERAL FAIR LENDING ACT prohibits discrimination in all areas of housing including mortgage lending. HUD enforces the compliance of the Fair Lending Act and the Equal Credit Opportunity Act (ECOA). The Fair Lending Act prohibits the refusal to make a loan, provide information, refuse to purchase a loan, or to provide different terms such as interest rates and fees based on any of the following:

- Race
- Color
- National origin
- Sex

- Religion
- Familial status
- Disability

ALTERNATIVE MORTGAGE TRANSACTION PARITY ACT (AMTPA) of 1982 over-rides state laws that restricted MLOs from providing loans other than those with conventional fixed interest rates and terms. The law allowed the industry to offer loans that had terms such as adjustable and negative amortization.

Although most of these loans were good for many situations and for the more sophisticated borrower, many MLOs put borrowers into loans that they did not understand. This practice of putting borrowers in loans that do not fit their needs and qualifications can jeopardize the homeowners' situation by compromising their ability to make payments.

The most common abuse or act of predatory lending occurred when the MLO did not inform the borrower that the interest rate and, therefore, the payment, were going to increase. The Truth-in-Lending form clearly provides a space to disclose the potential future payments, as well as the terms and index that the adjustments would be based on. It is unethical for an MLO to fail to disclose this information to the borrower.

FEDERAL TRUTH IN ADVERTISING ACT falls under the auspices of the Federal Trade Commission. The act requires that all advertising for those engaged in the mortgage industry must be non-deceptive and truthful. Advertisers must be able to verify that all claims in their advertising is accurate.

> *Example:* Broker James advertises that he can provide a 30-year fixed-rate loan with an interest rate of 4.75%. Broker James would need to show proof that the interest rate available at the time of placing the advertisement was in fact 4.75%, which would best be done by retaining a copy of the rate sheet from a lender that he uses on a regular basis.
>
> If 4.75% was not available on that date, he would be guilty of false or fraudulent advertising.

DISCLOSURES THAT ARE REQUIRED TO BE INCLUDED IN ADVERTISING include:

- Agency providing the mortgage broker's license.
- License # of the broker/owner of the business.
- APR/annual percentage rate if there is a disclosure of terms in any form such as:
  - Interest rate
  - Term in years or months
  - Payment amount
  - Closing costs
  - Down payment
  - LTV

DECEPTIVE ADVERTISING, as defined by FTC's Deception Policy Statement, is "advertising that omits material information that is pertinent to the consumer's ability to make a proper decision." Deceptive advertising misleads by not providing all of the information that a consumer needs in choosing a service or product.

UNFAIR ADVERTISING, as defined by the FTC's Unfairness Policy Statement, is "advertising or a business practice that causes or may cause injury to a consumer which they could not reasonably avoid based on the claims of the advertiser." The loss to the consumer cannot be outweighed by the benefit gained by the consumer.

> ***Example:*** *Broker James advertises a loan with an interest rate of 3.5%. He does not disclose that it is an adjustable-rate loan program and that the rate and payment may increase. Borrower Green cannot afford the payments after the rates adjust and must sell his home or lose it to foreclosure.*
>
> *The benefit of having a low payment for the first year is not a sufficient benefit to the borrower to offset his loss of both money, time, investment, and credit.*

PREDATORY LENDING

PREDATORY LENDING is a term used to describe the abusive practices of unethical people in the mortgage industry. The term was coined following the lending abuses that contributed to the mortgage meltdown of 2006.

The term "predatory lending" describes practices of deception, fraud, and unfair acts perpetrated by various parties in the mortgage industry for the purpose of making money or gaining property. There were many unethical and improper acts practiced by brokers, MLOs, lenders, closers, appraisers, and consumers.

Various state and federal laws cover the different practices that are considered predatory lending; there is no one law that directly covers the general act.

Some of the abusive practices that fall under the predatory lending term are as follows:

- Failure to disclose terms and conditions.
- Altering documentation.
- Failure to notify borrowers that loan terms are negotiable.
- Charging higher fees and rates when the loan file is not justified as a high-risk loan based on creditworthiness and guidelines, as one would be under the "risk-based pricing" parameters.
- Requiring insurance that is unnecessary for the lender's guidelines, such as requiring credit life or single-premium credit insurance.

PREDATORY LENDING LAWS initially addressed the implementation of the **Federal Good Faith Estimate of Closing Costs** and the **Truth-in-Lending Act.**

CHAPTER 6
CALIFORNIA SPECIFIC REAL ESTATE INDUSTRY

CALIFORNIA-SPECIFIC SAFE ACT

SAFE ACT OR THE SECURE AND FAIR ENFORCEMENT FOR **MORTGAGE LICENSING ACT** was implemented in January 2010, as a part of the Housing and Economic Recovery Act of 2008 to place federal controls on the mortgage industry. Through this act, mortgage loan originators (MLO) have new licensing requirements in California. *States that do not comply with this federal requirement will only have HUD and government loans available to their citizenry.*

Licensees are required to obtain the California Department of Real estate (DRE) licensing designation as an MLO; this is required to be on the license of anyone engaged in the mortgage industry. This designation applies to those who make, arrange, or service loans secured by real property and applies to both residential and commercial activities.

A licensee currently active in the mortgage industry in California must complete a report to the DRE at *www.dre.ca.gov* using Form 866, Mortgage Loan Activity Notification.

New licensees will need to meet the licensing requirements of the DRE or CFL (California Finance Lender) license issued by DBO (California Department of Business Oversight), complete the NMLS (National Mortgaging Licensing System) 20-hour education requirements, and take both the federal and the state-specific examinations prior to becoming an MLO.

Failure by those actively working as mortgage loan originators to obtain the appropriate licensing and endorsement may result in the assessment of the following fees:
- Fifty dollars ($50) per day for the first 30 days.
- One hundred dollars ($100) per day for every day thereafter up to a maximum of $10,000.

These fines apply in the future to any person acting as an MLO without the proper licensing and endorsement.

MORTGAGE LOAN ORIGINATOR

As mentioned earlier, the following requirements are required of all DRE real estate licensees who conduct Residential Mortgage Loan Originator (MLO) activities to qualify for the MLO real estate license endorsement:
- Obtain a unique identifier number from NMLS&R.
- Pass the national written exam (100 questions).
- Pass the California-specific components of the SAFE written exam.
- Complete 20-hours of pre-license education. (Some licensees may have met the requirements through other DRE education.).
- File an online MLO License Endorsement Application (MU4) and pay the fee on the NMLS&R website.
- Submit a new set of fingerprints using an NMLS&R live scan vendor. Vendor information is available in the application process.
- Provide authorization to run a credit report.

Derogatory credit explanations may be acceptable. Bankruptcy or foreclosure activity within the previous three years is not acceptable. The M L O m a y reapply after the 3-year period has passed.

Contract loan processors and underwriters will also be required to be licensed under the NMLS&R. Those working in these positions that are direct employees or W2 employees of the broker or lender will not be required to become licensed.

A California Department of Real estate (DRE) broker license is required in California to own and operate a mortgage company. A DRE salesperson licensee is allowed to function as a loan agent or mortgage consultant under the guidance and license of a DRE broker licensee.

DRE licensees can broker loans to those licensed under the DRE, the California Department of Financial Protection and Innovation (DFPI), or who are a residential mortgage lender.

California Finance Lender (CFL) licensees under the **California Department of Financial Protection and Innovation (DFPI)** may perform lending duties in much the same way as mortgage brokers licensed under the **DRE**. To operate as a mortgage broker in California without a **DRE broker's license**, one can obtain the **CFL license**.

The broker of record operating under the CFL must be licensed; however, the loan agents working for the broker do not need to be licensed under DOC, however, they are required to be registered under NMLS. Every MLO is required to take the 20-hour SAFE training and pass both the federal and the state-specific NMLS exams.

Many banks are licensed under the CFL and use these laws to perform their mortgage transactions. A broker licensed under CFL must provide the GFE/LE, but not the DRE MLDS.

A broker working under a CFL license can only submit loans to lenders licensed under the DOC with a CFL license.

The California Department of Real estate (DRE) is within the Business, Consumer Services, and Housing Agency. The DRE is headed by a commissioner who is appointed by the governor to oversee the activities of the DRE. The commissioner is responsible for:
- Licensing
- Regulation of the various business under licensing.
- Regulation of licensing, rules & regulations, and laws.
- Protect consumers and services to businesses.

The Department of Financial Protection and Innovation (DFPI) licenses and regulates securities brokers and dealers, investment advisers, financial planners, consumer and commercial lenders, including mortgage lenders, deferred deposit or payday lenders, escrow companies, and certain other fiduciaries. The DFPI also regulates the offer and sales of securities, franchises, and off-exchange commodities.

- *The DFPI's Financial Services Division* licenses and regulates payday lenders, mortgage and other non-bank lenders, mortgage servicers, escrow agents and companies, and other financial service providers.

Residential Mortgage Lender (RML) licensing is used by many banks and direct lenders. Many banks are licensed under RML or the DOC as a licensed banking corporation. Loan officers working for a bank do not require any state license; however, they do need to conform to the NMLS requirements of registration and education, but do not need testing.

An RML lender can only broker loans to other RML lenders or to state- or federally- chartered institutions.

The **California Residential Mortgage Lending Act** applies to those who service mortgages or make loans against 1-to-4-unit residential dwellings. The Commissioner of Corporations issues the license for the activities performed. The following are exempt from the requirement of the California Residential Mortgage Lending Act because they are operating under licensing by another agency:

- Real estate broker licensed by DRE.
- Broker licensed with CFL under the DOC.
- Institutional lender licensed under the DOC or federal licensing.
- Non-institutional lenders licensed under the DOC or federal licensing.
- Trustee of a trust fund or account.
- Individuals lending personal funds.
- Court-appointed representatives.
- Government employees.
- Pension fund administrator.

LICENSING

REAL ESTATE SALESPERSON'S LICENSE REQUIREMENTS are as follows:

- **Education:** 45 hours in each of three courses equal to three college-level courses
  - Real estate principles: 45 Hours
  - Real estate practice: 45 Hours
  - One elective which may be a previous college class if acceptable to DRE: 45 Hours
- **Experience:** None

TESTING is the first requirement of the California Department of Real Estate (DRE) for a person to enter the real estate industry in California, as it is in most States.

The DRE has established specified education requirements that must be met prior to being allowed to take the examination that is administered by the Department.

1. **REAL ESTATE PRINCIPLES** is the main required course that concentrates on the laws set forth by the California Business and Professions Code, as well as other relevant state and federal laws. The DRE also governs California real estate licensees through its rules and regulations. These laws, rules, and regulations govern the real estate industry and its licensees.

This essential course provides a solid understanding of the guidelines that a licensee should remember when working in the real estate industry.

2. **REAL ESTATE PRACTICE** is also required by the DRE as a course to prepare a potential licensee for the behavior and ethics necessary for a real estate professional. Both courses provide guidance in the use of the various forms and documentation that are part of the everyday real estate transactions. Real Estate Practice requires the completion of a mandatory Fair Housing Interactive Component.

3. **ONE ADDITIONAL COURSE WILL BE REQUIRED,** in addition to the two courses required for the real estate license exam. The following courses are approved by the DRE as electives:

   - Mortgage Loan Brokering
   - Real Estate Finance
   - Real Estate Appraisal
   - Legal Aspects of Real Estate
   - Real Estate Economics
   - Real Estate Office Administration
   - Business Law
   - Property Management
   - Real Estate Economics

A potential licensee can apply to take the state exam after the two required courses and the elective course have been successfully completed. Upon successful completion of each course, the school will provide a **CERTIFICATE OF COMPLETION**. In order to verify that an applicant is qualified to take the exam, one copy of the Certificate of Completion must be submitted to the DRE, along with the application to take the exam. *The applicant should always make at least one copy of every Certificate of Completion received at any point in their career.*

The application to take the state exam can be obtained online at the DRE website *https://www.dre.ca.gov*. The form must be completed and submitted to the DRE along with the Certificates of Completion for the three courses completed. The DRE will provide a letter with the test date and the exam location. The DRE letter, along with the application, must be taken to the exam, as it will be required for admission on the scheduled exam date.

If a computer is not available to an applicant, the DRE can be contacted at:
California Department of Real Estate
Examination Section
P.O. Box 137001
Sacramento, Ca. 95818-7001

The DRE REAL ESTATE SALESPERSON'S LICENSING EXAM consists of the following:
- 25% Practice of Real estate and Disclosures
- 15% Property Ownership and Land Use Controls & Regulations
- 9% Financing
- 17% Laws of Agency and Fiduciary Duties
- 12% Contracts
- 14% Property Valuation and Financial Analysis
- 8% Transfer of Property

The successful applicant will receive a packet of forms from the DRE within a few weeks of passing the exam. The following are included in the packet:
- **An application** to be completed by the applicant and signed by a broker. *A salesperson licensee cannot work independently.* If no broker has been chosen, the applicant may leave that blank and the license will be considered "inactive."
- A **fingerprint card** to be completed at an authorized fingerprinting service, including a police department. Most service providers will require an appointment to be made in advance. The fingerprints may then be forwarded directly to DRE from a facility if they have computer capability.
- **Additional information** that will be important to the new real estate salesperson licensee.

The application must be mailed to the DRE along with the licensing fee. Depending on the amount of workload, the real estate salesperson's license will be mailed back within a few weeks. The licensee cannot begin working until the date the license is issued. A broker may allow a new licensee to begin working in the office in order to become familiar with office practices, however, the new licensee cannot quote prices or interest rates, sign contracts, or perform any other duties that require a real estate license until the license is in hand.

Any misstatement of facts made on the license application through fraud, deceit, or misrepresentation may result in suspension of the license within 90 days of the application without a hearing. A real estate licensee is expected to be of good moral character. Conviction of certain felonies or crimes involving moral turpitude may result in the denial of their application for a real estate license.

Real estate salesperson's licenses are issued for four years. Real estate salespersons renewing an original license for the first time, must complete forty-five clock hours of DRE-approved *continuing education* consisting of:

- Five separate three-hour courses in the following subjects: Ethics, Agency, Trust Fund Handling, Fair Housing, Risk Management; and
- A minimum of eighteen clock hours of consumer protection courses; and
- The remaining clock hours required to complete the 45 hours of continuing education may be related to either consumer service or consumer protection courses.

A real estate license will be suspended if education requirements have not been met by the expiration date displayed on the license.

CHILD SUPPORT IN ARREARS will not be allowed for a DRE licensee or applicant. The DRE will not renew a real estate broker's license or a real estate salesperson's license to a licensee who owes back child support. A temporary or restricted license may be issued for a period of 150 days to allow time to pay the child support that is in arrears. If evidence of payment of that debt is not provided to DRE within the 150-day period, the license will be suspended.

License cancelation is temporary and is different from revocation. A real estate salesperson's license is canceled under two situations:

- Broker of record dies, is suspended, revoked, or holds an expired license.
- Licensee quits or is terminated.

During the time that the license is canceled, the licensee cannot perform any duties that require a real estate license.

CALIFORNIA REAL ESTATE LAW

REAL ESTATE LAW is found in the Business and Professions Code. The State of California recognizes a need for appropriate laws for the protection of the public from fraudulent acts on the part of unscrupulous sellers and agents. These laws have evolved over the years and continue to change in response to the ever- changing influences of society, the economy, and new business practices. The Department of Real estate provides a regular newsletter which offers updated information regarding laws, rules, and regulations relevant to licensees. *There is a space on the license application that asks if the applicant would like to receive mailings. Indicating "yes" will provide the licensee with the newsletters.*

The Real Estate Commissioner enforces real estate law by issuing the following licenses:
- Real Estate Broker License
- Real Estate Salesperson License
- Restricted Salesperson License
- Prepaid Rental Listing Service (PRLS)

ENFORCEMENT OF REAL ESTATE LAWS, RULES, AND REGULATIONS, other than as they apply to licensing, are the responsibility of the District Attorney (DA) in the county where a violation has occurred. Any criminal violations against a real estate licensee filed by members of the public are prosecuted by the local DA. Complaints must be in writing from the party filing the complaint and verified by the DA prior to prosecution being pursued. The DRE may suspend or cancel a real estate license based on the findings of the local courts and on the DA's recommendation. The local DA and the courts can levy fines and order imprisonment or house arrest. *The Commissioner does not have the authority to fine licensees or to collect penalties for fines that have been levied against licensees.*

The Commissioner does not get involved with commission disputes. Commission disputes are generally managed by the local Board of Realtors or through arbitration.

The REAL ESTATE EDUCATION AND RESEARCH FUND is held by the DRE as a way to provide relief to any member of the public who has obtained a judgment against a real estate licensee. Twenty percent of the amount collected by the DRE from license fees is placed into the fund, which also supports research projects and educational programs.

If a licensee has had a judgment against them and has not paid the fees associated with that judgment, the creditor who holds the judgment can request relief from the DRE Commissioner. Their license will be suspended until the amount that has been paid on their behalf has been repaid to the DRE Relief Fund. The Relief Fund will pay up to $20,000 per transaction on behalf of a licensee, up to a total of $100,000 per licensee.

REAL ESTATE LICENSE LAW

A REAL ESTATE BROKER'S LICENSE allows a person to perform a variety of duties for another person for a fee. These duties include:

- Listing
- Selling
- Managing
- Leasing
- Exchanging
- Negotiating options
- Arranging mortgage loans
- Commercial or business transactions as they pertain to the transaction.
- Mobile or manufactured homes transactions that have previously been used and placed in a park or otherwise on a privately owned. *The sale of new mobile homes must be conducted by a person licensed under the HCD.*

REAL ESTATE BROKER LICENSING is required for any of the aforementioned duties to be performed on behalf of a client. There is a distinction between a broker and a salesperson. To own and operate a real estate business, one must be a licensed real estate broker. The "broker of record" is the owner of the business.

Each partner in a **PARTNERSHIP** owning a real estate business must hold a real estate broker's license. A salesperson's license is not acceptable for an owner of a real estate business.

A **CORPORATION** must have a licensed real estate broker as an officer. A corporation may hold a real estate license as a legal entity, however, there must also be a person who holds an active real estate broker's license as an officer of the corporation.

An abusive practice sometimes referred to as **"RENT-A-BROKER"** involves the use of another broker's license, even though the broker has nothing to do with the real estate business being operated under their license. The broker is paid for the use of their license.

Rent-a-Broker is an illegal practice and is punishable by fines and loss of license for both the party operating the business and the one renting the license, and for the broker who is allowing their license to be used by another. A real estate professional must not participate in any actions involving this practice.

REAL ESTATE SALESPERSON'S LICENSEES must work for a licensed real estate broker. It is illegal for a salesperson licensee, other than their broker of record, to collect any payment from anyone. The broker of record is legally responsible for the actions of all salesperson licensees who have their license hanging under the broker's license. Files are not to be removed from the broker's office by the salesperson at any time since they belong to the broker, not the salesperson, and this is true even if the salesperson brought in the client and signed the contract.

UNACCEPTABLE AND/OR ILLEGAL ACTS committed by a salesperson licensee may be subject to fines, loss of license, and even imprisonment. The broker of record will bear the greatest liability for any illegal or unethical acts by a salesperson. A salesperson licensee has an obligation to act ethically and legally on behalf of the broker of record.

"HANGING YOUR LICENSE" refers to the legal requirement that all licensed persons working in an office in the business of real estate or requiring a real estate license must have their original license, **not a copy**, displayed in a conspicuous place on the business premises.

SELECTING A BROKER

SELECTING A BROKER is a process that should be approached with care and consideration. In most cases, the agent will be paid commission only rather than a salary, so it's advisable for the salesperson or agent to interview a broker, rather than the other way around. Every office is different in the way they conduct business and their areas of specialization.

When considering potential brokers/officers to work for, a new salesperson should consider some of the following:

- Most people prefer to do business locally. The new agent should decide on the neighborhood or locale where they would like to work and look for a broker within the area.
- A new agent should look at or study "Homes and Land Magazine" and similar publications. The types of properties a broker specializes in will be apparent. A new agent should choose the type of properties with which they wish to work.
- When a new salesperson walks into a broker's office for the first time, they should pay attention to the feeling of the office, how the receptionist treats them and the activities of the agents in the office. This is what the potential clients will see and feel when they come into the office. Some offices are more formal than others and some people prefer a casual atmosphere. A new agent should choose an office that suits their own personality.
- When interviewing a broker or manager, they should ask about benefits. Medical insurance is not likely to be available for most jobs in the real estate Industry. Benefits that may be available to an agent may include broker- paid business cards for the first order and assistance with annual dues for the Board of Realtors, MLS, or any other required memberships. Most real estate sales brokers belong to the Board of Realtors and the MLS. If the broker belongs, all agents **must** belong.
- Is floor time available? *Floor time is a way of obtaining potential clients. This will be discussed further in a later chapter.*
- Is there broker advertising?
- Does the broker provide training or a mentoring program?
- Are there computers in the office for agent use?
- What is the commission split? Does it increase? Is there a sliding scale?
- Request a copy of the employment contract for review prior to signing.

There are different areas of the real estate industry that a new licensee may be interested in, such as sales, property management, or mortgage loan brokering. Most of the considerations listed above will apply to any of these career choices, and they all apply to sales.

EMPLOYMENT CONTRACTS are used as a means to establish a real estate salesperson licensee as a self-employed person, but legally work under a real estate broker's license. This legal form of employment establishes an association between the broker of record and the salesperson licensee, creating the term, "**sales associate,**" when referring to a salesperson licensee in the employ of a real estate broker. The employment contract must state that the salesperson licensee is responsible to the broker of record and must obey their laws, as well as the rules and regulations that govern real estate professionals. A salesperson licensee is responsible to the broker of record to maintain ethical and legal practices.

LEAVING THE EMPLOY OF A BROKER or entering into employment by the broker of record requires notification to DRE of that change. The license change must be reported to DRE within ten business days of that change. The licensee may report the change online at the DRE website, *https://www.dre.ca.gov,* but the brokers of record for both the new and old companies are required to notify the DRE or confirm the change.

The **BROKER OF RECORD** retains the legal right to have access to all files and records at all times and is responsible for reviewing documentation during the time a transaction is in process. *For example*: the **DRE requires** that the broker of record review the purchase offer as soon as possible after the contract has been exercised. The broker is also required to review the MLDS/GFE within three business days of the original MLDS/GFE being prepared or signed by the borrower in a loan transaction. A broker may assign written authority to another holder of an active real estate broker's license to review files on their behalf. A person with an active real estate salesperson's license, two years' experience in the real estate industry and written authority from the broker of record may also be designated to review files for the broker.

A Salesperson may not remove files from the broker's office when leaving the employment of that broker. All files belong to the broker, not the salesperson licensee. Salesperson licensees will often expect to take any open files or files in process with them to their new broker's office. They have procured the client and worked on that transaction, and they would like to get paid for their work. Since a salesperson is not allowed to perform acts requiring a real estate unless they are working under the auspices of a broker of record, they may not remove the file. The proper way to ensure payment on a file is to discuss the situation with the current broker and arrange for payment to the new broker, who in turn, will pay the sales associate or salesperson licensee.

An **UNLICENSED PERSON** performing duties requiring a real estate broker's license or representing themselves as a real estate broker are subject to a fine of $10,000 per incident. Unlicensed persons working in a broker's office may assist with files and transaction, but without a real estate license that person is not allowed to perform any of the following duties:

- Sign contracts.
- Discuss price.
- Quote interest rates.
- Solicit clients.
- Discuss terms.

NOTE

A real estate salesperson licensee may not work independently.

EXCEPTIONS to the real estate license requirement that allow for persons acting under certain situations to perform real estate related duties without a license are:

- **DEALING WITH ONE'S OWN PROPERTY** A property owner may list, sell, lease, exchange or perform other real estate related duties that would otherwise require a real estate license for property that they own.

- **BUYING and/or SELLING REAL ESTATE PAPER OR PROMISSORY NOTES** secured by real property, more commonly referred to as **mortgage loans,** is the exception to this exception. A real estate broker's license is required for a person who is buying and/or selling **eight or more promissory notes secured by real property within one calendar year.** A person who makes eight or more real estate transactions in a year is considered to be working in the industry and is thus required to hold a real estate license.
  - Many investors loan money to homeowners using their property as security for the loan. This is **REAL ESTATE PAPER**. Investors can lend, buy, and sell real estate paper on a regular basis as an income-producing investment. The collection of the monthly principal and interest payments creates a steady income flow. This does not require a real estate license.

- **CORPORATIONS** dealing with their own properties in their own offices may conduct duties normally requiring a real estate license. When this occurs, the employees of the corporation are not allowed to be paid special compensation, such as a commission, for these duties.

- **POWER OF ATTORNEY** allows a person to transact business on behalf of the party giving the power of attorney. This constitutes transacting duties as an individual and therefore does not require a real estate license. Most real estate transactions can be performed only under a **specific power of attorney** versus a **general power of attorney**. A specific power of attorney is specified for that transaction *only,* as a means of preventing unscrupulous acts by the person assigned that role.

- **ATTORNEYS** performing an act or duty on behalf of a client or as a part of their duties as an attorney that would otherwise require a real estate license are exempt.

- **COURT APPOINTED PERSONS** acting on behalf of the court in a capacity that would normally require a real estate license are exempt from the licensing requirement.
    Example: Mary's grandmother has passed away and the will is to be managed by the probate court. Mary has been appointed as the executor for her grandmother's estate. As the executor, Mary can sell, lease, exchange, or otherwise dispose of the property without obtaining a real estate license.

- **BANKS, SAVING & LOANS, CREDIT UNIONS,** and their employees are exempt from real estate licensing when transacting on their own behalf. These entities are licensed and governed by the Department of Financial Protection and Innovation (DFPI).

- **ESCROW COMPANIES** and their employees are exempt from real estate licensing when transacting on their own behalf. These entities are licensed and governed by the Department of Financial Protection and Innovation (DFPI). Escrow companies are limited in the duties they are allowed to perform regarding real estate transactions. In their capacity as an escrow company, they may discuss terms, interest rates, and details that would otherwise require a real estate licensing; however, they are not allowed to sell, lease, or dispose of property.

REAL ESTATE BROKER LICENSE

REAL ESTATE BROKER'S LICENSE REQUIREMENTS are as follows:
- **EDUCATION: Eight college level courses of 45 hours each**
    - **5 MANDATORY CLASSES**
        1. Real Estate Practice
        2. Legal Aspects of Real Estate
        3. Real Estate Finance
        4. Real Estate Appraisal
        5. Real Estate Economics or Accounting
    - **ELECTIVES COURSES (3):** Choose from options such as
        1. Real Estate Principles
        2. Business Law
        3. Property Management
        4. Escrow
        5. Real Estate Office Administration
        6. Mortgage Loan Brokering and Lending
        7. Advanced Legal Aspects of Real Estate
        8. Advanced Real Estate Finance
        9. Advanced Real Estate Appraisal
        10. Computer Applications in Real Estate
        11. Common Interest Developments

- **EXPERIENCE:**
    - Either, a minimum of two years full-time licensed salesperson experience within the last five years, or two years of unlicensed equivalent experience, or a four-year degree with a major/minor in real estate is required.

- **PASS AN EXAM:** Prepared by the DRE consisting of 200 multiple-choice questions and completed within 4 hours, with a score of 75% or more, with a minimum of 150 correct answers.

The **BROKER'S EXAM** is compiled of the following:
- 25% Practice of Real Estate and Disclosures
- 15% Property Ownership and Land Use Controls & Regulations
- 9% Financing
- 17% Laws of Agency and Fiduciary Duties
- 12% Contracts
- 14% Property Valuation and Financial Analysis
- 8% Transfer of Property

REAL ESTATE BROKER'S LICENSES are issued for four years. At the end of the four-year license term, real estate brokers renewing an original license must complete forty-five clock hours of DRE-approved **continuing education** consisting of:

- Six separate three-hour courses in the following subjects: Ethics, Agency, Trust Fund Handling, Fair Housing, Risk Management, and Management and Supervision; and
- A minimum of eighteen clock hours of consumer protection courses; and
- The remaining clock hours required to complete the 45 hours of continuing education may be related to either consumer service or consumer protection courses.

REAL ESTATE BROKERAGE

REAL ESTATE BROKERAGE can be a business that works in any of a variety of real estate businesses. *Brokerage* refers to a kind of business that does not have items for sale as a retail business would offer. A brokerage is a type of business that conducts business on behalf of their clients or acts as an intermediary between a party who wants to obtain a particular item, product, or service. and the party who has that item, product, or service. A real estate brokerage business may sell a parcel of real estate on behalf of the property owner. The business does not own the parcel of land itself, but finds a purchase, and assists with the sale of the property by bringing the buyer and seller together, then assisting in the completion of that transaction.

"DOING BUSINESS AS" OR DBA is a fictitious name that a business uses instead of using the name of the business owner. A real estate broker may choose to operate their business under their own name; however, most businesses will operate under a fictitious name. A fictitious name must be recorded with the county recorder's office, and then advertised in a local newspaper under "public notices." The local newspaper personnel know the laws regarding fictitious name filings and will see that the requirements for the filing are met. The DRE must be provided with a copy of the fictitious name filing to be placed on the Real estate Broker's License.

CHANGE TO THE NAME OR ADDRESS of the broker or the business does not require obtaining a new license from DRE. The DRE allows for changes to be made manually by the broker as long as the changes have been reported to DRE.

A REAL ESTATE BUSINESS can operate under one of several different structures. Regardless of the business structure, it must be recorded with the county recorder's office and registered with the DRE. Whatever the form of ownership, the broker of record is responsible for the actions of the business and its employees. Because of this, *the broker of record is responsible for all decisions regarding the operation of the business.*

- **SOLE PROPRIETOR** is a business owned by one person. In the real estate industry, a sole proprietor must hold an active real estate broker's license. The broker of record/owner is solely responsible for all activities within that business.

- **PARTNERSHIP** is a business owned and operated by more than one person and can include any number of partners. **All** partners are required to hold an active real estate broker's license. This was not a requirement until 2004, when the DRE recognized the need to have a broker of record on site in real estate businesses as a way to help prevent fraud by unscrupulous business owners.

- **CORPORATION** is a form of business ownership that is considered to be a legal entity and can hold a real estate broker's license. It does require that a person holding an active real estate broker's license be an officer of the corporation. *It is recommended that the broker of record be the president of the corporation.*

- **BRANCH OFFICES** are allowed to be operated by a person holding only an active real estate salesperson's license with a minimum of two years' experience in the real estate industry.

REAL ESTATE BUSINESS OPPORTUNITIES

BUSINESS OPPORTUNITIES available to a person holding a real estate license offer a variety of interests.

REAL ESTATE SALES is the business most commonly sought by a real estate licensee. A real estate sales office performs a variety of duties and can specialize in an area. The duties that are performed in a real estate sales office include:

- Listing real property for sale.
- Showing homes to buyers.
- Negotiating purchase offer contracts.

- Leasing real property on behalf of property owners.
- Showing property to potential tenants.
- Preparing leases.
- Managing the property.
- Preparing legal documents such as a **notice to vacate.**

1. **PROPERTY MANAGEMENT** is the management of small SFRs, multi-unit residential properties, and all types of commercial properties. Specialization is usually exercised in the property management business. *It is important to remember that residential units of 16 or more are required to have a resident manager.*

   The duties performed in a property management business include:
   - Leasing real property on behalf of property owners
   - Showing property to potential tenants
   - Preparing leases
   - Managing the property
   - Preparing legal documents such as a notice to vacate
   - Managing maintenance
   - Bookkeeping

2. **MORTGAGE BROKERS** and **MORTGAGE LOAN ORIGINATORS working under the supervision of a broker** obtain mortgages for potential borrowers by locating a lender who matches their needs.
   The duties performed by a mortgage broker include:
   - Preparing loan applications
   - Working with client's financial needs
   - Providing credit advice
   - Working with lenders
   - Understanding appraisals

   As of January 1, 2010, all DRE licensees who choose to work as mortgage loan originators or to negotiate rates or terms in the process of obtaining a mortgage loan for a consumer must obtain a license through the Nationwide Mortgage System (NMLS) under the Safe Act, SB 32 and obtain a federal license in addition to the California license endorsement.

3. **PREPAID RENTAL LISTING SERVICE (PRLS)** is a business that provides, for a fee, listings of residential properties available for rent. Unlike other real estate- related fees, these fees are charged in advance. The PRLS can be operated by a licensed real estate broker or a person holding an active Prepaid Rental Listing Service License.

   The Prepaid Rental Listing Service (PRLS) License is a separate license provided by the Department of Real estate valid for a two-year period.

4. **MANUFACTURED/MOBILE HOME TRANSACTIONS** may be performed by a person holding an active real estate license if the manufactured home has been used and is located on a lot in a mobile home park for more than one year. The Department of Housing and Community Development (HCD) regulates licensing for the sale of new mobile homes by issuing dealer's licenses.

5. **MANUFACTURED/MOBILE HOMES IN PARKS** are considered chattel, or personal property, and are licensed by the Department of Housing and Community Development (HCD). They are required to be recorded with the state's Department of Housing and Community Development (HCD).

   Because the property is personal and not real property, mortgage brokers licensed under the Department of Real Estate are not licensed to broker these loans. The required license is a **California Finance Lender** (CFL) license provided through the California Department of Financial Protection and Innovation (DFPI). DRE Mortgage Brokers may prepare these loans and submit them to a California Finance Lending Broker and collect a fee; however, the California Finance Lending Broker is the acting broker and will collect their own commission and processing fees. *A DRE Broker may find it cost prohibitive to perform these loans since the commissions collected are considerably less than usual, but the California Finance Lending Broker will do most of the work.*

6. **REAL PROPERTY MANUFACTURED HOMES** are manufactured homes on private lots and are considered to be real property only if the home is **permanently fixed** on a private lot. Generally, this refers to mobile homes that have been placed on a permanent foundation with the wheels and axles removed. Mobile home manufacturers began building homes with the axles permanently attached in the mid-1990s. If this is the case, it is documentable and can be waived by the underwriter.

When a manufactured home has been permanently affixed to a foundation, the contractor will provide a state-required certificate. A copy of this certificate must be included as part of the transaction documentation required for a loan.

HUD began establishing guidelines for manufactured homes in 1976. Any homes built prior to 1976 are more difficult to finance because they do not meet building standards.

Single-wide mobile homes are not considered acceptable property to residential mortgage lenders even when permanently attached to a private lot.

7. **Real estate licensees may manage MINERAL, OIL, AND GAS TRANSACTIONS.** *The former licensing designated as a Mineral, Oil, and Gas (MOG) Broker License is no longer provided. New MOG licensing is no longer offered as the real estate broker's license provides for the licensing requirements.* The duties performed by a real estate licensee in a Mineral, Oil, and Gas Transaction include:
   - List for sale.
   - Solicit prospective buyers and sellers.
   - Negotiate and prepare purchase offers.
   - Lease.
   - Manage leases.
   - Exchange.
   - Assist with the filing of the application for purchase or lease of related property owned by the federal government.
   - Options.
   - Offer mining claims.
   - Be a principal.

Commercial real estate includes the various acts of selling, leasing, or financing commercial properties. Commercial lending will require an NMLS (National Mortgage Licensing System) license.

8. **A real estate licensee often oversees BUSINESS OPPORTUNITY BROKERAGE** even though the sale may be for personal property only. **Bulk sale of goods** refers to the sale of a business and all of its associated merchandise. A business sale will involve the sale of the:
   - **Business name and goodwill**: Goodwill is the continuing and ongoing patronage of the clientele.
   - **Inventory of business equipment**: Cash register, display shelves, machinery, or any equipment that is part of operating the business.

- **Inventory of retail product**: *A person purchasing a clothing store could expect to purchase the clothing that is currently for sale in the store.* Whatever the product the business offers will be included as part of the business purchase transaction.
- **Lease of real property**: If the current business is located in a leased space, the transfer of that lease (and perhaps new lease terms) will be a part of the business purchase transaction.
- **Sale of real property**: If the real property is a part of the business sale transaction, a **real property purchase offer** will be a part of the overall transaction.

The negotiations of the real property, whether a Lease or a purchase offer, is usually handled as a separate simultaneous transaction. A business sale does not require a real estate license; however, if the negotiation of real property is a part of the transaction, a real estate **broker's license** is required. A business sale that does not involve real property negotiations is rare.

AGENT'S RESPONSIBILITIES IN SALE OF A BUSINESS

- Review of the records to include current Profit & Loss Statement, and tax returns from at least the two most recent years.
- Seller's books and records.
- The consideration of the business location and the flow of business being generated
- Assisting the buyer with the review and consideration of all aspects of not only the purchase but also the operations of the business being purchased.

LOCAL LICENSING LAWS regarding the operation of a business and those specific to certain businesses are an important part of purchasing a business. The real estate professional specializing in the sale of businesses should be fully prepared to provide advice and assistance with the local requirements.

THE CALIFORNIA DEPARTMENT OF TAX AND FEE ADMINISTRATION (CDTFA) is responsible for collecting sales tax from businesses that collect sales tax as a part of their business operations, such as retail sales, and offers seminars for business owners on a regular basis. The seller of a business must obtain a tax certificate from the CDTFA to verify the amount of sales taxes due at the time of close of escrow (COE). The owner of a business required to collect sales tax must register the business with the California Department of Tax and Fee Administration. The CDTFA will provide the forms that will be needed for filing taxes.

UNIFORM COMMERCIAL CODE (UCC) is a federal code that has been adopted by California. The purpose of the UCC is to regulate the transfer of goods being held for sale by a business. Most retailers or sellers of goods purchase their stock or items for resale on credit. Retail businesses are typically able to pay for their stock over time, while generating profits through the resale of those goods. If the merchandise is part of a business sale, the creditor needs assurance of payment for the merchandise in the business being sold.

A BULK SALE is the transfer of a substantial part of the business inventory in a commercial transaction. Inventory will fluctuate as products are sold to customers and an inventory will be conducted. To protect the creditors, the UCC provides that:

- Creditors be notified of the transfer of business ownership.
- Notice be made at least 12 business days prior to transfer.
- Notice be recorded with the county recorder's office.
- Transfer be published in a local newspaper.
- Notice to county tax collector be notified by certified mail.
- Notice of the transfer be posted in a conspicuous place at the place of business.

FRANCHISES are businesses that sell to a party, or franchisee, the right to operate a business using their name, product, and trademark in the operation of their business. The franchisee purchases the right to operate under an already established business name and reputation.

> *Example: McDonald's is perhaps the best-known franchise. The franchisee, or the party that purchases a McDonald's franchise, purchases the right to use the name, sign, recipes, building design and all else that McDonald's offers. They obtain the right to purchase food from the McDonald's main corporation, which is the franchisor. The franchisee receives the right to advertise as McDonald's.*

The franchisee pays to purchase a franchise, and often pays a fee or a percentage of the profits as ongoing payment to operate the franchise. The franchisee is generally required to purchase supplies from the franchisor as part of the agreement. There are a number of large real estate companies that are franchises.

PROFESSIONAL ASSOCIATIONS

PROFESSIONAL ASSOCIATIONS are available to the real estate professional and should be considered excellent educational resources. They also offer numerous personal benefits. Many real estate sales offices require membership in the Board of Realtors and the Multiple Listing Service (MLS) as a part of doing business.

REALTOR® is a registered trademark of the **BOARD OF REALTORS** organization and may not be used by any persons who is not a member of the association. A real estate professional **must be** a member of the Board of Realtors in order to advertise and call themselves Realtor®. Membership in the **CALIFORNIA ASSOCIATION OF REALTORS (CAR)** constitutes membership in the **NATIONAL ASSOCIATION OF REALTORS (NAR)**. The organization provides online forms created by the *CAR* attorneys for use in preparing contracts, such as a purchase contract. If the broker of record is a member, all associate licensees working for that broker are required to be members, per the terms of the organization. *www.car.org*, *www.realtor.com*

CAR offers training for new licensees, especially in the use and completion of the real estate forms.

MULTIPLE LISTING SERVICE (MLS) is an organization of real estate sales professionals which provides access to the listings of all member brokers in the organization. It allows a broker to advertise their listing to other member brokers who are providing information to potential buyers. Members have an agreement to pay commissions to any other member office that procures a party to a transaction. Nonmember offices must obtain a contract agreeing to pay commissions for each transaction. If the broker of record is a member, all associate licensees working for that broker are required to be members per the terms of the organization. MLS is a localized organization in conjunction with the local Board of Realtors. *MLS also offers training for new licensees.*

REALTIST is a member of the **NATIONAL ASSOCIATION OF REAL ESTATE BROKERS, INC. (NAREB)**. This organization began in Florida in 1947 as an organization of predominantly African American members. It is now a nationwide organization with a number of local groups. *www.nareb.com*

CALIFORNIA ASSOCIATION OF MORTGAGE PROFESSIONALS (CAMP) (formerly BROKERS CAMB) is a professional organization for those involved in the mortgage business. Membership in this state association constitutes membership in the NATIONAL ASSOCIATION OF MORTGAGE BROKERS (NAMB).
https://www.thecampsite.org

INSTITUTE OF REAL ESTATE MANAGEMENT (IREM) is an association of property managers originally created for management companies but is now represents individuals working as property managers.

The following list provides some associations of interest to real estate professionals:
- **California Association of Realtors** *www.car.org*
- **Asian American Real Estate Association** *https://areaa.org*
- **National Association of Hispanic Real Estate Professionals** *www.nahrep.org*
- **California Association of Real Estate Brokers** *www.careb.org*
- **California Association of Mortgage Brokers** *www.cambweb.org*
- **California Mortgage Bankers Association** *www.cmba.com*
- **California Association of Business Brokers** *www.cabb.org*
- **California Association of Community Managers** *www.cacm.org*
- **California Building Industry Association** *www.cbia.org*

VIOLATIONS OF THE REAL ESTATE LAWS

The most common prohibited real estate violations are found in the Business and Professions Code Section 10176. The acts by a real estate licensee may result in license suspension, revocation, cancellation, fines, or imprisonment:

- Undisclosed dual agencies
- Misrepresentation of material facts
- Commingling of funds
- False promises
- Lack of providing a termination date for a real estate listing
- Violation of the Transfer Disclosure Civil Code
- Secret profits by licensee
- Dishonest dealing
- Fraud
- Theft
- False advertising
- Criminal activities
- Misuse of trade Negligence
- Negligent supervision of salespersons
- Trust fund violation
- Mishandling of clients' funds
- Inducing panic selling

CHAPTER 7

LOAN APPLICATION AND TRANSMITTAL SUMMARY

LOAN APPLICATION/1003

 **THE LOAN APPLICATION** provides all the information that makes up a complete loan package. All the verifications are created from the information provided in the original 1003. The final determination of qualification is made from the information compiled and provided by the processor on the final 1003 and the transmittal summary, or 1008.

The **LOAN AGENT'S JOB** is to provide the loan processor with as much information as possible when they take the original application. The loan processor determines if there is missing information while entering the information into the loan originating software (LOS) and will then notify the loan agent and borrower of any missing information necessary to complete the processing.

The following is an explanation of information needed to be provided on the 1003 by section:

THE TOP OF PAGE 1 OF THE LOAN APPLICATION states that the form is designed to be completed by the borrower and co-borrower with the help of the lender. There is also a disclosure regarding the borrower's rights as they pertain to loan qualifications, income, assets, and their liability for the accuracy of their information. The rights of the borrower and co-borrower as they pertain to community property are also disclosed. *California is a community property state.*

If the borrower and co-borrower agree that they are preparing the loan application jointly, they are required to sign directly below the disclosure. All joint borrowers will sign in this space even if they are not married co-borrowers.

> **NOTE**
>
> *Only married co-borrowers will be on the same application form. Co- borrowers do not need to be related in any way, but if they are not married, each borrower will complete a separate 1003 to become part of the one loan file.*

I. TYPE OF MORTGAGE LOAN:

Mortgage Applied For:

VA and FHA are common throughout the country, but less so in large metropolitan areas because the maximum loan amounts are restricted. FHA and VA loans were limited to the FNMA/FHLMC conforming loan limits. FHA loan limits were increased from 75% of the FNMA loan limits to 100% of the loan limits in 2008. The VA loan limit was increased to the FNMA maximum loan amount in January 2002.

CONVENTIONAL LOAN refers to conforming or jumbo loans, in first trust deed position, on 1-to-4-unit residential property, with a conventional lender except for the VA or FHA loans.

USDA/RURAL HOUSING are loans offered under the auspices of the U. S. Department of Agriculture. These loans are made by specific lenders and brokers working under DRE generally will not handle this type of loan.

OTHER includes all other loan types such as second trust deeds and equity lines. *The processor must know what type of loan they are processing in order to provide the proper input and documentation.*

CONFORMING LOANS are loans that meet or conform to the Fannie Mae (FNMA) guidelines. FNMA has established maximum loan limits as a part of their guidelines. Loans that exceed the FNMA loan limits are considered **jumbo loans.**

California has requested that HUD declare the entire state a 'high-cost area,'' which would qualify all conforming loans done within the state to qualify as a conforming loan at the higher loan limits currently used in Hawaii and Alaska. As of this writing the FNMA/FHLMC loan limits in most other states are as follows, and California is considered high cost.

The loan limit may be lower or vary for a specific high-cost area. Loan limits can vary from county to county: Refer to FHA at the following link to determine the limits for the county in which the loan is made: *http://www.fhfa.gov/DataTools/Downloads/Pages/Conforming-Loan-Limits.aspx.* These limits are revised each year. Most loan originating software will have these limits built in.

Pursuant to the *American Recovery and Reinvestment Act*, loans originated in 2009 may be delivered to FNMA using the higher of either the high-cost area loan limits or the temporary high-cost area loan limits in place for the year 2008. **Whether these loan limits continue or become permanent figures is unknown and are subject to change.**

Although FNMA has established these limits, lenders do not necessarily have to adhere to them. Many lenders will work within FNMA guidelines without approving loans for the maximum available amount. *Lenders do not want to be unable to sell loans at a later date because the loan limits have changed. Because of this, many lenders are not making loans for the maximum limit allowed.*

When FNMA decides to change the conforming loan limit, the new limit will generally go into effect in the month of January. Because of inflation in the early years of this century, FNMA adjusted the maximum loan limit every January for several years. When the country's economy improved, these changes slowed, and maximum conforming loan limit did not change for several years. The economy and changes in property values have a direct effect on changes to loan limits.

AGENCY CASE NUMBER: Brokers are required by law to keep a **loan log** of all files received in their office as shown in *figure 20*. The processor is generally responsible for maintaining this log and assigning the number. The number assigned to the file can go in this space, on the loan log, and on the file cover for easy reference. The exception to this will be VA and FHA loans, in which case the lender will assign the number.

NOTE

Loan amounts above the conforming limit are called jumbo loans for a single-family residence (SFR) and for properties with additional units. Brokers should check the loan limits on a regular basis as they are subject to change and the interest rates and charges will be affected.

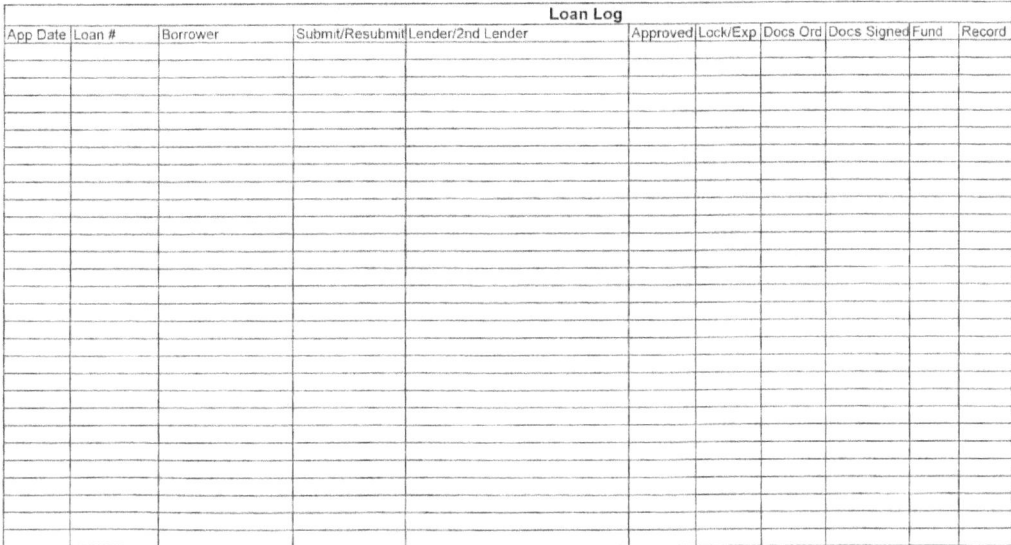

Figure 20 – LOAN LOG

LENDER CASE NUMBER: This will be assigned by the lender and put in this space before the lender sells in the secondary mortgage market. This space will be left blank by the broker. The only deviation is with VA and FHA loans. Once submitted, the lender will assign the agency number and lender case number assigned by VA or FHA. The broker is still required to assign an agency number; however, it will not appear on the 1003.

AMOUNT: Although loan agents will often leave this blank until they are sure of the amount needed, there must be a figure to work from to determine eligibility and the **law requires full disclosure before the borrower signs the loan application.** *There must also be a loan amount in order to prepare the loan application (1003) and the loan estimate (LE).*

The loan agent must provide a figure as close as possible, and it must be included in the original 1003. **This space must not be left blank.** The loan amount can be changed at any time during the processing according to the borrower's needs and qualifications along with the lender's guidelines.

It is best to use a higher loan amount to start the process because it is easier to reduce an amount later.

If the amount needs to be increased after it has been submitted to the lender, the loan will need to be re-underwritten and re-disclosed to make that change. It does not need to be re-underwritten to reduce a loan amount or an interest rate.

Under RESPA, there is ZERO TOLERANCE for the change of some of the fees on the loan estimate and the closing disclosure. A reason for the change of terms should be documented in the conversation log and the broker should obtain a letter from the borrower agreeing to the changes to any loan terms. If the terms change dramatically, the broker may choose to cancel the original loan application and create a new loan based on the terms that can be obtained. If this is done, the broker must wait a minimum of 10 days before the new loan application can be submitted to the lender.

INTEREST RATE: The same rule applies to this space as for the loan amount. Up- front disclosures cannot be made or a determination of qualification provided without the information in these two spaces. The figures provided by the loan agent should represent the figures that were discussed with the borrower.

NUMBER OF MONTHS: This figure tells whether the loan is for 40 years or 480 months, 30 years or 360 months, 20 years or 240 months, 15 years or 180 months, 10 years or 120 months, 5 years or 60 months, or another period of amortization. *The mortgage industry refers to months more often than years because amortization is the period of time in which the loan will be repaid, determining the amount of monthly payment.*

A variety of combinations, such as 360/180, are used. The first figure tells you the amortization period the payments will be based on, and the second figure shows when the balance is due. This example is called a **balloon payment,** meaning the the total balance becomes due and payable in a set period of time or on a predetermined date.

360/180 means the payments are calculated to repay the loan in 360 months, but the balance will be due in 180 months. The most common amortization is 360/360, or fully amortized for thirty years.

> **NOTE**
>
> *Any change to the loan terms will require re-disclosure to the borrower of the costs of obtaining a loan. The broker will require a new LE. The broker will also need to document the reason for the change. The terms of the initial LE are binding.*

AMORTIZATION TYPE

The amortization type refers to a **fixed rate**, **adjustable rate mortgage (ARM)**, **graduated payment mortgage (GPM)**, or any other variation or particular repayment method.

- **FIXED-RATE** means that the payment and interest rate will remain the same throughout the life of the loan. A **buydown** is a fixed-rate loan that begins with a lower interest rate and will adjust at given intervals until it reaches the actual rate. The borrower pays an additional fee or percentage of the loan amount to buy the initial interest rate down for a set period of time.

- **ARM LOANS** will adjust at predetermined periods. *ARMs will be discussed at length in Chapter 15, Types of Loans.*

- **GPM LOANS** OR **GRADUATED PAYMENT MORTGAGES** have a fixed-rate for the life of the loan, but the payment starts at a lower rate and then adjusts on a pre-determined date for a set period of time, usually between three to five years until the payment reaches the **note rate (actual rate)**. GPMs are rarely used when the economy is good but are popular during times of high interest rates. *They will be explained in more detail in Chapter 15, Types of Loans.*

There are a number of variations to any given type of loan and many of them will be discussed at length in different sections. Lenders will change loan programs occasionally as a way to compete in the market. Economic conditions determine the need for and use of various types of loan programs.

II. PROPERTY INFORMATION AND PURPOSE OF LOAN:

SUBJECT PROPERTY ADDRESS: The complete address of the property to be financed must be included. The address on the final 1003 must match the address shown on the preliminary title report (prelim) and the appraisal. The prelim is assumed to contain the correct information as this is the information recorded with the county recorder's office. If there is a major difference from the original 1003, an explanation may be necessary. Any variation on the appraisal must be corrected by the appraiser. *Common variations or discrepancies are the use of street instead of avenue.*

PRE-QUALIFYING for a loan is done before a property is chosen, when a borrower wants to determine whether they qualify for a home loan. The LE (loan estimate) must still be provided, however, and the broker should identify the disclosure by writing across the form in a visible manner: "This is not an LE." This will avoid the problem of disclosing extreme changes to the terms of the loan. Once the property is located, the LE can then be created with accurate terms disclosed.

NOTE

If there is no property, there is no loan according to Truth-in-Lending Law.

NO. OF UNITS: 1-to-4 units are acceptable for **conventional residential loans**. Lenders will usually have additional costs for more than two units. Properties with more than four units are considered **commercial properties,** and the application and processing will be handled differently. The broker must verify the number of units on page 1 of the appraisal once it is received.

LEGAL DESCRIPTION: It is acceptable and even advisable to write "**See Prelim**" in this space. There may be legal ramifications to the broker if the legal description proved has errors.

Often the legal description of the property is too lengthy and attaching a copy of the page providing the information may be necessary. The prelim provides the complete legal description as recorded by the county. The escrow officer will provide the legal description with the grant deed and other necessary documentation.

YEAR BUILT: If the borrower does not know this information, it will be found on Page 1 of the appraisal.

PURPOSE OF LOAN: This is self-explanatory and must be completed. The documentation that will be required will vary based on the borrower's reason for obtaining the loan.

If the loan is a **CONSTRUCTION LOAN** or a **CONSTRUCTION-TO-PERM**, also called a **TAKE OUT LOAN**, the borrower will need to provide receipts for all costs of the construction and acquisition, including the HUD-1/CD from the original purchase. The value will be the lesser of total costs or appraised value. *This is not a conventional loan and will be discussed at length in a later chapter.*

YEAR ACQUIRED: Loan agents rarely fill in this space, however, it is important and **should always be completed** because it determines **"seasoning,"** which has an effect on the value used.

Whether the loan is **"CASH-OUT" (C/O)** or **"NO-CASH-OUT" (N/C/O)** will also affect the "pricing" or the interest rate and fees charged by the lender. If the borrower has owned the property less than one year, the property is not seasoned, therefore the loan amount will be based on the lesser of the purchase price or the appraised value. A refinance loan will be considered cash-out if a second trust deed (TD) is being paid off, unless the TD was used for the purchase of the property or purchase money loan. The date of the loan must coincide with the date purchased.

REFINANCING an unseasoned loan is considered cash-out. If refinancing a second TD, the refinance will be considered a cash-out loan unless it was a "purchase money second." This FNMA/FHLMC guideline was established in 2002.

Prior to 2002, the loan was considered no-cash-out (N/C/O) as long as the first TD and second TD were more than 12 months after origination or date of closing escrow. If the borrower had taken a draw of $2,500 or more from an equity line in the past 12 months, it was considered cash-out (C/O). Otherwise, it was considered no cash out. This is no longer the rule and will not be considered anything less than cash- out.

ORIGINAL COST: Is equally important as the year acquired and for the same reasons: it determines seasoning and influences value. If the property was purchased within the last few years and has increased considerably in value, this space may also support the purpose of refi, low cash reserves, and excessive debt, as it may indicate remodeling/renovations. *A property that has been owned for a long period of time will establish the borrower as a more solid credit risk.*

NOTE

The basic information and documentation that is discussed applies to all loan types. When there is additional or different documentation required for a particular loan type, it will be stated. Documentation particular to a purchase loan will be discussed in a later chapter.

AMOUNT OF EXISTING LIENS: This figure can be derived from the credit report or the most recent mortgage statement if provided by the borrower. The loan agent should obtain the mortgage statements from the borrower whenever possible.

PURPOSE OF REFINANCE: RATE & TERM refers to no-cash-out and means the borrower is refinancing to reduce the interest rate, payment, or change the amortization term.

Closing costs may be included in a no-cash-out or rate and term refinance. Since it is impossible to calculate the exact closing costs, lenders will allow the borrower to receive up to a certain amount (generally $2,000 cash-out) on a rate & term refinance.

This amount may vary between lenders. Lenders like to see that the borrower is obtaining cash to upgrade or remodel their home because the value is going to increase. It shows pride of ownership and indicates stability.

A DEBT CONSOLIDATION LOAN is considered to be a **CASH-OUT LOAN** if the funds are being used to pay consumer debts such as cars or credit cards.

When the cash is being used to pay off debt, the lender will view this positively because it is reducing the borrower's monthly obligation. Most lender's guidelines do not allow revolving debt being paid through escrow to be deducted from the debt ratio in order for the borrower to qualify because the credit is still available, and the borrower may use the credit cards again. If the borrower needs to pay revolving debts to qualify, an alt-A or sub-prime lender would be needed.

These are the most common reasons for refinancing, but you may see college expenses for children, which is acceptable.

NOTE

Lenders will not accept a loan when the cash-out is being used to start a business. This indicates that the borrower's current income will not continue. The borrower's income is going to change and current income cannot be used for qualifying especially if the borrower has no proven history of being successfully self-employed. Most new businesses fail within the first three years and if the borrower has no history of being self-employed, the failure rate is a consideration to the lender.

COST OF IMPROVEMENTS: If the borrower is taking cash-out to pay remodeling debts or replenish cash reserves after remodeling, this space must be completed, be clearly explained, and may need to be verified with receipts especially when costs are in excess of $50,000. A lender may consider remodeling expenses a construction loan instead of a refinance. The determination will depend on the costs and type of work to be done.

If a building permit is required, the lender will most likely view the loan as a construction loan.

TITLE WILL BE HELD IN WHAT NAMES: This space carries legal ramifications and is best to state "TBD (To Be Determined) in Escrow," unless the loan is a refinance in which case the names will be taken from the prelim.

The processor should ask the borrower for the exact spelling of their name and how they want it to appear on title.

MANNER IN WHICH TITLE WILL BE HELD: Also holds legal ramifications. **The broker and employees must never advise a borrower how to hold title.**

If the loan is a refinance, the prelim will state how title is currently held. If the loan is a purchase, escrow will provide that information before docs are ordered. Examples of ownership or vesting are husband and wife as joint tenants (HWJT), tenants in common, unmarried man/woman (previously married), single man/woman (never married), married man/woman as sole and separate property. "TBD in escrow" is advisable if not on prelim.

SOURCE OF DOWN PAYMENT: Settlement charges and/or subordinate financing: On purchase loans, this space could say **savings**, **cash on hand**, or **gift**. A refinance may say any of these or "**equity in subject property**" meaning that the loan amount is going to be sufficient to pay existing liens and closing costs so that the borrower will not need to bring in funds to close.

On a **NO-CASH-OUT LOAN**, the amount can be increased to pay closing costs as long as the amount of cash left over does not exceed $2000, or 1% of loan, rate & term loan. *Most computer programs designed to process mortgage loans will have options from which to choose.*

ESTATE WILL BE HELD IN:

- **FEE SIMPLE** is the standard form of holding title and means the borrower owns the property with no restrictions as to use.
- **LEASEHOLDS OR LAND LEASES** are types of ownership where the borrower owns the improvements (buildings/structures on the land) and another person owns the land itself. They are generally written for terms of one hundred years. The lease must have a minimum remaining term greater than five years of the loan term if less than 50 years.

Lenders used to require a minimum of 50 years remaining on the lease; however, since land leases were commonly used in the early 1900s, the majority of land leases no longer have that amount of time remaining. The logic of requiring a remaining term of five years more than the loan term is to protect the lender's investment for more than the term of the loan. The land lease payment is included in the housing expense for qualifying purposes. Leasehold is uncommon but may be seen. This is a common form of ownership in areas such as Newport Beach, California.

> **NOTE**
>
> *The leasehold is irrevocable and runs with the land.*

III. BORROWER INFORMATION:

If there are multiple borrowers that are not married, a separate 1003 and credit package will be required for each borrower. Following the primary borrower's application and credit information, the secondary borrower's application and credit documentation will be placed in the same file folder and in the same stacking order. All subsequent borrowers' applications and documentation will follow in the file and be placed ahead of the property documentation or escrow instructions, purchase agreement, and appraisal. The borrower with the highest credit score will be the primary borrower.

> **NOTE**
>
> *Only married borrowers will be on the same loan application.*

BORROWER'S NAME: The correct spelling of the borrower's name is imperative. This is how it will show on all documentation and title. Double check with the borrower and, if a refi, check the prelim. The lender will usually draw loan documents according to the 1003. It must be accurate before submission to the lender.

SOCIAL SECURITY NUMBER: Required to run a credit report and if any discrepancies appear, a letter of explanation will be required and a copy of the Social Security card is required as part of the loan application.

HOME PHONE NUMBER: When recording the phone number, common sense could save trouble prior to funding.

> *Example: If a borrower states that they live in a certain area, but the area code or prefix do not match the address, ask questions, and clarify the situation. Borrowers will often try to obtain an owner-occupied loan on a non-owner- occupied property to save money.*

DOB (DATE OF BIRTH): This section has been added as a result of the Patriot Act and the establishment of the Department of Homeland Security. It helps establish the borrower's identity if needed.

The borrower's birth date is also advantageous to the loan agent as a reason to stay in touch with the client by conveying birthday wishes after the transaction has closed.

YEARS SCHOOL: This information is important and necessary as it confirms a variety of statements.

> *Example: Retirement income may be greater for a person with a higher level of education or recent college graduate with less than two years job history working in their field of education.*

MARITAL STATUS: The marital status of the borrower has obvious legal ramifications, especially in a community property state such as California.

A married borrower taking title as **SOLE AND SEPARATE** will require a **QUITCLAIM DEED** from the spouse, and the escrow officer should be notified to have the proper documents prepared at signing. A divorced person may have child support, spousal support, alimony, or separate maintenance expenses and will require a copy of the divorce decree.

NOTE

An incorrect Social Security number on a loan application can cause the borrower trouble with their credit for years to come. Accuracy is imperative.

DEPENDENTS, NUMBER AND AGES: This information may substantiate other information, such as cash-out for college expenses or recent credit issues caused by a loss of income due to a pregnancy.

PRESENT ADDRESS: This information will provide the lender with a history of stability. Whether they currently **own or rent** and **the length of time at that address are imperative**.

The lender will require a two-year history of housing payments, whether at the subject address or previous addresses. All addresses for the last two-year period are required by the lender.

If the borrowers are **CURRENTLY RENTING**, obtain the landlord's name and address to provide a verification of rent (VOR) or canceled checks for the last 24 months' rent.

MAILING ADDRESS: Allows for post office boxes or other address to facilitate communication with the borrower. Not all borrowers receive mail at their primary residence. The lender may require an explanation if obtaining an owner-occupied loan.

FORMER ADDRESS: Lenders require a two-year history for the borrower. All addresses for the borrower for the previous 24 months must be included. Page 5 of the 1003 is provided for any information that does not fit on the other pages.

IV. EMPLOYMENT INFORMATION:

NAME & ADDRESS OF EMPLOYER: This information is needed to provide verifications of employment (VOE).

If not self-employed, the borrower needs to provide prior 2-year **W2s** and **YTD** paystubs for the most recent 30-day period. Two complete years of employment are required and VOEs should be obtained from all employers during that time period. *Not all lenders will require VOEs. See Figure 22: verification of employment (VOE).*

YEARS ON THE JOB AND MONTHLY INCOME: Information on the original 1003 should be close to the figures verified by the processor. If not, question the loan agent and clarify before submission to lender.

Borrowers will often provide net income (after tax/take-home). Lenders use gross income (before tax) for qualifying. Consider whether this makes sense for the type of job, age of the borrower, etc.

POSITION/TITLE/TYPE OF BUSINESS: The underwriter will use a common sense approach when evaluating this information consider this information in relation to the rest of the application and as confirmed by the VOE.

> *Example: A 22-year-old has probably not been self-employed for 10 years and a chemical engineer probably has more than 12 years of education.*

BUSINESS PHONE: The lender will call the phone company's "information" to verify the business phone is listed as stated on the 1003, especially if the borrower is self-employed. They will also do a verbal verification of employment.

If the borrower's direct line is provided on the 1003, the main phone number for the business should be obtained. This is an opportunity for the broker to do some quality control on the file and perhaps ward off any problems prior to submitting the file to the lender.

There are spaces for additional employment whether working more than one job or to include all jobs during the previous two-year period.

V. MONTHLY INCOME AND COMBINED HOUSING EXPENSE INFORMATION:

GROSS MONTHLY INCOME: Before tax income is used for qualifying and is **always based on a two-year history.**

CURRENT MONTHLY INCOME is used for **salaried employees only;** however, the lender does want to see two years of similar stable or increasing income. Salary income is income that is the same whether the party misses work, works overtime, or any other change in work hours.

A two-year average is used to calculate **hourly employee's** income. Salaried and hourly income will require year-to-date (YTD) paystubs for the most recent 30-day period and the most recent two years of W2s. An 18-month average may be acceptable if there has been a job change and/or pay increase. Always check with the lender prior to submission if circumstances are out of the ordinary.

Request for Verification of Employment

Sample

Privacy Act Notice: This information is to be used by the agency collecting it or its assignees in determining whether you qualify as a prospective mortgagor under its program. It will not be disclosed outside the agency except as required and permitted by law. You do not have to provide this information, but if you do not your application for approval as a prospective mortgagor or borrower may be delayed or rejected. The information requested in this form is authorized by Title 38, USC, Chapter 37 (if VA); by 12 USC, Section 1701 et. seq. (if HUD/FHA); by 42 USC, Section 1452b (if HUD/CPD); and Title 42 USC, 1471 et. seq., or 7 USC, 1921 et. seq. (if USDA/FmHA).

Instructions: Lender - Complete items 1 through 7. Have applicant complete Item 8. Forward directly to employer, named in item 1.
Employer - Please complete either Part II or Part III as applicable. Complete Part IV and return directly to lender named in Item 2.
The form is to be transmitted directly to the lender and is not to be transmitted through the applicant or any other party.

Part I - Request

1. To (Name and address of employer)	2. From (Name and address of lender)

I certify that this verification has been sent directly to the employer and has not passed through the hands of the applicant or any other interested party.

3. Signature of Lender	4. Title	5. Date	6. Lender's No. (Optional)

I have applied for a mortgage loan and stated that I am now or was formerly employed by you. My signature below authorizes verification of this information.

7. Name and Address of Applicant (include employee or badge number)	8. Signature of Applicant

Part II - Verification of Present Employment

9. Applicant's Date of Employment	10. Present Position	11. Probability of Continued Employment

12A. Current Gross Base Pay (Enter Amount and Check Period)
- [ ] Annual
- [ ] Hourly
- [ ] Monthly
- [ ] Other (Specify)
- [ ] Weekly

$

13. For Military Personnel Only	
Pay Grade	
Type	Monthly Amount

14. If Overtime or Bonus is Applicable, Is Its Continuance Likely?

	Yes	No
Overtime	[ ]	[ ]
Bonus	[ ]	[ ]

12B. Gross Earnings

Type	Year To Date	Past Year ___	Past Year ___
Base Pay	Thru ___ $	$	$
Overtime	$	$	$
Commissions	$	$	$
Bonus	$	$	$
Total	$	$	$

Base Pay	$
Rations	$
Flight or Hazard	$
Clothing	$
Quarters	$
Pro Pay	$
Overseas or Combat	$
Variable Housing Allowance	$

15. If paid hourly-average hours per week

16. Date of applicant's next pay increase

17. Projected amount of next pay increase

18. Date of applicant's last pay increase

19. Amount of last pay increase

20. Remarks (if employee was off work for any length of time, please indicate time period and reason)

Part III - Verification of Previous Employments

21. Date Hired	23. Salary/Wage at Termination Per (Year)(Month)(Week)			
22. Date Terminated	Base	Overtime	Commissions	Bonus
24. Reason for Leaving	25. Position Held			

Part IV - Authorized Signature

Federal statutes provide severe penalties for any fraud, intentional misrepresentation, or criminal connivance or conspiracy purposed to influence the issuance of any guaranty or insurance by the VA Secretary, the U.S.D.A., FmHA/FHA Commissioner, or the HUD/CPD Assistant Secretary.

26. Signature of Employer	27. Title (Please print or type)	28. Date
29. Print or type name signed in Item 26	30. Phone No.	

Calyx Form - voe.frm (11/07)

Figure 22: Verification of Employment (VOE)

SOCIAL SECURITY INCOME or any other income that is not taxed will require an award letter and proof of the current amount. Each January, Social Security sends recipients a letter stating the amount to be received monthly for the following year. The award letter, current check, or a bank statement showing a direct deposit is all acceptable for verification. The monthly allotment can be grossed up by 15% or multiplied by 115% to derive the usable income.

The reason for this is to compensate for the fact that taxes are not paid on this money which allows the borrower more spendable cash in comparison to other borrowers that are qualified on their gross or before tax income.

- OVERTIME, BONUS, COMMISSION, DIVIDENDS/INTEREST, and RENTAL INCOME will all require the most recent tax returns from the last two years and YTD verification *to be discussed further in the chapter on income.*

- RENTAL INCOME will, in addition, require current leases/rental agreements or the prior 2-years 1040s including Schedule E.

- SELF-EMPLOYED Borrowers will be required to provide the prior 2-year 1040 Tax Returns, Schedule C if a sole proprietorship, 1120s if a corporation, 1065s and K1s if a partnership, and a signed YTD Profit & Loss Statement (P&L) through the most recent quarter.

Self-employed borrowers should also be asked to provide current and prior 2-years' business license. Twenty-four bank statements can be used as verification of self- employment or commission income (generally limited to sub-prime lenders or non- conforming loan programs). Seventy-five percent of the monthly average will be used to determine income if the business bank statement is used because the deposits do not reflect the expenses, or 100% if the statements are on a personal account because they have taken the gross profits for their income. *Other calculations apply and will be discussed at length in Chapter 12.*

The exception to the above requirement is for stated income or alternative (alt) doc loan programs, which will be discussed in Chapter 15, Types of Loans.

There are additional lines at the bottom of Page 2 of the 1003 that allow for other income, such as alimony and child support.

NOTE

Lender's requirements will change depending on the economy and the current market.

COMBINED MONTHLY HOUSING EXPENSE:

Current-housing expenses are whatever the borrower currently pays for housing.

This amount will be compared against the proposed amounts for **"PAYMENT SHOCK."** If the proposed housing expenses are more than 50% higher than current payments, the lender will ask the borrower to provide a letter addressing payment shock. This letter needs to address the borrower's means of adapting the personal budget to a considerable increase in expenses. This letter also makes the borrower aware of the increase.

If the loan is a refinance transaction, the actual payment will be taken from the credit report and the actual tax amount will be established from the preliminary title report (prelim). The insurance amount will be determined from the declarations page of the insurance statement. Lenders will always require a copy of the insurance dec page when the insurance will be impounded with the loan. Taxes are paid twice a year, and insurance is usually paid once a year. Some insurance companies now offer a variety of payment plans to allow for smaller payment amounts whether monthly, quarterly, or bi-annually. The figures must be broken down to a monthly figure.

For a purchase loan, the tax information will be obtained by using a factor of 1.25% of the purchase price divided by twelve to calculate the monthly amount.

Homeowner's insurance can be estimated by using a factor of approximately .28% to multiply the loan amount. This calculation will provide an annual amount, which must then be divided in 12 months to derive the monthly figure. For the average-priced home in California, homeowner's insurance will usually run $600 to $800 per year, depending on the location and value of the property. Lenders will require the subject property to be insured at all times during the life of the loan. If the homeowner allows the insurance coverage to lapse, the lender will obtain insurance through their choice of insurance company and will notify the borrower of the additional amount to be paid along with the monthly house payment. The amount will be considerably higher than the insurance the borrower can obtain.

MORGAGE INSURANCE (MI) is insurance that protects the lender from loss in case of default on loans that are greater than 80% of the value of the property. It is also referred to as PMI, private, or primary mortgage insurance. Lenders usually do not require MI on loans that are less than 80% of the value.

Mortgage insurance is used by lenders as a way to protect their investment. Mortgage insurance is required on loans that are greater than 80% of the value of the property or 80% loan-to-value (LTV).

When the loan amount is greater than 80% LTV, the lender is at a higher risk of losing a portion of the money they have invested in making the loan. If the borrower defaults on the loan or otherwise does not fulfill the contract, the costs that will be incurred in collecting through foreclosure or any other recourse will be costly. By the time the lender has undergone foreclosure and sold the property again, they may actually have lost money on the transaction. If a property does not sell at the foreclosure sale, the lender then needs to hire a real estate agent and list the property for sale, which will add to their expense.

Mortgage insurance insures the loan down to 75% to 78% LTV for the lender. This means that any amount of the original loan that is lost will be reimbursed to the lender by the insurance company, down to an amount equal to but no less than 75% of the original loan amount.

Example:

	$100,000	*Value of Property*
	90,000	*Loan Amount*
	90%	*Loan-to Value (LTV)*
	$10,000	*Equity*

If the lender forecloses on the loan, the following estimated costs are incurred by the lender:

$4,000	*Foreclosure filing*
3,000	*Lost interest from the time of last payment made*
3,500	*Delinquent property taxes*
1,500	*Foreclose sale and sheriff's costs*
$12,000	*Total costs*
$2,000	*Loss after foreclosure sale*

The lender will be paid $2,000 by the mortgage insurance company.

The higher the LTV, the more a borrower will pay for the mortgage insurance because the risk is greater. The borrower pays for the mortgage insurance that will protect the lender based on the risk assessment. It is insurance that the insurance company charges based on the risk the same, much like a driver with a history of accidents and tickets will pay more for auto insurance than a driver with a clean driving record.

The following chart is an example of the PMI premiums that may be charged according to the risk assessment which is established by the LTV:

Loan Terms	Loan to Value (LTV)	Annual Premium Factor
30-Year Fixed	95.1% thru 98%	.0097/.97%
	90.1% thru 95%	.0078/.78%
	85.1% thru 90%	.0050/.50%
	80.1% thru 85%	.0030/.30%
15-Year Fixed	90.1% thru 95%	.0067/.67%
	85.1% thru 90%	.0042/.42%
	80.1% thru 85%	.0024/.24%

The most commonly used factor is .30%; since the mortgage meltdown of 2006-2008, the amount of MI has increased to a factor of .60%. This will vary depending on the borrower's risk factors and the LTV. The higher the LTV, the higher the rate. The loan amount is multiplied by the factor, then divided by twelve to ascertain the monthly payment amount. Mortgage insurance companies provide schedules for calculating more closely; however, the underwriter will provide the exact figure for the final 1003. The premium amount is included in the monthly mortgage payment.

IMPOUND, OR ESCROW, ACCOUNTS are used by lenders to collect the monthly amounts for the homeowner's insurance and property taxes. When the insurance premium and the property taxes come due, the lender forwards the payment on behalf of the borrower. The lender will calculate the amount that will be held at close of escrow (COE) so that they will have sufficient funds available when the debt is due.

NOTE

Once the borrower feels they owe less than 80% of the property's value, they can contact the lender and request the MI be canceled. The borrower will need to acquire an appraisal at that time to verify value for cancellation of MI.

The lender will generally hold two months' insurance payments in reserve. The first mortgage payment will be due between 30 and 60 days after **COE (close of escrow)** as allowed by law. The lender will count the number of payments that will be collected by the time that the next annual premium is due in 12 months from COE. Eleven monthly payments should be collected by the due date. If the eleventh payment is late, the lender would lack sufficient funds to pay the premium, so they will collect an additional two months of payments to ensure the availability of funds. Otherwise, the bill would not be paid on time and the insurance policy would be cancelled.

IMPOUNDING PROPERTY TAXES works the same way, except that property taxes are due twice a year. The first payment is due on November 1 and is late if not paid by December 10. The second payment is due February 1 and is late if not paid by April 10. A lender will count the number of months of payments that will be collected before the next payment is due and will allow for a two-month cushion, as with the insurance impounds. When estimating the amount to be collected for the impound account, the broker/mortgage loan originator must consider not only the amount due for the first tax payment, but also that the second payment is due only three months later.

> *Example: Sue is purchasing a home that will close on July 15. She wants to have her taxes and insurance impounded. Her first payment cannot be due less than 30 days after COE or more than 60 days after COE, so her first mortgage payment will be due on September 1. The lender will most likely collect four monthly tax payments because they will collect the September and October payment before the bi-annual payment comes due November 1.*
>
> *The lender will also collect an additional three months of tax payments because the second bi-annual tax bill will be due on February 1. This means that they will have collected payments for November, December, and January when the tax bill comes due on February 1.*
>
> *At COE Sue will be required to deposit an amount equal to approximately 7 months of tax payments in order to provide the lender with sufficient funds to pay the tax bills.*

These calculations will vary with lenders, but RESPA does not allow the lender to hold more than two months of payments beyond the amount that will be due. Impound accounts used to be allowed to accumulate large amounts. RESPA now requires that the funds be returned to the borrower when they exceed the two-month cushion.

Not all borrowers will choose to have impound accounts; however, the lender can require such an account if the LTV exceeds 90%. Many lenders offer incentives by giving better pricing for borrowers who agree to have their taxes and/or insurance impounded. This is a particularly good option for borrowers who are first-time homebuyers and for those who are not good at saving.

The MLO must know that with the introduction of NMLS, many states do not use an escrow company to close real estate transactions. Most states use title companies or attorneys to function as closing agents. In those states, the term "escrow" is used to describe what is referred to in California as **impound accounts**. Understanding the variation in terminology is also important when working with clients from other states.

 **HOMEOWNERS' ASSOCIATION (HOA) DUES** should be checked for accuracy when the HOA cert and appraisal are received. If the borrower provides an HOA fee, the processor must check the prelim for classification as a condo, planned urban development (PUD), co-op, or a single family residence with common grounds.

The name and address of the HOA will be requested along with the name of the manager or the management company to mail an HOA certificate, which is a questionnaire to be completed by the association or the manager. Because of the increased use of computers in the industry, many HOA certs can now be obtained on the internet at *www.condocerts.com*. Lenders will require that their own cert be used. Lenders also have the capability to verify through FNMA (Fannie Mae) whether the condo is approved or will be acceptable for lending. These guidelines change every few years and it is advised to check with the lender before pursuing the proper HOA documentation.

- The main items that lenders are looking for on the condo cert are lawsuits pending.
- Owner occupancy greater than 65% (FNMA).
- Less than 10% are owned by developer.
- Percentage sold (applies to new complexes).

Many lenders check for FNMA approval of a project if built before a certain date. Newer condo associations may not be found on the FNMA list because the method of FNMA approval changed in the early 2000s. Most lenders have the capacity to verify FNMA approval through the FNMA website.

A copy of the conditions, covenants & restrictions (CC&Rs), the articles of incorporation, current budget, and property insurance to include the fidelity bond will be requested.

A fidelity bond insures the association against fraud, such as embezzlement by an employee. Lenders like to see an amount in reserves that is equal to at least six months of HOA dues for all units. The HOA dues will be checked for accuracy on receipt of the HOA cert and the first page of the appraisal.

The CC&Rs (covenants, conditions & restrictions) and additional documentation should be requested from the owner, escrow, manager, or the management company. Management companies will often require a fee, generally ranging from $25 to $300, for the preparation of this documentation. The borrower is responsible for this fee, and it can be included on the **broker demand** when loan docs are ordered if the broker has paid the fee upfront. Make a note of this fee on the file cover sheet for collection at close of escrow (COE).

For a purchase loan, the HOA dues along with the payment, taxes, and homeowner's insurance information will be calculated on the LOS and obtained by the processor. The listing agent (realtor) should provide the amount of HOA dues. Escrow is a good source for the CC&Rs.

PROPOSED HOUSING for owner-occupied properties will be the figures for the loan being obtained. *Non-owner-occupied property figures for the subject property will also be included in Section VI.*

VI. ASSETS AND LIABILITIES:
Assets/Cash or Market Value

CASH DEPOSIT TOWARD PURCHASE HELD BY: This space will provide the name of the escrow company or any other entity holding the borrower's deposit, or earnest money, and the amount of the deposit. Escrow will provide a copy of the check and the deposit receipt for verification. As this is generally done by personal check, the lender may require a copy of the front and back of the canceled check from the borrower.

LIST CHECKING AND SAVINGS ACCOUNTS BELOW: The name and address of the bank, savings & loan (S&L), or federal credit union (FCU) to include the type of account, account numbers, and current balances, are necessary to complete the verifications of deposit (VOD). These spaces must be completed in full. The loan agent should request the bank statements when taking the loan application. Lenders may require the most recent three bank statements to include all pages. Any large deposits may need explaining and documentation verifying the source. Lenders want to verify that the borrower has not created a new debt in order to close the transaction unless they qualify for it. It is also important to the lender that the borrowers have at least 5% of their own money vested in a purchase transaction.

The information should be taken from the statements for accuracy. Several of the larger banks/repositories have specified addresses or branches for preparation of VODs. Generally, the address of the bank branch where the borrower's account is maintained will suffice. If the borrower has more accounts than the 1003 has spaces for, Page 5 of the 1003 is a blank page provided for any additional information. *See Figure 23, Verification of Deposit (VOD).*

STOCKS & BONDS (COMPANY NAME/NUMBER & DESCRIPTION): This space does not allow room for addresses as these assets are generally considered reserves and not verified. In instances when the borrower needs these funds to close the loan, it will be necessary to list them in the above sections, including addresses, because a VOD may be required to close escrow.

LIFE INSURANCE NET CASH VALUE: Face amount is value at death and cash value is the amount the owner can draw at this time. It is not necessary to complete this section. If the borrower has provided this information, those figures should be used and there is no need to verify unless the funds are required to close escrow.

In situations where life insurance or retirement funds are to be used, verification from the entity involved will need to be obtained to show that the funds do not need to be repaid, and if they do need to be repaid, the terms of repayment will need to be stated. This will be in the form of a letter from the company or the fund's manager.

SUBTOTAL LIQUID ASSETS: The figures the borrower provided should be totaled. The computer will automatically calculate this. This does not need to be completed by the borrower or the loan agent when completing the initial application.

AUTOMOBILES, OTHER ASSETS, ETC. are non-liquid assets, which is an indicator of income, assets, and debt. An underwriter will consider whether the income, assets, and debts make sense.

Many loan agents will leave these sections blank; however, it should always be completed and will often make the difference in obtaining loan approval when the loan is otherwise boarder-line.

It is much better for qualifying if they have a lot of assets to offset debt or lack of verifiable assets.

OTHER ASSETS (itemize): may include household belongings, computer equipment, and tools of the trade (such as for a carpenter), boats, jewelry, art, collectibles, etc.

REAL ESTATE OWNED (enter market value from schedule of real estate owned) (SREO): If the borrower does not provide this information, the loan agent needs to obtain the value of all properties owned by the borrower. If the borrower does not know, the broker can obtain the information from *www.zillow.com.*

> **NOTE**
>
> *Missing information can be handwritten in the appropriate space on the original 1003 as it is provided. The broker should be certain of the accuracy before completing any missing information. Whiteout is not allowed on any forms. If the form is provided with whiteout on it, it will be necessary to redo the entire page. Changed information should be lined through and will require the borrower's initials. If these changes are drastic, the lender will question the information; therefore, it may be best to redo a page before submission.*

> **NOTE**
>
> *It is an accepted rule of thumb that a borrower must have six months' stated income in reserves.*

Request for Verification of Deposit

Sample

Privacy Act Notice: This information is to be used by the agency collecting it or its assignees in determining whether you qualify as a prospective mortgagor under its program. It will not be disclosed outside the agency except as required and permitted by law. You do not have to provide this information, but if you do not your application for approval as a prospective mortgagor or borrower may be delayed or rejected. The information requested in this form is authorized by Title 38, USC, Chapter 37 (if VA); by 12 USC, Section 1701 et. seq. (if HUD/FHA); by 42 USC, Section 1452b (if HUD/CPD); and Title 42 USC, 1471 et. seq., or 7 USC, 1921 et. seq. (if USDA/FmHA).

Instructions: Lender - Complete items 1 through 8. Have applicant complete item 9. Forward directly to depository named in item 1.
Depository - Please complete items 10 through 18 and return directly to lender named in item 2.
The form is to be transmitted directly to the lender and is not to be transmitted through the applicant(s) or any other party.

Lender's Phone No.

Part I - Request

1. To (Name and address of depository)

2. From (Name and address of lender)

I certify that this verification has been sent directly to the bank or depository and has not passed through the hands of the applicant or any other interested party.

3. Signature of Lender	4. Title	5. Date	6. Lender's No. (Optional)

7. Information To Be Verified

Type of Account	Account in Name of	Account Number	Balance
			$
			$
			$
			$

To Depository: I/We have applied for a mortgage loan and stated in my/our financial statement that the balance on deposit with you is as shown above. You are authorized to verify this information and to supply the lender identified above with the information requested in items 10 through 13. Your response is solely a matter of courtesy for which no responsibility is attached to your institution or any of your officers.

8. Name and Address of Applicant(s)	9. Signature of Applicant(s)
	X
	X

To Be Completed by Depository

Part II - Verification of Depository

10. Deposit Accounts of Applicant(s)

Type of Account	Account Number	Current Balance	Average Balance For Previous Two Months	Date Opened
		$	$	
		$	$	
		$	$	
		$	$	

11. Loans Outstanding To Applicant(s)

Loan Number	Date of Loan	Original Amount	Current Balance	Installments (Monthly/Quarterly)	Secured By	No. of Late Payments
		$	$	$ per		
		$	$	$ per		
		$	$	$ per		

12. Please include any additional information which may be of assistance in determination of credit worthiness (Please include information on loans paid-in full in item 11 above)

13. If the name(s) on the account(s) differ from those listed in item 7, please supply the name(s) on the account(s) as reflected by your records.

Part III - Authorized Signature

Federal statutes provide severe penalties for any fraud, intentional misrepresentation, or criminal connivance or conspiracy purposed to influence the issuance of any guaranty or insurance by the VA Secretary, the U.S.D.A., FmHA/FHA Commisioner, or the HUD/CPD Assistant Secretary.

14. Signature of Depository Representative	15. Title (Please print or type)	16. Date

17. Please print or type name signed in item 14	18. Phone No.

Calyx Form - vod.frm (11/07)

Figure 23: Verification of Deposit (VOD)

VESTED INTEREST IN RETIREMENT FUND: The borrower should be able to provide a statement, which is generally an annual form. If they do not retain these and the funds are not needed to close the loan, the figure provided by the borrower will be used. Unless the funds are required for qualifying, the stated amount is sufficient.

NET WORTH OF BUSINESS OWNED (attach financial statement): This space is rarely completed. There are a few circumstances that require this information. A self-employed borrower obtaining a full-doc loan will be the only time this is used, and a **P&L Statement** is generally used in place of a financial statement.

AUTOMOBILES OWNED (make and year): Borrowers will give an estimated value. Use their figure as this item is not verified and the lender uses this as a commonsense tool in comparison with other statements and documentation.

The exception to this is when the borrower owns a new car or one of high value and there is no loan on the vehicle. In that instance, the lender may ask for a copy of the pink slip to verify the vehicle is owned free and clear. This information is not crucial to the loan, but the information should be obtained to make a strong file.

OTHER ASSETS (itemize): Generally, use "personal property." This includes all household belongings. Borrowers will usually provide a figure. If not, estimate based on the income and what you already know about them.

*Example: $4,000/mo. income will have approximately $20,000-$35,000 in furniture, clothing, electronics, jewelry, and kitchenware. $20,000/mo. income will have $75,000-$200,000 in the same items. An antique dealer will likely have $50,000-$200,000 in antiques listed separately. A computer programmer will probably have $15,000 in computer equipment. **This is a commonsense issue. If it does not seem right, ask.***

LIABILITIES/MONTHLY PAYMENT & MONTHS LEFT TO PAY/ UNPAID BALANCE:

NAME AND ADDRESS OF COMPANY/ACCT. NO.: It is imperative to obtain the complete address and accurate loan number of any mortgage lender that is to be paid-off through the loan. The escrow officer will ask for this information when you open escrow.

The **CREDIT REPORT** will provide this information. The LOS allows the broker/MLO (mortgage loan originator) to run the credit report from most agencies from the program and download the information into this area. It is not required to have a signed approval from a borrower prior to running a credit report; however, the broker/MLO should have the signed request as a matter of good business practice. The approval can be a letter, a broker-created form, or the 1003. *Page 4 Section IX of the 1003 provides a credit authorization.*

The largest unpaid debt, which is usually the mortgage, generally appears first and will descend to the smallest debt. The lender will use the disclosed debts as a way of calculating **debt ratio (DR),** or the percentage of the borrower's income that is obligated to pay their debts. *This will be explained at length in the chapter on credit reports and the transmittal summary.* The basic calculation is as follows:

> Housing expense ÷ income = Front End Debt Ratio
> Housing + other debt ÷ income = Back End Debt Ratio

> *FNMA guidelines allow 36% Front End DR and 45% Back End DR*

The **MORTGAGE HISTORY** will generally appear on the credit report and be included in the liabilities section. Some lenders do not report the information, or the mortgage maybe held by a private party, in which case the name and address must be obtained for a verification of mortgage (VOM). Twenty-four months of canceled checks may be acceptable for some lenders. Because the borrower is applying for a mortgage loan, the payment history is the most important of the borrower's liabilities.

Account numbers are scrambled on the credit report for security reasons, so that information is unreliable. When a mortgage statement is provided, take the needed information directly from the mortgage statement rather than the credit report.

When there is a private second TD, the complete name and address is required to obtain a **VOM (verification of mortgage)** and a **demand to close** the loan.

All other debts can be taken directly from the credit report; however, the only information that is required on debts other than the mortgage is the company name, type of payment (revolving, installment, etc.), balance of loan, payment amount, and number of months remaining. Occasionally a lender will require the account number on all debts; in that case, the statements will need to be obtained from the borrower. If there are several accounts with the same creditor, account numbers should be included for clarification. This may also imply duplication. Since most brokers are computerized, the information automatically populates the form when the credit report is ordered through the LOS.

The number of months remaining on the debt applies to loans such as car loans. This number is derived by dividing the balance due by the payment amount.

> *Example: $3,000 balance divided by $300=10 meaning there are 10 months payments remaining on the loan. In the computer, this information will appear as ($300)/10. The parentheses indicates to the computer that this amount will not be included in the totals. This applies only to consumer loans with a set period of repayment and equal monthly payments. Revolving debts do not qualify because they are ongoing, and the consumer may restart the debt once the balance is paid in full.*

UNPAID BALANCE: This figure will be taken from the most recent statement or the credit report.

ALIMONY/CHILD SUPPORT/SEPARATE MAINTENANCE PAYMENTS OWED TO:

A divorce decree or other court documentation is required for these figures. This space is for amounts paid by the borrower and is a monthly or regular liability. If the borrower indicated that he/she pays child support, a copy of the divorce decree will be required. Any funds received by the borrower are income and therefore belong in Section V, under "other income." Income from child

> **NOTE**
>
> *Any loans with a set period of time, such as a car loan, need not be included in the debt ratio if there are fewer than ten payments remaining. When putting this information into the computer, any qualifying figures are to be placed in parentheses ( ).*

> **NOTE**
>
> *Throughout this section, remember that the figures on the credit report are considered accurate unless the borrower provides actual statements. Do not use the figures provided by the borrower on the original 1003 unless proven.*

support and alimony must continue for an additional three years. In other words, if a borrower has a child who is 14 years old and the child support payments will continue until the child turns eighteen, that debt should be reported. This rule also applies to a borrower that claims these items as income.

SCHEDULE OF REAL ESTATE OWNED (SREO):

PROPERTY ADDRESS: All properties owned by the borrower are to be listed in this section. The subject property should be listed first. Vacant land or commercial properties should be placed on the form after any SFRs or 1–4-unit residential properties.

If the property is being **sold** and is currently in escrow, the box to the right of the address must display "PS" for pending sale. If the property has recently sold and the proceeds are to be used for this loan, "S" for sold should be marked.

If the property is a **rental and income is derived** from that property, indicate with "R" in this box. This space is left blank for any other situation.

TYPE OF PROPERTY: This box indicates whether the property is SFR, units, land, or commercial. Most computer programs have a pop-up giving these selections.

When the property is 2, 3, or 4 units, it is best to type in the exact number of units rather than using the generic "1-4" for clarification when dealing with leases and rental income. More than four units are considered commercial property.

Rental properties will require 1040 tax returns/leases. If neither is provided in the package, add these items to your needs list. If tax returns, including Schedule E, are provided to verify rental income, 100% of that verified amount can be used for qualifying. If only leases are provided, the amount of rental income used for qualifying will be 75% of the lease amount.

PRESENT MARKET VALUE: The value of the subject property will be taken from the appraisal. At this point, the estimated value provided will be used. The borrower must provide an estimate if no value is provided. The loan agent/borrower must provide all other property values.

> **NOTE**
>
> *Remember that the two most recent year's tax returns are required for validation of income. Schedule E provides a breakdown of gross and net rental income.*

If the values of other properties owned are not verified, however, they must make sense. The broker will become familiar with values and neighborhood areas as they gain experience. There are websites available that provide estimated values such as *www.zillow.com*. The values obtained on the website or estimates derived from the Multiple Listing Service (MLS) comparables (comps) are all acceptable.

AMOUNT OF MORTGAGES & LIENS: The amount for this space will be taken from the credit report. If the credit report is not yet available, the borrower's figures should be used until it is received.

GROSS RENTAL INCOME: The figure provided by the borrower will be used until the Schedule E of the borrower's 1040s or current leases are received. *To be discussed in detail in Chapter 10, Verifying and Calculating Income.*

MORTGAGE PAYMENTS: These amounts will be determined from the credit report.

INSURANCE, MAINTENANCE, TAXES & MISC.: The borrower's stated amounts can be used until the tax returns are received, or if the leases are the only documentation used for properties other than the subject. *The figures used for the subject property will be completed in Chapter 10, Verifying and Calculating Income.*

NET RENTAL INCOME: The borrower's stated amounts can be used until the tax returns, or the leases are received. *The final or actual figures used will be completed in Chapter 10 on income and the amount will be placed in Section V, monthly income, and Page 2 of the 1003.*

LIST ANY ADDITIONAL NAMES UNDER WHICH CREDIT HAS PREVIOUSLY BEEN RECEIVED: AKA (also known as) will often appear in divorce decrees and on the

> **NOTE**
>
> *If there is an SFR declared as rental property and the declared value is greater than that of the owner-occupied (O/O) property, the validity of the application should be questioned. Lenders will assume that a borrower will live in the most valuable or nicest property and rent the less desirable property. If the borrower states that the subject property is owner-occupied and they own more valuable SFRs in more desirable areas, the lender will require proof of occupancy, such as a phone bill.*

credit report. If none appear in other documentation, leave this blank. If there are AKAs, a letter may be required to explain the additional names. The lender will require an AKA statement to be signed with the loan docs.

VII. DETAILS OF TRANSACTION:

This section is rarely completed by the MLO/loan agent and will be completed in detail by the computer program. It is important to provide as much information as possible with information drawn from other areas, such as the good faith estimate to complete this section. Line I will need to be completed by the MLO or the person putting the information into the LOS. This line will include any credits to the borrower, such as seller-paid costs or lender credits.

VIII. DECLARATIONS:

The borrower must answer all questions. The loan agent is required to obtain any missing information. The questions in this section may indicate the borrower is not qualified for the type of loan expected or quoted by the loan agent. If any of the questions "a" through "i" are answered "yes," further documentation and a letter of explanation will be required. The broker/loan agent should discuss the ramifications with the borrower and ask questions to clarify any potential problems. Some circumstances may be cause for decline by the lender:

a. **OUTSTANDING JUDGMENTS** will be required to be paid in full or document that it has been paid in full prior to closing. This may indicate that the loan may not be "A" paper, and the lender and the interest rate may need to be reconsidered.

b. **BANKRUPTCY** in the last seven years will require a copy of the complete bankruptcy documentation, an LOE, as well as documentation of the borrower's **re- established credit, with at least three creditors since the bankruptcy dismissal.**

A bankruptcy within the last 3-4 years, depending on the lender, will disqualify the borrower for an "A" paper loan. Any late payments since the date of bankruptcy dismissal also will generally disqualify the borrower for an "A" paper loan. There are lenders that will fund a loan that is currently in bankruptcy. The loan to value (LTV) will be considerably lower and the interest rate and costs considerably higher. This will happen when the borrower has filed bankruptcy to prevent losing their home to foreclosure and is a difficult loan to do.

c. **PROPERTY FORECLOSED** on, or given title or deed in lieu of foreclosure, will require a strong LOE and supporting documentation.

A foreclosure must have been at least five years ago; however, lenders do not want the expense of a foreclosure and sale of real property. They look at the applicant's history to determine creditworthiness and borrower attitude. This will be a difficult loan to place. Following the "mortgage meltdown," most lenders will not consider an application that shows a foreclosure or deed in lieu of foreclosure on the credit report. This means that it must have been at least seven years since the completion of the foreclosure or deed in lieu of foreclosure.

TITLE OR DEED IN LIEU OF FORECLOSURE is an action in which the borrower, finding foreclosure unavoidable, voluntarily transfers title of their property back to the lender. This gives the lender the advantage of avoiding the expense of foreclosure and allowing the sale or disposal of the property to begin immediately.

> **NOTE**
> *Many lenders will not approve a loan that has a foreclosure on the credit report. A foreclosure will remain on the credit report for seven years.*

d. **PARTY TO A LAWSUIT** may affect any and all property owned by the borrower. In such a case, the lawsuit must be settled prior to funding a new loan. If the case has been settled and the borrower is refinancing to obtain cash to pay a settlement, the loan can be completed and the funds will be paid through escrow to the recipient of the settlement, provided there are sufficient funds to pay the debt in full.

LIS PENDENS is a notification that there is legal action pending which may affect the property and its ownership. A preliminary title report will show if a lis pendens has been filed. Depending on the type of lawsuit, property may or may not be affected. Information, documentation, and an LOE are required. It may not be possible to obtain a loan.

e. **HAVE BEEN OBLIGATED TO PAY ANY LOAN RESULTED IN TRANSFER OF TITLE IN LIEU OF FORECLOSURE, OR JUDGMENT:** This is a catch-all category includes most of the other items and repeats items already addressed.

f. **TAX LIENS** filed against the borrower can be subordinated by the IRS; however, few lenders will accept this. If the loan is a refinance, they may take cash-out to pay the income taxes in full. Verification of the tax debt will appear on the credit report and prelim.

g. **ALIMONY, CHILD SUPPORT, OR SEPARATE MAINTENANCE** will require the court documentation to verify. A complete divorce decree will be required. Any differences in the amount owed should be documented.

h. **DOWN PAYMENT BORROWED** is acceptable as long as the borrower has an acceptable percentage (generally a minimum of 5%) of their own money.

Documentation or a loan agreement will be required. The payment must be included in the debts on page 2, liabilities of the 1003, and the lender of that second TD must provide a **SUBORDINATION AGREEMENT** if the loan is to be secured by the property. This is acceptable if the borrower qualifies with the additional debt. A second TD is shown by using the acronym **CLTV (COMBINED LOAN TO VALUE)** on their rate sheet in the section for the requested loan program.

i. **CO-MAKER** or endorser on a loan for another person will require that the debt be included in the borrower's debts or verification that the borrower does not make the payments. Six to twelve months of canceled checks proving payment will be required. The number of canceled checks required for verification will vary according to the lender, so it is best to request a minimum of 12 months.

j. **US CITIZEN** if the answer is "no," see item k.

k. **RESIDENT ALIEN** will require a copy of the borrower's green card/resident alien registration.

Some lenders will grant a loan to a non-resident alien without a green card, but only under certain circumstances. Generally, the lender is looking for an alien that will be living in the country for at least three years. It is best to check with the desired lender as soon as possible to know what they will require, or if they will consider the loan at all.

l. **OCCUPY PROPERTY AS PRIMARY RESIDENCE** qualifies a loan as either an owner-occupied or a rental property and may require verification of the borrower's occupancy by way of utility bills, especially if the lender does not feel the documentation makes sense or does not believe the borrower will, or does, occupy the property.

Lenders often do occupancy checks by way of knocking on the door and asking for the borrower. It is a general rule of thumb that the lender expects the borrower to occupy a property with an owner-occupied loan for at least six (6) months after the loan has closed, while some expect a year of occupancy. The interest rate and costs are higher for a non-occupied property loan.

In the case of fraud, the broker may have to buy the loan back from the lender, lose their license, be fined, or even be imprisoned. The lender will notify the borrower of such findings and give them a period of time to refinance or notify them of an increase in interest rate to the higher non-occupied rate. If this space is marked to indicate non-owner-occupied, the appraiser needs to know this when ordering the appraisal. The appraiser must include a rent survey and comparable rental properties as part of the appraisal.

NOTE

Knowingly submitting a loan as an owner-occupied that will be non- owner-occupied is fraud.

m. **OWNERSHIP INTEREST IN PROPERTY IN THE LAST THREE YEARS** tells the lender whether the borrower has a history as a homeowner. If the borrower answers yes, but there are no properties listed in the SREO, a HUD-1/CD verifying sale of that property may be required.

m1. **TYPE OF PROPERTY** asks if the borrower owns/owned a principal residence, second home, or investment property. The way this question is answered may give the lender cause to question occupancy or to require the borrower to provide a history of residency.

This may be the case, especially if the subject property is an investment property. This could indicate the borrower's experience in handling rentals and may ultimately affect the lender's attitude towards the borrower and the amount of reserves required. The lender may require a title search to verify ownership of properties. The title search can be ordered from the escrow or title officer.

m2. **HOW TITLE WAS HELD** indicates responsibilities for other properties and may indicate needed documentation required to close the loan. For instance: a refinance for a married couple with both borrowers on the application, but this is marked "S" for sole ownership, a grant deed to add a spouse will be required by escrow. The letter "O" may indicate that not all proceeds stated on a HUD-1/CD from a recent sale are available to the borrower, as the property may have had other owners that owned a portion of the equity.

IX. ACKNOWLEDGMENT AND AGREEMENT:

THE UNDERSIGNED SPECIFICALLY ACKNOWLEDGES AND AGREES spells out to the Borrower that by signing, they are authorizing the broker to obtain financing for their real property on their behalf.

This is an agreement between the borrower and broker authorizing the broker to obtain a mortgage loan on their behalf. Signing this agreement does not bind the borrower to accept any loan obtained, even if it matches the original figures. Signing and dating this section effectively "agrees and acknowledges" that the information provided by the borrower/applicant is true and correct. Signing also authorizes the broker to obtain any information necessary to this loan only and to order a credit report. If a separate credit authorization is not provided, this section may be copied and used in lieu of that form.

As of January 1, 2010, this section provides additional disclosure per **MORTGAGE DISCLOSURE INFORMATION ACT (MDIA)** requirements. This is information previously provided on separate forms. The possibility of the loan servicing being transferred to another lender is stated, along with the borrower's right to obtain a copy of the appraisal.

If the borrower wishes to request a copy of the appraisal, they should do that within 90 days. The address to which the borrower is to send their request, along with the address of the Broker/MLO, is clearly spelled out for the borrower's information.

NOTE

Without the signatures of all borrowers, there is no loan. If they are not on the loan, they will not be on title.

X. INFORMATION FOR GOVERNMENT MONITORING PURPOSES:

THE FEDERAL GOVERNMENT REQUESTS THE FOLLOWING INFORMATION...

BORROWER: This information is used by the government to audit the activities of lending institutions in order to prevent prejudicial or unfair lending activities, such as redlining. This is a requirement of **RESPA** and the **Home Mortgage Disclosure Act (HMDA)**.

It is up to the borrower whether they provide the information; however, if the loan application has been taken face-to-face, as indicated in the next section, the broker is required to answer to the best of their ability on the 1003 the following, even if the borrower has elected not to provide the information:

- **Ethnicity:** Every borrower is to indicate whether they are Hispanic/Latino or not.
- **Race:** All borrowers are asked to answer this, in addition to the response to the previous question.
- **Sex:** Respond accordingly.

TO BE COMPLETED BY INTERVIEWER must have all the spaces filled in. If the application was taken face-to-face, the loan agent must provide the above information to the best of their ability if not completed by the borrower.

If an application is taken any way other than face-to-face, the interviewer is not required to provide the information in the previous section. If the Application was not taken face-to-face, the MLO would not necessarily know the correct response to the questions.

The broker should complete any blank spaces. Any time the loan agent/MLO is not available to sign this or any other form, the broker can sign for them as long as they also write by the signature "by (their initials)." The broker should discuss this with all loan agents/MLOs and get a verbal approval, so it is understood and agreed to, prior to actually signing for someone else. There could be legal ramifications associated with signing for someone else, and the practice should be avoided as much as possible.

Uniform Residential Loan Application

This application is designed to be completed by the applicant(s) with the Lender's assistance. Applicants should complete this form as "Borrower" or "Co-Borrower", as applicable. Co-Borrower information must also be provided (and the appropriate box checked) when ☐ the income or assets of a person other than the "Borrower" (including the Borrower's spouse) will be used as a basis for loan qualification or ☐ the income or assets of the Borrower's spouse or other person who has community property rights pursuant to state law will not be used as a basis for loan qualification, but his or her liabilities must be considered because the spouse or other person has community property rights pursuant to applicable law and Borrower resides in a community property state, the security property is located in a community property state, or the Borrower is relying on other property located in a community property state as a basis for repayment of the loan.

If this is an application for joint credit, Borrower and Co-Borrower each agree that we intend to apply for joint credit (sign below):

Borrower _____   Co-Borrower _____

I. TYPE OF MORTGAGE AND TERMS OF LOAN

Mortgage Applied for:	☐ VA ☑ Conventional ☐ Other (explain):		Agency Case Number	Lender Case Number
	☐ FHA ☐ USDA/Rural Housing Service			

Amount $	Interest Rate %	No. of Months	Amortization Type:	☑ Fixed Rate ☐ GPM	☐ Other (explain): ☐ ARM (type):

II. PROPERTY INFORMATION AND PURPOSE OF LOAN

Subject Property Address (street, city, state, & ZIP)	No. of Units

Legal Description of Subject Property (attach description if necessary)	Year Built

Purpose of Loan ☑ Purchase ☐ Construction ☐ Other (explain): ☐ Refinance ☐ Construction-Permanent

Property will be: ☑ Primary Residence ☐ Secondary Residence ☐ Investment

Complete this line if construction or construction-permanent loan.

Year Lot Acquired	Original Cost $	Amount Existing Liens $	(a) Present Value of Lot $	(b) Cost of Improvements $	Total (a+b) $

Complete this line if this is a refinance loan.

Year Acquired	Original Cost $	Amount Existing Liens $	Purpose of Refinance	Describe Improvements Cost: $	☐ made ☐ to be made

Title will be held in what Name(s)	Manner in which Title will be held	Estate will be held in: ☑ Fee Simple ☐ Leasehold (show expiration date)

Source of Down Payment, Settlement Charges and/or Subordinate Financing (explain)

III. BORROWER INFORMATION

Borrower	Co-Borrower
Borrower's Name (include Jr. or Sr. if applicable)	Co-Borrower's Name (include Jr. or Sr. if applicable)
Social Security Number / Home Phone (incl. area code) / DOB (mm/dd/yyyy) / Yrs. School	Social Security Number / Home Phone (incl. area code) / DOB (mm/dd/yyyy) / Yrs. School
☐ Married (includes registered domestic partners) ☐ Unmarried (includes single, divorced, widowed) ☐ Separated — Dependents (not listed by Co-Borrower) No. ___ Ages ___	☐ Married (includes registered domestic partners) ☐ Unmarried (includes single, divorced, widowed) ☐ Separated — Dependents (not listed by Borrower) No. ___ Ages ___
Present Address (street, city, state, ZIP/country) ☐ Own ☐ Rent ___ No. Yrs. / United States	Present Address (street, city, state, ZIP/country) ☐ Own ☐ Rent ___ No. Yrs. / United States
Mailing Address, if different from Present Address	Mailing Address, if different from Present Address

If residing at present address for less than two years, complete the following:

Former Address (street, city, state, ZIP) ☐ Own ☐ Rent ___ No. Yrs.	Former Address (street, city, state, ZIP) ☐ Own ☐ Rent ___ No. Yrs.
Former Address (street, city, state, ZIP) ☐ Own ☐ Rent ___ No. Yrs.	Former Address (street, city, state, ZIP) ☐ Own ☐ Rent ___ No. Yrs.

Freddie Mac Form 65 6/09
Calyx Form - Loanapp1.frm (11/09)

Borrower _____   Co-Borrower _____

Fannie Mae Form 1003 6/09

Figure 24: Uniform Residential Loan Application (URLA)/1003
Page 1 of 5

| Borrower | IV. EMPLOYMENT INFORMATION | Co-Borrower |

Name & Address of Employer	☐ Self Employed	Yrs. on this job	Name & Address of Employer	☐ Self Employed	Yrs. on this job
		Yrs. employed in this line of work/profession			Yrs. employed in this line of work/profession
Position/Title/Type of Business		Business Phone (incl. area code)	Position/Title/Type of Business		Business Phone (incl. area code)

If employed in current position for less than two years or if currently employed in more than one position, complete the following:

Name & Address of Employer	☐ Self Employed	Dates (from-to)	Name & Address of Employer	☐ Self Employed	Dates (from-to)
		Monthly Income $			Monthly Income $
Position/Title/Type of Business		Business Phone (incl. area code)	Position/Title/Type of Business		Business Phone (incl. area code)

Name & Address of Employer	☐ Self Employed	Dates (from-to)	Name & Address of Employer	☐ Self Employed	Dates (from-to)
		Monthly Income $			Monthly Income $
Position/Title/Type of Business		Business Phone (incl. area code)	Position/Title/Type of Business		Business Phone (incl. area code)

Name & Address of Employer	☐ Self Employed	Dates (from-to)	Name & Address of Employer	☐ Self Employed	Dates (from-to)
		Monthly Income $			Monthly Income $
Position/Title/Type of Business		Business Phone (incl. area code)	Position/Title/Type of Business		Business Phone (incl. area code)

Name & Address of Employer	☐ Self Employed	Dates (from-to)	Name & Address of Employer	☐ Self Employed	Dates (from-to)
		Monthly Income $			Monthly Income $
Position/Title/Type of Business		Business Phone (incl. area code)	Position/Title/Type of Business		Business Phone (incl. area code)

V. MONTHLY INCOME AND COMBINED HOUSING EXPENSE INFORMATION

Gross Monthly Income	Borrower	Co-Borrower	Total	Combined Monthly Housing Expense	Present	Proposed
Base Empl. Income*	$	$	$	Rent	$	
Overtime				First Mortgage (P&I)		$
Bonuses				Other Financing (P&I)		
Commissions				Hazard Insurance		
Dividends/Interest				Real Estate Taxes		
Net Rental Income				Mortgage Insurance		
Other (before completing, see the notice in "describe other income." below)				Homeowner Assn. Dues		
				Other		
Total	$	$	$	Total	$	$

* Self Employed Borrower(s) may be required to provide additional documentation such as tax returns and financial statements.

Describe Other Income   Notice: Alimony, child support, or separate maintenance income need not be revealed if the Borrower (B) or Co-Borrower (C) does not choose to have it considered for repaying this loan.

B/C		Monthly Amount
		$

Freddie Mac Form 65 6/09
Calyx Form - Loanapp2.frm (11/09)

Borrower _____
Co-Borrower _____

Fannie Mae Form 1003 6/09

Figure 24: Loan Application/1003 Page 2 of 5

VI. ASSETS AND LIABILITIES

This Statement and any applicable supporting schedules may be completed jointly by both married and unmarried Co-borrowers if their assets and liabilities are sufficiently joined so that the Statement can be meaningfully and fairly presented on a combined basis; otherwise, separate Statements and Schedules are required. If the Co-Borrower section was completed about a non-applicant spouse or other person, this Statement and supporting schedules must be completed by that spouse or other person also.

Completed [✓] Jointly [ ] Not Jointly

ASSETS Description	Cash or Market Value	Liabilities and Pledged Assets. List the creditor's name, address and account number for all outstanding debts, including automobile loans, revolving charge accounts, real estate loans, alimony, child support, stock pledges, etc. Use continuation sheet, if necessary. Indicate by (*) those liabilities which will be satisfied upon sale of real estate owned or upon refinancing of the subject property.	Monthly Payment & Months Left to Pay	Unpaid Balance
Cash deposit toward purchase held by:	$			
		LIABILITIES		
List checking and savings accounts below		Name and address of Company	$ Payment/Months	$
Name and address of Bank, S&L, or Credit Union				
		Acct. no.		
		Name and address of Company	$ Payment/Months	$
Acct. no.	$			
Name and address of Bank, S&L, or Credit Union				
		Acct. no.		
		Name and address of Company	$ Payment/Months	$
Acct. no.	$			
Name and address of Bank, S&L, or Credit Union				
		Acct. no.		
		Name and address of Company	$ Payment/Months	$
Acct. no.	$			
Stocks & Bonds (Company name/number description)	$			
		Acct. no.		
		Name and address of Company	$ Payment/Months	$
Life insurance net cash value	$			
Face amount: $				
Subtotal Liquid Assets	$	Acct. no.		
Real estate owned (enter market value from schedule of real estate owned)	$	Name and address of Company	$ Payment/Months	$
Vested interest in retirement fund	$			
Net worth of business(es) owned (attach financial statement)	$	Acct. no.		
Automobiles owned (make and year)	$	Alimony/Child Support/Separate Maintenance Payments Owed to:	$	
Other Assets (itemize)	$	Job-Related Expense (child care, union dues, etc.)	$	
		Total Monthly Payments	$	
Total Assets a.	$	Net Worth (a minus b) => $	Total Liabilities b.	$

Schedule of Real Estate Owned (if additional properties are owned, use continuation sheet)

Property Address (enter S if sold, PS if pending sale or R if rental being held for income)	Type of Property	Present Market Value	Amount of Mortgages & Liens	Gross Rental Income	Mortgage Payments	Insurance, Maintenance, Taxes & Misc.	Net Rental Income
		$	$	$	$	$	$
Totals		$	$	$	$	$	$

List any additional names under which credit has previously been received and indicate appropriate creditor name(s) and account number(s):

Alternate Name	Creditor Name	Account Number

Freddie Mac Form 65   6/09
Calyx Form - Loanapp3.frm (11/09)

Borrower _____
Co-Borrower _____

Fannie Mae Form 1003   6/09

Page 3 of 5

Figure 24: Loan Application/1003 Page 3 of 5

VII. DETAILS OF TRANSACTION		VIII. DECLARATIONS				
		If you answer "Yes" to any questions a through i, please use continuation sheet for explanation.	Borrower		Co-Borrower	
			Yes	No	Yes	No
a. Purchase price	$	a. Are there any outstanding judgments against you?	☐	☐	☐	☐
b. Alterations, improvements, repairs		b. Have you been declared bankrupt within the past 7 years?	☐	☐	☐	☐
c. Land (if acquired separately)		c. Have you had property foreclosed upon or given title or deed in lieu thereof in the last 7 years?	☐	☐	☐	☐
d. Refinance (incl. debts to be paid off)		d. Are you a party to a lawsuit?	☐	☐	☐	☐
e. Estimated prepaid items		e. Have you directly or indirectly been obligated on any loan which resulted in foreclosure, transfer of title in lieu of foreclosure, or judgment?	☐	☐	☐	☐
f. Estimated closing costs		(This would include such loans as home mortgage loans, SBA loans, home improvement loans, educational loans, manufactured (mobile) home loans, any mortgage, financial obligation, bond, or loan guarantee. If "Yes," provide details, including date, name, and address of Lender, FHA or VA case number, if any, and reasons for the action.)				
g. PMI, MIP, Funding Fee						
h. Discount (if Borrower will pay)						
i. Total costs (add items a through h)		f. Are you presently delinquent or in default on any Federal debt or any other loan, mortgage, financial obligation, bond, or loan guarantee? If "Yes," give details as described in the preceding question.	☐	☐	☐	☐
j. Subordinate financing						
k. Borrower's closing costs paid by Seller		g. Are you obligated to pay alimony, child support, or separate maintenance?	☐	☐	☐	☐
l. Other Credits (explain)		h. Is any part of the down payment borrowed?	☐	☐	☐	☐
		i. Are you a co-maker or endorser on a note?	☐	☐	☐	☐
		j. Are you a U. S. citizen?	☐	☐	☐	☐
		k. Are you a permanent resident alien?	☐	☐	☐	☐
		l. Do you intend to occupy the property as your primary residence? If "Yes," complete question m below.	☐	☐	☐	☐
m. Loan amount (exclude PMI, MIP, Funding Fee financed)		m. Have you had an ownership interest in a property in the last three years?	☐	☐	☐	☐
n. PMI, MIP, Funding Fee financed		(1) What type of property did you own-principal residence (PR), second home (SH), or investment property (IP)?				
o. Loan amount (add m & n)						
p. Cash from/to Borrower (subtract j, k, l & o from i)		(2) How did you hold title to the home-solely by yourself (S), jointly with your spouse (SP), or jointly with another person (O)?				

IX. ACKNOWLEDGEMENT AND AGREEMENT

Each of the undersigned specifically represents to Lender and to Lender's actual or potential agents, brokers, processors, attorneys, insurers, servicers, successors and assigns and agrees and acknowledges that: (1) the information provided in this application is true and correct as of the date set forth opposite my signature and that any intentional or negligent misrepresentation of this information contained in this application may result in civil liability, including monetary damages, to any person who may suffer any loss due to reliance upon any misrepresentation that I have made on this application, and/or in criminal penalties including, but not limited to, fine or imprisonment or both under the provisions of Title 18, United States Code, Sec. 1001, et seq.; (2) the loan requested pursuant to this application (the "Loan") will be secured by a mortgage or deed of trust on the property described in this application; (3) the property will not be used for any illegal or prohibited purpose or use; (4) all statements made in this application are made for the purpose of obtaining a residential mortgage loan; (5) the property will be occupied as indicated in this application; (6) the Lender, its servicers, successors or assigns may retain the original and/or an electronic record of this application, whether or not the loan is approved; (7) the Lender and its agents, brokers, insurers, servicers, successors and assigns may continuously rely on the information contained in the application, and I am obligated to amend and/or supplement the information provided in this application if any of the material facts that I have represented herein should change prior to closing of the Loan; (8) in the event that my payments on the Loan become delinquent, the Lender, its servicers, successors, or assigns may, in addition to any other rights and remedies that it may have relating to such delinquency, report my name and account information to one or more consumer credit reporting agencies; (9) ownership of the Loan and/or administration of the Loan account may be transferred with such notice as may be required by law; (10) neither Lender nor its agents, brokers, insurers, servicers, successors or assigns has made any representation or warranty, express or implied, to me regarding the property or the condition or value of the property; and (11) my transmission of this application as an "electronic record" containing my "electronic signature," as those terms are defined in applicable federal and/or state laws (excluding audio and video recordings), or my facsimile transmission of this application containing a facsimile of my signature, shall be as effective, enforceable and valid as if a paper version of this application were delivered containing my original written signature.

Acknowledgement. Each of the undersigned hereby acknowledges that any owner of the Loan, its servicers, successors and assigns, may verify or reverify any information contained in this application or obtain any information or data relating to the Loan, for any legitimate purpose through any source, including a source named in this application or a consumer reporting agency.

Right to Receive Copy of Appraisal. I/We have the right to a copy of the appraisal report used in connection with this application for credit. To obtain a copy, I/we must send Creditor a written request at the mailing address Creditor has provided. Creditor must hear from us no later than _____ days after Creditor notifies me/us about the action taken on this application, or I/we withdraw this application.
If you would like a copy of the appraisal report, contact:

Borrower's Signature	Date	Co-Borrower's Signature	Date
X		X	

X. INFORMATION FOR GOVERNMENT MONITORING PURPOSES

The following information is requested by the Federal Government for certain types of loans related to a dwelling in order to monitor the lender's compliance with equal credit opportunity, fair housing and home mortgage disclosure laws. You are not required to furnish this information, but are encouraged to do so. The law provides that a Lender may not discriminate either on the basis of this information, or on whether you choose to furnish it. If you furnish the information, please provide both ethnicity and race. For race, you may check more than one designation. If you do not furnish ethnicity, race, or sex, under Federal regulations, this lender is required to note the information on the basis of visual observation and surname if you have made this application in person. If you do not wish to furnish the information, please check the box below. (Lender must review the above material to assure that the disclosures satisfy all requirements to which the lender is subject under applicable state law for the particular type of loan applied for.)

BORROWER	☐ I do not wish to furnish this information		CO-BORROWER	☐ I do not wish to furnish this information	
Ethnicity:	☐ Hispanic or Latino	☐ Not Hispanic or Latino	Ethnicity:	☐ Hispanic or Latino	☐ Not Hispanic or Latino
Race:	☐ American Indian or Alaska Native ☐ Asian ☐ Black or African American ☐ Native Hawaiian or Other Pacific Islander ☐ White		Race:	☐ American Indian or Alaska Native ☐ Asian ☐ Black or African American ☐ Native Hawaiian or Other Pacific Islander ☐ White	
Sex:	☐ Female	☐ Male	Sex:	☐ Female	☐ Male

To be Completed by Loan Originator:
This information was provided:
☐ In a face-to-face interview   ☐ By the applicant and submitted by fax or mail
☐ In a telephone interview   ☐ By the applicant and submitted via e-mail or the internet

Loan Originator's Signature X		Date
Loan Originator's Name (print or type)	Loan Originator Identifier	Loan Originator's Phone Number (including area code)
Loan Origination Company's Name	Loan Origination Company Identifier	Loan Origination Company's Address

Figure 24: Loan Application/1003 Page 4 of 5

Continuation Sheet/Residential Loan Application

Use this continuation sheet if you need more space to complete the Residential Loan Application. Mark **B** for Borrower or **C** for Co-Borrower.	Borrower:	Agency Case Number:
	Co-Borrower:	Lender Case Number:

This Page Intentionally Left Blank

I/We fully understand that it is a Federal crime punishable by fine or imprisonment, or both, to knowingly make any false statements concerning any of the above facts as applicable under the provisions of Title 18, United States Code, Section 1001, et seq.

Borrower's Signature	Date	Co-Borrower's Signature	Date
X		X	

Freddie Mac Form 65   6/09
Calyx Form - Lnap5cnt.frm (11/09)

Fannie Mae Form 1003   6/09

Figure 24: Loan Application/1003 Page 5 of 5

CONTINUATION SHEET/RESIDENTIAL LOAN APPLICATION, PAGE 5 is used for any additional information that does not fit in the previous spaces of the 1003. For example, Section VI, Page 3, allows spaces for three bank accounts. Any additional accounts will automatically appear on the continuation sheet, Page 5. Additional credit accounts, addresses, employers, etc., will appear on this page. If there is no additional information appearing on this page, the MLO should either draw a diagonal line across the page or write "This page intentionally left blank" and have the borrower sign at the bottom of the page.

The 1003 and the input into the computer is now complete and the information will be updated as verifications are received. The next step is to complete the MLDS and the GFE/LE and all required disclosures. The disclosures must be mailed to the borrower within three days or 72 hours of the date the borrower signed the 1003, if not completed at the time of taking the original 1003.

XI. BORROWER INFORMATION

Contains the borrower's name, Social Security number, and property address.

PROPERTY TYPE:

1 UNIT is a single-family residence, or a residence built to accommodate one family.

2- to 4- UNITS are residential properties that are built to accommodate from two to four separate families. Most lenders charge more for the additional units.

CONDOMINIUM (Condo) is a project wherein each property owner owns their unit separately from the other property owners and all owners own the common property jointly. The common property would be the driveways, sidewalks, pool, and any green areas.

> **NOTE**
>
> *Borrowers should never sign a blank document.*

> **NOTE**
>
> *If possible, it is always advisable to provide disclosures at the time the original 1003 is taken. The exception is the GFE/LE and TILA because they must be as accurate as possible. It is best to check with the title company/closer and the lender for accurate fees before disclosing to the borrower.*

Condominium owners pay dues to a homeowners' association (HOA) for the maintenance of common ground. The legal distinction in the structure of a condominium is that it is apartment-like. Townhouses are considered to be a row-house style, in which homes have adjoining walls and are generally more than one story. They are usually legally viewed as condominiums, but owners often prefer to call them "townhomes."

PUDs or PLANNED UNIT DEVELOPMENTS are basically the same as a condominium because the homeowners own their individual unit and share the common grounds. This is a legal form of ownership that is established at the outset by the developer. These often appear to be SFRs or they may have adjoining walls. The common grounds are usually less extensive than those at a condominium, and may have public streets, where the streets in a condominium are private. The common areas in PUDs are usually grassy areas and may include a swimming pool or tennis courts. Many PUDs are gated communities, and the association dues pay for the maintenance and management of the gate and streets, and the salaries of any guards at the gates.

A CO-OP is similar to a condominium, especially in appearance, with the primary difference being that the owners of a co-op own shares in a corporation, with all owners having an equal share of the entire project. Each owner essentially leases or maintains the use of their individual unit from the corporation. When processing a co-op, the borrower's stock shares and the corporation papers are obtained in lieu of CC&Rs. Co-ops are not common in all areas of the country and many lenders will not accept loan applications for co-ops.

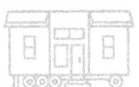

MANUFACTURED HOUSING is also known as mobile homes or prefabricated homes.
> **Single Wide** Most lenders will not lend on a single wide.
> **Multi-wide Homes** built since July 1, 1976, are built under HUD guidelines and are easier to get a loan against.

PROJECT CLASSIFICATION indicates which phase of construction the project is in. These classifications were established by FNMA and FHLMC. The classifications are usually used in regard to condo or PUD projects, but may occasionally refer to a **SUBDIVISION,** especially if low-income housing and HUD are involved.

FREDDIE MAC (FMLMC):

1. **STREAMLINED REVIEW:** must meet certain standards per FHMLC.
   - Owner occupied.
   - Completed project per appraisal.
   - Insured.
   - Established project.
   - Non-owner occupied (N/O/O) not to exceed 20% of the year.
   - Investor-owned units not to exceed 30% of the year.

2. **ESTABLISHED PROJECT:**
   - Ninety percent or more of the units have been sold and closed.
   - Project 100% complete.
   - Homeowners' association (HOA) turned over to unit owners.
   - No more than 115% of HOA dues delinquent more than 30 days.
   - If the subject unit is owner-occupied or second home, there is no maximum investor concentration.
   - No single entity can own more than 10% of the units.
   - No more than 20% of the project can be for commercial use.
   - Budget must have more than 10% replacement reserves for capital expenditures and replacement costs for common elements, and adequate funds for insurance.
   - Insurance.
   - Project complies with state and local laws and requirements.
   - Non-owner occupied (N/O/O) not to exceed 20%.
   - Max 30% investor occupancy.

3. **NEW PROJECT:** Still under construction or less than 90% sold. May be approved at various stages of construction.

4. **DETACHED PROPERTY** is a stand-alone structure, generally a single-family-residence (SFR). This may or may not have an attached garage. Garages are not considered when determining property type. An attached property has a common wall with the living area of another structure but not the garage.

5. **2-to 4-UNITS PROJECT:** Many lenders will not lend on projects with 4 units or less because they have a high risk of loss due to the lack of HOA dues in reserve, decision making by the association, and the potential for disputes that cannot be resolved.

6. **RECIPROCAL REVIEW:** Requires
   - FNMA form 1028
   - FNMA Condo Project Manager (CPM) which is a program available to lenders.
     -OR-
   - FHA approved.

FANNIE MAE:

1. **LIMITED REVIEW NEW DETACHED:**
   - Owner occupied.
   - Completed project per appraisal.
   - Insured.
   - Established project.
   - Non-owner occupied (N/O/O) not to exceed 20% of the year.
   - Investor-owned units not to exceed 51% for the year.
   - The developer has established the CC&Rs and is still in control of the HOA.
     FNMA can provide the forms to apply for approval by either the broker or the lender. This is most commonly done by the lender, but the broker/processor may choose to apply to expedite a loan and with the prospect of obtaining additional business from the developer. This process takes about two weeks once submitted to FNMA.

2. **LIMITED REVIEW ESTABLISHED:**
   - Completed project per appraisal.
   - Insured.
   - Established project.
   - Non-owner occupied (N/O/O) not to exceed 20% of the year.
   - Investor-owned units do not exceed 30% of the year.

3. **EXPEDITED REVIEW NEW:** A FNMA condo approval can be requested through Project Eligibility Review Service (PERS) by completing the application and submitting it to FNMA.

Condominiums under this classification have not been approved for lending purposes and the homeowners have obtained control of the HOA, however, the construction is not complete.

The prelim for either of these types will show a large blanket loan as the **lender-of-record**. The new lender will require this to be removed at closing and the existing lender will collect a proportionate amount of cash to pay-down the blanket loan with the balance applied to the remaining units. A **442** is a form to be obtained from the appraiser stating the unit is complete and ready for occupancy. The developer must provide a **certificate of completion** from the county/city inspector.

4. **FANNIE MAE REVIEW:** This approval is also obtained through PERS.
5. The project is **FHA-APPROVED**.
6. REFI PLUS: FNMA LOAN PROGRAM.

The **PUD** and **CO-OP** classifications follow the same rules with **E PUD** and **1 co-op** being new/under construction and **III PUD** and **2 Co-op** being completed.

1. **PROJECT NAME** is the name of the project or association such as "Shady Glen Condos."
2. **OCCUPANCY STATUS** tells the lender whether the property will be:
   - Primary residence or owner-occupied
   - **Second home** or **vacation home**: *A second home must make sense, such as being in a resort area and a reasonable distance from the borrower's primary residence or the lender may consider it an investment property and may apply add- ons accordingly.*
   - **Investment Property:** such as a rental property or spec property. *An investment property will have a higher interest rate and add-ons to the cost of the loan.*
3. ADDITIONAL PROPERTY INFORMATION:
   - **Number of Units** will be 1, 2, 3, or 4:
   - **1 unit** is a **single-family residence**.
   - **2- to 4- units** are residential properties that are built to accommodate 2, 3, or 4 separate families.
     Most lenders charge more for the additional units. All others will be commercial loans.

4. **SALES PRICE** applies to a purchase transaction and is the amount the buyer has agreed to pay to purchase the property according to the contract terms.

5. **APPRAISED VALUE** is the value of the subject property as determined by the appraiser.

6. **PROPERTY** RIGHTS:
   - **FEE SIMPLE** means that there are no limitations on the borrower's rights.
   - **LEASEHOLD** is property in which the land is owned by another party with the improvements owned by the lessee.

XII. MORTGAGE INFORMATION:

LOAN TYPE: These have been identified on page 1 of the 1003.
- **CONVENTIONAL** refers to conforming or jumbo loans, in first trust deed, on 1-to-4-unit residential property, with a conventional lender (except for the VA or FHA loans).
- **VA AND FHA** are commonly seen throughout the country although less often in the large metropolitan areas because the maximum loan amounts are restricted. FHA and VA loans were limited to the FNMA/ FHLMC conforming loan limits. FHA loan limits were increased from 75% of the FNMA loan limits to 100% of the loan limits in 2008. The VA loan limit was increased to the FNMA maximum loan amount in January 2002.
- **USDA/RHS (RURAL HOUSING)** is the U. S. Department of Agriculture. These loans are made by specific lenders who provide this type of loan. The broker working under DRE will generally do this type of loan.
- **Other** includes all other loan types such as second trust deeds and equity lines. *The broker/processor must know what type of loan is being processed in order to provide the proper input and documentation.*

AMORTIZATION TYPE means the way in which the payments are to be made such as **fixed, adjustable, balloon,** or **other**. When adjustable or balloon is marked, a space is provided to give brief details such as **libor, 2-year fixed, or due in 5 years.** Amortization may also refer to the term or number of monthly payments required to pay the loan in full.
- **Fixed-rate monthly payments:** The payment and interest rate will remain the same throughout the life of the loan with payments being made once a month.
- **Fixed-rate biweekly payments:** The payment and interest rate will remain the same throughout the life of the loan with payments being every two

weeks. *Because there are 52 weeks in a year, there will be two extra payments made each year, which will provide for an early pay-off and a savings in interest.*

- **Balloon:** This type of loan establishes payments based on an amortization period: however, the balance of the loan will come due in a shorter period of time, creating one large payment on the final due date, thus the name balloon.
- **ARM loans** will adjust at predetermined periods. ARMs will be discussed at length in Chapter 15, Types of Loans.
- **Other:** Allows for any other type of payment and amortization.

LOAN PURPOSE:

Purchase: Buying a home

- **Cash-Out Refinance:** This type of loan involves borrowing more than the loan being paid off and the closing cost. The cash-out may be used for remodeling, debt consolidation, or college expenses, among other things. If the borrower states they are taking funds out to start a new business, the lender will assume the income used to qualify will not be continuing and therefore will not use it.
- **Limited Cash-Out Refinance (Fannie Mae):** FNMA allows for cash up to usually $2,000 after the current loan is paid-off and the closing costs arc paid.
- **No Cash-Out Refinance (Freddie Mac):** FHLMC allows for cash up to a range of $250 to $1,000 after the current loan is paid off and the closing costs are paid. *It is extremely difficult to estimate the closing costs prior to the day of closing, so this program allows for a minimal amount to cover the incidental differences on the settlement fees.*
- **Home Improvement:** This category can cover a variety of loan programs, including community improvement programs.
- **Construction to Perm:** Refinances a temporary construction loan and replaces it with a permanent conventional loan.

LIEN POSITION states whether the loan is a
- **First Mortgage:** (first trust deed [TD])
- **Amount of Subordinate Financing:** If a HELOC, the balance and total credit limit must be included in the qualifying calculations. Subordinate financing is completed only when there is a second TD to be behind a first TD. If the loan being processed is a second TD, the amount of the first TD will be placed in the space "original loan amount of first mortgage".
- **Second Mortgage:** (second TD) or the legal position it holds.

A first TD is in first position on the chain of title, or it is in the priority position and the second TD is recorded in the second position. When reading the preliminary title report, items are always listed in the order of priority or the chain of title.

Property taxes and state and federal tax liens are always listed first. Likewise, trust deeds are listed first, second, then any subsequent TDs. This clarifies which lien is to be paid first, such as in the case of a foreclosure. Unrecorded liens will not appear in the county records or on a prelim.

NOTE INFORMATION provides the amount of the loan being applied for, the initial principal and interest (P&I) payment, the initial note (interest) rate, and the loan term in months.

MORTGAGE ORIGINATOR is to be marked as **third party** by a broker and would be marked as **seller** only in the case of being a direct lender. If the broker is a **correspondent lender**, it must be disclosed. The name of the broker or seller, as the case may be, is completed on the lines directly following.

BUYDOWN states whether the loan rate or program that allows the borrower to pay an extra amount upfront to reduce the payments for a preset period of time, usually 2- to 5-years. The amount prepaid is equivalent to prepaying interest. *This term will be discussed further with loan programs and actually has several different connotations.*

IF SECOND MORTGAGE, specify who owns the first TD. The broker rarely completes this section. The lender completes this when selling the loan on the secondary mortgage market. If the information is known, the processor can complete it if they choose, but it is not necessary.

ORIGINAL LOAN AMOUNT OF FIRST MORTGAGE must be completed for the lender to be able to establish the combined LTV (CLTV) for guideline purposes. If a second TD is to remain and subordinate behind a new first TD, it is important to know the LTV, which is the percentage of the value that is the loan amount. The combined LTV (CLTV) is the total loan amount of the first and second (or any additional TDs) divided by the value of the property to determine the percentage of the value that is dedicated to loans.

XIII. UNDERWRITING INFORMATION

UNDERWRITER'S NAME will be completed by the lender before selling the loan on the secondary mortgage market.

APPRAISERS NAME AND LICENSE # AND APPRAISAL COMPANY NAME will be
found at the bottom of page two of the appraisal.

STABLE MONTHLY INCOME will be transferred directly from the 1003 when working on a computer program. This space is for the income totals from page two of the 1003. If there are additional co-borrowers on separate 1003s, the combined transmittal summary will combine the incomes.

- BASE INCOME will include the income from the borrower's primary job or employment.

- OTHER INCOME includes all other sources including overtime, bonuses, second jobs, dividend and interest, and rental income.

PRESENT HOUSING PAYMENT is especially helpful when working on a non-owner-occupied loan application, as this space is designed for the housing expense of the borrower's primary residence. It is also helpful when comparing for payment shock.

PROPOSED MONTHLY PAYMENTS include the figures from the 1003, page 2, Section V, which are the basic housing expenses associated with the requested loan. Included in this section is the monthly amount for principal and interest for the first TD, principal and interest for the second TD, hazard insurance, property taxes, mortgage insurance, HOA dues, and land lease. Any other expenses that may be required as a result of owning the subject property may also be included in this section, such as required flood insurance.

OTHER OBLIGATIONS include negative cash flow for the subject property, which applies if the subject property is income-producing or rental property. This applies to investment property only and will be used if the figure from the 1003, page 3, Section VI, net income is a negative or a loss or, in other words, the costs are greater than the income.

- ALL OTHER MONTHLY PAYMENTS is the total of all consumer debts and other obligations such as child support (*1003, page 2, Section VI*).

- TOTAL ALL MONTHLY PAYMENTS is the total amount the borrower is obligated to pay monthly. The total includes housing expenses, consumer debt, and legal obligations to include alimony and child support.

BORROWER FUNDS TO CLOSE establishes the amount that is required to close escrow, including settlement costs and down payment, for purchase transaction. Verified reflects that the funds have been documented with bank statements and VOD.

- SOURCE OF FUNDS states where the funds came from, such as savings or gift.

- NUMBER OF MONTHS RESERVES is important for the lender to verify that the borrower will be able to make payments for a minimum of three months (usually) if they are unable to work.

- INTERESTED PARTY FUNDS such as gift funds are also disclosed here for ease in reviewing the overall loan package. The gift donor must be an immediate family member.

DEBT RATIO OR QUALIFYING RATIOS: The percentage of debt in relation to the income or the amount of income that is dedicated to the housing expense and the consumer debt. Lenders will qualify a borrower by calculating these expenses to establish the percentage of the income that is the borrower's monthly obligation.

PRIMARY HOUSING EXPENSE/INCOME: also known as the **front-end debt ratio** is the percentage of the borrower's income that is dedicated to the basic housing expenses. The percentage of the income that is obligated to pay the monthly debt is derived by totaling all amounts included in the *proposed monthly payment* section and dividing that amount by the total income.

This is referred to as the **front-end ratio** and FNMA guidelines suggest that this ratio should not exceed 28% (36% in common practice). The figure can exceed this guideline with compensating factors in the package, which strengthen the creditworthiness of the borrower. If excessive, the borrower may qualify for another loan program, the loan amount may be reduced, or additional income may be available for use in the calculations.

> *Example:*
>
> | | |
> |---|---|
> | $1,500 | *Monthly Mortgage Payment* |
> | 200 | *Monthly property taxes ($2,400÷12 =$200)* |
> | + 50 | *Monthly insurance ($600÷12=$50)* |
> | $1,750 | *Total Monthly Housing Expense* |
> | ÷$4,700 | *Gross Monthly Income* |
> | = 37.23% | *Front-End Debt Ratio (FNMA guideline 28%)* |

Total primary housing expense divided by the total income equals the front-end debt ratio:

TOTAL OBLIGATIONS/INCOME is the percentage of all monthly obligations, including housing plus consumer debt, and is derived by dividing the total of all monthly payments by total income.

Total primary housing expense plus the consumer debt divided by the total income equals the back-end debt ratio:

> *Example:*
>
> | | |
> |---|---|
> | $1,750 | *Total monthly housing expense* |
> | 350 | *Car payment* |
> | + 150 | *Credit card payments* |
> | $2,250 | *Total monthly expense* |
> | ÷ $4,700 | *Monthly income* |
> | = 47.87% | *back-end debt ratio (FNMA guideline 36%)* |

This is the **BACK-END DEBT RATIO**. This example is an unacceptable ratio. FNMA's guidelines suggest that this figure should not exceed 36% (45% in common practice), but some lenders will accept a greater percentage with strong compensating factors. **Debt ratios** are most commonly displayed: 28/36 or in our example: 37.23/47.87.

Debt-to housing gap ratio (Freddie) is calculated by the lender when selling the loan on the secondary mortgage market, especially when being sold to FHLMC on particular loan programs.

> **NOTE**
>
> *Debt ratio may be referred to as DR for or DTI for debt-to-income.*

LOAN-TO-VALUE RATIO (LTV) shows the percentage of the value of the property that is the loan amount.

> *Example 1: A lender will loan a particular borrower 90% of the value of the property or a 90% LTV.*

> $350,000 *Purchase price*
> _X 90%_ *Maximum LTV*
> = $315,000 *Loan amount*

> *Example 2: A borrower is refinancing their home, and they are looking for a loan of $360,000. The lender has approved them for an LTV of 85%.*

> $360,000 *Loan amount needed*
> ÷ 85%   *Maximum LTV*
> =$423,530 *Appraised value that will be necessary in order to obtain the loan desired*

LTV is used in reference to the first TD or mortgage.

CLTV/combined loan-to-value or the **TLTV/total loan-to-value** is the combination of the first and second TDs plus any additional TDs or mortgages there may be against the property.

HCLTV is the HELOC combined loan-to-value or the percentage of the value that is a *home equity line of credit (HELOC).*

The LTV, CLTV, HCLTV and TLTV are each derived by dividing the loan amount(s) by the appraised value.

> *Example:*

> *$450,000 (Loan amount) ÷ $550,000 (appraised value)*
> *= .818 or 82%*

Lenders use these figures to establish and set guidelines that will affect the allowable loan amount, interest rates and fees, and the documentation that will be required. For example, the lender's guidelines may say that they will do a cash-out loan up to 80% <=80%) or a stated-income loan cannot exceed 70%. A lender may have an add-on for a rate & term loan amount that is greater than 80% (>80%). These guidelines/restrictions are generally shown on the lenders' rate sheets.

At this point in preparing the loan, the 1008 is used to view the overall package to
- Establish whether the loan can be done.
- If more income is needed.
- Which lenders will accept the ratios and LTV.
- It will help to establish any needed or missing documentation. If any of the figures exceed most lenders guidelines, it should be discussed with the borrower to point out the issues and work with them to determine the strategy that should be taken to complete the loan. This may also determine that the loan cannot be done at this time.

In the case of extenuating circumstances or compensating factors, there is a space labeled **UNDERWRITER COMMENTS**. The broker/processor can use this space to comment on strong points in the file such as good credit scores.

QUALIFYING RATE is the interest rate a borrower must be able to afford to make payments on based on their income. It is a rate that may be different from the **note rate** or the **start rate**. The qualifying rate is most important when obtaining an adjustable-rate loan and is used to determine whether the borrower will be able to qualify for the loan if the rate increases or changes.

NOTE RATE is the actual or nominal rate that the borrower will be paying on the loan. This is the interest rate that is stated on the loan note.

% ABOVE NOTE RATE is used for qualifying based on what the note rate may adjust to by the end of the first year or one full adjustment period. This amount is generally 2%.

> **NOTE**
>
> *The lender will base the usable LTV on the lesser of the sales price or the appraised value.*

The lender wants to be certain, especially in a period of increasing interest rates, that the borrower will in fact be able to meet any increasing payments.

% BELOW NOTE RATE is similarly used for loan programs that will begin with a rate less than the note rate such as a graduated payment mortgage (GPM) or a buy down. Various lenders will have different requirements subject to change based on the economy. *When this space is completed on the 1008, the calculations will carry throughout the computer software program.*

LEVEL OF PROPERTY REVIEW will indicate the type of appraisal performed, if any.

EXTERIOR/INTERIOR is the standard appraisal performed for conventional lending purposes. The appraiser will inspect and provide the property's value on the condition and amenities of both the inside and the outside of the subject property.

EXTERIOR ONLY Appraisals are rarely used in the conventional lending market. During certain economic conditions, lenders may allow this type of appraisal, but it is rare.

NO APPRAISAL is a very rare occurrence because lenders are using the property as security, and they need to know the value to make a proper credit decision as well as the possibility of foreclosure.

FORM NUMBER: refers to the appraisal forms, which are numbered the same as lending forms.
- **1004-** Standard exterior/interior appraisal is the 1004.
- **1004D-** Updated.
- **1007-** Rental survey.
- **216-** Income.
- **1007 + 216-** Rent survey + income.
- **2055-** Exterior only.
- **2070-** Exterior only with no comps.
- **2055-** FHA exterior only with no comps.

RISK ASSESSMENT: describes the type of underwriting performed on the loan application.

MANUAL UNDERWRITING is done by an underwriter as opposed to an automated underwriting system. The underwriter personally reviews the file to determine the creditworthiness of the borrower and the solidity of the property for security purposes.

AUS is an Automated Underwriting System and means that the loan file is input into a computer program to determine that the loan file meets all of the required guidelines. These programs are helpful and save time, but a person will still be needed to verify that the documentation confirms the information provided.

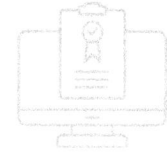

AUS or Automated Underwriting Systems are computerized systems of underwriting that are available in a variety of ways and places. Many lenders now offer an AUS on their websites. Most can be populated from the software program used by brokers for processing loan applications, or the information can be put directly into the AUS. By using an AUS, it can quickly be determined whether the loan fits the lender's guidelines, which program will work, and the rates and costs. If a loan application does not work, the loan agent or processor can adjust the loan until it does fit, such as LTV or required assets. Approval and conditions are obtained immediately but may be subject to underwriting review on receipt of the file by the lender, and additional conditions may be required. This can all be done while the client waits. *Immediate loan approval is a powerful tool for loan agents.*

DU (DESKTOP UNDERWRITING) is an AUS developed by FNMA for the purpose of providing approval on a loan acceptable for purchase by FNMA. Generally, lenders will accept a DU approval without change or addition on verification of the application because it is saleable to FNMA on the terms stated.

LP (LOAN PROSPECTOR) is the AUS designed and used by FHLMC. The same applies to an LP approval as for DU. Both the LP and DU approvals are usually easier than a manually underwritten approval.

AUS RECOMMENDATION is accepted by the lender as the underwriting decision with the verification of the assets. If the recommendation is "declined," the broker will not submit the file as is under the loan program originally requested.

DU CASE ID/LP AUS Key# are used by the lenders before sale on the secondary mortgage market.

LP DOC CLASS (FREDDIE MAC) is used by the lenders before sale on the secondary mortgage market.

FHA uses TOTAL SCORECARD GUIDE.

REPRESENTATIVE CREDIT/INDICATOR SCORE is the middle credit score from a Tri-Merge Credit report. The credit score is the primary indicator of a borrower's creditworthiness because it shows a clear picture of the way the borrower pays their debts.

UNDERWRITER'S COMMENTS can be used to make notes of loan highlights or issues for the underwriter's consideration.

ESCROW (T&I): YES OR NO is asking if there is an Impound or Escrow Account to be established for Taxes or Insurance.

COMMUNITY LENDING/AFFORDABLE HOUSING INITIATIVE AND HOME BUYERS HOMEOWNERSHIP EDUCATION CERTIFICATE IN FILE: refer to programs designed under FNMA and HUD to provide affordable housing for lower income families. FHA and FNMA programs both require that the borrower take a class on home ownership prior to the close of escrow (COE). Once the class has been completed successfully, a certificate of completion is provided and must be forwarded to the lender.

XIV. SELLER, CONTACT, AND CONTACT INFORMATION

is the last section of this form to be completed by the broker/processor.

- **Seller Name and Seller Address** is the broker's name and address.
- **Contact name, contact title, and contact's phone number** is to contain the processor's name and phone number where they can be reached by the lender. The processor will sign and date the corrected/complete 1008 at time of submission.

Uniform Underwriting and Transmittal Summary

I. Borrower and Property Information

Borrower Name_____

Total # of Borrowers_____

Property Address_____

Occupancy Status
❑ Primary Residence
❑ Second Home
❑ Investment Property

Sales Price$_____

Appraised Value $_____

Property Type
❑ 1 unit
❑ 2 units
❑ 3 units
❑ 4 units
❑ Condominium
❑ PUD   ❑ Co-op
❑ Manufactured Housing
❑ Single Wide   ❑ Multiwide

Project Classification
Freddie Mac
❑ Streamlined Review
❑ Established Project
❑ New Project
❑ Detached Project
❑ 2- to 4-unit Project
❑ Exempt from Review
❑ Reciprocal Review

Fannie Mae
❑ E Established PUD Project
❑ F New PUD Project
❑ P Limited Review - New Condo Project
❑ Q Limited Review - Established Condo Project
❑ R Full Review - New Condo Project
❑ S Full Review - Established Condo Project
❑ T Fannie Mae Review through PERS - Condo Project
❑ U FHA-approved Condo Project
❑ V Condo Project Review Waived
❑ 1 Full Review - Co-op Project
❑ 2 Fannie Mae Review through PERS - Co-op Project

Property Rights
❑ Fee Simple
❑ Leasehold

Project Name_____

Fannie Mae Condo Project Manager™ Project ID# (if any) _____

II. Mortgage Information

Loan Type
❑ Conventional
❑ FHA
❑ VA
❑ USDA/RD

Amortization Type
❑ Fixed-Rate—Monthly Payments
❑ Fixed-Rate—Biweekly Payments
❑ Balloon
❑ ARM (type)
❑ Other (specify)

Loan Purpose
❑ Purchase
❑ Cash-Out Refinance
❑ Limited Cash-Out Refinance (Fannie)
❑ No Cash-Out Refinance (Freddie)
❑ Home Improvement
❑ Construction Conversion/Construction to Permanent

Lien Position
❑ First Mortgage
Amount of Subordinate Financing
$ _____
(If HELOC, include balance and credit limit)
❑ Second Mortgage

Note Information
Loan Amount $_____
Note Rate _____ %
Loan Term (in months) _____

Mortgage Originator
❑ Seller
❑ Broker
❑ Correspondent
Broker/Correspondent Name and Company Name:
_____

Temporary Buydown
❑ Yes
❑ No
Terms _____

III. Underwriting Information

Underwriter's Name

Appraiser's Name/License #

Appraisal Company Name

Stable Monthly Income

Borrower 1	$_____
Borrower 2	$_____
Borrower 3	$_____
Borrower 4	$_____
Other Borrowers (5+)	$_____
Rental Income - subject property	$_____
Net Rental Income - other properties	$_____
Total Borrower Income	$_____

❑ At least one borrower is self-employed

Loan-to-Value Ratios
LTV_____%
CLTV/TLTV_____%
HCLTV/HTLTV_____%

Proposed Monthly Payment for the Property

First Mortgage P&I	$_____
Subordinate Lien (s) P&I	$_____
Homeowner's Insurance	$_____
Supplemental Property Insurance	$_____
Property Taxes	$_____
Mortgage Insurance	$_____
Association/Project Dues (Condo, Co-Op, PUD)	$_____
Other	$_____
Total	$_____

Qualifying Ratios
Primary Housing Expense/Income _____%
Total Obligations/Income(DTI) _____%

Level of Property Review
❑ Exterior/Interior
❑ Exterior Only
❑ No Appraisal
Form Number_____

All Other Monthly Payments Used in Qualifying $_____

Qualifying Rate
❑ Rate Used for Qualifying _____%
❑ Initial Bought-Down Rate _____%
❑ Other _____%

Escrow (T&I)   ❑ Yes ❑ No

Borrower Funds to Close
Required $_____
Verified Assets $_____

No. of Months Reserves_____

Interested Party Contributions_____%

Risk Assessment
❑ Manual Underwriting
❑ AUS
   ❑ DU ❑ LPA ❑ Other
AUS Recommendation _____
DU Case ID/LP AUS Key# _____
LPA Doc Class (Freddie) _____
Representative Credit/Indicator Score _____

Affordable Housing Initiative
❑ Yes ❑ No

Homeownership Education Certificate in File
❑ Yes ❑ No

Underwriter Comments
_____
_____
_____
_____

IV. Seller and Contact Information

Seller Name_____

Seller Address_____

Seller No._____

Seller Loan No._____

Contact Name_____

Contact Title_____

Investor Loan No._____

Contact Phone Number_____
_____

Freddie Mac Form 1077   12/18   Page 1 of 1   Fannie Mae Form 1008   12/18

Figure 25: Transmittal Summary/1008

When the loan file is first input into the computer, a copy should be printed and placed on the top of the file as a working copy along with a working copy of the 1003. As information is obtained, inputting that information into the computer system is a convenient way of providing accurate information and will help prevent omissions and errors.

TRANSMITTAL SUMMARY/1008 TRANSMITTAL SUMMARY

Most commonly referred to as the **1008,** this form was originally designed for use when selling loans on the secondary mortgage market. It provides a one-page summary of the loan file including information about the property, borrower, and loan. This information will include the LTV, debt ratios, value, income, and expenses. This form is helpful to the MLO, processor, and underwriter when determining the borrower's creditworthiness. *See Figure 25, Transmittal Summary/1008*

CHAPTER 8
CREDIT

REVIEWING THE CREDIT REPORT

REVIEWING THE CREDIT REPORT to analyze the creditworthiness of a borrower is the main tool used by a lender when a consumer requests a loan. "Packaging" a loan application is preparing it to be as thorough and compelling as possible to a given lender. The credit report is one of the most important documents in the file. It gives the clearest picture of how the borrower views their debts and obligations. *See Figure 26, Credit report.*

The loan application requires a mortgage, therefore past mortgage history is of particular importance to the lender. A borrower should always put their home first in priority of payments because that is where they live. Car payments should be in the second priority position because that is how they get to their job to earn the money to pay for their lifestyle. Credit cards are last, and if payments are to be deferred because of lack of funds, the creditor may want to consider the credit cards to be paid last.

On receipt of the credit report, the information is input into *Section VI of the 1003* as it appears, unless otherwise verified in a statement from the creditor. The ability to run a credit report online provides the capability to order the credit report directly from the software program or from the credit reporting company's website. Balances and payments on the credit report are assumed to be accurate.

Review the **GENERAL, APPLICANT, and SPOUSE'S INFORMATION** at the top of *Page 1 of the 1003* to ensure that the information is accurate prior to ordering the credit report. The information does not need to match exactly, but misinformation may affect the borrower's credit for many years. A Residential Mortgage Credit report (RMCR) was generally used prior to internet access because the information was verified.

An **IN-FILE CREDIT REPORT** looks basically the same as a Residential Mortgage Credit report (RMCR) and is currently the accepted form because of the ease of running a new report to verify the validity of the existing report.

CREDIT REPORT

FILE #	FNMA #	DATE COMPLETED	10/20/2009	RQD' BY
PREPARED FOR		DATE ORDERED	10/20/2009	
		REPOSITORIES	XP/TU/EF	PRPD' BY
		PRICE	$17.55	LOAN TYPE
		REF. #		

PROPERTY ADDRESS

APPLICANT   CO-APPLICANT

APPLICANT		CO-APPLICANT	
SOC SEC #	DOB	SOC SEC #	DOB
MARITAL STATUS		DEPENDENTS	
CURRENT ADDRESS			LENGTH
PREVIOUS ADDRESS			LENGTH

SCORE MODELS

EQUIFAX/FACTA BEACON 5.0 -
SCORE: **732**
00039 - SERIOUS DELINQUENCY
00008 - TOO MANY INQUIRIES LAST 12 MONTHS
00010 - PROPORTION OF BALANCES TO CREDIT LIMITS IS TOO HIGH ON BANK REVOLVING OR OTHER REVOLVING ACCOUNTS
00012 - LENGTH OF TIME REVOLVING ACCOUNTS HAVE BEEN ESTABLISHED

TRANSUNION/FICO CLASSIC (04) -
SCORE: **738**
039 - SERIOUS DELINQUENCY
005 - TOO MANY ACCOUNTS WITH BALANCES
008 - TOO MANY INQUIRIES LAST 12 MONTHS
013 - TIME SINCE DELINQUENCY IS TOO RECENT OR UNKNOWN
FA - INQUIRIES IMPACTED THE CREDIT SCORE

EXPERIAN/FAIR, ISAAC (VER. 2) -
SCORE: **729**
39 - SERIOUS DELINQUENCY
10 - PROPORTION OF BALANCE TO HIGH CREDIT ON BANK REVOLVING OR ALL REVOLVING ACCOUNTS
13 - TIME SINCE DELINQUENCY IS TOO RECENT OR UNKNOWN
08 - TOO MANY INQUIRIES LAST 12 MONTHS

TRADE SUMMARY

	#	BALANCE	HIGH CREDIT	PAYMENTS	PAST DUE
MORTGAGE	9	322873	368250	2156	0
AUTO	3	0	0	0	0
EDUCATION	7	65379	65423	480	0
OTHER INSTALLMENT	0	0	0	0	0
OPEN	0	0	0	0	0
REVOLVING	30	18784	142350	368	0
OTHER	0	0	0	0	0
TOTAL	49	407036	576023	3004	0

SECURED DEBT	322873	OLDEST TRADELINE	10/69
UNSECURED DEBT	84163	DEBT/HIGH CREDIT	66%

DEROGATORY SUMMARY

CHARGE OFFS:	0	30 DAYS:	2	INQUIRIES:	2
COLLECTIONS:	0	60 DAYS:	1	MOST RECENT LATE:	undetermined
BANKRUPTCY:	0	90 DAYS:	1		
PUBLIC RECORDS:	0	OTHER:	0		

PUBLIC RECORDS
*** NONE ***

ECOA KEY: B=BORROWER; C=CO-BORROWER; J=JOINT; U=UNDESIGNATED; A=AUTHORIZED USER; P=PARTICIPANT; S=CO-SIGNER

Figure 26: Credit report - Page 1 of 3

FILE #		FNMA #		DATE COMPLETED 10/20/2009		RQD' BY	
PREPARED FOR				DATE ORDERED 10/20/2009			
				REPOSITORIES XP/TU/EF		PRPD' BY	
				PRICE $17.55		LOAN TYPE	
				REF. #			

PROPERTY ADDRESS

APPLICANT   CO-APPLICANT

APPLICANT		CO-APPLICANT	
SOC SEC #	DOB	SOC SEC #	DOB
MARITAL STATUS		DEPENDENTS	

OPEN ACCOUNTS

ECOA	WHOSE	CREDITOR	DATE REPORTED	DATE OPENED / DLA	HIGH CREDIT OR LIMIT / ACCT TYPE	BALANCE / TERMS	PAST DUE	MO REV	30	60	90+	STATUS / SOURCE
B	B	BAC HOME LOANS SERVI 339	09/09	06/03 / 09/09	$293250 / MTG	$263931 / 360 $1619	$0	73	0	0	0	AS AGREED / XP/TU/EF
		CONVENTIONAL REAL ESTATE LOAN, INCLUDING PURCHASE MONEY FIRST										
B	B	US DEPT OF EDUCATION 97	09/09	04/09 / 09/09	$65423 / EDU	$65379 / UNK $480	$0	1	0	0	0	AS AGREED / XP/TU/EF
B	B	BAC HOME LOANS SERVI 603	09/09	11/06 / 09/09	$75000 / MTG	$58942 / 180 $537	$0	31	0	0	0	AS AGREED / XP/TU/EF
		SECOND MORTGAGE										
B	B	CITI 66524	10/09	05/00 / 10/09	$21430 / REV	$11772 / MIN $176	$0	99	0	0	0	AS AGREED / XP/TU/EF
B	B	CITI 4431	09/09	11/99 / 09/09	$23420 / REV	$4631 / MIN $128	$0	99	0	0	0	AS AGREED / XP/TU/EF
B	B	CHASE 7865	09/09	04/91 / 09/09	$24000 / REV	$1553 / MIN $39	$0	99	0	0	0	AS AGREED / XP/TU/EF
		ACCOUNT PREVIOUSLY IN DISPUTE-NOW RESOLVED-REPORTED BY SUBSCRIBER										
B	B	GEMB/LOWES 429	09/09	08/09 / 09/09	$3600 / REV	$828 / $25*	$0	2	0	0	0	AS AGREED / XP/TU/EF
B	B	SEARS/CBSD 7968	10/09	05/09 / 05/09	$2800 / REV	$0 / $0	$0	6	0	0	0	AS AGREED / XP/TU/EF
B	B	MCYDSNB 12320	10/09	06/09 / 07/09	$1200 / REV	$0 / $0	$0	5	0	0	0	AS AGREED / XP/TU/EF
B	B	DISCOVER FIN SVCS LL 006	09/09	08/96 / 09/09	$12000 / REV	$0 / $0	$0	99	0	0	0	AS AGREED / XP/TU/EF
J	B	DISCOVER FIN SVCS LL 37060	09/09	03/86 / 10/05	$18000 / REV	$0 / $0	$0	99	0	0	0	AS AGREED / XP/TU/EF
B	B	OITECH 5355	08/09	02/00 / 06/04	$40000 / MTG	$0 / $0	$0	99	0	0	0	AS AGREED / XP/TU/EF
		HOME EQUITY LINE OF CREDIT - REVOLVING TERMS										
B	B	KOHLS/CHASE	10/09	09/08 / 10/09	$1500 / REV	$0 / $0	$0	13	0	0	0	AS AGREED / XP/TU/EF
B	B	HSBC/BSBUY 431	10/09	01/06 / 01/09	$3600 / REV	$0 / $0	$0	45	0	0	0	AS AGREED / XP/TU/EF
B	B	VISDSNB	09/09	06/09	$5000	$0	$0	1	0	0	0	AS AGREED

ECOA KEY: B=BORROWER; C=CO-BORROWER; J=JOINT; U=UNDESIGNATED; A=AUTHORIZED USER; P=PARTICIPANT; S=CO-SIGNER

Figure 26: Credit report - Page 2 of 3

Credit

Page 5 of 10

FILE #	FNMA #	DATE COMPLETED 10/20/2009	RQD' BY
PREPARED FOR		DATE ORDERED 10/20/2009	
		REPOSITORIES XP/TU/EF	PRPD' BY
		PRICE $17.55	LOAN TYPE
		REF. #	

PROPERTY ADDRESS
APPLICANT   CO-APPLICANT
APPLICANT
SOC SEC #   DOB   CO-APPLICANT
MARITAL STATUS   SOC SEC #   DOB
                                      DEPENDENTS

CLOSED ACCOUNTS

ECOA	WHOSE	CREDITOR	DATE REPORTED	DATE OPENED / DLA	HIGH CREDIT OR LIMIT / ACCT TYPE	BALANCE / TERMS	PAST DUE	MO REV	30	60	90+	STATUS / SOURCE
J	B	CAP ONE 39	08/00	06/96 07/99	$35 REV	$0 $0	$0	50	0	0	0	PAID XP/TU/EF
		ACCOUNT CLOSED AT CONSUMER'S REQUEST										
B	B	CHASE 92	06/03	12/00 04/01	$7400 REV	$0 $0	$0	31	0	0	0	PAID XP/TU/EF
		ACCOUNT CLOSED AT CONSUMER'S REQUEST										
B	B	BAC HOME LOANS SERVI 31	06/03	06/02 05/03	$290000 MTG	$0 360 $0	$0	9	0	0	0	PAID XP/TU/EF
		CONVENTIONAL REAL ESTATE LOAN, INCLUDING PURCHASE MONEY FIRST										
B	B	GDYR/CBSD 0062	05/04	11/00 02/01	$1600 REV	$0 $0	$0	43	0	0	0	PAID XP/TU/EF
B	B	BAC/FLEET-BKCARD 969	05/02	06/99 06/00	$10000 REV	$0 $0	$0	39	0	0	0	PAID XP/TU/EF
		ACCOUNT CLOSED AT CONSUMER'S REQUEST										
D	B	WELLS FARGO HM MORTG 616	07/02	02/01 05/02	$242000 MTG	$0 360 $0	$0	14	0	0	0	PAID XP/TU/EF
		CONVENTIONAL REAL ESTATE LOAN, INCLUDING PURCHASE MONEY FIRST										
B	B	AUTONATION FINANCIAL 2	07/02	04/01 07/02	$25473 AUTO	$0 060 $0	$0	15	0	0	0	PAID XP/TU/EF

DEROGATORY ACCOUNTS

ECOA	WHOSE	CREDITOR	DATE REPORTED	DATE OPENED / DLA	HIGH CREDIT OR LIMIT / ACCT TYPE	BALANCE / TERMS	PAST DUE	MO REV	30	60	90+	STATUS / SOURCE
B	B	BANK OF AMERICA 4104	10/09	10/01 04/09	$25800 REV	$0 $0	$0	97	1	0	0	CUR WAS 30 XP/TU/EF
		Late Dates: 5/08-30										
B	B	BANK OF AMERICA 0079	04/08	10/02 10/06	$15000 REV	$0 $0	$0	67	1	1	2	PD WAS 120 XP/TU/EF
		Late Dates: 10/06-120, 9/06-90, 8/06-60, 7/06-30										
		ACCOUNT CLOSED AT CREDIT GRANTOR'S REQUEST										

OTHER CREDIT HISTORY
*** NONE ***

INQUIRIES (LAST 90 DAYS)

TU	08/20/09	GEMB/LOWES
XP/TU/EF	07/30/09	LANDSAFE

EQUIFAX SAFESCAN

ECOA KEY: B=BORROWER; C=CO-BORROWER; J=JOINT; U=UNDESIGNATED; A=AUTHORIZED USER; P=PARTICIPANT; S=CO-SIGNER

CCIS MORTGAGE SERVICES: 1502 MILL ROCK WAY, SUITE 140, BAKERSFIELD, CA 93311 (P) 661-398-4700 (F) 661-398-4705

This information is furnished in response to an inquiry for the purpose of evaluating credit risks. It has been obtained from sources deemed reliable, the accuracy of which this organization does not guarantee. The inquirer has agreed to indemnify that reporting bureau for any damage arising from misuse of this information, and this report is furnished in reliance upon that indemnity. It must be held in strict confidence and complies with the provisions of Public Law 91-508, the Fair Credit Reporting Act. Reporting bureau certifies that all Residential Mortgage Credit Reports meet the standards prescribed by FNMA, FHMC, FHA, VA and the Farmers Home Administration.

Figure 26: Credit report - Page 3 of 3

8-4

The first page of the credit report has the borrower's name, Social Security number, and the price charged for the report, which is necessary for the MLDS/GFE (LE). The following information contains the credit score as determined by each of the credit repositories used. The largest and most commonly used credit bureaus are **EXPERIAN (XPN)** (formerly TRW), **TRANS UNION (TUC)**, and **EQUIFAX** (EFX).

Experian uses the name **Fair, Isaac, and Company (FICO)** for their credit scoring system. Trans Union's scoring is called **EMPIRICA** but they also use FICO. Equifax uses **BEACON**. These scoring systems are similar, and the scores are usually close. If one of the agencies has a score that is considerably different than the other two, it may indicate that the agency has an item reported that has not been reported to the others. This may also indicate an error. Since lenders use the mid-score, a variation between the scores will usually not be an issue unless the difference is substantial.

DEROGATORY ITEMS OR REMARKS Section indicates that public records have been checked for:
- Judgments,
- Bankruptcies,
- Foreclosures or other records.
- Derogatory credit such as late payments, repossessions, or collections

Any items listed in this section will require an explanation, documentation, and may cause lenders to decline a loan.

Any accounts that are listed as being in collection, a bad debt, or charge-off with a balance owed will need to be paid through escrow and a letter of explanation (LOE) will be required. Any such accounts will also affect the credit evaluation and the lender to be used. Many lenders have guidelines based on minimum credit scores. Many sub-prime lenders do not require pay-off of medical collections, especially for an amount of less than $500.

The past seven years of **PUBLIC RECORDS** are reported, with a few exceptions. Tax liens remain on a report until paid; bankruptcy remains on the records for ten years; judgments remain for ten years and can be renewed for an additional ten or until paid.

The public records section of the credit report discloses tax liens, tax lien releases, and judgments along with any currently owed balances. These debts must be paid in full at closing or verification that the debt has been paid in full must be provided. An LOE is required. Any pending lawsuits must be finalized before a loan can be funded or a copy of the suit provided to verify the subject property will not be affected.

A-PAPER LENDERS will require a time period of three or four years since the bankruptcy was discharged and verification that there has been no new derogatory credit since that time.

- **CHAPTER 7 BANKRUPTCY:** the elimination of debt will require a three- to four-year time period from the date the bankruptcy is dismissed.
- **CHAPTER 11 BANKRUPTCY:** a reorganization of debt where the lender may provide a loan to repay the debts and bring the borrower out of bankruptcy. *An A-Paper lender will not provide this type of loan; usually only sub-prime lenders will approve such loans.*

Borrowers must also have re-established credit with a minimum of **three** accounts. Sub-prime lenders offer a variety of guidelines including One-Day Out of Bankruptcy.

CREDIT HISTORY is generally broken down into ten columns and may vary with different credit agencies. The order in which the information is disclosed will vary, but the information will be the same. The information on the report that is shown in *Figure 26* is as follows:

1. **Column one:** provides the name of the creditor and the account number. The account numbers on a credit report are usually scrambled to some extent for security reasons but are identifiable, if necessary, in order to avoid duplication of accounts. Mortgage account numbers, or a recent mortgage statement, need to be obtained from the borrower because escrow needs accurate information for the lender to obtain a **Demand for Pay-Off** if the loan is a refi.
2. **Column two:** provides the date the account was last reported or date of last activity.
3. **Column three:** discloses the date the account was opened and the date of the last activity.
4. **Column four:** tells the maximum amount of credit or **"high"** that was extended to the borrower. For a revolving account, this figure will be the maximum amount of the credit limit for the account.

Account type or type of payment:
- **REV or R** is a revolving account such as a credit card or an equity line.
- **M** is a mortgage account.
- **Inst or I** or a set number indicates an installment, or a loan with a set payment amount that will be paid in full, and the account closed on receipt of the last payment.

  Example: 48x550 marked "I" may indicate a car payment that is financed for 48 months with a monthly payment of $550. Car loans are generally for terms of 36, 48, or 60 months.

5. **Column five:** shows the current balance of the debt, the terms of repayment, and the amount of payment due.
6. **Column six:** shows any amount currently past due. *This column should be checked first for any potential problems.*
7. **Column seven:** tells the number of months reported.
8. **Column eight:** tells if there have been late payments made in the past and whether they were 30, 60, or 90+ days past due. The figure in each of those columns shows how many times they were late.
9. **Column nine:** provides the status, such as whether it has been paid as agreed and states which credit repository provided the information.

The credit report covers a seven-year period. Late payments more than two years old are generally not a problem with most lenders but do require an LOE from the borrower. Each late payment is required to be addressed and explained individually. This column also discloses the number of monthly payments that are included in this report.

The date when the last late payment occurred will be disclosed within these columns and may vary even within the same credit report. Each credit reporting company will use their own format; however, most of the information provided will be the same. Read the heading of each column prior to reviewing the individual accounts.

NOTE

Mortgage history requires 24 months or a 2-year history. If the mortgage account is showing less than a 24-month history, additional verification will be needed. If the mortgage is less than 2-years old, check the report for additional mortgages.

If the transaction is a refinance and the borrowers have owned the property more than two years, there will probably be another mortgage account. If the loan is a purchase transaction, they may have owned other properties that had mortgages. The credit reporting agency may be able to acquire additional history on request, or canceled checks (front and back) from the borrower will suffice as mortgage verification. Rental verification may be required to generate a complete a 2-year history, in which case, the borrower must provide landlord information or canceled checks.

The credit report will show any discrepancies such as name variations, different Social Security numbers, and additional addresses not previously disclosed. Most items are easily explained; however, some items may be the result of another person with the same or similar name. A borrower's work address may appear as an additional address. A Social Security number or a name discrepancy may be a typo from the current or a previous request. All items should be discussed with the borrower to determine the cause and the explanation.

Inaccurate items can often be removed by the credit agency on request and with verification. To do this, they will require documentation from the borrower, and they may also need to contact the creditor reporting the item. There are times, especially with child support, that the reporting DA's office can be contacted and can verify by using the Social Security number, that the creditor is in fact another person.

CREDIT SUPPLEMENTS can be provided by the reporting agency to remove an erroneous item or provide a new report by confirming it with the creditor.

If the creditor does not correct an error, the borrower will need to provide proof, such as canceled checks or letters from the creditor, stating corrections or other communication. The agencies cannot remove items arbitrarily or on the borrower's word. **Documentation must be provided.**

Because of the cost and use of the Tri-Merge In-file Credit report, the credit reporting agencies do not often provide the service of verifying and removing erroneous items reported. It may be best and most efficient to obtain the documentation and LOE from the borrower for submission to the lender.

A **RAPID RESCORE** is available to correct items and to correct the credit score based on the corrected information. Credit reporting agencies do charge per item and per repository. It is advisable to determine the value of correcting items before doing a loan. *There are situations that are best left untouched and corrected after the loan has been completed.*

> *Example: The borrower has a small collection account showing on the credit report and the "last activity date" is more than two years ago. Paying that account in full, or verifying that it was paid in full, will make the "last activity date" current, thereby lowering the credit score because of recent activity on a collection account. It would be advisable in this case to provide an LOE and have the borrower pay the collection after COE to avoid the adverse effect on their credit score.*

Debts are usually listed from the largest balance to the smallest balance, followed by 0 balance accounts. Mortgages are the most important entries in regard to late payments. For an A-paper loan, there must be no late payments within the last two-year period. If a mortgage foreclosure appears on the credit report, the borrower will not get an A-paper loan. Lenders used to require that a foreclosure be more than five years old with a strong LOE. Depending on the economy, many lenders may refuse to accept a loan with a foreclosure showing on the credit report, therefore it must have been more than seven years since the foreclosure was completed.

PAYMENT SHOCK occurs when the new housing payment is more than 50% higher than the current payment. If payment shock is an issue, the borrower will need to write a "payment shock letter" addressing how they plan to cope with the new payment amount. The purpose of this letter is to make the borrower aware of the increase.

> *Example:*
>
> | | |
> |---|---|
> | $3,649 | *New payment amount* |
> | -$1,559 | *Current payment amount* |
> | =$2,090 | *Payment difference* |
> | ÷1559 | *Current payment amount* |
> | =134% | *Increase in housing payment* |

The name of the person providing the information should be checked to see if the verification is for rent, a land contract, or a lease purchase option. If the preparer's name indicates a family relationship, such as parents, canceled checks must be obtained to ensure that there is an **arms-length transaction**.

The updated information is to be placed appropriately on the *1003, Section V, Page 2,* present housing expense for the current payment and *Section VI, Liabilities for Current Loan Information.*

If there are **REVOLVING DEBTS,** such as credit cards or equity line mortgages, provide the current balance and payment amount based on that balance. If a payment is not provided on a revolving debt, the computer will calculate 5% of the balance owing.

> *Example:*
> | | |
> |---|---|
> | $3,000 | *Balance* |
> | x 5% | *Standard percentage of balance used to determine the minimum payment* |
> | = $150 | ***Monthly payment*** |

This will be the payment amount used to calculate total debt and the debt ratio. If the borrower's debt ratios are high, request the most recent statement from the borrower to obtain the actual payment amount, which is usually less than 5% of the balance.

Few conventional lenders will allow revolving debt to be paid off to qualify for a mortgage, but sub-prime lenders often will. The opinion is that they will continue to use credit cards in the same way they have in the past. A revolving debt can be paid in full, and the borrower can reuse the account the following day up to the credit limit.

Occasionally a lender will allow credit cards to be paid off to qualify and they may require the account to be closed. This is most often used in the case of an equity line of credit because closing the account requires a Reconveyance Deed and proof of closing through escrow because it is a lien against real property. Paying off revolving debt to qualify is more commonly allowed for sub-prime loans.

INSTALLMENT LOANS such as car loans, with the exception of car leases, can be paid off to qualify, as these accounts will be closed once paid in full.

Divide the balance of the loan by the monthly payment to ascertain the number of months remaining. When a borrower needs to reduce debt, but there are insufficient funds to pay a loan in full, the debt can be paid down to a balance that will be paid off in less than 10 months.

NOTE

If the number of months remaining on an installment debt is 10 months or less, it does not need to be included in the debt ratio.

Example:

$18,500	*Balance*
÷ $475	*Payment*
= 39	***Months left to pay***
$475	*Payment*
X 10	*Months left to pay*
= $4,750	***Balance needed***
$18,500	*Current Balance*
-$4,750	*Required Balance*
= $13,750	***Amount needed to pay down debt to eliminate from Debt Ratio***

CREDIT SCORING has become the most commonly used method of determining creditworthiness. FAIR, ISAAC, AND COMPANY or FICO, is Experian's scoring model, EMPIRICA is Trans Union's scoring model, and BEACON is the scoring model for Equifax.

These will reflect a historical status with a series of numbers following the score. These numbers are the rating system used by the bureaus to calculate the borrower's credit score, commonly referring to FICO as a generic term. These credit score numbers reflect the likelihood that the borrower will repay the debt. The numbers shown after the credit score are assigned to a designated credit issue, such as age of accounts, ratio of debt to credit limit, number of late pays, public records, and others. Lenders rely heavily on the scores and many loan programs require a minimum score to be considered acceptable. The score will also affect the loan type, LTV, and the quality of paper (A, B, C, or D).

Most lenders use the middle score of those provided by the three agencies, or the lowest if there are only two scores. The preferred credit report is called a **TRI-MERGE** or, in other words, information from three agencies has been incorporated, as well as all three scores. The following will give a range to be followed for most lenders:

- 740 to 850 score is excellent.
- 680+ acceptable with compensating factors.
- 640+ may be accepted as A- paper but is scrutinized very closely and few A- paper lenders will provide a mortgage loan to borrowers with this score.
- 620 is no longer considered A paper by most lenders. This is considered a B-paper loan.
- 580 to 620 is workable but with lenders that provide B- or C-paper loans.
- <580 is more difficult to find a lender to accept and will be very costly. *Private money or hard money loans are the probable lenders.*

When the economy is good, and the value of property is increasing, loans will be more readily available for borrowers with lower scores.

Borrowers with credit scores less than 620 are sub-prime or alt-A borrowers and are often best put in a two-year fixed-rate loan, advised how to correct their current credit situation, then refinanced into a better loan in two years. This gives the broker future business if managed well. If properly advised, many clients will be A- paper when the 2-year period has passed.

Lenders view credit history as a clear picture of how people pay bills, and few people change these habits. Remember the borrower is asking the lender to give them large sums of money and the broker must convince them this loan is a good investment.

Credit scoring was created in the late 1960s and early 1970s by the automotive industry as a means to determine quickly if a potential car buyer was qualified for financing. Sears and Roebuck further refined it as a means to qualify their customers quickly.

It was not adopted by the mortgage industry until the mid-1980s. At that time 620 was an excellent credit score and a score greater than 680 was rarely seen. Over the years, the system was refined, and many changes were made.

In the late 1990s and early 2000s the major bureaus revised their credit scoring programs and the credit scores of today are considerably different. A score that was once 620 will now appear as 740. The broker must be aware that these programs do change occasionally, and credit scores will shift with these changes.

At the end of the credit report are the addresses and phone numbers of the creditors who are showing an account on the report. If the borrower chooses to dispute any of the items, they can contact the creditor directly. In order for another person, such as the broker, to assist the borrower with a disputed debt, they will need to have the credit authorization from the borrower available to send to the creditor.

The creditor cannot speak to anyone other than the borrower without written authorization.

DEBT RATIOS

DEBT RATIOS are a major consideration for creditworthiness.

FRONT-END DEBT RATIO is the total of monthly housing expenses divided by the monthly income:

> *Example:*
> $2,574.60   *Principal & interest payment (P&I)*
> + 504.38   *Taxes*
> + 76.00   *Insurance*
> =$3,154.98   *Total monthly housing expense*
>
> *$3,154.98 (monthly housing expense) ÷ $11,533.25 (monthly income) =*
> *.28.335% Front-End Debt Ratio*

BACK-END DEBT RATIO is calculated by adding the total monthly housing expenses to all other monthly obligations (payments, child-support, etc.) and dividing that figure by the total monthly income:

Example:

$3,154.98	*Total monthly housing expense*
+1,195.00	*Total monthly payments per Sect. VI 1003*
=**$4,462.96**	**Total monthly obligation**
÷$11,533.25	*Monthly Income*
=**38.696%**	**Back-End Debt Ratio**
-OR-	
$4,462.96 ÷ $11,533.25 = 38.696%	

36/45% or less is the standard accepted A-paper debt ratio even though FNMA states that the debt ratios should not exceed 28/36. Higher debt ratios are considered and will require the underwriter to make a judgment call based on compensating factors. FNMA will allow up to 45% debt ratio; however, most lenders will not allow higher than 42 to 44%. For a borrower with a high debt ratio, compensating factors could be excellent credit, adequate reserves, disposable income, and having owned a home for a long period.

Remember **gross income, or pre-tax income,** is used for qualifying. The average taxpayer pays 35% of their income in income taxes. Using the figures above:

Example:

$11,533	*Gross monthly income*
X 33%	*Average income tax*
=**$3,806**	**Total income tax**
$11,533	*Gross monthly income*
-$3,806	*Income tax*
=**$7,727**	**Net Income**
-$4,463	*Monthly obligations*
=**$3,264**	**Disposable monthly income**

In this case the borrower has $3,264 monthly disposable income or money left for necessities such as food, utilities, and clothing. Based on this debt ratio, this is an example of a very good borrower.

COMPENSATING FACTORS

Compensating factors are factors that demonstrate that the borrower is a stronger borrower than normal documentation shows. Some items that give the file strength by off-setting derogatory issues are:

- Long time owning the subject property.
- Long employment history.
- Good savings history.
- Few debts/obligations.
- Tangible assets that may be sold or financed to generate cash.
- Good credit.

CREDIT REPOSITORIES OR CREDIT REPORTING AGENCIES

CREDIT REPOSITORIES OR CREDIT REPORTING AGENCIES are three main agencies that oversee the information received from creditors regarding the payment history of their debtors or consumers. These are **EXPERIAN/XPN** (formerly TRW), **TRANS UNION/ TUC**, and **EQUIFAX/EFX**. They each have their own scoring system based on a variety of issues, some of which are:

- **Late payments.**
- **Number of active or open accounts.**
- **Balance of credit is too near the limit.**
- **Age of accounts:** too many new accounts will cause the score to go down or decrease.
- **Excessive number of recent inquiries.**

A late payment on a mortgage will have a more detrimental effect on the credit score than a late payment on a car. A late payment on a car will have a more detrimental effect on the credit score than a late payment on a credit card. There are many issues taken into consideration, only a few of which are mentioned here; however, these are among the most important and will have the greatest effect on a credit score.

For credit reporting purposes, a payment is considered 30-days late 30 days after the payment due date. The payment must be received in the office of the company extending the credit the day prior to the 30th day.

> **Example:** *A payment due on the 15th of the month must be paid by the 14th of the following month or it will be considered and reported as 30 days late.*

It may be arguable whether the payment was actually received in the office the day before the payment's due date (considered the 29th day). The person opening the payment will record the payment as being paid on the date that they actually open the envelope and enter the information into the computer. This is not necessarily the date the payment was received. Payments may at times be at the creditor's office for more than a week before being processed. If a payment is going to be made late (after the due date), every effort should be made to get the payment to the creditor within that 30-day period. Verifying receipt in the office of the creditor is imperative.

Many creditors now take "check by phone" payments by calling the borrower, who gives the checking information over the phone with a customer service representative. A confirmation number for the payment will be provided and the debtor should make a note of that number.

Payments can also be made online, and a receipt or confirmation can be printed out and retained by the debtor as verification of the payment and the date paid.

Overnight mail, such as **FedEx** or **Priority Mail** through the post office with a signature and return receipt, can verify the date of receipt of a payment, if necessary, to correct a credit report. **Western Union** provides a receipt when funds are wired. Bank wire transfers are also an excellent way to transmit funds within the same day. All of these receipts are acceptable proof of time of payment.

Documentation provided to the credit bureaus for correction of errors may include canceled checks (front and back) and proof of mail receipt. A copy should also be sent along with a letter to the creditor requesting a correction either by removal or correcting the information.

CREDIT REPORTING AGENCIES are required by law to contact the creditor within 30 days of receipt of a letter to verify the accuracy of the reported information. The creditor then has 30 days to respond to the credit-reporting agency, which in turn has 30 days to respond to the borrower with the outcome of their inquiry.

It may take several tries to get the information corrected if the creditor is being obstinate or is not fully reviewing the documentation or has wrong information in their records. Contacting the creditor directly by phone may be beneficial and may expedite the correcting of an error. The consumer should be prepared to fax information directly to the person they spoke to as soon as possible following the phone conversation while the issue is still fresh in their mind.

If an uncooperative person is contacted, the consumer should hang up and call again later when it is likely that a different person will answer the phone call. Persistence will pay off and the borrower will see a change in their credit score within three months of the correction. The best way to expedite credit corrections is by email or fax and is well worth any cost incurred from these services. These companies are generally advertised as **office services** or **mail services**.

When lenders review a borrower's credit history and credit scores, they assume that most people continue to pay bills and spend money in the same manner throughout their life. The creditor considering lending money will assume that the payments due to them will occasionally be paid late if the borrower has a history of late payments to others.

Credit problems require explanations. If any problems were all within a short period of time, exceptions can be made with good explanations. If late payments have been continuous or consistent over a long period of time, it is assumed that the borrower will continue to make late payments in the future.

When a consumer feels they are ready to seriously look to purchase a home, they should contact their mortgage broker/loan agent and have a credit report run so they can begin to determine and prepare for the interest rate and loan program for which they will qualify. This initial credit report will provide the pertinent information needed for proper planning. If there are errors in the credit report, time should be taken to repair some issues before actually finding a home. Realistically, this process may take at least three months.

It is still possible to obtain a mortgage with credit problems, even with a recent bankruptcy, but the interest rate will be higher and a lower loan to value (LTV) will be required. Credit issues stay on a credit report for seven years from the date that the late payment was received or the date that it was reported.

*Bankruptcy is the exception to this, and it remains on the credit report for **ten years** from the date of dismissal.*

Collection accounts affect the score adversely, but most lenders will accept small medical collections as a normal circumstance in our society if the balance is less than $500. If the collection is old and the date reported is one year or more, the borrower *should not pay it prior to applying for the loan*. Paying it off brings the "date reported" to the current date and the credit score will drop because it will now appear as a recent adverse account. The borrower should be prepared to pay the account through escrow since many lenders will require full payment. *If payoff is not required, the debt should be paid shortly after the close of escrow so the score will begin to improve prior to future credit needs.*

The following addresses and phone numbers are for contacting the credit repository companies:

EQUIFAX
P.O. Box 740241
Atlanta, Ga. 30374
Phone (800)685-1111
www.equifax.com
TRANS UNION
P.O. Box 1000
Chester, Pa. 19016
Phone (800)888-4213
www.transunion.com

EXPERIAN
P.O. Box 2006
Allen, TX 75013
Phone (888)397-3742
www.experian.com/reportaccess

FEDERAL ACTS AND LAWS AND CREDIT

FEDERAL ACTS that pertain to credit reporting and the use of credit reports include the **FAIR AND ACCURATE CREDIT TRANSACTIONS (FACT) ACT** and the **FAIR CREDIT REPORTING ACT (FCRA)**.

1. **FAIR AND ACCURATE CREDIT TRANSACTIONS (FACT) ACT** requires creditors to provide borrowers with information regarding their personal credit history to include:
   - Credit scores.
   - Range of scores for the program that created the credit profile.
   - Credit bureaus provide the information.
   - Scoring models or the computer program used to create the scores/profile.
   - Factors affecting the credit score (such as late payments).

FACT ACT also provides that every consumer is allowed to request one free credit report per year from each of the three national repositories: Equifax, Trans Union, and Experian. The purpose of providing the information is to give the consumer the ability to verify and/or dispute information in their report. The Act helps provide for the reduction of identity theft by allowing the consumer to review their credit information for accuracy and to place alerts on their report if there has been or could be an incident of identity theft or other fraudulent use of the credit information.

RED FLAG RULES were implemented into the FACT ACT on November 1, 2008, requiring financial institutions to comply with the following regulations as a means to identify and help prevent identity theft crimes as soon as possible:

- Develop and implement an **Identity Theft Prevention Program** of reasonable policies and procedures for detecting and preventing identity theft for both new and existing accounts. The program must also include methods to follow through on the discovery of such acts.
- Businesses using credit reports as a means of determining creditworthiness must respond to all **Notices of Address Discrepancies**.
- Issuers of credit are required to *assess the validity* of a request for a change of address if that request is followed by a request for a replacement card within a short period of time.

Address discrepancies are an indicator of identity theft since the person stealing another's identity will often provide a change of address to a credit provider for the victim's account then request a new card shortly after. This action provides a credit card to the criminal and the statements will also go to the criminal allowing them considerable time to use the account before the victim is made aware of the illegal usage.

2. **FAIR CREDIT REPORTING ACT (FCRA)** protects the consumer from inaccurate credit reporting. The consumer is allowed to inspect their credit report for errors. The consumer has the right to provide explanations of credit incidents and derogatory credit, such as accounts that were obtained or abused by someone through identity theft.

   The consumer must be informed if the credit in their report has been used against them or has caused them to be declined or to pay a higher interest rate or fees.

Any business taking adverse action against the consumer based on the information provided must inform the consumer by providing the agency's name, address, and phone number. The consumer can then contact that agency directly to correct any errors or identify any issues.

The consumer has a right to know what is in their credit file and they are entitled to a free report once per year from each repository per the FACT ACT. Consumers may also be entitled to a free report under the following circumstances:

- **Adverse action** has been taken against them based on the credit report.
- **They are the Victim** of identity theft.
- **Inaccurate fraudulent information.**
- **They are on public assistance.**
- **They are unemployed** but anticipate employment within 60 days. *Many employers now run credit reports prior to hiring.*

Consumers have a right to know their credit score since the scores are an integral part of creditworthiness. Consumers also have the right to dispute inaccurate information that has been reported and is adversely affecting their score. The credit repository is required to investigate any valid disputes within 30 days of receiving a consumer dispute. The consumer is responsible for providing any documentation to confirm the statements. The credit repository will contact the creditor for verification or confirmation. The creditor will also have 30 days to respond to the credit repository.

During this time, the credit repository may have the right to continue reporting the disputed credit information, or if they removed it while investigating, they may replace it with the new information if the creditor has verified its accuracy. It is often necessary for a consumer to contact the Federal Trade Commission if they receive an unsatisfactory response. Frivolous disputes will not be investigated. Verification, such as canceled checks, may be necessary to confirm the payment of a debt.

Access to a consumer's credit report is limited to those who require the information for the purpose of advancing credit or establishing a person's creditworthiness for a loan application or their character for employment. A Social Security number will be required for identity and a signature for authorization. The consumer's consent must be provided when a credit report is used for employment purposes.

Credit repositories must delete outdated detrimental credit information. Most information that is seven years old must be deleted from the report. Bankruptcies may be reported for a period not to exceed ten years. Judgments reported under "public record" are good for ten years and may be renewed for an additional ten-year period.

Unsolicited prescreened offers based on credit information may be blocked, or the consumer can **"opt out."** Businesses using this method of extending credit must provide an 800- or toll-free number for the consumer to contact in order to be removed from any lists providing their information. Consumers have the right to opt out by contacting the nationwide credit bureaus or calling (888) 567-8688. The consumer has a right to seek damages from any violators of these rights and may sue in either state or federal courts.

Victims of identity theft and those serving in the military under active duty have rights beyond those listed. For further information about these rights, the consumer may contact the following:

FEDERAL TRADE COMMISSION
Consumer Response Center-FCRA
DC 20580
877-382-4357
www.ftc.gov/credit

OFFICE OF THRIFT SUPERVISION
Consumer Complaints Washington,
Washington, DC 20552
800-842-6929
www.occ.gov

FEDERAL RESERVE BOARD
Division of Consumer &
Community Affairs
Washington, DC 20551
202-452-36963
www.federalreserve.gov

**OFFICE OF THE COMPTROLLER
OF THE CURRENCY**
Compliance Management
Washington, DC 20219
800-613-6743
www.occ.treas.gov

CHAPTER 9
QUALIFYING INCOME

INCOME DOCUMENTATION

Lenders require a **2-YEAR HISTORY OF INCOME IN THE SAME FIELD OF EMPLOYMENT.** If the borrower has changed professions within that period of time, a letter of explanation (LOE) will be required and in some cases, the new income cannot be used to qualify if the borrower has changed their line of work. There are some acceptable changes.

A. **A SALARIED EMPLOYEE** is one who is paid the same amount for a determined period of time, usually monthly or bi-monthly. A salaried borrower's current income can be used because the income will not change, but a two-year history must be verified to confirm the consistency of that salaried amount. The most important thing to determine regarding a salaried borrower's income is that the income has not been reduced during the two-year time frame. This can often be explained by loss of time on a job due to illness or a change of jobs for a future improvement.

B. **WAGE EARNER'S INCOME** must be averaged because it changes regularly. An employee who receives wages is paid by the number of **hours** they work, or some other increment of measuring work actually done or completed.

C. **SELF-EMPLOYED FOR LESS THAN TWO YEARS** for a borrower that had been a salaried employee **is not** usable income. Likewise, if a borrower is currently salaried and they are refinancing to take cash out to start a new business, the current income will not be ongoing and, therefore, not usable.

D. **RECENTLY GRADUATED FROM COLLEGE** and the borrower is now employed in the field of study, the current income **is** usable. The college transcripts and the diploma are required to establish a 2-year history.

E. **18 MONTHS OF INCOME** will occasionally be accepted by lenders. This would include the prior year's W2 and 6-months income for the current year, or the W2 for the most recent years and six months income from the previous year.

The previous year's W2 must still be included to verify a 2-year history, but if the borrower has had an increase in pay, the most recent 18 months' income may be used to determine average pay. There would need to be good reasons depending on the borrower's circumstances and the lender's underwriter would have to approve the decision.

This will also vary in different economic climates. It will be more acceptable during good economic times when property values are steady or increasing. If 18 months of income is needed to qualify, the lender should be given the scenario prior to submitting the application because this practice is not as commonly used as it has been in the past.

> *Example: The borrower has been employed by the same company for more than five years and was promoted to a management position one year ago. They were a wage earner prior to the promotion and they are now a salaried employee with a considerable increase in pay.*

There are many circumstances that could apply to different borrowers and every underwriter will view them differently. What one underwriter will decline, another underwriter will approve. The broker/processor can call the lender and speak to the representative (rep), the underwriter, or the processor to discuss an unusual situation prior to submission if there is any doubt. If there is a situation that the broker/processor views as acceptable, they should work with it and do their best to convince the lender of the validity. *A strong cover letter with the submission package to explain any circumstances is always helpful.*

SALARIED EMPLOYEES' INCOME does not vary and determining the current monthly income establishes the qualifying income to be used for the borrower. Averaging is not necessary. The net income or before tax income is used for qualifying.

> Salaried employees are the easiest to calculate. *Part II Section 12A* of the verification of employment (VOE) states the current gross base pay and states how the income is paid:

1. **ANNUAL:** Divide the figure provided by twelve. Verify by comparing to YTD paystub by dividing the YTD income by the number of months worked. For example, 6/1/01 would require that the YTD income be divided by 5 because the employee has been paid from January through May. As a confirmation, add the previous two years W2s and divide that figure by 24 (total number of months). *These figures are not likely to match exactly but should be close enough to confirm the current income and the probability of*

continued income.

The W2s will be considered accurate, but large differences will be questioned and may be an **indication of fraud.** Compare the current-year income with the amount stated on the YTD paystub. Most paystubs will show a "base pay" amount and will include a year-to-date (YTD) income amount. Divide the YTD figure by the number of months to compare with the monthly income figure derived. Does it match? **The broker/ processor must use common sense.** If the figures are not comparable, the borrower should be questioned.

2. MONTHLY: The amount stated on the VOE is used and confirmed by comparing it to the YTD paystub by dividing the YTD income and adding the previous two years' W2s and dividing that figure by 24 (total number of months). *These figures are not likely to match but should be close enough to confirm the current income and the probability of continued income.*

3. BI-WEEKLY (every two weeks): Bi-weekly refers to being paid every 2 weeks. The bi-weekly amount is multiplied by 26 (52 weeks per year divided by 2 = 26) then divided by 12 to determine the monthly income. Twenty-six is one half of 52, so again, the annual amount is derived in order to determine the most accurate monthly income. Bi-weekly paystubs will have a pay date for the same day every other week such as every other Friday.

> *Example: A person receives $1,500 every two weeks:*
> *$1,500 x 26 =$39,000 annual income*
> *$39,000 ÷ 12 = $3,250 monthly income*

4. BI-MONTHLY (twice monthly): Using the same figures is less and easily confused with bi-weekly. Bi-monthly (usually paid the first and 15th of every month) in which case, the monthly income is calculated by multiplying the bi- monthly net income by two to obtain the monthly income. Checking the dates on the paystubs will verify the type of pay schedule, whether bi-weekly or bi- monthly. Requesting that the borrower provide a full month of pay stubs helps to clarify and confirm the pay schedule to determine the qualifying income properly.

> *Example: Using the same $1,500 twice a month:*
> *$1,500 x 2 = $3,000 monthly income*

5. **WEEKLY:** Is calculated by multiplying the figure provided by fifty-two for each week of the year and dividing by 12 to derive the monthly income. *There are not four weeks in every month*; therefore, multiplying weekly income by 52 weeks will properly calculate the annual income.

> *Example: Using $750 per week:*
> *$750 x 52 = $39,000 annual income*
> *$39,000 ÷ 12 = $3,250 monthly income*

WAGE EARNER INCOME varies and will need to be averaged over a two-year period.

1. **HOURLY EMPLOYEES:** must be averaged for at least 18 months, but most lenders require that a full 24-month period and 2 years of employment in the same line of work must be verified. The following steps are used to determine the average income allowable for an hourly employee.
   a.) Add the figures in Section 1 of the W2 from the two prior years and add this figure to the YTD gross income on the paystub. Divide the total by the number of months' income being used. *See Figure 27, W2s; and Figure 28, Paystub.*

> *Example 1:*

$67,832.86	'08 W2
+64,362.16	'07 W2
$132,195.02	*Total*
+ 55,168.62	'09 YTD Gross thru 10/18/09 or 9.5 months (Note: OT included)
$187,363.64	**Total income months (12-'07 + 12-'08, + 9.5 mos. YTD/'05)**
÷ 33.5	Months (12- '07 + 12-'08 + 9.5 mos. YTD/2009)
=**$5,592.94**	**33.5 mos. average monthly income**

If the loan application was taken in June or later, an 18-month average may be considered. This may result in a higher monthly income if the most recent year and YTD include pay raises, and there have been 6 months of verified income for this year. You will note the borrower recently received a pay raise in section 19 of the VOE. If the pay raise had been so recent that it has not yet appeared on the paystub, a new paystub showing that raise would be required to be able to use that income for qualifying.

If section 16 indicates a pay raise is due before close of escrow, verification on receipt of that raise will be acceptable if needed for qualifying or as a compensating factor for a high debt ratio.

b.) The W2s do not give a breakdown of base pay and overtime so the total is all calculated as base income on the 1003. The VOE asks to have these forms of income declared separately; however, this section of the VOE is not always prepared in detail by the employer. This is acceptable, but the underwriter may request the details. If this happens, the person who prepared the VOE must be contacted requesting that they complete the form in more detail.

A new VOE can be faxed to them including a copy of the original VOE which will be helpful. It may be requested that they return the completed VOE by fax as soon as possible and mail the original. If it is not possible to obtain a more complete VOE, requesting year-end paystubs from the borrower for the two W2 years will provide a complete breakdown of base pay and overtime pay. The broker/processor should also write a processor's cert explaining the situation.

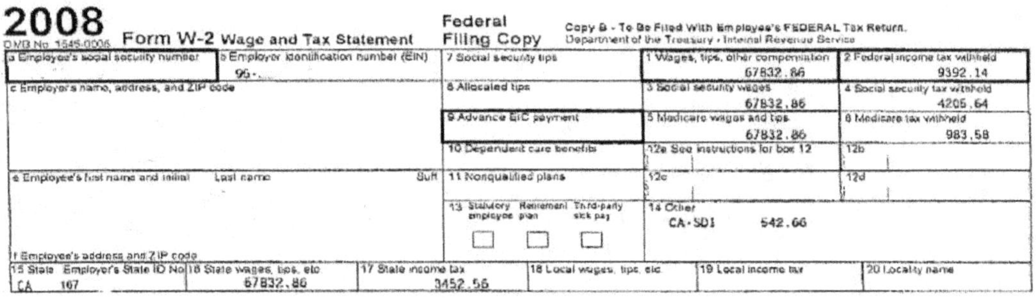

2008 Form W-2 Wage and Tax Statement
OMB No. 1545-0008
Federal Filing Copy
Copy B - To Be Filed With Employee's FEDERAL Tax Return. Department of the Treasury - Internal Revenue Service

a Employee's social security number
b Employer identification number (EIN): 95-
c Employer's name, address, and ZIP code
e Employee's first name and initial | Last name | Suff.
f Employee's address and ZIP code
1 Wages, tips, other compensation: 67832.86
2 Federal income tax withheld: 9392.14
3 Social security wages: 67832.86
4 Social security tax withheld: 4205.64
5 Medicare wages and tips: 67832.86
6 Medicare tax withheld: 983.58
7 Social security tips
8 Allocated tips
9 Advance EIC payment
10 Dependent care benefits
11 Nonqualified plans
12a See instructions for box 12 | 12b | 12c | 12d
13 Statutory employee | Retirement plan | Third-party sick pay
14 Other: CA-SDI 542.66
15 State: CA | Employer's State ID No: 167
16 State wages, tips, etc.: 67832.86
17 State income tax: 3452.56
18 Local wages, tips, etc.
19 Local income tax
20 Locality name

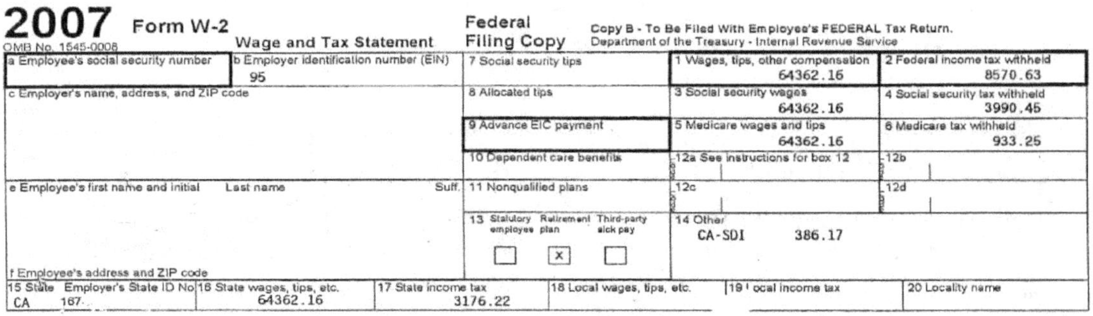

2007 Form W-2 Wage and Tax Statement
OMB No. 1545-0008
Federal Filing Copy
Copy B - To Be Filed With Employee's FEDERAL Tax Return. Department of the Treasury - Internal Revenue Service

a Employee's social security number
b Employer identification number (EIN): 95
c Employer's name, address, and ZIP code
e Employee's first name and initial | Last name | Suff.
f Employee's address and ZIP code
1 Wages, tips, other compensation: 64362.16
2 Federal income tax withheld: 8570.63
3 Social security wages: 64362.16
4 Social security tax withheld: 3990.45
5 Medicare wages and tips: 64362.16
6 Medicare tax withheld: 933.25
7 Social security tips
8 Allocated tips
9 Advance EIC payment
10 Dependent care benefits
11 Nonqualified plans
12a See instructions for box 12 | 12b | 12c | 12d
13 Statutory employee | Retirement plan [X] | Third-party sick pay
14 Other: CA-SDI 386.17
15 State: CA | Employer's State ID No: 167
16 State wages, tips, etc.: 64362.16
17 State income tax: 3176.22
18 Local wages, tips, etc.
19 Local income tax
20 Locality name

Figure 27: W2s

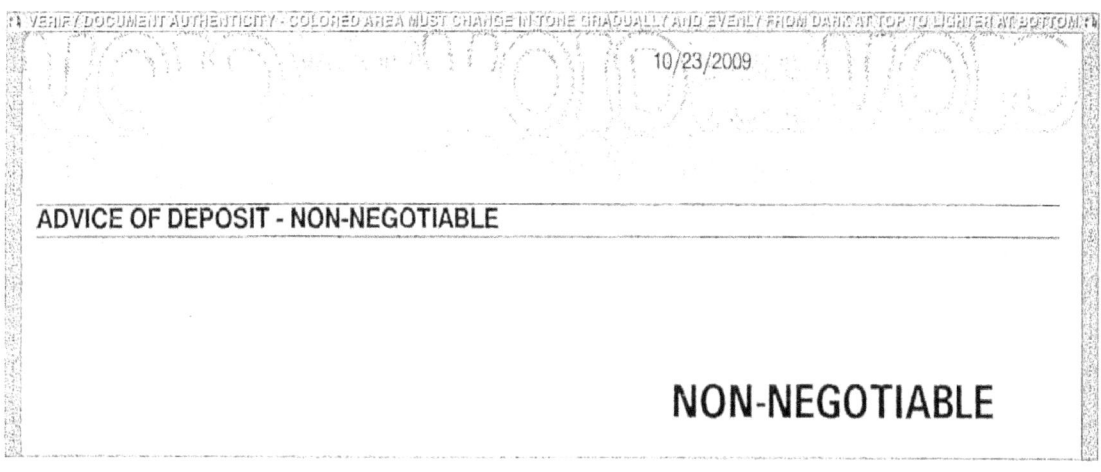

VERIFY DOCUMENT AUTHENTICITY - COLORED AREA MUST CHANGE IN TONE GRADUALLY AND EVENLY FROM DARK AT TOP TO LIGHTER AT BOTTOM

10/23/2009

ADVICE OF DEPOSIT - NON-NEGOTIABLE

NON-NEGOTIABLE

THE ORIGINAL DOCUMENT HAS AN ARTIFICIAL WATERMARK ON THE BACK   HOLD AT AN ANGLE TO VIEW WHEN CHECKING THE ENDORSEMENT.

REMOVE DOCUMENT ALONG THIS PERFORATION

Employee			Emp ID	Social Security	Status		Exemptions/Allowances		Number
					Single		US-4/0 CA-4/0		
Code		Paygroup	Division	Department	Hire Date	Period Start	Period End		Pay Date
		2	01			10/05/09	10/18/09		10/23/09

Taxable Earnings	Rate	Units	Current	Year To Date	Paid Time Off	Current Accrued	Current Taken	Balance	Limit
Regular Pay	30.1200	78.75	2,371.95	44,434.53	Plan				
Overtime	45.1800	0.50	22.59	4,845.62	SICK	-	-	-	48.00
Sick Pay	-	-	-	1,204.80	VACATION	3.02	-	41.03	80.00
Vacation Pay	-	-	-	1,777.08					
Holiday Pay	-	-	-	1,686.72					
Correction Regular	-	-	-	835.83	Direct Deposit Accounts				Amount
Correction Overtime	-	-	-	203.32	Checking -				1,720.10
MEAL BREAK	30.1200	-	30.12	180.72					
Total			2,424.66	55,168.62					

Taxes		Current	Year To Date
Federal Income Tax		263.18	6,384.45
Social Security (FICA)		146.43	3,334.72
Federal Medicare		34.24	779.89
California Income Tax		108.12	2,505.63
California State Disability		25.97	591.64
Total		577.94	13,596.33

Pre-Tax Deductions			
Dental Insurance Pre-Tax		22.62	500.86
Medical Insurance Pre-Tax		39.23	856.48
Vision Insurance Plan Pre-Tax		1.16	25.52
Total		63.01	1,382.86

After-Tax Deductions			
Meals		31.85	631.71
Critical Illness		11.76	94.08
Whole Life		20.00	440.00
Total		63.61	1,165.79

W2 Gross		2,361.65	53,785.76

Net Pay		1,720.10	

Figure 28: Paystub

This is the preferred calculation for hourly employees and the figure should be placed in *page 2, Section V, "Base Income" of the 1003*.

Example 2:

$62,649.60	'08 Base pay
+58,489.60	'07 Base pay
=121,139.20	Total
+50,323.00	'09 YTD Gross pay thru 10/18/09 or 9.5 months (Note: OT not included)
$171,462.20	Total
÷ 33.5	months' income

c. *Part II section 12A of the VOE* confirms the borrower is an hourly employee or a wage earner, and the hourly rate. Section 15 states he is paid for 40 hours per week. Using the information provided, multiply the hourly rate by the hours worked per week. Multiply that figure by 52 weeks per year and divide that total by twelve to derive a monthly income figure.

Example 3:

$30.12	Per hour
x40	Hours per week
=$1,204.80	Weekly income
x 52	Weeks per year
=$62,649.60	Annual income
÷ by 12	Months per year
=$ 5,220.80	Average monthly income

This figure compares very closely to the figure derived in **Example 1** thereby confirming the accuracy of that figure. *This is done merely to confirm the accuracy of the other amounts; this figure is not used as it is not the actual amount of income earned by the borrower.* If there had been a large difference in the figures, the broker/ processor would then look for the reason. In the case of frequent layoffs such as for construction workers or field hands, unemployment income will be averaged for 2-years and used as "other income". Two-year unemployment must be verified using 1099s. Extended illness and maternity leaves are also acceptable reasons for decreased income. In instances where the actual income is less, the broker/ processor should look for overtime (OT) or bonus income.

The broker/processor may choose to discuss any discrepancies or missing information on the VOE by phone with the person who signed the VOE in Part IV. They can request their fax number and that they complete the needed information and re-sign, providing an original signature. It should be requested that the form be faxed back when completed (ASAP) and the original mailed to the broker's office as soon as possible. Most employers are willing to accommodate. *The broker/processor must be certain to provide the complete office address on the fax cover sheet.*

2. **OVERTIME INCOME:** will also be calculated using the information provided on the VOE in section 12B and the YTD paystub.

Example:

$ 5,183.26	'08 Overtime
+ 5,872.56	'07 Overtime
$ 11,055.82	Total 2 Year Overtime
+4,845.62	YTD Overtime
$15,901.44	Total
÷ 33.5	Total Months
=$474.67	Average Monthly Overtime

This figure is placed in Section V, Page 2 of the 1003 under borrower "overtime". Note that '09 would be included even if the overtime income for that year was $0.

Example 2 provides an actual income total earned by the borrower for a 33.5-month income figure of $5,118.28. The $5,220.80 calculated in *Example 3* shows a greater income; however, the **actual** amount calculated from paystubs and W2s will be used. The calculation in *Example 3* provides confirmation of the expected amount of qualifying income. The figure from *Example 2* is the figure to be used for qualifying this borrower and may be placed in *Section V, Page 2 of the 1003* under the borrower's "base employee income".

Lenders will each have their own required method for calculating income and because some methods may not be acceptable, the broker/processor should check with the underwriter if the debt ratio is high (greater than 40% for the front-end ratio and 46% for the back-end ratio).

3. **COMMISSIONED EMPLOYEES'** income will be calculated by using 2-years' 1099s and verification of YTD. A commissioned employee's paystubs may or may not show the YTD gross income amount, in which case, all paystubs received for the current year will be required. The underwriter may require 2-years' 1040s for commissioned employees because they generally will have unreimbursed employee expenses. These expenses are written-off their income on *IRS form 2106* and disclosed on *IRS Schedule A Line 21.*

Some commissioned employees work as independent contractors and will declare income to the IRS on *IRS Schedule C, Profit or Loss from Business.*

Salespeople, such as realtors and loan agents, are examples of commissioned employees. When doing a loan for a realtor or a mortgage broker, a lender will generally require 2-years' 1040s because they know the amount of write-offs used and the cyclical nature of the industry and the income.

Entertainment industry employees' income will be averaged for two years using W2s, 1099s, and YTD income using all YTD paystubs. They will have many employers and there will be many W2s, 1099s, and YTD paystubs. They all must be totaled and averaged by dividing the total income figure by the total number of months included.

4. **SOCIAL SECURITY INCOME,** or any other income that is not taxed, such as certain retirement incomes, will require an **award letter** and proof of the current amount. Each January, Social Security sends recipients a letter stating the amount to be received monthly for the following year. This letter, a current check, or a bank statement that shows a direct deposit, are all acceptable for verification. The monthly allotment can be grossed up by 15% or multiplied by 115% to derive the usable income.

NOTE

Underwriters will often scrutinize W2s for evidence of fraud. Federal income tax withheld should be approximately 8% or more of the wages depending on the IRS sliding scale for income tax purposes. Social Security tax withheld should be approximately 6% of the Social Security wage.

The reason for this is to compensate for the fact that taxes are not paid on this money, which allows the borrower more spendable cash in comparison to borrowers who are qualified on their gross or before-tax income.

5. **SELF-EMPLOYMENT INCOME** will be taken from the most recent two years' 1040s, *Schedule C: Profit or Loss from Business.* They may also be required to provide an YTD Profit & Loss Statement (P&L) or YTD bank statements to verify current income.

6. **RENTAL INCOME** can be taken directly from lease agreements when tax returns are not used. The total amount of rent shown on the lease is multiplied by 75% and that figure is placed in *Section VI, Page 3 of the 1003* as gross rental income. *One hundred percent of the calculations derived from Schedule E of the tax returns is used because everything is verified, unlike when the lease is used for calculating rental income.*

The purpose of using 75% of the current lease allows for vacancy loss and undisclosed maintenance expenses that are included on the tax returns. The logic is that the current tenant may move out and the property may be vacant for several months, creating a loss to the owner. This loss percentage also takes into consideration the expenses listed on Schedule E that will not appear on a lease. The figures included in Section VI, Page 3 of the 1003 under Insurance, Maintenance, Taxes, & Misc., will be figures provided by the borrower unless it is the subject property.

Example:

$1,200	*Rent per month*
x 75%	*Vacancy allowance*
=$900	*Gross rental income*

A YEAR-TO-DATE PROFIT AND LOSS STATEMENT (YTD P&L) may be required by the lender in addition to the two years' 1040s and appropriate tax schedules. The P&L may go through the end of the last quarter or through the last month. The borrower may choose to show whichever way is more desirable. The P&L will include the year-to-date gross income, all business expenses, and the net income. If the borrower prepared the P&L, they must sign it as a way of stating they prepared the document and are also taking the responsibility for the figures used. *See Figure 29, Profit & Loss Statement (P&L).*

Borrowers may have a bookkeeper, or a CPA prepare the P&L, and if so, that preparer must sign as such. The expense of having a CPA prepare a current P&L is generally prohibitive because a CPA will not prepare such a document without full documentation or without auditing the books. The cost is similar to having taxes prepared because CPAs must prepare a P&L in the same manner and with the same documentation that they require for tax returns.

If the borrower is unsure or seems to need help preparing a P&L, the broker/processor may offer to assist. The borrower may not realize or understand what is required for a P&L, in which case, offering to type the P&L on the computer for the borrower can be helpful. By doing this, the broker, processor, loan agent can ask the borrower for the gross income and direct them by explaining what is meant and what is required. Often the borrower needs to be led through the expenses by suggesting items that they actually have, such as office rent, telephone, postage, advertising, etc. Using the information and expenses provided on the previous year's Schedule C as a guide can be useful because it helps remind the borrower of their actual expenses.

The processor should compare the P&L to the prior 2-years' income generally found on IRS Schedule C. The same items should be used as expenses and YTD income should be in line with prior years. If the P&L is showing a large increase, a LOE may be required.

Examples of explanations for an increased or decreased income amount may be: ill health during an income period; perhaps the business is new and is considerably more equitable during the last quarter than the previous two years; or the business began part of the way through the first tax year provided and, therefore, was not a full year of business. Few lenders will use YTD income from a P&L, but they will look at it for comparison and confirmation from the borrower that they are still earning the same income. If a borrower provides a P&L prepared and signed by their CPA, it may be used to qualify.

NOTE

The broker/processor and MLO must never make-up figures or falsify documents. All figures and statements must come from the borrower since the figures are the borrower's. The broker/processor must only provide the service of typing and giving guidance as to the needed information. The borrower must sign the P&L.

```
Profit & Loss for XYZ Incorporated
01/01/2009 through 09/30/2009

Income:

    Income derived from sale of product:        $156,445
    Income derived for services rendered:         21,399
    Total YTD gross income:                     $177,844


Expenses:
    Rent                                         $22,500
    Phone                                          4,500
    Utilities                                      3,876
    Repairs                                        1,002
    Equipment                                      8,687
    Wages                                         28,450
    Commissions                                   18,600
    Total Expense:                               $87,615

YTD Net Income:                                  $90,229
```

Figure 29: Profit & Loss Statement (P&L)

NOTE

Borrowers must have been self-employed in their current line of business for a minimum of two years to be considered for a mortgage loan.

ALTERNATIVE DOCUMENTATION (ALT DOC) can be used for the self-employed borrower as well as salaried and hourly borrowers. Some lenders will allow other documentation to verify income, and it is referred to as "alt-doc." Lenders' terminology and required documentation varies. The use of alt docs will change according to economic circumstances. There are times when the required documentation is strict, especially when there is an economic downturn and there is not as much money available. When property values are increasing and money is available, the use of alt docs will become more common.

If alt-docs are to be used, ask the chosen lender what they require and what will be acceptable for their alt-doc loan programs. Most lenders consider the following to be alt docs:

- SALARIED AND HOURLY EMPLOYEES:
  - **YTD paystub and the last 2-years W2s:** 1040s are not included in the loan package.
  - **Year-end paystub is acceptable** for a missing W2 for one year, (the last paystub in December for that year).
- **SELF-EMPLOYED BORROWERS** are more common and can include many options.
  - **24-months personal bank statements:** This is rarely accepted for standard A-paper loans.

All that is needed is Page 1 of the statement showing total deposited amounts for each month. Occasionally an underwriter will require all pages of the statements, so it is good to make a copy of all pages and keep them on the left side of the file in case they are needed later. Add the total deposits for the entire 24-month period and divide by twenty-four to acquire the average monthly income. This method has been most common with sub-prime lenders and has recently become acceptable with some A-paper lenders. If this method is to be used, the underwriter will need to verify that it meets their guidelines.

- **BUSINESS BANK STATEMENTS** will be required by some lenders. They will calculate the income by using 75% of the average monthly balance divided by the number of months.

  The logic of this method is that it confirms the total funds available to the owner of the business after expenses have been paid.

- **P&LS FOR THE LAST TWO YEARS and YTD prepared and signed by a CPA** are also considered alt docs. P&Ls prepared by a CPA are expensive because the CPA audits them, and it is not acceptable to require audited P&Ls. They are rarely used because of the extra cost associated with them.

STATED-INCOME LOAN PROGRAMS and **NO-INCOME NO-ASSET (NINA) LOAN PROGRAMS** were major contributing factors in the recent loan crisis and are no longer available.

The lender will usually perform a **QUALITY CONTROL (QC) AUDIT** prior to funding the loan or, in some cases, prior to approval.

The lender will contact the information operator and request the phone listing for the business to confirm the information given in Section IV Page 2 of the original 1003. If the borrower has provided a number that is their own extension, the main phone number for the company should be acquired.

This is a good opportunity for the broker/processor to do some quality control work by calling the information operator and handling any issues before the loan is submitted to the lender. The company's main line should be the number on the type 1003 because they will need to speak to someone other than the borrower to confirm employment. The lender may choose to contact the person that prepared the VOE to confirm that the information is accurate.

For a self-employed borrower, the lender will call information to obtain the phone number for the borrower's business and call the number to verify the business exists and that the phone is answered in the business name. Small businesses may use their **home phone as their business phone,** which will be questioned by the lender and must make sense for the type of business. If this is the case, the lender will call the number during business hours to see if it is answered as the business stated. A cleaning service or consultants are examples of small, in-home businesses. Many small businesses will use a cell phone number as their business number, and this is acceptable for many types of businesses.

ANALYZING TAX RETURNS

ANALYZING TAX RETURNS, IRS 1040s: The complete and most recent two years' income tax returns are required when qualifying the borrower's income. If the prior year is not available because the borrowers have filed for an extension, the extension must be in the file and the two prior years' returns must be provided.

The broker/processor should begin reviewing the income tax returns by comparing the names and addresses on the 1040s with the information the borrower has provided on the original 1003. Any question of occupancy should be addressed.

The information is to be averaged for the 2-year term, and it will be helpful to flag the first page of each year while calculating income since this requires going back- and-forth between the two.

The basic logic of the figures that will be added or subtracted is that the "hard costs" that the IRS allows the taxpayer to deduct will be subtracted from the gross income because it was a real expense. Any deductions that were not hard costs, such as depreciation, will be added back into the gross income because there was no actual cost or out-of-pocket expense to the borrower.

SELF-EMPLOYED INCOME ANALYSIS, also known as the **cash flow analysis,** is a form that was created by FNMA and FHLMC to be used by underwriters to calculate income from tax returns. They are now available to the broker/processor on the LOSs for convenience and guidance while calculating income from tax returns. It can be helpful to use one of the two forms because they walk the broker/ processor through the complete income calculations line-by-line. Only one of the forms is needed, and the broker/ processor should choose the one they prefer working with. *See Figure 30, Self-Employed Income Analysis/ Adjusted Gross Income Method.*

> **NOTE**
>
> *The examples used here to demonstrate income calculations from tax returns will be for one year only. The broker/processor needs to remember to repeat the calculations for two years the of client's income and combine the figures and divide the total by 24 months.*

For the following explanations and uses, the adjusted gross income (AGI) method will be used. The scheduled analysis method may be more useful when calculating income for a borrower that has only self-employment income.

IRS 1040s (INDIVIDUAL INCOME TAX RETURNS) and all other IRS forms will be explained line-by-line, according to the entries allowed by the lender to determine the borrower's gross income used for qualifying for a mortgage loan.

Self-Employed Income Analysis

Borrower Name   **Sam Sample**

Property Address

General Instructions: This form is to be used as a guide in Underwriting the Self-employed borrower. The underwriter has a choice in analysing the individual Tax return by either the Schedule Analysis Method or the Adjusted Gross Income (AGI) Method.

The AGI Method begins with adjusted gross income from the individual tax returns and either increases or decreases that figure after analysing specific lines and schedules of the return. This method derives total income (both business and non-business).
If the borrower has passive activity unallowed losses or loss carryovers, use the Schedule Analysis Method of analysing income.

Adjusted Gross Income (AGI) Method

A. Individual Tax Return (1040)

  1. Adjusted Gross Income

Income Section:

  2. Wages, salary considered elsewhere   (-)

  3. Taxable Interest Income   (-)

  4. Tax-exempt Interest Income   (+)

  5. Dividend Income   (-)

  6. Taxable Refunds   (-)

  7. Alimony   (-)

  8. Business Income or Loss - Schedule C

       a. Depletion   (+)

       b. Depreciation   (+)

       c. 50% Meals and Entertainment Exclusion   (-)

  9. (-) Capital Gain or (+) Capital Loss - Schedule D

  10. IRA Distributions (non-taxable)   (+)

  11. Pensions and Annuities (non-taxable)   (+)

  12. Schedule E - Depreciation   (+)

  13. Schedule F - Depreciation   (+)

  14. Unemployment Compensation   (-)

  15. Social Security Benefits (non-taxable)   (+)

  16. Other

Adjustment Section:

  17. IRA Deduction   (+)

  18. One-Half of Self-Employed Tax   (+)

  19. Self-Employed Health Insurance   (+)

  20. Keogh Retirement Plan   (+)

  21. Penalty for Early Withdrawal   (+)

  22. Alimony Paid   (+)

Additional Schedules:

  23. Form 2106 Unreimbursed Expenses(not fully deductible)   (-)

  24. Form 4562 Amortization   (+)

  25. Total

Figure 30: Self-Employed Income Analysis
Page 1 of 2

Complete sections B, C, and D, only if the borrower needs more income to qualify for the loan than is shown in section A and the borrower has the legal right to draw additional income from the business to qualify for the loan.

B. Corporate Tax Return Form (1120) - Corporate Income to qualify the borrower will be considered only if the borrower can provide evidence of access to the funds.

1. Taxable Income (Tax and Payments Section)	(+) _____	_____	_____
2. Total Tax (Tax and Payments Section)	(-) _____	_____	_____
3. Depreciation (Deductions Section)	(+) _____	_____	_____
4. Depletion (Deductions Section)	(+) _____	_____	_____
5. Mortgages, notes bonds payable in less than one year (Balance Sheets Section)	(-) _____	_____	_____
6. Subtotal	_____	_____	_____
7. Times individual percentage of ownership	x _____ %	x _____ %	x _____ %
8. Subtotal	_____	_____	_____
9. Dividend Income reflected on the borrower's individual income tax returns	(-) _____	_____	_____
10. Total Income available to borrower	_____	_____	_____

C. S Corporation Tax Returns (Form 1120s) or Partnership Tax Returns (Form 1065) - Partnership or S Corporation income to qualify the borrower will be considered only if the borrower can provide evidence of access to the funds.

1. Depreciation (Deductions Section)	(+) _____	_____	_____
2. Depletion (Deductions Section)	(+) _____	_____	_____
3. Mortgages, notes bonds payable in less than one year (Balance Sheets Section)	(-) _____	_____	_____
4. Subtotal	_____	_____	_____
5. Times individual percentage of ownership	x _____ %	x _____ %	x _____ %
6. Total income available to borrower	_____	_____	_____
Total Income Available (add A, B, C)	I _____	II _____	III _____

D. Year-to-Date Profit and Loss

Year-to-Date income to qualify the borrower will be considered only if that income is in the line with the previous year's earnings or if audited financial statements are provided.

1. Salary/Draws to Individual $ _____
2. Total Allowable add back _____ x _____ % of individual ownership = $ _____

3. Total net profit _____ x _____ % of individual ownership = $ _____
4. Total $ _____

Combined Total I, II, III, YTD = $ _____ divided by _____ months = $ _____ Monthly Average

This form is only a reference to help organize information from the tax returns.

Figure 30: Self-Employed Income Analysis
Page 2 of 2

INCOME

LINE 7 is the borrower's base income that has already been figured using the W2s. The CFA refers to this income as non-self-employed wages.

LINES 8a, 8b, 9a, and 9b are dividend and interest income that is totaled for both years of the 1040s. Divide the 2-year total by 24 (months) and put the figure in *Section V, Page 2 of the 1003* as dividend/interest income.

Bank statements and VODs should be used as comparatives to verify sufficient funds to continue producing the income as averaged. If the loan is a purchase transaction and the funds will be depleted to complete the purchase, the dividend and interest income should not be used for qualifying. Common sense should be used to determine the amount of funds needed to close escrow and the remaining balance required for asset reserves. Place the amounts for each year on the appropriate line of the *Self-Employed Income Analysis; Section A, Lines 3, 4, and 5 appropriately.*

These figures will be subtracted for the total income on the self-employed income analysis form, as the adjusted gross income (AGI) because it is being credited to the borrower's Income on the 1003.

LINE 10: includes taxable refunds and state tax refunds. These items cannot be used for income and must be deducted. Tax refunds are actually income that was already claimed. These figures should be placed on *Line 6 of Section A of the Income Analysis Form.*

LINE 11 is alimony that has been received. Add this figure with the figure in Line 11 of the previous year and divide it by 24. Place this figure in *Section V, Page 2 under other income.*

In the other income section, it must be determined whether the income belongs to the borrower (B) or the co-borrower (C) in the first column. Describe the income as "alimony" in the second column and place the total income amount in the third column. A copy of the complete divorce decree will be required as part of the package. If the alimony will not continue for at least three additional years, it cannot be included as qualifying income. The figure will be placed in *Section A Line 7 of the Income Analysis.*

LINE 12 tells us if the borrower is **self-employed** and will be using **Schedule C** to calculate the income. *Income Analysis Section A, Lines 8a-8c*

LINE 13 and 14 refers to Schedule 4797 or Schedule D capital gains and losses. *Schedule D will be used to calculate this income.*

LINES 15a and b, and 16a and b are either draws from retirement accounts or may indicate ongoing retirement income. The amounts shown in 15a or 16a were tax exempt according to IRS, but the income was received by the borrower and can be added into the total income figure.

If the borrower is drawing a regular income from these sources, the income will be used if it is ongoing. An **award letter** is required for documentation. This will be requested from the Borrower. *Section A, Line 10 of the Income Analysis.*

If the income is received as one large draw, such as from an annuity or a 401k, it must be clarified as a draw and not included in the total income figure because this is a one-time occurrence and will not continue.

LINE 17 is supplemental income such as rental, royalty, corporation, or partnership income. Rental or royalty income is calculated on Schedule E. If a partnership income, the borrower must provide an IRS K1 or partner's share of income and form 1065, return of partnership income. Corporation income will be on a form 1120 or 1120S.

LINE 18 is farm income and if there is a figure in this space, Schedule F must be checked for several issues to the loan file as a conventional loan.

If the property that is producing the farm income is the subject property, and the income derived from this property cannot exceed 25% of the borrower's total income, as it may indicate that the property is a commercial or agricultural property. Residential lenders will not provide a loan on this property.

The broker/processor can run a property profile through the title company to check the property for zoning and acreage. Property zoned as agricultural or commercial can only be financed as such. Few lenders of residential mortgages will loan on properties of more than 25 acres and many lenders limit acreage to seven acres. The lender should be contacted for guidelines prior to submission if there are any questions.

LINE 19 shows unemployment income and is acceptable with jobs that have regular layoffs, such as farm workers, construction laborers, and the entertainment industry. This income must be documented with two years averaged and verified with the 1099s. Income Analysis Section A, Line 14.

Example:

$690   *'08 1099G*
+5,060   *'07 1099G*
=$5,750   *Total 2-year income*
÷ 24   *Months*
$239.58   *Average monthly Unemployment Income rounded to $240*

This figure is placed in *Section V, Page 2 of the 1003* as unemployment under **other income.**

LINE 20a and 20b are Social Security income. The figure in 20a is tax exempt, but is actual income, and is therefore usable with the full amount received used for qualifying. The 1099s, award letter for the current year, and a current check, or bank statement if automatically deposited, are required.

The current amount received may be increased by 115% because the recipient is not usually paying income tax on this income. If the borrower is being taxed on any part of the Social Security income, that amount will be in the right-hand column and will not be grossed up by 115%. The figure is placed in Section V, Page 2 of the 1003 as either base income or other income depending on other income received. Income Analysis Section A, Line 15.

LINE 21 is for other income and can be used if there is a 2-year average and is documented. If the income amount displayed is a negative figure, it will be subtracted, which will reduce the total income. CFA, Sect. A, line 9.

ADJUSTED GROSS INCOME

LINE 31a is alimony paid by the borrower and requires documentation in the form of a divorce decree.

This is a debt owed by the borrower.

The figure is a monthly obligation, and the monthly amount will not be taken directly from the divorce decree. It will be derived by dividing the figure on line 31a of the two most recent years 1040 by twenty-four.

The divorce decree is used to verify the obligation and to prove that it will be ongoing for at least three more years. If it will not last for three additional years, it does not need to be included in the borrower's obligations. The figure derived is to be included in the liabilities in Section VI, Page 3 of the 1003 under assets and liabilities. Income Analysis Section A, Line 22.

LINE 37 is the adjusted gross income. This is the figure used for determining the amount of income taxes to be paid. *Income Analysis Section A, Line 1.*

When using the income analysis, the broker/processor will start with this amount and add or subtract accordingly to arrive at the income amount acceptable to a lender.

SIGN HERE at the bottom of Page 2 of the 1040 is checked to confirm the borrower's occupation is the same as stated on the 1003.

SCHEDULE A- ITEMIZED DEDUCTIONS:
SCHEDULE A
LINE 6 is confirmation of real estate or property taxes.

The broker/processor should make note of the amount of property taxes paid in comparison to the property they currently own. This can signify or suggest the value of property owned and may be helpful if the borrower owns more than one property. Since this is used only for the taxpayer's principal residence, this should be compared to the subject property's tax amount shown in the prelim and the 1003 Section V, Page 2, combined monthly housing expense. This may disclose the borrower's residence if there is a question of occupancy, or it may reflect the sale of a former home, which may also establish assets. It must make sense.

LINES 10 AND 11 TAXES YOU PAID AND INTEREST YOU PAID will be looked at merely as a comparison to confirm the borrower's residence the same as Line 6.

LINE 21 UNREIMBURSED EMPLOYEE EXPENSES must be checked for any expenses that are necessary for the job but are not paid by the employer.

These expenses are those that are a real part of the borrower's employment and are not reimbursed by the employer. Included in these expenses are items such as tools for a mechanic, uniforms for a waitress, or mileage for a salesperson. A form 2106 must be included with the 1040s if the taxpayer is claiming the expenses. These expenses are subtracted from and reduces the borrower's total W2 income. Income Analysis Section A, Line 23.

SCHEDULE C PROFIT OR LOSS FROM BUSINESS SCHEDULE C:

Schedule C, profit or loss from business and is used for self-employed borrowers.

- **LINE A** confirms the type of industry or employment as declared by the borrower on the original 1003.
- **LINE 31** is the **net profit or loss** and will be used as our basis to add or subtract the usable income.
- **LINES 12 and 13 depreciation and depletion** are not hard cost. They are deductions allowed for decreasing value of equipment, etc. These figures are **added to** the total net income figure from line 31. Income Analysis Section A, Line 8a and 8b.
- **LINE 24** is an actual hard cost as it is entertainment for clients; however, the IRS allows only half of these costs to be deducted.
- **LINE 24b** is one half of this **actual cost** and is to be **subtracted** from the total net income figure. Income analysis Section A, Line 8c.

> *Example: Only one year is included in this calculation. When actually calculating income from the tax returns, repeat the steps for the previous year and combine both to derive at a 24-month period.*

$36,000	*Net annual income*
+2,000	*Depletion*
+500	*Depreciation*
-200	*½ deduction for entertainment expense*
$5,000	*Business use of home*
=$43,300	**Total net annual income**
÷12	**Months**
=$3608.33	**Monthly average income**

This figure is placed in *Section V, Page 2 of the 1003* unless the borrower has income from another job in which case the figure will be placed under "**other income**" and described as "**schedule C income**".

- **LINE 30 expenses for business use of home** is added to the net income or loss figure as this figure is a deduction for the actual monthly housing expense that has already been calculated in *Section V, Page 2 of the 1003*. Leaving this figure as a reduction of income would be the same as deducting the housing expense twice form the borrower's income. This is not allowed on the income analysis form but is an actual and usable adjustment to the income.

Schedule D Capital Gains and Losses

Schedule D: Capital gains and losses

- **LINE 7**, if there is a positive or negative figure, there is a short-term gain (positive) or a short-term loss (negative).
  - **Short-term gains** are **subtracted** from the total income figure because this is income that will not continue. The figures will be averaged for 24 months.
  - **Short-term losses** are **added** into any total income figure because the loss will not be continuing.

- **LINE 15** is **Long-term gain or loss** and will be included in the total income figure. This figure is to be placed in Section V, page 2 of the 1003 under other income as capital gain (plus) or loss (minus).

  - **CAPITAL GAINS** that continue for at least three years (long term) will show as a positive (plus) figure and can be added to the income.

  - **CAPITAL LOSSES** that will continue for at least three years (long term) will show as a negative (minus) and must be deducted from the borrower's income. This is not allowed in the income analysis, but the gain or loss has an actual effect on the income and should be calculated if it will continue.

> **NOTE**
>
> *The rule of thumb is that any income that will not continue for more than three years cannot be used for qualifying.*

This income is considered to be continuing for more than three years because it is an investment, and investment accounts are typically rolled over to other investment accounts on an ongoing basis. The logic regarding investment accounts is much the same as the logic regarding savers: that a person who saves regularly will continue to save, and a person who pays their debts on time will continue to pay their debts on time. The broker/ processor must confirm that the investment funds are not being used to close the transaction.

Schedule E supplemental income: This form is most often used for rental income and royalty Income.

- **LINE 22 income or loss** is the figure to begin with and to add or subtract the other figures.

- **LINE 20 depreciation** is added to that amount. Depreciation is not a hard expense or an actual cash out-of-pocket expense and can, therefore, be included in the qualifying income.

- **LINES 9, 12, and 16 insurance, interest paid, and property taxes** are housing expenses that have been included on the 1003 in Section V, proposed housing expense. If the loan is a refinance for a rental property, these expenses will be included in Section VI, assets & liabilities, schedule of real estate owned (SREO), if the loan is for another property.

The same calculations of the prior year's returns are averaged, and the amount is derived by dividing by 24 months. The figure remaining is the rental income figure to be placed in Section VI, Page 3 of the 1003 as gross rental income.

The figures from lines 9 and 16 from both years are to be added and divided by 24 months. This figure is placed in Section VI, Page 3 as insurance, maintenance, taxes, & misc. The other expenses are all variable and controllable and therefore not used for qualifying purposes. For instance, the borrower (landlord) can eliminate a gardener and require that the tenant maintain the yard.

> **NOTE**
>
> *Not all underwriters will allow this income, whether positive or negative. They may view it as an uncertain income, even though FNMA and FHLMC allow it.*

The mortgage amount for Section VI, Page 3 of the 1003 is figured either from the credit report or, if it is the subject property, the amounts for the new loan will be used.

> *Example: Only one year is included in the following calculation. When actually calculating income from the tax returns, repeat the steps for the previous year and combine for a 24-month period.*

-$568	*Line 22 Net income/loss*
+9,294	*Line 20-depreciation*
+850	*Line 9-insurance*
+7,244	*Line 12-mortgage interest*
+1,875	*Line 16-taxes*
=8,695	***Total income***
÷ 12	*Number of months*
=$1,558	***Average monthly income***

Prior year calculations will be included and divided by twenty-four for an actual rental income figure.

RENTAL INCOME can be taken directly from lease agreements when tax returns are not used. The total amount of rent shown on the lease is multiplied by 75%, and the figure is placed in Section VI, Page 3 of the 1003 as gross rental income.

One hundred percent of the calculations derived from Schedule E of the tax returns is used because everything is verified, unlike when the lease is used in calculating rental income. The purpose of using 75% of the current lease is to allow for vacancy loss and undisclosed maintenance expenses that are included in the tax returns. The logic is that the current tenant may move out and the property may be vacant for several months, creating a loss to the owner. This loss percentage also takes into consideration the expenses listed on Schedule E that will not appear on a lease. The figures included in Section VI, Page 3 of the 1003 under insurance, maintenance, taxes, & misc., will be figures provided by the borrower unless it is the subject property.

$1,200	*Rent per month*
x 75%	*Vacancy allowance*
=$900	*Gross rental income*

The figures calculated in Section VI, Page 3 of the 1003 will also be entered in Section V, Page 2 as net rental income if Column 2 has been marked "R," as rental property.

SCHEDULE F, PROFIT OR LOSS FROM FARMING

If the borrower has filed a Schedule F, the broker/processor must check the address of the agricultural property. If it is the subject property, the amount of farm income cannot exceed 25% of the borrower's gross income to be considered a residential property. If the income does exceed the 25% limit, the property is considered agricultural or commercial, even if it is zoned as residential. The borrower will need to obtain an appropriate loan.

1065 U. S. PARTNERSHIP RETURN OF INCOME

The 1065 is the schedule used for the actual partnership entity. This should be looked at merely as a confirmation of the total income. Schedule K-1 (Form 1065) is the form for income earned by each individual partner. The 1065 must be included in the loan file as part of the 1040s.

- **LINE 16a and 16c** include depreciation and depletion, which are not actual expenses and therefore, are added back into the borrower's income using Schedule K1.

Schedule K-1 Partner's share of income, credits, deductions, etc.

K-1: Partner's identifying number, or Social Security number, name and address should match the rest of the 1040s and loan file.

- **LINE J** states the percentage of ownership of the business the individual partner owns.

If the borrower is claiming a business account as personal assets, the percentage of ownership is particularly important. If not 100% ownership, all other partners would need to write a letter releasing the needed funds to the borrower.

- **LINE L** declares the total amount of capital contributed during the year by the individual partner. This amount must be subtracted from the income.

Partnership income must have a 24 month, or 2-year, history. If there is only a 12- month history, the figure is still divided by twenty-four because all income is averaged for a 2-year period. This may provide an insignificant figure and has to be included in the income section of the 1003. This may actually be helpful if the debt ratio is high, and the loan is questionable. If the K-1 shows the borrower owns 25% or more of the partnership, IRS form 1065 is required and this is considered a major part of the borrower's income.

1120 CORPORATE RETURNS: Check and compare Sections A through E against information given and question any discrepancies. Form 1120 is used for corporations. An 1120S is for corporations that fall under Sub-Chapter S Incorporation Laws. For loan qualifying purposes, both forms are viewed the same.

- **LINE 28 Taxable Income** is the figure used to begin the calculations.
- **LINES 20 - 21 Depreciation and Depletion** are added to the figure because they were not actual "out-of-pocket" costs. Place this figure on the CFA, Section IV, line A.

PAGE 2, SCHEDULE E COMPENSATION TO OFFICERS discloses the borrower's percentage of ownership. If the borrower owns 100% of the corporation, the income derived can be credited to them for qualifying because it is their income, even if they did not remove the additional funds from the business. It is theirs to take any time they choose to do so. There are many underwriters and lenders who do not accept the funds as income if it were not removed from the business accounts to the personal accounts. If the additional income is needed for the borrower to qualify for the loan, it is recommended that the broker/ processor contact the lender for their guidelines.

PAGE 5, Schedule L, Line 1 and Line 28 will disclose any cash assets available to the borrower which may be required to close escrow or may be used to establish reserves. If the borrower owns less than 100% of the corporation, the other owners and officers must provide a letter stating the amount of cash assets owned by the borrower for use as private funds. CFA, Section IV, line F-b.

If the borrower owns 100% of a corporation, the return will be scrutinized more thoroughly as the income or loss will probably have more effect on the determination of eligibility for the loan.

VALIDATION OF INCOME

4506-T REQUEST FOR TRANSCRIPT OF TAX FORM is used to verify income with the IRS. The 4506-T requests that IRS provide the transcripts, which are a line-by-line printout of the figures reported on the returns. The lender will generally require this form to verify income prior to docs. The form is valid for 90 days from the date it is signed. This is a two-page form, and the borrower must be provided both pages, although only Page 1 is shown here. Page 2 provides general instructions.

The lender uses the form to verify income if they feel there is a question about the income used to qualify. Lenders used to hold the 4506, which only requests the AGI figure, as a means of verifying income if the borrower defaulted on their loan within the first three months after close of escrow. Now the 4506-T is used as a Prior to Doc Condition to verify the income before it becomes a problem.

The lender cannot legally require these forms for a stated-income loan, but they can refuse to grant the loan if the borrower refuses to sign. Borrowers often feel uncomfortable signing these forms and should be assured that it is standard practice by the lender. If the borrower is uncomfortable signing either form, it may be an indication of fraud, and the broker/ processor and loan agent should discuss the issue and be diligent with verification.

IRS will not accept or process any 4506-T forms that are:
- Incomplete.
- Handwritten.
- Have whiteout.
- Illegible in any way.
- Small font size.
- Reduced size of the faxed form.
- Name, address, or SS# cannot have been scratched out, or changed in any way.
- Line 5 cannot have changed in any way the original company is the only acceptable one; Cannot use "c/o."
- A married couple on the 1040s requires only one signature; tt can be either spouse.
- Telephone number of the taxpayer must be included.

CHAPTER 10
VERIFICATION AND DOCUMENTATION

VERIFICATION OF ASSETS

VERIFICATION OF DEPOSIT (VOD) provides the current balances of the borrower's bank and investment accounts. The current balance is always the figure used on the final/typed 1003. See Figure 31, Verification of Deposit/VOD.

COMPUTERIZATION has allowed many changes to the financing process. Banking on-line has become so commonplace that the VOD is no longer used on a regular basis. It is easy for a borrower to obtain a copy of the current statement online, eliminating the need for the VOD. The lender has the right to request a VOD and may do so if there is a reason to question the information provided or for a borrower who is not computerized. It is important to remember that the majority of the population is computerized.

VOD, PART II: States the type of account, account number, current balance, average balance for previous two months, and the date the account was opened. The depository's current figures are recorded in the cash or market value column of Section VI, Assets, on Page 3 of the 1003. Changes by the depository to any account numbers or additional accounts should be noted. Corrections are made on page three of the 1003.

The depository must provide the average balance for the previous 2-month period. If this information is not provided, the person in Part III who prepared the form can be contacted and requested to provide that information. Some depositories will not provide this information; in this situation, a processor's cert will suffice according to the actual conversation with the preparer of the VOD.

If they are willing to provide the additional information requested, the broker/ processor can forward the VOD and request a new signature before returning the original signature by mail. In the past, live signatures have been required; however, use of the computer has enabled the broker/lender to accept documents that have been emailed or faxed.

Whiteout cannot be used on these forms. Faxing or emailing a copy to the preparer who requests that changes where the whiteout was used be initialed, as well as a live signature, is acceptable. This verifies accurate figures in spite of the use of whiteout.

Request for Verification of Deposit

Privacy Act Notice: This information is to be used by the agency collecting it or its assignees in determining whether you qualify as a prospective mortgagor under its program. It will not be disclosed outside the agency except as required and permitted by law. You do not have to provide this information, but if you do not your application for approval as a prospective mortgagor or borrower may be delayed or rejected. The information requested in this form is authorized by Title 38, USC, Chapter 37 (if VA); by 12 USC, Section 1701 et seq (if HUD/FHA); by 42 USC, Section 1452b (if HUD/CPD); and Title 42 USC, 1471 et seq., or 7 USC, 1921 et seq (if USDA/FmHA).

Instructions: Lender - Complete items 1 through 8. Have applicant complete item 9. Forward directly to depository named in item 1.
Depository - Please complete items 10 through 18 and return directly to lender named in item 2.
The form is to be transmitted directly to the lender and is not to be transmitted through the applicant(s) or any other party.

Lender's Phone No.

Part I - Request

1. To (Name and address of depository)

2. From (Name and address of lender)

I certify that this verification has been sent directly to the bank or depository and has not passed through the hands of the applicant or any other interested party.

3. Signature of Lender | 4. Title | 5. Date | 6. Lender's No. (Optional)

7. Information To Be Verified

Type of Account	Account in Name of	Account Number	Balance
			$
			$
			$
			$

To Depository: I/We have applied for a mortgage loan and stated in my/our financial statement that the balance on deposit with you is as shown above. You are authorized to verify this information and to supply the lender identified above with the information requested in items 10 through 13. Your response is solely a matter of courtesy for which no responsibility is attached to your institution or any of your officers.

8. Name and Address of Applicant(s)

9. Signature of Applicant(s)

X

X

To Be Completed by Depository

Part II - Verification of Depository

10. Deposit Accounts of Applicant(s)

Type of Account	Account Number	Current Balance	Average Balance For Previous Two Months	Date Opened
		$	$	
		$	$	
		$	$	
		$	$	

11. Loans Outstanding To Applicant(s)

Loan Number	Date of Loan	Original Amount	Current Balance	Installments (Monthly/Quarterly)	Secured By	No. of Late Payments
		$	$	$ per		
		$	$	$ per		
		$	$	$ per		

12. Please include any additional information which may be of assistance in determination of credit worthiness (Please include information on loans paid-in full in item 11 above.)

13. If the name(s) on the account(s) differ from those listed in item 7, please supply the name(s) on the account(s) as reflected by your records

Part III - Authorized Signature

Federal statutes provide severe penalties for any fraud, intentional misrepresentation, or criminal connivance or conspiracy purposed to influence the issuance of any guaranty or insurance by the VA Secretary, the U.S.D.A., FmHA/FHA Commisioner, or the HUD/CPD Assistant Secretary.

14. Signature of Depository Representative | 15. Title (Please print or type) | 16. Date

17. Please print or type name signed in item 14 | 18. Phone No.

vod.frm (11/07)

Figure 31: Verification of Deposit (VOD)

If the current balance is considerably greater than the average balance, the borrower will need to explain the increase and, in most cases, will need to document the source of the increase or source of funds. An LOE will be helpful. A canceled check and deposit receipt are normally used to verify transfer of funds from another account or gift funds. The lender wants to know that the funds have not been borrowed to close the loan, especially for a purchase.

The lender needs to confirm that if the funds have been borrowed, the borrower is able to afford repayment of that debt by including the payment in the debt ratio.

BANK STATEMENTS

BANK STATEMENTS can be used in lieu of VODs. The borrower must provide the three most recent months' bank statements. All pages of each statement will be required. Lenders may require both, but generally the statements are sufficient. There are many depositories that charge to prepare a VOD, in which case bank statements are generally accepted.

Depending on the loan package and the lender's guidelines, the underwriter may condition for a VOD if it has not been provided. This will generally happen when the borrower has barely enough funds to close escrow or if the assets are questionable. To obtain a VOD quickly, the processor may call the depository and request the email address or the fax number and the name of the person or department to whom it should be directed. On the cover letter, express the need for expediency; request a copy by return email or fax, with the original to be returned by mail.

When using bank statements only, the broker/processor should be certain that the statements do not reveal a history that is derogatory such as non-sufficient-funds (NSF) charges or negative balances. If the bank statements show consistent NSFs, it may be best to not use them and to wait for the VODs. If there are undesirable items on the bank statements, the broker/loan agent may want to discuss this with the borrower in the form of both consulting and of discovery.

NOTE

The lender should be consulted when there is a problem obtaining the requested information.

OTHER ASSETS

OTHER ASSETS may be used to close escrow and the lender will find them acceptable as long as they are verified and makes sense.

BORROWED FUNDS must be disclosed and include the terms of that loan. The payment will be included in the debt ratio. In the case of borrowed funds, the CLTV needs to be addressed if the funds are in the form of a lien or a second TD against the subject property. If the loan is a personal loan and not a lien against the property, the debt must be included in Section VI, Page 3, Liabilities, of the 1003.

GIFT FUNDS can **ONLY** be from an immediate family member such as a parent, sibling, aunt, or uncle. A copy of the check from the donor and a deposit receipt are required. Most lenders require a copy of the donor's bank statement verifying that they have the funds to give. This practice has been debated and the donor will occasionally decline to provide that information. In that event, a letter from the donor stating that they are concerned about their privacy may suffice, depending on the lender, underwriter, and the economic climate.

A GIFT LETTER will be required from the donor stating that the money is a gift and does not need to be repaid, as well as their relationship to the borrower (parent, sibling, aunt, or uncle). The donor will also be required to provide bank statements verifying that they have adequate funds to give the gift.

401K OR RETIREMENT FUNDS are generally considered a loan. The depository of such accounts will provide the borrower with a statement clarifying whether the draw on the account is a loan or merely a draw. A copy of this letter must be included in the file, and if the funds are a loan, the figure must be included as an obligation in Section VI, Page 3 of the 1003 under liabilities.

The funds actually belong to the borrower, and they will be repaying themselves. If the borrower does not repay these funds within a set period of time (usually 18 months), they will pay income taxes on the withdrawn amount. For this reason, some lenders do not require the payment to be included in the obligations. A copy of the check and deposit receipt are also required.

CASH-ON-HAND OR REPAYMENT OF A LOAN are both common explanations for balance increases. Cash-on-hand cannot be verified and is often accepted, especially with certain cultures that tend to avoid banks and keep "mattress money." An LOE is required, and it is up to the underwriter to accept or reject the explanation. Repayment of a personal loan, usually by a close friend or a relative, requires a copy of the check and the deposit receipt verifying transfer of funds. A letter from the person repaying or a copy of a written agreement between the borrower and the person who received the loan is also required.

SALE OF OTHER PROPERTY funds must be verified by a Final HUD-1/CD if escrow has closed, or an estimated closing statement from the escrow officer, and the purchase contract if escrow has not closed. The close of escrow for the property providing funds to close this loan must be prior to close of escrow, or there must be a concurrent closing.

CONCURRENT CLOSING means that escrow will close at the same time as the sale of the current property, or on the same day as the close of escrow on the purchase of the new property. Often on a purchase transaction, the borrower needs the funds from the sale of their current residence to make the down payment and cover the closing costs for their new home. Even in situations when the borrower does not need the funds from the sale of another property, the lender will require the close of the other transaction prior to funding, or they must qualify for both the new mortgage and the old mortgage including reserves.

> **NOTE**
>
> *The lender will probably run a credit report prior to funding to verify that no accounts have increased dramatically, or no new accounts have been opened indicating borrowing of funds.*

VERIFICATION OF MORTGAGE (VOM)/VERIFICATION OF RENT (VOR)

VERIFICATION OF MORTGAGE/RENT (VOM AND VOR) forms are used to verify that the borrower has been making their payments on time, the amount of those payments, how long they have been paying, the current balance, and that they are current on their payments. The information is provided in Section VI Liabilities of the 1003. **A two-year history of payments is required for this information.** Some banks will not provide the mortgage history because they report to the credit reporting agencies, or they may charge a fee to complete the form. Mortgage information can generally be verified by credit reports. The borrower may provide 24 months of canceled checks (front and back) as verification of this information.

If the borrower has been at their current residence less than two years, the processor must also send a VOM/VOR to the previous recipients of payments to complete a 24-month payment history. It is best to mail forms to all landlords or private money lenders listed on the 1003 as **time is of the essence**. If they do not respond or require a fee and the information is not on the credit report, the borrower can provide 24-months of canceled checks as verification of payment. The front and back of all checks will be required to verify that the check was actually cashed, and some underwriters will look at the date cashed as verification of timely payments.

If the borrower is currently delinquent, encourage them to bring the payment current immediately, then confirm through the credit bureau or with new verifications. The interest rate will be higher and the terms more stringent if the loan/rent is delinquent or if the borrower has a history of late payments ('lates'). In these cases, the borrower will not qualify for an A-paper loan. Hard money/sub- prime loans will be discussed later. In some instances, the lender will require 24- months of canceled checks for verification. Generally, this is necessary when verifying rent, when the borrower has been renting from the seller, or in a situation where the person providing the information has a personal interest or is a private individual, rather than an institutional lender. The lender may be concerned that the landlord or current recipient of payments may have ulterior motives for providing inaccurate information regarding the borrower's payment history.

The loan agent must obtain the necessary information, such as names and addresses, from the borrower immediately. VORs often require a second request, especially when requesting information from an individual. Record the date the request was mailed on the tracking log. The form must be signed, a credit authorization attached, and it must be mailed as soon as possible. Highlighting the areas that need to be completed and signed is helpful for the recipient of the form in order to complete it quickly and properly.

These forms should be mailed with a return envelope and the broker should provide return postage. Expect a turnaround time of two weeks, on average, for verifications.

> **NOTE**
>
> *The front and back of canceled checks must be provided. The endorsement on the back of the check must match the recipient appropriately. There will be a series of numbers below the payer's signature on the front of the check. If that space is blank, the check may be fraudulent. The check was never cashed.*

VERIFICATION OF EMPLOYMENT (VOE)

The VOEs are to be sent to the borrowers' employers to be completed by them. VOEs are used only for salaried, hourly, or commissioned employees; they are never for self- employed borrowers. When the employer returns the completed form, the information will be compared to the W2s and paystubs for accuracy and conformity. The information is placed in Section V, Income, of the 1003. Discrepancies should be questioned and corrections made before submission to the lender.

The VERIFICATION OF DEPOSIT (VOD) is mailed to banks and other repositories, such as companies that manage investment or retirement accounts to verify the borrower's assets and liquidity.

For a purchase transaction, there must be sufficient funds to make the down payment, pay closing costs, and, generally, to leave an amount equal to three months' principal, interest, taxes, and insurance (PITI). A refinance transaction will require sufficient funds to close escrow and leave an amount equal to three months PITI. The exception to both transactions will be for a stated-income or investment property loans, which will generally require six months in reserves. This information is provided in Section VI, Assets, of the 1003. The bank/repository will provide you with a 3-month average balance and the current balance.

THREE MONTHS BANK STATEMENTS from the borrower may be used in lieu of the VOD, however, some lenders may still require the VOD, so it is best to send the request even when bank statements have been provided. Record the date sent in the tracking log. Sign the form; attach a credit authorization; highlight needed information; and mail with a self-addressed, stamped return envelope.

Alt-A and sub-prime lenders will accept less seasoning or, in some cases, none at all.

If any of the verifications are returned incomplete, the processor should contact the person that completed the form and explain the need for the missing information.

The form may be faxed to that person to be completed. They can fax the corrected form back to the processor and mail the copy with the corrections initialed and resigned by the preparer.

NOTE

Any returned forms with whiteout must be replaced. Whiteout is unacceptable.

A CREDIT REPORT is ordered immediately through the chosen agency. These are usually ordered online through the LOS or the credit reporting agency's website. For brokers who are not fully computerized, a credit report can also be ordered by faxing the first four pages of the 1003 to the credit reporting agency with a cover sheet stating the type of report being requested. The borrower must have signed *Section X* of the original 1003 for the credit report to be released when requesting a standard factual or residential mortgage credit report.

A RESIDENTIAL MORTGAGE CREDIT REPORT (RMCR) is rarely used but is available if a fully audited report is needed or will be helpful to the borrower. Lenders will rarely require an RMCR **or Standard Factual Credit report.** This report will have information drawn from three credit reporting agencies, and much of the information will have been confirmed by the credit reporting agency or can be at your request. An RMCR usually cost $50 to $65 and is considered thorough. It may be 24-to 48 hours before this report is received. RMCRs are considered the most accurate reports.

IN-FILE CREDIT REPORTS are generally ordered on the internet when taking the loan application or during the initial interview. Computers have made this process easy and quick. In-file reports are not audited, and the information is drawn directly from the credit repositories. The ability of lenders to immediately run a report has eliminated the need for RMCRs. The lender can quickly confirm the accuracy of the provided information. The information is drawn from one to three credit repositories and is not verified. Most brokers use three repositories and the reports that are generated are therefore called Tri-Merge Credit reports. These reports usually cost $15 to $24 and will give the processor and the agent a good idea of the borrower's credit standing immediately. An in-file credit report is ordered by providing the borrower's name, address, length of time at current address to include a two-year history, and the Social Security number.

The credit report should be dated the same day as the loan application, especially for a refinance. If the transaction is for the purchase of real property, the file is not considered a loan application until a property is chosen. If the file is for the purpose of pre-qualification, the credit report may not need to be ordered the same day as the actual 1003; however, it is good practice. Disclosures must be provided when the credit report is ordered if there is a loan application. Lenders will often require disclosures dated the same day as the credit report, and again when the 1003 is signed if the dates are different based on the personal interpretation of RESPA.

RESPA defines an application as including:
- Property
- Credit report
- Name
- Social Security number
- Loan Amount

Credit agencies are fully automated, giving brokers the ability to get an immediate response upon request for an in-file report.

APPRAISALS have historically been chosen by the **loan agent/broker**. Beginning May 1, 2009, appraisals were required to be ordered through the lender according to HVCC guidelines. That law was overturned in 2010; however, FNMA and FHLMC did not change the rule within their guidelines. All loans being sold to FNMA and FHLMC must still be ordered through the lender's choice of appraisal management companies (AMCs). Other lenders may accept appraisals from a private appraiser if they choose. The broker needs to know both ways of ordering an appraisal because this is subject to change.

HOME VALUATION CODE OF CONDUCT/HVCC was implemented to establish standards for solicitation, selection, compensation, and conflicts of interest by appraisers. HVCC also helps eliminate abuses by those who were elevating property values beyond a realistic value for personal gain. This unscrupulous practice caused consumers to lose equity, which ultimately caused many to owe more than the property was worth. *The appraisal is ordered through the lender and is not chosen by the mortgage broker.*

The appraiser will need the property address, and the borrower's name and phone number to contact them for access. The borrower's email address is now requested for the AMC to email the appraisal directly to them upon completion. The appraiser will ask the type of loan, a copy of the prelim, and the purchase contract will be requested for a purchase transaction.

The appraiser must provide a fair value, but having an idea of what is needed will be helpful and they will do their best to accommodate. If the appraiser will not be able to evaluate the property as needed, they will let the processor or loan agent know prior to completing the report. Under these circumstances, the loan agent will determine whether the appraiser should complete the appraisal with the value they have determined, or they may be able to provide additional information to the appraiser that will help establish a higher value.

Depending on the loan, the amount may be reduced, the borrower may not be able to receive cash-out, or in the case of a purchase, the buyer may choose to cancel the transaction if the appraised value is less than the sales price. *Contracts to purchase property generally have an appraisal clause allowing the buyer to cancel the contract if the appraised value is less than the purchase price.*

Depending on how busy the appraiser is, the report should arrive within three days of the physical inspection or approximately five to seven days from the date the appraisal is ordered. They will let the borrower know what the turnaround time is and whether it will take longer.

At this point, the processor has completed **opening the loan**. The turnaround time for verifications and all other documentation is about two weeks. During that time, figures will be corrected and updated as verifying documents are received, then filed in the loan package in the proper stacking order.

THE STACKING ORDER shown below is the standard FNMA/FHLMC stacking order. Some lenders will require a variation on this order, which will be provided with their submission sheet. For working purposes, this order should be maintained throughout processing and not changed until submitting the file to the lender, unless the lender requires a different order. The stacking order should follow a "common sense" order for underwriting, with the items of greatest importance appearing first and items of lesser importance further down.

1008 IS A SUMMARY OF THE FILE including the primary information required for loan approval.

TYPED 1003 is the loan application with the information that has been verified by the broker/processor prior to submission. *The term "typed" comes from the time when the borrower completed the 1003 by hand then submitted it to the broker, who then typed the information onto a 1003 following verification.* Use of the computer has changed this process; however, the term still is used as a means to distinguish between the application with information as yet unverified and the information provided by the credit report.

ORIGINAL 1003 is the application as received from the borrower. This may also be referred to as the HW or handwritten 1003. The original is important because it has the borrower's signature and also because this is the information as stated by the borrower. The underwriter will review and compare the information from the borrower against the final information verified by the broker and processor for inaccuracies or indication of fraud.

After reviewing these forms for the summary of what is being requested, the rest of the file consists of documentation and verification provided on the 1008 and the 1003s.

CREDIT REPORT tells the lender how the borrower views their obligations and if they are responsible and creditworthy.

INCOME DOCUMENTATION verifies that they are capable of making the payments.

ASSET DOCUMENTATION in the form of bank statements and VODS verifies that the borrowers have the funds to close the transaction and also that they will be able to make payments for at least three months if they were to lose their income or employment.

ESCROW AND PRELIMINARY REPORT provide evidence that the property is transferable, or that the owners are actually the borrowers, and that there are no liens against it that will prevent the transaction from closing.

APPRAISAL verifies that the property is adequate security for the requested loan. The lender considers the condition of the property and the legality by ensuring that the structures have building permits and are up to building codes and standards. The value is not the only concern of the lender.

DISCLOSURES are last in the file because they do not affect the borrower's creditworthiness but verify that the borrower has been provided with all of the important and necessary information that requires disclosure, such as rights and costs.

Forms and documentation will be easily located once one is used to this order. Many brokers/processors find it helpful to place a copy of the attached list on the top of the loan package as a checklist. See Figure 32, stacking order.

Stacking Order

_____ Transmittal Summary/1008.

_____ Loan Application/Typed 1003.

_____ Original Signed 1003.

_____ Credit report.

_____ VOM/VOR/Canceled Checks.

_____ Letter of Explanation/LOE.

_____ Credit Documentation (Creditor Letters, Creditor Statements, canceled checks, etc.).

_____ Mortgage Statement (Current loan for a Refinance).

_____ December Page of Homeowner's Insurance.

_____ Verification of Employment/VOE-primary Borrower first.

_____ Paystubs-most recent 30-days-primary Borrower first.

_____ Profit & Loss Statement.

_____ 4506T/signed.

_____ W2s - most recent 2 years - primary Borrower first, most recent year first.

_____ Tax Returns-most recent 2 years to include 1120s, K1s, 1065s if self-employed-the most recent year first.

_____ Lease Agreements (if Borrower owns rental property and will use the rents as income to qualify).

_____ Verifications of Deposit/VOD.

_____ Bank Statements/most recent 3 months - most recent month first.

_____ Purchase Contract/Deposit Receipt.

_____ Receipt for funds deposited with escrow/down payment.

_____ Escrow Instructions.

_____ Prelim.

_____ HOA Cert.

_____ Budget, Insurance, Articles of Incorporation.

_____ CC&Rs.

_____ Appraisal.

_____ Loan estimate & Closing Disclosure.

_____ ECOA and Fair Lending.

_____ Credit Authorization.

_____ Credit Disclosure.

_____ Request for Appraisal.

_____ Patriot Act.

_____ Privacy Policy.

_____ Servicing Disclosure.

_____ Mortgage Loan Origination and California Real Estate Agency.

_____ Any additional documentation such as Tax Statements, Property Profiles, etc.

Figure 32: Stacking Order

AUTOMATED UNDERWRITING SYSTEMS (AUS)

AUTOMATED UNDERWRITING SYSTEMS (AUS) are computer-generated underwriting systems that review the information, then give an approval or decline based on the information provided. The AUS will generate a list of conditions based on the standard documentation that is required, such as the original 1003, income documentation, and asset verification.

RESPA requires that all information being sent online must be password protected. All efforts must be made to protect the borrower's personal information. Identity theft is a potential problem that must be considered at all times when working with this information.

DESKTOP UNDERWRITER (DU) is the AUS that is used by FNMA and **Loan Prospector (LP)** is the AUS or computer program used by FHLMC. They provide automatic underwriting for lenders and for the broker's benefit by being able to obtain immediate loan approval. The broker must be aware that the loan approval obtained through automated underwriting systems (AUS) will be reviewed and verified once the lender receives the loan documentation or the loan file.

> **NOTE**
>
> *The AUS approval is only as good as the documentation being provided, meaning that the documentation provided must support the information stated.*

CHAPTER 11
LOAN PROGRAMS

TYPES OF LOAN PROGRAMS

 **Loans** are available in many forms, and they are redesigned and changed according to the economic climate. Terminology often changes when the loans change.

Questions about loan programs should be discussed with the lender. Rate sheets will disclose a great deal of information regarding different loan programs. The lender's representatives (reps) or loan agents are the salespeople for the lender and are helpful in determining the ability of their company to provide a loan under particular circumstances.

1. **CONVENTIONAL LOANS** are standard first trust deeds with a mortgage lender and are for any amount for a 1-to 4-unit residential property. They are not insured or guaranteed by the federal government in any way.

2. **CONFORMING LOANS** are conventional loans that go up to a maximum amount established by FNMA and FHLMC guidelines. The current amount, as of 2024, for an SFR is $766,550. These limits are subject to annual adjustments based on changes in average home prices. Many lenders will not accept a loan amount of less than $40,000. A conforming loan can be a fixed-rate, adjustable-rate, convertible, or a balloon loan, as long as it is no more than the current FNMA/ FHLMC limit and will be underwritten to FNMA/FHLMC guidelines.
Loans that do not fall under the conforming loan limits are funded by a variety of other investors and are called jumbo loans. Because of the new high-cost loan limits, FNMA is now doing certain jumbo loans. Most lenders, including those outside of the FNMA guidelines, use many of the guidelines established, even when not selling to FNMA.

CONVENTIONAL LOAN LIMITS

The general loan limits for 2024 have increased and apply to loans delivered to FNMA in 2024 (even if originated before 01/01/2024). Conventional loan limits are subject to change and should be verified by the broker prior to quoting rates and programs to a borrower.

Number of Units	Contiguous States, District of Columbia, and *Puerto Rico		Alaska, Guam, Hawaii, and U.S. Virgin Islands	
	General	High-Cost	General	High-Cost*
1/SFR	$766,550	$1,149,825	$1,149,825	Not Applicable
2/Duplex	$981,500	$1,472,250	$1,472,250	Not Applicable
3/Triplex	$1,186,350	$1,779,525	$1,779,525	Not Applicable
4/Fourplex	$1,474,400	$2,211,600	$2,211,600	Not Applicable

A number of states (including Alaska and Hawaii), Guam, Puerto Rico, and the U.S. Virgin Islands do not have any high-cost areas in 2024.

CONFORMING LOAN PROGRAMS

The best or lowest interest rates are available for conforming loans, and these are generally the easiest loans to obtain from a lender.

California has a stricter predatory lending law, which will not allow NRCCs (non-recurring closing costs) in excess of 4.99% of the loan amount. This restriction makes it almost impossible for a mortgage broker to provide their services to a borrower on a small loan amount and make any money for their work.

3. **NON-CONFORMING AND JUMBO LOANS** are conventional loans that do not meet FNMA/FHLMC guidelines or are for an amount greater than $766,550. Because of the recent designation of certain parts of California as High-Cost Property areas according to FNMA Guidelines, many lenders are able to offer what is called FNMA Jumbo Loans. Only certain counties in California have been officially designated as high-cost areas. This will allow loans that would normally be considered jumbo loans to qualify as conforming and meet FNMA/FHLMC guidelines.

   FNMA/FHLMC may choose not to purchase or guarantee these loans, so they are underwritten according to the investor's guidelines. Investors in the secondary mortgage market set their own guidelines, which generally conform to other investor's guidelines, including FNMA and FHLMC.

These loans are conventional and are packaged the same as a FNMA/FHLMC loan. Jumbo guidelines will vary with loan amounts and the lenders will charge more as the loan amount increases. Lenders will also require lower LTVs as the amount increases.

There are many lenders who will not accept a loan greater than $750,000, but others will accept a loan amount as high as $2,500,000. Each lender will set their limit, and it will often vary from one program to another.

Stated-income loans are usually done under jumbo loan programs.

4. **ALT-A LOANS** are loans that do not fit into an A-paper program for a variety of reasons, such as credit problems, property issues, lack of reserves, or excessive debt ratio. Borrowers with a credit score of 600 to 630 are generally considered alt-A borrowers.

   An alt-A loan will cost more than a conventional loan and the interest rate will be higher. FNMA and FHLMC will generally not offer loan programs that accept alt-A loans.

5. **SUB-PRIME LOANS** have various issues that are not A-paper or alt-A. In addition to the issues listed under alt-A, sub-prime loans are used for credit scores that are not acceptable to A-paper lenders. The actual credit score will determine the grade of paper and, therefore, the interest rate and terms available to the borrower. Sub-prime loans, like alt-A loans, are used when either the borrower or the property do not fit the guidelines of A-paper lenders.

   The credit scores are generally between 500 and 620. The interest rates are always higher than a conventional loan and the loan programs are usually 2-year fixed-rate or 3-year fixed-rate loans. This is to allow the borrower two to three years to repair their credit and to be able to qualify for a conventional loan at that time. There is usually a pre-payment penalty on these loan programs.

   Sub-prime lenders are private mortgage banks, private money, or private investors. Sub-prime loans often fall under Section 32 of the Truth-in-Lending Act, which was amended by the Home Ownership and Equity Protection Act (HOEPA). This law addresses deceptive and unfair lending practices that apply to high-cost transactions.

By amending the LE (loan estimate), HOEPA establishes requirements for loans with high interest rates and high cost/fees. The rules that pertain to high-cost loans are contained in Section 32 of Regulation Z/TIL, which is the reason that high-cost loans are commonly referred to as Section 32 loans.

The following loans are covered under this law:
- First lien or the original mortgage on the property with an APR exceeding the rates on the Treasury Securities of comparable maturity by 8%.
- Second lien or a subordinate mortgage with an APR exceeding the rates on the Treasury Securities of comparable maturity by 10%.
- Total fees and points paid by the borrower at or before closing exceeding $583 or 8% of the total loan amount.

In 2009, $583 was established as the amount. The Federal Reserve Board can adjust that amount annually based on the Consumer Price Index. Credit/mortgage insurance premiums are considered and included in this calculation.

The broker/lender must provide written notice that the loan does not need to be completed, even though the loan application has been signed and the required disclosures have been delivered. This disclosure is provided at the bottom of the Truth-in-Lending form in bold typeface. If provided in another form, the lettering can be no smaller than 10-point typeface. The borrower has three (3) business days to rescind the loan after receiving this disclosure. The notice must also inform the borrower that they could lose their home and any equity as a result of the loan because the lender will have a lien against the property. This disclosure has the same 10-point typeface rules as previously stated.

As with all mortgage loans that fall under the Truth-in-Lending Law, the APR must be disclosed along with:
- Payment amount.
- Increases that may be expected as a result of an adjustable-rate loan program.
- Maximum possible monthly payment and interest rate.
- Balloon payment that may be allowed as permitted by law.
- Credit insurance required as either PMI or Credit Life/Health.

The following terms are not allowed on a Section 32 loan:

- Balloon mortgage terms are illegal if the required balloon payments do not pay off the balance of the loan and if the balloon payment is more than twice the amount of the regular payment for loans with less than a five-year term.
- Negative amortization or terms that allow payments of less than a sufficient amount to cover the interest due, causing an increase in the loan balance.
- Default interest rates that are greater than the pre-default rates.
- Rebates of interest based on the default calculated by any method less favorable to the consumer than the actuarial method.
- Repayment schedule requiring advance payment from the loan proceeds that are in excess of two or more payments.
- Pre-payment penalties including refunds of unearned interest calculated by any method less favorable to the consumer than the actuarial method with the exception of the following:
  - The lender verifies that the total monthly debt, including the mortgage, is less than 50% of the borrower's monthly gross income.
  - Money to prepay the debt is from a source other than the lender being paid or an affiliate of that lender.
  - Lender exercises the pre-payment penalty clause within five years of the inception of the loan.
- Due-on-Demand Clause with the following exceptions:
  - Fraud or material misrepresentation by the borrower in the loan application file.
  - Borrower defaults on the payments as agreed to in the note.
  - Actions by the borrower that adversely affects the lender's security.
- Loans may not be based on security only with no regard to the borrower's ability to repay the debt.
- Home improvement loan proceeds must be delivered directly to the borrower, the borrower and contractor jointly, or to an escrow agent, **not to the broker or lender.**
- Refinance a Section 32 loan within 12 months of inception of the existing loan unless it is in the best interest and a benefit to the borrower. This prohibition also applies to loans being held by an affiliate of the original lender and any servicers of the loan.
- Documenting a closed-end high-cost loan as an open-end loan, such as an equity line of credit when there will knowingly not be any expectation of repeat transactions or draws against the loan.

Compliance violations on the part of the lender may be pursued by the borrower through lawsuit, allowing damages both real and punitive, plus court and attorney fees. The borrower will have the right to rescind or cancel the loan for up to three years of the loan's inception. See *www.ftc.gov* for additional information or clarification.

Those lending their own funds, or sellers that are carrying the loan for the buyer/borrower are exempt from providing the disclosures as stated under Truth- in-Lending laws unless they are considered to be "in the business." A person or entity is legally considered to be "in the business" if they lend, trade, or sell ten (10) or more loans/paper within a twelve-month period, or one calendar or fiscal year.

6. **INTEREST-ONLY LOANS** require that the borrower pay only the interest due for a pre-set term. At the end of that term, which is usually five or ten years, the full principal amount of the original loan will still be owed. These terms are often suggested and used to acquire a higher loan amount for a borrower who will likely have an increase in income in the future. These loans are also useful for investors and investment property.

7. **FIXED-RATE** refers to any loan with a set payment amount over a set term (number of years), which is referred to as fully amortized. Currently, most fixed- rate loans are amortized for 15 years (180 months) or 30 years (360 months). Some lenders have programs for 20 years (240 months) or 40 years (480 months).

8. **CONVERTIBLE LOANS** offer an adjustable rate for a set period of time, usually three or five years. At that time, the loan will convert to a fixed-rate loan for the remainder of the loan's term.

9. **BUY-DOWN LOANS** are basically fixed-rate loans. The difference is that with a buy-down, the initial or beginning interest rate is a set rate less than the final or actual note rate and can increase according to the original agreement or the loan note. The lender charges a fee at close of escrow to compensate for the decreased interest rate. The fee charged is the difference between the initial interest rate charged and the actual interest rate. In other words, the borrower literally buys the rate down for a temporary period of time. The fee may be paid by the seller, which is commonly done when buying in a new development.

The buy-downs are referred to as a 2/1 buy-down or a 3/1 buy-down. Additional terms may be offered but are not common. A 2/1 buy-down will adjust twice before reaching the actual interest rate for the remaining term of the loan. The adjustment is generally made on an annual basis.

Example:

8.50%	*Interest rate 30 year fixed*
3.00%	*Fee to Lender (par) or the cost to borrower for 2/1 buy-down*
6.50%	*Rate for the first year (2% difference)*
7.50%	*Rate for the second year (1% difference)*
2.00%	*first year difference*
+1.00%	*second year difference*
=3.00%	*Total charge for the buy-down*

The borrower "bought down" the interest rate for a cost of 3.00% of the loan amount which reimbursed the lender. This is the difference between the interest rates of 2.00% for the first year, and 1.00% for the second year. The amortization is not negative and there are no shortages to add-on to the balance of the loan because the borrower paid for the difference upfront.

The term "buy-down" can also reference a borrower choosing an interest rate below par or a lower interest rate that the lender will offer versus a higher interest rate, which would provide a rebate. This is referred to as a one-time buy-down.

10. **GRADUATED PAYMENT MORTGAGES (GPM)** are adjustable-rate mortgages that also start at a lower interest rate like buy-downs. GPM's will adjust at predetermined amounts for a period of either three or five years. There is no margin or cap.

The purpose of these loans is to help qualify borrowers who can expect their income to increase over the period, such as a recent college graduate. These loans are also commonly used when interest rates are high. The borrower may choose this type of loan in anticipation of rates lowering during the GPM period. GPMs are rarely seen during periods of low interest rates.

The difference between a buy-down and a GPM is that the interest rate actually adjusts with a GPM and the rate is not bought-down. Once the loan reaches the end of the term for the payment to increase, the payment will remain fixed for the remainder of the loan term.

Example:

> 5.00%   *first year*
> 6.00%   *second year*
> 7.00%   *third year and the remainder of the loan term*

11. **ADJUSTABLE-RATE LOANS** are amortized over a set period of time, but the interest rate and payment will adjust on preset dates according to a predetermined margin over the predetermined index. The adjustable-rate programs that are most commonly used and available are monthly adjustable, which uses the Cost of Funds Index or Monthly Treasury Average Index; six month adjustable using the LIBOR; and one year adjustable using the T-Bill for an index. The adjustment period is determined by the index used.

    IN TODAY'S MARKET, LENDERS WILL OFTEN QUALIFY BORROWERS AT THE ACTUAL RATE (INDEX + MARGIN) FULLY AMORTIZED. THIS GIVES THE LENDERS, AS WELL AS THE BORROWERS, A BETTER ESTIMATE OF THE BORROWER'S ABILITY TO PAY OFF THE LOAN.

    INDEX is the actual rate that the funds cost the investor, or the interest rate that one bank pays another bank to borrow funds. Most mortgage lenders print the daily index on the rate sheet. Indexes vary according to changes in the economy and are printed in the business section of the newspaper and can also be found online.

    MARGIN is the investor's profit and the amount above the index that the borrower is charged for use of the funds. The margin is established at the time of locking the loan and will vary according to the loan and the desired interest rate. *For instance, a higher LTV constitutes a higher margin.* The margin establishes the amount of the interest rate and payment will adjust at the given adjustment date. Marins are currently at about 2.50% to 3.5%. **It is essential that the margin is always added to the index to determine the actual rate; the rate for the payment calculation is based on this rate.**

CAP is the maximum amount the interest rate can adjust within any given period. Caps are all determined by the loan program and the index used for the program. The terms are always included in the note. Caps on sub-prime loan programs are generally higher on all adjustments. The various caps include:

- **ADJUSTMENT CAP:** The maximum amount the rate can adjust at each adjustment date determined by the loan program chosen, such as once every six months for a 6-month adjustable program. The adjustment cap is usually 1% if the adjustment period is less than one year, such as for a COFI or a LIBOR loan program. It is typically 2% if the adjustment period is one-year or more.

- **ANNUAL CAP:** is the maximum amount the interest rate can adjust within a one-year period. The annual cap is usually 2% and the life cap is usually 6% on conforming loans and is disclosed as 2/6 on rate sheets.

  Example:

5.00%	*Start rate or teaser rate.*
+2.0%	*Annual cap*
= 7.0%	*Maximum interest rate within 1 year*

- **LIFE CAP:** is the maximum amount the interest can adjust to over the entire term or life of the loan.

  Example:

5.00%	*Start rate.*
+6.0%	*Life cap*
=11.0%	*Maximum interest rate for life of loan*

- **PAYMENT CAPS:** were offered as the maximum amount the payment can adjust to over the current payment, such as 7.5% annually for a monthly adjustable. **THEY ARE NO LONGER OFFERED, AS THEY CAN CAUSE NEGATIVE AMORTIZATION.**

- **FLOOR:** establishes the lowest amount the interest rate will be allowed to be. This amount is often the start rate or the starting index.

  Example:

4.75%	*Start ate -or Lesser of-*
3.75%	*Index*
= 3.75%	*Floor or lowest amount the Rate can be for Life of the Loan*

Example: A six-month adjustable or **LIBOR** (Index) will be used for a loan amount of $450,000 for a 30-year amortization:

Start Rate	4.75%
Adjustment Cap	1.00%
Life Cap	6.00%
Margin	2.25%
Index	3.75%

1.) The payment for the first six months of the loan will be: $2,347.41 at an interest rate of 4.75%.

2.) On the sixth month, when the first adjustment is due, the index is still 3.75%. The margin allows the lender to add the:

2.25%	Margin amount onto the
+3.75%	Index which would make
=6.00%	Interest rate

The annual cap, or the maximum the interest rate can increase, is 2.00% per year; however, on most LIBOR loans the adjustment cap will generally be 1% at each 6-month adjustment period:

The lender will use the lesser of the index + margin or current interest rate + adjustment cap:

4.75%	Start Rate/Current Rate
+1.00%	Adjustment Cap
=5.75%	Interest Rate

The new interest rate will be 5.75% because it is less than the index + margin figure of 6%. The new payment amount is $2,626.08. The note will clarify the terms for the borrower.

3.) At the second adjustment period (6 months after the last adjustment date) the interest rate can adjust 1% more as long as it does not exceed the index plus margin on that date. Again, it will adjust to the lesser of the two ways of calculating the new interest rate.

The broker/processor can use the Regulation Z to calculate the amortization based on these figures. Regulation Z will calculate adjustments based on the original Index as there is no way to determine what the Index will be at any future date. All of the adjustable-rate loan programs can be calculated using the above guidelines. The loan origination software can generate the information required for these calculations.

12. **12.T-BILL OR TREASURY BOND LOANS** adjust annually based on the federal bond market. This Index is the most volatile; however, the caps control the maximum amount that the interest rate can adjust. The adjustment is annual or once a year. Generally, the caps are 2% annually and 6% for the life of the loan.

13. **LIBOR (London Inter-Bank Offered Rate)** Loans adjust every six months, and the Index historically does not move very much, as it is based on interest paid on savings accounts, or on money borrowed from banks investing money from their depositors' savings accounts.

    LIBOR began to be used for the Monthly Adjustable or Negative Amortizing Loan Programs in the early 2000s because of the relative stability of the Index.

    Using the example above, the highest the interest rate could go for the life of the loan on this particular loan is 10.75%, creating a monthly loan payment of $4,536.72.

    > *Example:*
    > 4.75%   *Start rate.*
    > + 6.00%   *Life cap.*
    > =10.75%   *Maximum interest rate for the life of the loan.*

    This is not likely to happen unless there is an extreme inflationary period. The interest rate and payment can also decrease if the Index decreases. If a borrower were to obtain a LIBOR loan during an inflationary period when the Index was high, the interest rate may decrease with the onset of a recession.

14. **COFI (Cost of Funds Index)** is a monthly adjustable loan program, and many lenders may offer COFIs with a 3-month fixed start rate, meaning that the first three payments will not adjust.

    These loans have been called **NegAm** (negative amortization) but are now more commonly referred to as **OPTION ARMS**. The term option arm is preferred because of the negative connotations of the term NegAm.

Lenders offer three or four different payment options, including a payment based on the low start rate, interest-only, or fully amortized. The start rate, or the interest rate of the initial payment, on these loan programs is extremely low, often starting as low as 1.00% to 1.95%.

These loans are often negatively amortized (NegAm), meaning the actual rate owed is greater than the amount of the monthly payment.

> *Example: Based on a $450,000 loan amount:*
>
> | $951.36 | *Initial payment based on a start rate of interest due based on the Index* of 2.622%* |
> |---|---|
> | $1,921.88 | *+ margin of 2.5% for an actual rate of 5.122 %* |
> | =$970.54 | *Shortage or negative payment amount* |
> | $2,449.36 | *Fully amortized payment* |
>
> *The minimum payment is not enough to cover the full amount due. Therefore, the shortage is added to the principal balance of the loan the borrower now owes:*
>
> | $450,000.00 | *Original loan balance* |
> |---|---|
> | +970.54 | *Interest shortage* |
> | =$450,970.54 | *Principal balance after the first monthly payment* |
>
> *This is how the loan program came to be called "negative amortization." The term "Option ARM" indicates the three options available for the payment amounts.*

*While some lenders base the fully amortized payment on the Index, others will establish an actual interest rate at the time of locking the interest rate with the lender. The interest rate will then appear on the rate sheet and in the note.

Monthly Treasury Average Index (MTA) is also an index for a monthly adjustable loan program with the potential of being a NegAm. A NegAm loan typically starts to balance out and pay the principal around the thirty-sixth payment, or the third year of the loan.

These loans are especially good to help get a borrower into a property at the high-end of their budget, or to free up the borrower's cash flow during a period of renovation. They are also good for a buyer who can anticipate a steady pay increase over the next few years. It can be viewed that the borrower will borrow an additional amount from the lender each month.

Because of the mortgage meltdown, many borrowers who had option arms lost their homes because they were unable to make the higher payments following the multiple adjustments. Borrowers were often placed in these loans without understanding the potential increases, which they often could not afford. These loans may or may not become available at some time in the future because of the problems they have caused in the past. They are excellent loans under the right circumstances, but the loan program is not suitable to every borrower. Careful scrutiny and a thorough explanation to the borrower are crucial to the successful management of the loan.

Both the COFI and MTA loans have an annual payment cap, usually at 7.5%. This means that the lender will figure the new payment based on:

Index + Margin

-Or-

Payment + Cap

-Or-

7.5% of the current payment + the current payment

The lowest figure will be used.

MINIMUM DOWN PAYMENTS FOR MORTGAGES

The minimum down payment for a mortgage is:

- VA loan: 0% down payment
- USDA loan: 0% down payment
- Conventional 97% mortgage: 3% down payment
- HomeReady™ mortgage: 3% down payment
- FHA loan: 3.5% down payment

In addition to the above programs, down payment assistance programs are often available and provide, on average, more than $11,000 to today's buyers.

ZERO DOWN PAYMENT MORTGAGES

A no down payment mortgage allows first-time home buyers and repeat home buyers to purchase property with no monies required at closing. Mortgage insurance premiums typically accompany low and no down payment mortgages, but not always. In the current US housing market, home buyers are no longer bound to a 20 percent down payment.

The likely reason buyers believe a 20% down payment is required is because, with one specific mortgage type -- the conventional mortgage -- putting twenty percent down means *private mortgage insurance* (PMI) is not required. And for much of the twentieth century, a down payment of 20 percent was standard. For today's home buyers, however, there are numerous options, and making a down payment should not be the only consideration. Home affordability is not about the size of a down payment -- it's about whether they can manage the monthly payments and still have cash left over for "life."

1. VETERANS ADMINISTRATION LOANS (100% FINANCING)

The VA Loan is a no-money-down program available to members of the U.S. military and surviving spouses. Guaranteed by the U.S. Department of Veteran Affairs, VA loans are similar to FHA loans in that the agency guarantees repayment to lenders making loans.

VA loan qualifications are straightforward. Any active duty and honorably discharged service personnel are eligible to receive a VA loan. In addition, home buyers who have spent at least six years in the Reserves or National Guard are eligible, as are spouses of service members killed in the line of duty.

Some key benefits of the VA loan are:
- You may use intermittent occupancy.
- Bankruptcy and bad credit do not immediately disqualify a borrower.
- No mortgage insurance is required.

VA loans also allow for loan sizes of up to $1,094,625 in high-cost areas. This can be helpful in areas such as San Francisco, California; and Honolulu, Hawaii, which are home to U.S. military bases.

2. UNITED STATES DEPARTMENT OF AGRICULTURE LOANS (100% FINANCING)

No money down options also exist for non-military borrowers. The U.S. Department of Agriculture offers a 100% mortgage. The program is formally known as a Section 502 mortgage but is more commonly known as a Rural Housing Loan.

The good news about the USDA RURAL HOUSING LOAN is that it's not just a "rural loan" -- it's also available to buyers in suburban neighborhoods. The USDA's goal is to reach "low-to-moderate income homebuyers," wherever live. Financing a home via the USDA can be the most affordable path to homeownership.

Many borrowers using the USDA Single Family Housing Guaranteed Loan Program make a good living and reside in neighborhoods which do not meet the traditional definition of rural. For example, college towns including Christiansburg, Virginia; State College, Pennsylvania; and even suburbs of Columbus, Ohio meet USDA eligibility standards, as do some of the less-populated suburbs of some major cities.

Some key benefits of the USDA loan are:
- Eligible home repairs and improvements can be included in the loan.
- There isn't a maximum home purchase price.
- Guarantee fee added to loan balance at closing.
- Mortgage insurance collected monthly.
- Rates are often lower than rates for comparable, low- or no-down payment mortgages.

LOW DOWN PAYMENT LOANS

The FHA Loan, the HomeReady™ mortgage and the Conventional 97 loan offer low down payment options, with a little as 3% down.

1. FEDERAL HOUSING AUTHORITY LOANS (3.5% DOWN)

The FHA mortgage is somewhat of a misnomer because the FHA does not actually make loans but rather insures them. The FHA publishes a series of guidelines for the loans it will insure; when a bank underwrites and funds a loan which meets these guidelines, the FHA agrees to insure that loan against loss. FHA mortgage guidelines are famous for their liberal approach to credit scores and down payments. The FHA will typically insure a home loan for borrowers with low credit scores provided there is a reasonable explanation for the low FICO. The agency allows a down payment of just 3.5 percent in all U.S. markets, with the exception of a few FHA-approved condos.

Other benefits of an FHA loan are:
- The down payment may consist entirely of "gift funds."
- The credit score requirement is only 500.
- Mortgage insurance premiums are paid upfront at closing, and monthly thereafter.
- Homeowners who have experienced recent short sales, foreclosures, or bankruptcies, receive assistance through the agency's Back to Work program.
- Insures loan sizes up to $625,500 in designated "high cost" areas.

The FHA loan requirements are:
- A credit score of at least 500.
- Income which can be verified using W-2 statements and paystubs, or federal tax returns.
- No history of bankruptcy, foreclosure, or short sale within the last 12 months.
- No delinquency on federal taxes, student loans, or any other federal debt.

FHA DOWN PAYMENT ASSISTANCE PROGRAMS

FHA down payment assistance programs are available to home buyers and 87% of U.S. single-family homes potentially qualify. Programs vary by state. The average home buyer using down payment assistance receives $11,565.

2. THE HOMEREADY™ MORTGAGE (3% DOWN)

HomeReady™ home loans were designed to help multi-generational households get approved for mortgage financing. However, the program can be used by anyone in a qualifying area or who meets household income requirements.

Backed by Fannie Mae and available from nearly every U.S. lender, the HomeReady™ mortgage offers:
- Below market mortgage rates.
- Reduced mortgage insurance costs.
- The most innovative underwriting idea in more than a decade. The income of everyone living in the home can be used to get qualified and approved.

For example: A homeowner living with their parents, children, or even boarders who earn incomes, can use these incomes to help qualify. Even income from a non-zoned rental unit paid in cash can be used.

3. CONVENTIONAL LOAN 97 (3% DOWN)

The Conventional Loan 97 was discontinued in December 2013 but was reinstated by the Federal Home Finance Agency in 2014. It is available from Fannie Mae and Freddie Mac. For many home buyers, it's a less expensive option compared to an FHA loan.

The Conventional 97 basic qualification standards are:

- A three percent down payment that can come from gifted funds from
- a relation.
- Loan size may not exceed $417,000, even if the home is in a high-cost market.
- The subject property must be a single-unit dwelling. No multi-unit homes are allowed.
- The mortgage must be a fixed-rate mortgage. No ARMs via the Conventional 97.
- Can be used to refinance a home.

4. THE "PIGGYBACK LOAN" (10% DOWN)

The "piggyback loan" program is typically reserved for buyers with above-average credit scores. It's actually *two* loans meant to give home buyers added flexibility and lower overall payments.

The beauty of the 80/10/10 is its structure. With an 80/10/10 loan, buyers bring a ten percent down payment to closing. This leaves ninety percent of the home sale price for the mortgage. But instead of giving one mortgage for the 90%, the buyer splits the loan into parts.

The first part of the 80/10/10 is the "80." The "80" represents the first mortgage and is a loan for 80% of the home's purchase price. This loan is typically a conventional loan via Fannie Mae or Freddie Mac; and is offered at current market mortgage rates.

The first "10" represents the second mortgage and is a loan for 10% of the home's purchase price. This is typically a home equity loan (HELOAN) or home equity line of credit (HELOC).

Home equity loans are fixed-rate loans. A home equity line of credit is an adjustable-rate loan. Buyers can choose from either option. HELOCs are more common because of the flexibility they offer over the long term.

And that leaves the last "10," which represents the buyer's down payment amount -- ten percent of the purchase price. This amount is paid as cash at closing.

80/10/10 loans are sometimes called piggyback loans because a second loan "piggybacks" on the first one to increase the total amount borrowed.

80/10/10 loans are meant to give buyers access to the best pricing available, so lenders may sometimes recommend an alternate structure.

For example, for buyers of condos, a 75/15/10 is advised because condo mortgages get better rates with LTVs of 75% or less.

As another example, interest rates on HELOCs are sometimes better at larger loan sizes. Your lender may recommend that you increase the size of your HELOC to lower your overall loan costs. The choice of the loan's structure, however, remains with the borrower.

You cannot be forced into borrowing more money on your second mortgage than makes you comfortable.

MORTGAGE DOWN PAYMENTS

Benefits to Putting More Money Down
Just as there are benefits to low and no money down mortgages, there are benefits to putting more money down on a purchase. The primary advantage of making a larger down payment is that because the mortgaged amount is smaller, the monthly mortgage payment is lower as well. Additionally, if a mortgage requires mortgage insurance, a larger down payment means that the mortgage insurance will "cancel" in fewer years.

A down payment can be funded multiple ways:
- Savings or checking account.
- Proceeds from the sale of an existing home.
- Cash gifts
  - The gift must be made using a personal check, a cashier's check,
  - or a wire.
  - The borrower should keep all paper records of the gift, including photocopies of the checks and of deposits, and make sure the deposit matches the amount of the gift exactly.
  - Verification that the gift is not a loan-in-disguise and does not require repayment.
- Borrow from a 401k or IRA.
- Down payment assistance programs that grant money to home buyers with the stipulation that they live in the home for a certain number of years, usually no more than five years.
- Home buyer grants, also known as down payment assistance (DPA) programs, are available to all U.S. borrowers. DPA programs are widely available but seldom used; eighty-seven percent of single-family homes potentially

qualify, but less than ten percent of buyers apply.

MORTGAGE INSURANCE

When a buyer makes a low down payment, they are more likely to pay mortgage insurance, but there are some programs in which this is not the case. For example, the VA Home Loan Guaranty program does not require mortgage insurance, so a borrower who uses a VA loan and makes a small down payment would not have mortgage insurance. Conversely, FHA and USDA loans *always* require mortgage insurance. Even with large down payments, borrowers who get an FHA or USDA loan will still have a monthly mortgage insurance charge.

The only loan for which a down payment affects the mortgage insurance is the conventional mortgage. The smaller the down payment, the higher the monthly PMI. However, once a home has twenty percent equity, the borrower is eligible to have the PMI removed.

If I make a low down payment, what are my lender fees?
The size of a down payment does not relate to lender fees. No matter how large or small the down payment, lender fees should remain equal. This is because mortgage lenders are prohibited from charging higher fees based on the size of down payments. It should be noted, however, that different loan types may require different services (e.g., home inspection, roof inspection, home appraisal), and this may affect the total loan closing costs.

CalHFA (California Housing Finance Agency) offers a variety of loan programs to help purchase a home in California.

FIRST MORTGAGE PROGRAMS CONVENTIONAL LOANS

CALHFA CONVENTIONAL LOAN PROGRAM
The CalHFA Conventional program is a first mortgage loan insured through private mortgage insurance on the conventional market. The interest rate on the CalHFA Conventional is fixed throughout the 30-year term.

CALPLUS CONVENTIONAL LOAN PROGRAM
The CalPLUS Conventional program is a conventional first mortgage with a slightly

higher fixed interest rate than our standard conventional program. This loan is fully amortized for a 30-year term and is combined with the **CalHFA Zero Interest Program (ZIP)** for closing costs, prepaid items, and principal reduction.

GOVERNMENT INSURED LOANS

CALHFA FHA LOAN PROGRAM
The CalHFA FHA program is an FHA-insured loan featuring a CalHFA fixed interest rate first mortgage. This loan is fully amortized for a 30-year term.

CALPLUS FHA LOAN PROGRAM
The CalPLUS FHA program is an FHA-insured first mortgage with a slightly higher fixed interest rate than our standard FHA program. This loan is fully amortized for a 30-year term and is combined with the CalHFA Zero Interest Program (ZIP) for closing costs, prepaid items, and principal reduction.

CAL-EEM + GRANT PROGRAM
The Cal-EEM + Grant program combines an FHA-insured Energy Efficient Mortgage first mortgage loan with an additional Cal-EEM Grant, making energy efficient improvements even easier. The interest rate on the Cal-EEM is fixed throughout the 30-year term.

DOWN PAYMENT ASSISTANCE PROGRAMS

The money put "down" or the down payment on a home loan can be one of the largest hurdles for many first-time homebuyers. That's why CalHFA offers several options for down payment and closing cost assistance. This type of assistance is often called a second or subordinate loan.

CalHFA's subordinate loans are "silent seconds," meaning payments on this loan are deferred so buyers do not have to make a payment on this assistance until their home is sold, refinanced, or paid in full. This helps to keep their monthly mortgage payment affordable.

MYHOME ASSISTANCE PROGRAM
This program offers a deferred-payment junior loan of an amount up to the lesser of three and half percent (3.5%) of the purchase price or appraised value to assist with down payment and/or closing costs.

EXTRA CREDIT TEACHER HOME PURCHASE PROGRAM (ECTP)
This program is for teachers, administrators, school district employees, and

staff members working for any California K-12 public school, which includes charter schools and county/continuation schools. Applicants must also be first-time homebuyers.

The program offers a deferred-payment junior loan of an amount not to exceed the greater of $7,500 or 3.5% of the sales price, or in CalHFA-defined high cost areas, an amount not to exceed the greater of $15,000 or 3.5% of the sales price. Assistance can be used for down payment.

OTHER PARTNERSHIP & PROGRAM OPTIONS

MORTGAGE CREDIT CERTIFICATE TAX CREDIT PROGRAM (MCC)

This is a federal credit which can reduce potential federal income tax liability, creating additional net spendable income which borrowers may use toward their monthly mortgage payment. This MCC Tax Credit program may enable first-time homebuyers to convert a portion of their annual mortgage interest into a direct dollar for dollar tax credit on their U.S. individual income tax returns.

INDIVIDUAL DEVELOPMENT ACCOUNTS

IDA's are special savings accounts designed to assist low-income borrowers on their path toward ownership of a long-term asset, such as a home, through matched contributions by nonprofit organizations and eligible banks. These organizations may offer up to a 3:1 savings match (i.e., if you save $1,000, you will receive an additional $3,000). To find an organization that offers an IDA program, please follow the link
https://ca.db101.org/ca/programs/job_planning/ida/program2.htm

DOCUMENTATION VARIATIONS

1. **ALTERNATIVE DOCUMENTATION OR ALT-DOC LOANS,** *as mentioned earlier,* **can** be used for the self-employed borrower as well as salaried and hourly borrowers. Some lenders will allow alternative documentation, referred to as "alt-doc" to verify income. Lenders' terminology and required documentation varies. If alt-docs are to be used, ask the chosen lender what they require and what will be acceptable for their alt-doc loan programs.

   Alt Doc by most lenders is considered to be:
   - **Salaried and hourly employees:**
     ◦ **YTD paystub and the last 2-years' W2s:** 1040s are not included in the loan package.
     ◦ **Year-end paystub is acceptable** for a missing W2 for one year, (the last paystub in December for that year).

- **Self-employed borrowers** are more common and can include many options.
  - **24-months' personal bank statements:** This is rarely accepted for standard A-paper loans.

All that is needed is Page 1 of the statement showing total deposited amounts for each month. Add the total monthly deposits for the entire 24-month period and divide by twenty-four to acquire the average monthly Income. This method has been most common with sub-prime lenders but has more recently become acceptable with some A-paper lenders. If this method is used, ask the underwriter if it is acceptable under their guidelines. Some underwriters will require all pages of the statements, so it is advisable to copy all pages and keep the additional pages on the left side of the file in case they are needed later.

- **Business bank statements** will be required by some lenders. They will calculate the income by using 75% of the average monthly balance divided by the number of months.

The logic of this method is that it confirms the total funds available to the owner of the business after expenses have been paid.

- **P&Ls for the last two years and YTD prepared and signed by a CPA** is also considered alt-docs. P&Ls prepared by a CPA are expensive because the CPA performs a full audit of them. In situations where a less meticulous review is acceptable, audited P&Ls should not be required because the extra time and expense simply isn't warranted. They are rarely used because of being cost prohibitive.

2. STATED-INCOME LOAN PROGRAMS were originally created for self-employed borrowers but are no longer available. In recent years, CPA professional associations determined that mortgage brokers were abusing the stated-income loan program by placing borrowers in loans that they could not afford.

   NO-INCOME NO-ASSET (NINA) LOAN PROGRAMS require no verification for the income or the assets. AS THESE LOANS WERE A CONTRIBUTING FACTOR IN THE MORTGAGE COLLAPSE, THEY ARE NO LONGER OFFERED.

3. BALLOON LOAN is defined as a loan that will receive a payment in excess of twice the minimum payment due in any payment period. Balloon loans are loans that are not amortized for the actual term of the loan. A balloon mortgage is a loan that has

the payments based on a term that is longer than the actual term of the loan. A balloon loan may have payments amortized over a period of 30 years, but the balance of the principal will be due in 15 years. Thus, the term "balloon," as the principal balance will be considerably more than any one payment. This is commonly used for second TDs or as a way to receive a lower interest rate on a first TD.

> *Example:* Tom has a balloon mortgage with ABC Bank for $100,000 at 6.0% interest. The loan is amortized for 30 years, requiring a monthly payment in the amount of $622.88. The loan will be due and payable in 15 years, meaning that the 180th payment will be for a total amount of $71,671.85.

> *Tom plans to refinance the property prior to that last payment coming due and payable so he will never actually make the last large payment out of his personal cash.*

> *If Tom had gotten a 15-year loan, his monthly payment would have been $867.19. The shortened term would have made the monthly payment more than $200 higher. He was able to obtain a loan for the same period of time but with a lower payment by getting a balloon loan for 30 years.*

A lender will consider that the borrower is requesting a loan of a considerable amount of money for a very long term. However, if the loan is paid back in half the time, it is a more appealing loan to the lender even though they will earn less interest.

4. **BUY-DOWN LOANS** are basically fixed-rate loans. The difference is that with a buy-down, the beginning rate is for a set interest rate which is less than the final or actual note rate and can adjust up or down according to the original agreement.

NOTE

The lender charges an upfront fee, which is the difference in the interest rates, at close of escrow to compensate for the decreased interest rate. The borrower actually buys the rate down for a temporary period of time. In some instances, the seller can pay the fee. This is commonly done when the property in question is in a new development and the developer may pay the fee as an incentive to buyers.

ALL INCLUSIVE TRUST DEED/ LAND CONTRACTS

ALL INCLUSIVE TRUST DEED (AITD), LAND CONTRACTS, OR CONTRACTS FOR DEED are methods of purchasing a home whereby the seller becomes the lender. The buyer makes payments to the seller and the seller retains title in most situations. These are often wrap-around loans because they "wrap-around" an existing mortgage. The buyer can usually get an AITD with minimal qualifying and the seller gets a tax benefit by receiving profit in smaller annual amounts.

When the buyer applies for a new loan to pay off or "take-out" the seller and obtain title, the broker, loan agent, and borrower will usually consider this a refinance; however, most lenders will consider this a purchase.

For a loan to be considered a refi, it has to meet certain criteria, which will vary among lenders. A copy of the original contract is required along with all canceled checks from the date of purchase, as well as the deposit or down payment check A rule-of-thumb establishing ownership is that if all payments have been applied to the principal, interest, and to the down payment. If the seller has retained part of the payments for a purpose other than the purchase price, the payments may be considered rent and that determines that the transaction might not be considered a purchase. A VOM (verification of mortgage) should also be provided. Possession by the borrower establishes intent.

Such transactions are often between immediate family members, which means that the purchase is a non-arms-length transaction. An arms-length transaction is one in which the parties have no connection to each other. A non-arms-length transaction must be fully documented, as anything less will be carefully scrutinized by the lender.

CALIFORNIA DEPARTMENT OF VETERANS' AFFAIRS (CALVET) provides contract for deed loans. CalVet closes the purchase transaction for the property in the name of that organization, then sells it to the buyer/ borrower using a contract for deed. CalVet then transfers the deed into the borrower's name when the loan is paid off, either by payment in full or refinance. Until that time, CalVet holds the title to the property.

SECOND TRUST DEEDS

Second TRUST DEEDS, OR JUNIOR LIENS, are generally smaller loans that may be used for a variety of reasons.

A purchase money second is often used when the lender on the first TD will not allow the borrower a high enough loan to value (LTV) to meet the borrower's needs or when the borrower lacks enough cash to close. A purchase money second TD will be used to obtain the additional cash needed.

When the borrower has a good first TD but wants additional cash for personal needs, such as remodeling, they will request a second TD to acquire the funds. Lenders look at the combined loan-to-value (CLTV). Lenders will place a maximum on the LTV, then allow an additional percentage or a higher CLTV. Rate sheets may show a program such as 80/10/10. This means that they will allow an 80% first, a 10% second, and 10% down-payment from the borrower.

Lenders do not like to place small seconds behind large first TDs because if the borrower defaults on the first, the lender of the second TD will have to bring the first loan current in order to be able to file a notice of default and collect their own funds through a foreclosure proceeding.

The holder of a junior lien is in a weaker position because they are subordinate to the first TD. In a foreclosure proceeding, the lien holder who filed the foreclosure will collect along with any lien holder in a priority position. Second TDs are a riskier position for the lender. Lenders also do not like to place a large second TD behind a smaller first TD for the same reasons. It is because of the lesser position that second TDs have a higher interest rate and fees than a first TD loan.

SUBORDINATION AGREEMENT is required in a situation where a borrower is refinancing their first TD and does not want to pay off the existing second TD. In other words, the holder of the second loan agrees to allow the new first lien holder to take a priority lien position, although the new lien is filed at a later date than the first one. The priority of any lien against a property is established by the date that the lien is recorded unless otherwise subordinated.

TAX LIENS may also be subordinated in this manner if acceptable to the lender. The IRS is generally easy to work with if the borrower has been making regular payments on their tax debt, but lenders will rarely agree to leave a tax lien against a subject property. If the IRS chose to have a tax sale, the lender could lose some of their investment even though the tax lien is subordinated to the mortgage lien.

Second TDs are generally amortized for a period of 15 years or 180 monthly payments, and 20 years or 240 monthly payments. Fixed seconds are fully amortized for that period, but lenders commonly offer a variety of amortization choices, such as 30 due in 15 or 30/15. *(30/15 means that the payment amount will be based on a 30-year amortization and the balance will be due at the 15-year anniversary date. This is known as a balloon payment.)*

EQUITY LINES of CREDIT or a HOME EQUITY LINE OF CREDIT (HELOC) work much like a credit card and the interest rate is a monthly adjustable. The borrower may draw or take out the entire amount at funding or they can draw on the funds over time using checks provided by the lender. When borrowers decide how much to draw at the close of escrow, they need to know that they will not be able to draw additional funds for a set period from the date of closing, which will be disclosed in the note. The funds will be frozen for a period of 15 to 45 days following the close of escrow.

The broker/processor will complete a disbursement schedule provided by the lender. This schedule will ask for the amount of the initial draw, or the amount of funds to be taken by the borrower when loan docs are ordered. The broker/loan agent must be sure that the borrower understands the process before completing this form. If the borrower is refinancing to pay off existing first and second TDs, the loan is considered a cash-out refinance unless the first and second were both purchase money loans. This means that both loans were taken by the borrower at the time of purchasing the property for that purpose.

Prior to 2002, the guidelines were that the refinance loan paying off a HELOC would be considered a cash-out loan if the borrower had drawn funds from the equity line in the last 12 months, generally in excess of $2,000 or 1% of the loan amount. Likewise, if any second TD is less than 12 months old at time of closing, the new loan is considered cash-out. Second TD loans had to have 12 months' seasoning to be considered a rate & term (R&T) refinance. *This is no longer an acceptable way of viewing refinances.*

A FORECLOSURE SALE may not necessarily relieve a borrower of the obligation of a second trust deed/mortgage or a junior lien. If a homeowner loses their home to foreclosure, it is important to know that if the holder of the second does not get paid through the foreclosure sale. The borrower will still be obligated to pay the balance of the loan if it was not used to purchase the property or was not a purchase money loan. If the loan was taken out by the borrower after the original purchase transaction, the lender will recognize the fact that the borrower took out cash and spent it, therefore, they are obligated to repay it. Any write-off of mortgage debt that has provided cash to the borrower is reported to the IRS as income to the borrower.

REFINANCES

REFINANCES of properties purchased less than a year prior may have specific guidelines, as some lenders will require a seasoning period, which is typically six months to a year. If a borrower is short of the 12-month seasoning period, the lender should be informed of this as well as the difference in cost to obtain a cash-out loan versus an R&T loan (rate and term refinance).

It may be advisable to get loan approval then set a closing date to be the day after the one-year-anniversary date if that date is near. This will appear on the lender's conditions as "not to close before ____date," and should be addressed by the broker/processor in a cover letter when the loan is submitted to the lender for underwriting.

REVERSE MORTGAGES

REVERSE MORTGAGES AS AN OPTION FOR SENIOR CITIZENS: There are many senior citizens across the country who are living on a reduced income, often consisting of only minimum Social Security, however, they may have a lot of equity in their home. This means that they do not owe nearly as much as the property is worth. HUD created reverse mortgages expressly for senior citizens. The loan was created in the 1950s but had some problems and was never used well. During the past twenty years, the program has been revised and re-organized into a feasible and practical loan option for senior citizens.

This loan was designed to create additional income for seniors who have either paid mortgage in full or have appreciated equity. The government's intention in creating the program was to give seniors a way to draw on the equity in their home without having the large monthly mortgage payment that a standard refinance or mortgage loan would have.

Unlike a conventional mortgage loan, the borrower of a reverse mortgage receives a monthly allotment, or draw against the loan, which creates an income instead of an expense. A homeowner who is living on Social Security alone, or a small pension, can increase their monthly income by an average of $1,500 to $2,000. This can substantially improve their lifestyle by creating a monthly income of between $2,100 to $3,500 per month.

QUALIFYING THE BORROWER does not require personal information, such as a credit report or income verification, because the lender holds the equity and gives it to the borrower in monthly installments instead of the borrower making monthly installments to the lender. The only requirement is that the youngest person in the household must be at least 62 years of age.

At the time the borrower takes the loan, a loan amount and interest rate is established. They do not receive the total amount of the loan at that time, however. Instead, they will begin to receive the monthly draw against the loan balance instead of making a monthly payment.

The borrower can draw this monthly amount for the entire term of the loan, or until they have moved out of the house for a period of at least nine months, as might be necessary for convalescent care, or until their demise. The homeowner will owe only the amount that has been borrowed and the accrued interest for that amount.

The reverse mortgage can be taken in the form of a monthly amount from the lender, as described above, or the funds can be drawn in one lump sum, in the form of an equity line of credit to draw as needed, or any combination of the above.

If the borrower outlives or stays in the home longer than the term of the loan, which is usually for either fifteen or twenty years, they can refinance the property again, taking any additional accrued interest. Property values will generally increase over a 15- to 20-year period, creating added equity in the property.

If the homeowner moves from the home for a period of twelve (12) months for any reason, the loan will become due and payable, but only for the amount actually drawn by the borrower. The homeowner or their heirs will be required to sell the property or refinance into a conventional loan to pay off the reverse mortgage. The balance of the equity will go to the homeowner or the heirs as the case may be. The lender, or HUD, is only entitled to the amount they are owed. Reverse mortgages got bad press in the past because some consumers believed that the property would revert to the lender upon the homeowner's demise, but this was a misunderstanding of how the loan works.

The program was created by the federal government as a way to assist senior citizens in keeping their home and maintaining a lifestyle they have worked many years to achieve. Many seniors receive financial assistance from their adult children, who may be financially burdened, especially if they still have children at home. Reverse mortgages provide a viable solution for everybody, giving independence back to aging parents and relieving children of the added expense.

The loan amount available to a homeowner is determined by HUD. They have actuary charts that determine future value in any given community. The loans are based on 75% of the value, which ensures that the homeowner will have cash remaining if they decide they need to sell their home. This practice also ensures that their heirs will receive an inheritance.

The closing costs for these loans are high in comparison to conventional loans; however, when it is considered that the lender will not receive any payment on the money for up to twenty years or more, it is worth the expense.

Deferred property taxes are available for senior citizens even if they do not feel this loan is an option for them. Senior citizens may choose to contact the county tax assessor's office to discuss the possibility of having the taxes deferred until they are no longer in the home. This is a substantial aid to those on a fixed income. This is a program available solely to senior citizens.

For more information, borrowers should contact AARP (American Association of Retired People). This organization is a supporter of this loan program. They have a great deal of information on their website, *www.aarp.org,* and they can be contacted by phone or mail. HUD also provides extensive information on *www.hud.gov.* The available loans and other information are determined by the county where the property is located. This information can also be found on the AARP and HUD websites.

VA LOANS

VA LOANS are loans which are guaranteed by the Veteran's Administration for the benefit of all veterans of the United States Military Services through the Servicemen's Readjustment Act of 1944, commonly known as the GI Bill. The mortgage banks fund the loans, and the VA guarantees the balance of the loan in case of default. When a VA borrower defaults on a loan, the VA will guarantee the balance due down to half of the property value, much in the way that mortgage insurance works. This will allow the lender enough equity in the property to be able to pay foreclosure costs and not lose money on the transaction.

The VA allows fixed-rate loans for terms of 15 or 30 years only. The loans are available to qualified veterans and their spouses only; however, a non-veteran may assume an existing VA loan on approval by the lender. Reservists and members of the National Guard are also provided VA benefits. The qualifying requirements for a VA loan are more liberal than with a conventional loan and will allow a front- and back- end ratio of 41%.

Eligibility is based on the length of continuous active service and the maximum loan amount had historically been 75% of the FNMA/FHLMC maximum loan amount.
The FNMA/FHLMC guideline for the maximum loan amount is currently $417,000. As of January 2002, the VA allows VA loan amounts to be 100% of FNMA/FHLMC loan limits, and the FHA followed several years later.

VA Loans will allow 100% financing plus the closing costs based on the veteran's entitlement or amount qualified to borrow. The loan file must be full doc and owner-occupied.

VA loans do not require a monthly mortgage insurance premium since there is an up-front funding fee charged, which may be as much as 2.25%, based on the LTV and up to 3.30 % for repeat users of the GI Bill.

LTV	Funding Fee
96% - 100%	2.25% (.0225)/3.30% (.033)
91% - 95%	1.50% (.015)
90% and below	1.25% (.0125)
All Streamline or	
Rate Reduction Refinances	0.5% (.005)

The VA allows a STREAMLINE REFINANCE is allowed by the VA for borrowers who currently have a VA loan when the purpose is to reduce the payment. The required documentation is minimal as long as the payments have been made in a timely manner. An appraisal is generally required, as verification that the value of the property is still equal to or greater than the amount of the loan will be necessary.

The VA will not allow the borrower to pay the non-recurring closing costs (NRCC) consisting of the broker's fees, lender's fees, and escrow fees. A purchase offer transaction to be completed using a VA loan must always specify that the seller will pay these costs. A funding fee is used to pay some of the closing costs and the lender pays a yield-spread premium to the broker, currently in the amount of .55% of the loan amount.

The documents will be prepared in basically the same manner with the addition of a few forms that are included in the processing programs under "VA." On receipt of a VA application, the broker/processor will immediately contact the lender to register the loan and request an application/loan number, which will be transferred to page one of the 1003, section I under agency case number. This number is called the *CAIVRS (Credit Alert Interactive Verification Reporting System)* numbers.

At the same time, the broker/processor will submit the form called *VA Request for Determination of Reasonable Value* and *HUD Application for Property Appraisal and Commitment.* The lender will order the appraisal through a VA-approved appraiser. The appraiser prepares a *Certificate of Reasonable Value,* which notifies the broker/processor of the property value and the maximum loan amount allowable.

The veteran must provide a copy of their *discharge papers,* and a form called the *Certificate of Eligibility* or the *DD214.* This form is provided to veterans at the time of their discharge from the service or is available on request for veterans and those currently active in the military. For identification purposes, the Certificate of Eligibility is a light green color that looks like a certificate. If the borrower does not have the form, the processor can print out a *Request for Certificate of Eligibility* to be signed by the veteran and forwarded to the nearest VA Office. The veteran can also carry the form to the VA Office and receive the Certificate immediately if there is a need to expedite the loan application. If the form is mailed, it may take up to six weeks for the original to be returned.

There are additional forms that are required to be signed by the borrower and will be provided by the broker/processor once the initial information has been input into the LOS processing program. These forms are:
- **Verification of VA Benefit**- the purpose of this form is to determine that the borrower currently has no additional open VA Loans.
- **Counseling Checklist for Military Homebuyers**- this form discloses terms and requirements set forth by VA and HUD.
- Interest Rate and Discount Statement
- **Borrower's Certificate**- certifies compliance with VA and HUD rules.
- **Request for Certificate of Veteran Status**- Confirms eligibility and status.
- **Borrower's Acknowledgement of Disclosures** verifies receipt of the good faith estimate and the Truth-in-Lending.

When the processor has entered the usual information into the LOS computer processing program, the information will carry over to the appropriate places in the VA forms. The broker/processor will have additional information to enter, most of which will be found on the borrower's *discharge papers*. These loans are available to eligible veterans, their spouses, as well as disabled veterans with a minimal amount of active duty. Some of the additional information required for VA loans will include:

- Date of birth.
- Date of discharge from military service.
- Branch of military service.
- If currently active in the service, date of entry, current rank, and status.
- Breakdown of withholding taxes on pay stub.
- Service number.

Military pay is different than civilian pay with a non-military employer. The VOE specifies Section 13 for military employees. The military includes in the pay certain items, including:

- Allowance for personnel to be away from home.
- Housing.
- Uniforms.
- Travel.

These are normal payroll items for military personnel and are included on a two-year average because they will vary with assignment.

Submission to the lender will include these additional VA forms, along with information required in the regular loan package:

- **Loan Analysis**- similar to the 1008.
- **HUD/VA Addendum to Uniform Residential Loan Application**-is an addendum to the 1003 loan application.
- **VA Loan Summary Sheet**
- **VA Transmittal List.** This form is to be used by the underwriter and the lender to verify that all forms are included at the time of funding and for shipping to the investor.
- **Request for CRV** is included and the lender orders the CRV or Certificate of Reasonable Value, which is the appraisal.

Loan approval from the lender will include the company's usual Conditional Approval Sheet and the *Direct Endorsement Approval for HUD/VA Loans or Commitment.*

This is minimal instruction for VA loans, but it is sufficient to prepare and submit to the designated VA Lender. Unless the employing broker does an unusual amount of VA business, most processors will rarely have the opportunity to process a VA loan.

Underwriters must complete training and testing to be approved to underwrite a VA loan; upon completion, they will receive a certificate called Designated Endorsement. VA underwriters are referred to as DE Underwriters. This designation also applies to FHA Loans. The VA, FHA, and HUD all provide seminars offering thorough training on government loans.

Unless the broker/processor prepares a number of these loans, knowing the factors and calculations is no longer necessary as the complicated equations are now done by computer programs.

Each mortgage broker must obtain approval to do VA loans, which is separate from the usual conventional broker approval. Brokers will generally be approved by only one VA lender, although they have the option of being approved by more than one. Since the broker has a designated VA lender, the underwriters generally understand the uniqueness of the loans and will work with the broker/processor to complete the forms properly.

FHA LOANS

FHA LOANS are similar to VA loans in that they are government-backed loans and must be underwritten by a DE underwriter. The Federal Housing Administration (FHA) was created in 1934 and became part of HUD in 1965. The FHA insures FHA loans and governs the loan program. FHA does not lend money directly to borrowers. Offering low down payments and no prepayment penalties, FHA loans were created to make home ownership possible to lower-income families.

The loan package must be full doc, and the loan amount can be 100% of the FNMA/FHLMC maximum loan limit. Loan limits vary greatly from county to county and are subject to change at any time. The amounts are published daily on the lender's rate sheets.

NOTE

FHA insures the loans against loss in case of default; they do not lend directly to the borrowers.

The broker and lender must both be approved by HUD in order to broker FHA loans. The broker approval by HUD for FHA has changed in recent years to make FHA loans more widely available. The approval process used to be a more expensive and lengthier process than for VA loans. The additional cost was mostly due to the requirement for a Profit & Loss Statement that was fully audited by a CPA. FHA has eliminated that requirement for brokers who can verify a minimum of $75,000 in liquid assets.

The FHA loans are intended for lower income families and will allow a loan amount of 96.5% of the purchase price, plus non-recurring closing costs in most situations. This is a down payment of 3.5% of the purchase price or appraised value, whichever is less. Gifts of up to 100% of the down payment and the closing costs are acceptable from an immediate family member only. Acceptable family members include parents, siblings, aunt, uncle, cousin, or grandparent.

There are maximum income limits based on the number of people in the household and the county of residence. These guidelines generally apply to variations or clones of FHA loan programs, such as a CHAFA program. The specifications and county limits can be obtained from the lender. The income limits usually change each January. See *Figure 33, FHA Loan Limits* for a sampling of current income limits in California. The county limits are available on the HUD website *www.hud.gov.*

Each loan is charged an upfront mortgage insurance premium (UFMIP) in the amount of 2.5% of the loan amount. This figure increased from 1.75% on April 1, 2010. The borrower also pays a monthly MI in the amount of .55% of the loan amount.

Example:

$100,000	*Loan Amount*
X 2.5%	*Upfront MIP Percentage*
= $2,500	*Upfront MIP Charge*

Example:

$100,000	*Loan Amount*
X .55%	*Monthly MI Percentage*
= $550	*Annual MI Charge*
÷ 12	*Months/Year*
= $45.83	*Monthly MI Charge*

The monthly MI amount is reduced annually until the balance reaches 78% of the original loan amount, or the value of the property if the borrower requests a revaluation on the property. Financed MI is not required on condominiums.

The maximum loan amount is 100% of the purchase price or appraised value, whichever is less. This LTV must include the UFMIP. The lender's rebate or premium pricing may be used to pay the borrower's NRCCs. Second TDs/ mortgages are not limited to 100% LTV.

Owner-occupancy is required on all FHA loans and must be on one-to-four-unit residential properties. FHA loans are assumable at the lender's discretion. The assuming party must apply to the lender for qualifying prior to being approved for assumption.

RENTAL INCOME on the borrower's current residence may be used for qualifying income when obtaining an FHA loan only if they are relocating due to new employment or job transfer beyond a distance of reasonable commuting distance. Rental income may also be used if the loan balance of the current residence is 75% or less of the current value. An appraisal no more than six months old will be required to establish that value.

The loan programs that are available to borrowers are as follows:
- FHA 203b- Fixed-rate loan
- FHA 251- adjustable-rate loan- 1 year ARM
- FHA 203k- Rehabilitation loan program

The purpose of FHA loans is to help those who would not otherwise be able to qualify for a mortgage to be able to enjoy homeownership. Because of this, the qualifying is more liberal than conventional lending. The qualifying debt ratios for an FHA loan are 31 frontend and 43 backend. FHA underwriting guidelines are also more flexible on credit scores than conventional loans. Bankruptcy and foreclosure are acceptable once three years have passed since dismissal.

FHA borrowers are required to complete a Homebuyer's Course and answer questions relating to debt management and homeowner's responsibilities. This is currently done online or over the phone.

The forms are similar to those required by VA with the exception of the military information. The basic mortgage loan application is used along with the FHA forms. An estimate of living expenses is used in qualifying including the utilities.

FHA allows a Streamline Refinance for borrowers who currently have an FHA loan when the purpose is to reduce the payment. The required documentation is minimal as long as the payments have been made in a timely manner. An appraisal is generally required as verification that the value remains.

The broker/processor or loan agent should contact the lender when an FHA loan is received to verify guidelines.

USDA/RURAL DEVELOPMENT LOANS (RD)

USDA (Department of Agriculture)/Rural Development Loans (RD) are for properties located in areas with a population of less than 15,000. RD loans are also known as Section 502 loans and are primarily for low-income families in rural areas who do not have adequate housing.

The funds from RD loans can be used to prepare, build, renovate, repair, or relocate a home. The funds can also be used to prepare the building site, including obtaining utilities and services including water and electricity.

Income limits are similar to that of FHA guidelines; however, the borrower may have a qualifying income of up to 115% of the median income for the county.

Income limits may be found on *www.rurdev.usda.gov.* The borrower must qualify for the housing/mortgage payments using income to PITI and total debt obligation. They must have an acceptable credit history as determined by the lender.
The terms are fixed rate only with a maximum LTV of 100%.

RD loans can be obtained from lenders who are approved under the Single-Family Housing Guaranteed Loan Program, which includes:
- State Housing Agencies.
- Lenders approved by
  - HUD for Federal Housing Mortgage Insurance or GNMA mortgage-backed securities.
  - VA
  - FNMA or FHLMC
  - Farm Credit System (FCS)
  - Farm Service Agency

CONSTRUCTION LOANS

Construction Loans provide funds to build or perform a major renovation to a property. They are interim or temporary loans for the term of the construction. The loan package must be full doc. The value of the property is determined by the acquisition cost or purchase price, plus the cost to build.

The following must be included in the loan package:
- Standard Mortgage Loan Application and supporting documentation.
- Copy of the HUD-1/CD or closing statement from the original purchase transaction verifying the original cost of the property even if the property has been owned for a long period of time.
- Receipts or canceled checks for any expenses already paid by the borrower towards construction.
- Contractors' estimates and the accompanying contract for work to be done.
- Building permits
- Blueprints and/or plans
- Description of materials to be completed by the borrower or contractor and to be signed by both.
- Line-item cost breakdown- a form to be provided by the lender, which combines all the information gathered in the receipts and contracts.
- Copy of the contractor's license.
- Proof of insurance for the contractor.
- Proof of adequate liability insurance on the property to be provided by the borrower

Any additional information or documentation that may be helpful to the lender in determining the eligibility of the borrower should be included because the loan amount will be based on the future value of the property, not the present value. The broker should contact the lender of choice for clarification of various forms that will be required in the application.

Not all lenders will provide construction loans. The terms of these loans are usually for a term of 6-, 9-, or 12-months. During the term of the loan, the escrow company holds the funds that have not already been dispersed and will provide payment to the various contractors or service providers on receipt of proof of completion or presentation of a bill. Funds may also be dispersed to the borrower on proof of payment or presentation of a paid receipt.

NOTE

The lender will not allow incidental costs such as meals and phone calls.

At the time of locking the loan, the borrower can decide to lock in the interest rate for the term of the construction loan only or may choose to have the construction loan roll over into a fixed 15- or 30-year loan once the work is complete. The interest rate during the construction term will be higher than a conventional mortgage loan.

Upon proof of completion of the building, the lender will disperse the remaining funds to the borrower and the loan will roll over into the previously chosen fixed interest rate. If the borrower has chosen not to roll over the loan terms, a new refinance loan must be obtained. This is commonly referred to as a "take-out" loan.

For either the roll over or the take-out, the broker/processor must submit the following items to the lender:
- Signed building permits with all items signed by the building inspector.
- Certificate of Completion from the contractor/appraiser.
- Certificate of Occupancy from the local Department of Planning
- 442 appraisal form which states that the appraiser has re-inspected the property, the work has been completed, and the subject is habitable.

REAL PROPERTY MANUFACTURED HOMES are manufactured homes on privately owned lots and are considered **real property** only if the home is **permanently affixed to a private lot.** Generally, this refers to mobile homes that have been placed on a permanent foundation and the wheels and axles have been removed. Mobile home manufacturers began building the homes with the axles permanently attached in the 1990s. If this is the case, it should be documented, and the condition can be waived by the underwriter.

When a manufactured home has been permanently affixed to a foundation, the contractor will provide a state-required certificate. A copy of this certificate must be included in the loan file.

NOTE

HUD began establishing guidelines for manufactured homes in 1976. Any homes built prior to July 1, 1976, are more difficult to finance because they were not built to HUD guidelines. Contacting the intended lender for guidelines is advisable.

CHAPTER 12
PURCHASE TRANSACTIONS

PURCHASE TRANSACTIONS

Purchase transactions vary from refinance transactions in several ways generally involving documentation. The purchase contract is a generic term for the form that is used by real estate agents to determine the terms of the purchase between buyer and seller. The contract is frequently referred to by real estate agents as a **deposit receipt.** In California, the most commonly used purchase offer or contract form is the Residential Purchase Agreement and Joint Escrow Instructions.

It must be understood that the deposit receipt and the escrow instructions refer to two completely different pieces of documentation when dealing with lending. The purchase agreement includes "instructions" to escrow regarding the transaction, which is the reason it is often referred to as escrow instructions. It is important to understand and differentiate between the meanings when processing a mortgage loan. Neither is wrong; the terms are merely used differently in various areas of the relating industries.

DEPOSIT RECEIPT REQUIRED FOR LENDING PURPOSES is the actual receipt from escrow to the buyer for the deposit funds paid to escrow as the buyer's security. The law requires that funds must be deposited as earnest money to establish an escrow for a real estate purchase transaction. The receipt must be accompanied by a copy of the check from the buyer disclosing the amount deposited. Copies of this documentation should be requested from escrow by the loan processor.

> **NOTE**
>
> *Many terms are used interchangeably, and some have different meanings in different areas of the industry. Real estate sales, mortgage brokers, mortgage lenders, and the government agencies involved in the real estate and lending industries all vary the terms and use them with different meanings. The broker should be aware of this and know the various uses of the same term.*

ESCROW INSTRUCTIONS for lending purposes are documents that are prepared by escrow that summarize the terms as agreed to by buyer and seller. In other words, these are the instructions that will be followed by escrow, the real estate agent, and the lender based on the terms agreed to in the purchase agreement.

When verifying assets, the processor should carefully check dates to determine if the deposit check was cashed before or after the stated balance on a VOD or a bank statement. The borrower may be required to verify whether the funds on the VOD are before or after the deposit check. The purpose is to verify sufficient funds to close escrow if the buyer's funds are limited. The borrower can usually obtain a statement online or at the ATM.

RESIDENTIAL PURCHASE AGREEMENT AND JOINT ESCROW INSTRUCTIONS, or the purchase contract must be included in the loan file for a purchase loan transaction. The contract must be "fully executed," meaning that it must have all pages and spaces appropriately signed by both buyers and sellers. A complete copy including any and all counteroffers and addendums can be obtained from the escrow officer. The escrow officer is usually the only one involved who actually has a fully executed copy. The real estate agents are required to have a fully executed copy for their file; however, they do not always get that copy until later in the transaction.

The real estate agent that listed the property for sale is referred to as the listing agent and is the one who works directly with the seller as the seller's agent. The real estate agent who sold the property is the buyer's agent or the selling agent and is the direct contact with the buyer.

The loan agent is responsible for communication with the buyer's agent. The broker/processor will rarely speak with the listing agent. The buyer's agent is responsible for contacting the listing agent who in turn contacts the seller. The processor should not take calls from the listing agent or the seller because there is an accepted chain to be followed, and the processor does not have the time to communicate the loan status to all parties concerned. Any calls or questions should be referred to the loan agent or the broker of record.

> ## NOTE
>
> *The most recent should be placed at the top of the purchase offer to reflect the most accurate and/or final terms agreed upon.*

The broker/processor should check the following items, which may affect the loan or require additional documentation. Some items may become issues that can render the contract invalid.

SECTION 1 of the contract will include the property address, which should be compared to the prelim for accuracy. The address on the prelim is considered to be accurate as it is the way it is recorded with the county recorder's office.

The purchase price will also be stated in this section, but if there are any counteroffers included, they should be checked carefully for the final and accurate purchase price.

SECTION 2 discloses the financing terms that have been agreed to. **Sections 2 A through J** - All apply to financing and should be looked at carefully by the broker/processor.

2C - FIRST LOAN IN THE AMOUNT OF: provides the loan terms.

The amount of the loan and the acceptable interest rate is an issue that can render the loan void. If the buyer/borrower cannot get a loan amount equal to or greater than the amount agreed to in this section, they may decide to cancel the transaction.

> *Example: If the contract states that the buyer will obtain a 90% LTV and the lender will approve the borrower for 80%, the borrower has the option to cancel.*

> *The borrower may be willing to continue with the transaction; however, they will need to pay the difference and verify the additional funds.*

The same applies to the interest rate as stated on the contract in 2C.

> *Example: the contract states that the maximum interest rate will be 6.00% and the interest rates have increased to 6.5%, the borrower may choose to accept the higher rate and continue with the transaction or cancel the file. The borrower will need to qualify at the higher interest rate.*

2D states any additional financing terms that the borrower is requesting such as a second trust deed or a seller carry back, which is a second TD that will be carried or financed by the seller.

These examples indicate additional qualifying, and the terms must be disclosed. The CLTV must be taken into consideration and the payment for the second TD must be figured into the debt ratio to qualify. There may be other terms that will affect the loan and should be fully considered.

2G - LOAN APPLICATIONS: States the number of days (usually 7) that the contract allows for the borrower to complete a loan application. This condition also requires that the broker or lender shall provide the seller with a letter stating that they are qualified for the loan based on the application and credit report.

2H - VERIFICATION OF DOWN PAYMENT AND CLOSING COSTS: Sufficient funds to close in a set number of days (usually 7)

2I - LOAN CONTINGENCY REMOVAL: Loan approval and acceptance of the terms by the buyer/ borrower within set number of days (usually 17).

A contingency is a condition specified in a purchase contract, such as a satisfactory home inspection.

If that date arrives and loan approval has not been obtained, the loan agent should contact the real estate agent to request an extension. The processor should discuss the issues and any problems with the loan agent prior to the request.

The buyer has the option to waive the approval contingency; however, it is not advisable. If the processor and loan agent cannot obtain an acceptable loan, the buyer will still be obligated to perform according to the terms of the contract and close escrow. This may be impossible for the buyer to do, and they may be obligated to take a loan that they cannot afford. The buyer and seller can each be sued for **specific performance for non-performance** or not meeting the terms.

2J - APPRAISAL CONTINGENCY AND REMOVAL: This contingency allows the buyer to cancel the contract if the property does not appraise for a value equal to the purchase price within a set number of days (usually 17)

If the appraised value is less than the purchase price, the buyer has the option to cancel the contract, renegotiate the contract with the seller, or continue the transaction. This section will also state the time period to obtain an appraisal and for the appraisal to be accepted by the buyer and the lender.

If the transaction is continued with a reduced appraised value, the lender will base the LTV on the reduced value. The term used in lending is "**the lesser of the purchase price or the appraised value.**" The buyer can choose to waive this contingency but must be prepared to accept the possibility that it may be worth less than the purchase price. The appraisal can only be waived for an "all cash" transaction. Lenders will not provide a loan without an appraisal.

2K - NO LOAN CONTINGENCY: Is similar to waiving an appraisal.

If the loan contingency is waived, but the borrower cannot get a loan, the contract is still valid, and the deposit may be forfeited to the seller if the buyer cannot perform without a loan.

2L – ALL-CASH OFFER: if this is marked, be certain that the buyer can actually perform with an all-cash offer if necessary.

This is the same as waiving any loan contingencies. Often a buyer will change their mind and apply for a loan instead of tying up all their cash in their home and forfeiting any tax benefits. This occurs frequently with high-end properties, especially those in excess of one million dollars.

Many buyers will write an all-cash offer during a seller's market in order to get the offer accepted. If the buyer cannot afford to pay cash, they may lose their deposit if they cannot obtain a loan. The buyer may also be obliged to accept a loan with undesirable terms or one for which they do not qualify.

SECTION 3 - CLOSING AND OCCUPANCY

3A - BUYER INTENDS: states whether or not the buyer will occupy the property as their primary residence. This statement will affect the interest rate and closing costs that will be charged.

A second home or an investment property will require additional costs. An investment property will generally be charged an increased interest rate approximately 1.5% higher than the normal rate. The loan agent and processor should check with the lender or consult the rate sheet and the add-ons. If the interest rate or fees are going to be increased, the processor must provide a new MLDS/GFE and advise the borrower immediately. This may affect the financing terms on page one, section 2 and may render the contract invalid at the buyer/borrower's discretion.

3B - SELLER-OCCUPIED OR VACANT PROPERTY: provides the date that escrow is to close. The broker/ processor should do everything possible to ensure that this date is met.

The close of escrow is constituted by the recording of the deed and will be discussed further in Chapter 16, Submission & Closing. If this date is not met, both buyer and seller may suffer additional costs such as having to pay rent.

If the broker or processor knows the predetermined date will not be met, the loan agent, buyer, and the selling agent should be notified immediately. The selling agent is responsible for notifying the listing agent, who will notify the seller.

When it is determined that the close of escrow date will be extended, or if the seller decides to cancel the contract based on non-performance, escrow will be notified by the real estate agents or the loan agent.

The broker/processor should be as accurate as possible when requesting a new closing date and should consider allowing an extra day or two. The processor will need to contact the lender to request an extension of the interest rate. The lender does not have to extend the rate and may charge an additional fee or increase the rate.

SECTION 4 ALLOCATION OF COSTS:

4A - WOOD DESTROYING PEST INSPECTION: allows the buyer to require a termite inspection be performed. This section states whether buyer or seller pays for this inspection and any required repairs that are necessary. Generally, the seller pays for the inspection and any repairs.

> **NOTE**
>
> *The broker, loan agent, and processor must make every effort to ensure a timely close of escrow. The consequences of not meeting the predetermined closing date can be extremely costly to all parties to the agreement and may even cause cancellation of the transaction.*

If repairs are required, and the seller is paying for repairs, there is usually a maximum amount that they will pay, which is usually in the range of $1,500 to $2,500. If the buyer is to pay for the report or repairs, the costs will need to be included in the closing costs and disclosed on the MLDS/GFE.

The buyer has the right to waive a termite inspection. If this is the case, the lender cannot require a termite report unless the appraiser comments on obvious damage. Unless this occurs, there will be no repairs required. The processor will request a copy of the termite report be forwarded from escrow once it has been completed. This will be discussed further at the end of this chapter.

4B through 4C allow for additional reports or repairs and states whether buyer or seller will pay. In most cases, the seller will pay for these reports. If the buyer is to pay, allow for the additional expense in the closing costs on the MLDS/GFE. Real estate agents can provide an estimate of costs to the processor if necessary.

4D ESCROW AND TITLE: Provides the escrow and title information and fee division between buyer and seller. The processor may need to get phone numbers for escrow from the loan agent or the selling agent for contact purposes.

4E OTHER COSTS: should be checked for additional costs to the buyer to be included in the closing costs for qualifying.

SECTION 8 ITEMS INCLUDED AND EXCLUDED

8B - ITEMS INCLUDED IN SALE: provides for any personal items that are included in the purchase. Commonly included items are washers and dryers, refrigerators, or chandeliers.

The broker/processor must be aware that the underwriter has the right to reduce the purchase price by the value of the item, which may affect the loan amount.

> **NOTE**
>
> *RESPA states that the buyer has the right to select the title company to be used. If the seller or real estate agent selects, they may be responsible for 3x the costs to be reimbursed to the buyer.*

The inclusion of personal items does not typically affect the loan amount, but that could happen if the personal item is a large or valuable item, such as a car or a piece of antique furniture. These items are considered unusual and are rarely included in a purchase. The broker/processor should read this section to be certain of any potential changes to the purchase price. The broker/processor should contact the lender if there are questions about the inclusion of personal property.

SECTION 13 SALE OF BUYER'S PROPERTY

13A and B will indicate the buyer's intention with their current residence. This also discloses whether the sale of the current residence is a contingency of this transaction.

If the purchase agreement is not contingent on the buyer's selling their current residence, the current housing expenses must be included in the debt ratio for qualifying purposes. If qualifying determines that the borrower can afford both properties, it is certain that the transaction can close as scheduled, even if the current property is not sold.

The buyer may be planning to retain that property as an investment property and rent it. If this is the case, the rent can be included at 75% of the actual monthly rental amount. If the rental income is required for the buyer to qualify for the new loan, a copy of the rental agreement or lease must be obtained prior to the close of escrow to verify that income for qualifying.

SECTION 14 TIME PERIODS; REMOVAL OF CONTINGENCIES; CANCELLATION RIGHTS:

14B and 14C: clarifies the time frames, terms, and rights for meeting and removing contingencies.

The broker/processor must be aware that the buyer must accept or reject, or request repairs, or corrections regarding any and all contingencies in writing. If a written response is not received, the seller has the right to cancel the contract. It is always best to put everything in writing.

The seller may assume a contingency has been met and is acceptable if there is no response from the buyer by the deadline. If a contingency is not acceptable, the buyer must respond prior to the date.

Any unacceptable items may be corrected or repaired as agreed between the buyer and the seller or the contract may be cancelled or considered invalid.

An example would be the appraised value is less than the sales price. As discussed earlier in this chapter, the buyer has the option to pay any difference if the allowable loan amount is affected. The seller may agree to reduce the sales price to an amount equal to the appraised value. If the reduced value is going to cause the transaction to be canceled, the loan agent may choose to have another appraisal prepared by another appraiser, or the loan agent or processor may be able to provide additional information to the appraiser to justify the value being increased. With the introduction of HVCC, the options are no longer as readily available but should be considered, and the appraiser and lender should be consulted.

The broker/processor is not responsible for any additional negotiations between buyer and seller but must be aware of the issues. The broker/processor will be most helpful with the financing contingencies and any issues directly affecting the loan and closing costs and should discuss any of the issues and make suggestions for resolution with the borrower.

SECTION 24 states that "time is of the essence." This is important in a real estate transaction and simply means that everything required by the purchase agreement must be done as quickly as possible, including the loan processing. Dates must be met if at all possible.

If there are any issues that may cause the need for an extension of time, the broker/processor must notify the borrower and real estate agent as quickly as possible.

SECTION 25E Other Terms and Conditions provides for any additional terms to the contract. The broker/processor should check for any contingencies that may affect the loan.

An example would be when the seller or real estate agent will pay a portion of the buyer's closing costs. Most lenders will allow up to 3% of the loan amount to be paid towards the buyer's non-recurring closing costs by someone other than the buyer.

NON-RECURRING CLOSING COSTS are the costs that will occur for this transaction only, such as the appraisal, credit report, lender's fees, escrow fees, and broker's fees.

SECTION 33 provides complete signatures of all buyers and sellers.

If there are counteroffers, the seller's signature will be on that form, not on page 8. In the case of counteroffers, the final one will be the only form with all complete signatures. All buyers and sellers must initial each page of the purchase agreement where indicated.

The broker/processor can obtain a copy of the complete contract from escrow. The lender will require a fully executed copy with all counteroffers and addendums.

The broker/processor must check for all buyers. All borrowers included in the loan application **must** initial and sign the purchase agreement and all buyers included on the purchase agreement must be included on the loan application.

If there is a buyer/borrower that is included in the purchase transaction, but who will not occupy the property, and the transaction is to be owner-occupied, the occupying borrower must qualify for the loan alone.

If the occupying borrower does not qualify alone, the loan will need to be prepared as a non-owner-occupied loan. Lenders do not allow the non-occupying borrower's income to qualify for the loan unless the transaction is non-owner occupied. If this is the situation, the broker/processor should discuss it with the borrower because this may adversely affect the interest rate and/or closing costs.

COUNTEROFFERS will be numbered, and the highest-numbered counteroffer will be considered the final terms. The broker/processor must read the terms in sections 1A, B, and C for any terms affecting the loan. The most frequent issue included in the counteroffer is the purchase price. All counteroffers must be read because once a term is agreed to it will not be carried over to the next counteroffer.

> **NOTE**
>
> *Interest on a loan, insurance (including title insurance), and property taxes are examples of recurring closing costs and must be paid by the buyer.*

The broker/processor should request clarification of any unusual items and consider any financing problems or issues. The loan agent is responsible for relaying any issues or information to the borrower for resolution and decisions.

A 1031 EXCHANGE is a real estate transaction in which the purchase of an investment property and the sale of another of the buyer's investment properties of similar value occur simultaneously. The purpose of doing a 1031 exchange is an income tax benefit affecting capital gains. By purchasing a property of equal or greater value, the buyer can defer or offset income taxes incurred through the capital gains.

This applies to investment properties **only** and must involve **similar properties,** meaning the same type of investment property. If the seller is selling rental property, they must be buying rental property; likewise, commercial property must be replaced by commercial property; developed property replaced by property to be developed.

The escrow officer and real estate agents handle the issues of the 1031 exchange and the mortgage broker and lender are basically doing a purchase loan. The legal requirements of a 1031 exchange are not part of the mortgage process other than the absolute need for timeliness. Full documentation of the entire transaction is required; therefore, the purchase agreement for the sale of the buyer's former property or the sale property will be required.

To complete a 1031 exchange, the purchase transaction will be a **concurrent closing**. In other words, the sale of the former property will close escrow at the same time as the purchase of the new property. The funds from the sale will be transferred according to the 1031 exchange, purchase contract and the lender's requirements to the purchase escrow. This is a purchase transaction and closing costs cannot be included in the loan amount. The closing costs have to be deducted from the funds from the sale of the former property. Otherwise, the buyer must bring in any additional funds required to close escrow.

Canceled listings may become a refinance transaction. Lenders are reluctant to accept these loans as owner-occupied, cash-out refinances because they feel that the borrower is taking cash-out to use as a down payment to purchase a new owner-occupied home, then putting their current home on the market once the loan has closed.

The other possibility is that they will rent the current residence even though they got an owner-occupied loan with this transaction. Either way, the lender stands to lose money. If this is a legitimate transaction, the lender will require a listing cancelation and a strong letter of explanation. *Many lenders will not consider this scenario at all, but it can be done if handled properly. Check with the desired enders prior to submission.*

TERMITE REPORT AND CLEARANCE

WOOD DESTROYING PESTS AND ORGANISMS' INSPECTION REPORT, OR TERMITE REPORT is prepared by a pest control company and is ordered by the real estate agent. Once the report is completed, it is forwarded directly to escrow. The processor will obtain a copy from escrow.

The termite report discloses wood destroying pests and dry rot damage among other possible related issues. The purpose is to locate any problems that will affect the integrity of the structure. See Figure 34, termite inspection report.

Page 1 provides the address of the property being inspected, the date of the physical inspection and the total number of pages included in the report. Also included on this page is information about the property and a general description. The **center of page one** has a section that discloses the obvious problems that were readily visible to the inspector. A diagram of the structure shows the areas of the property that have issues or evidence of dry rot, pest infestation, or other findings. Along with the diagram is an estimate of costs to cure the problems.

Page 2 of the termite report provides definitions and explanations of the work to be done by the inspector and a variety of other disclosures important to the buyer of the property.

Page 3, 4, and 5 of the report provides the summary of the damage and the recommendations with the item number coordinating to the diagram on page one and a reference as to the location of the problem. A written description of all findings of either dry rot or pest infestation and the recommendation of the licensed inspector is also provided. Beneath or immediately following the recommendation there will be a statement that will clarify the need for the repairs that must be made.

The classifications are as follows:

- **Section I (1) items** must be repaired prior to the close of escrow. Many lenders will require all section I Items to be repaired prior to drawing loan docs. Section I Items are serious and, if not repaired, will continue to cause damage, which will directly affect the integrity of the structure. These are the most seriously damaged areas.
- **Section II (2) items** are not as serious, but if not repaired will most likely become a section I problem in the future. Most lenders will not require section II items to be repaired as part of this transaction unless required by the purchase agreement.
- **Section III (3) items** are disclosed for the buyer's information and will rarely be required to be repaired. These are problem areas that should be watched by the buyer because they have the potential to become serious problems.

> **NOTE**
>
> *VA and FHA loans always require all Section 1 and Section 2 items to be repaired prior to closing.*

An example of a section III item is a damaged rain gutter that is leaking onto a window sill. If not repaired, the sill will eventually develop dry rot and need to be replaced. The property owner should consider repairing the rain gutter before this happens.

- **Page 6 following the disclosure** will include estimates for the required or recommended repairs. If the required repairs will cost more than the seller is willing to pay, the buyer can choose to cancel the transaction or pay the additional costs. If the buyer will pay the additional costs, the amount must be added to the closing costs for qualifying purposes.

Occasionally the buyer will agree to pay for the repairs but will not want to do this until they own the property. This is not acceptable to the lender. In the past, lenders would allow the loan to close and require escrow to hold the broker's check until the completion report was received. In some instances, however, the buyers were not in a hurry to complete the work once escrow closed. The lender lost money because they could not ship the file or sell the loan in a timely manner, and they were charged pair-off fees for not meeting their commitment. This would also lead to extended periods of time when brokers were deprived of payment for a completed job.

The solution is to have the repairs made and paid for through the close of escrow. This way, the borrower pays for the work and owns the property. If for any reason the transaction fell out of escrow, the seller will pay the bill for the work completed and will still own the property.

The various inspection companies will use different forms or different computer programs that provide the required information. The information will not vary even though the forms and the format does. The broker/processor needs to review the report and look for any section I items. If the loan is obtained through the VA or FHA, the broker should also look for section II items.

Standard Notice of Work Completed and Not Completed is referred to as the termite completion and the form is required by the lender. See figure 35, Standard Notice of Work Completed and Not Completed/Termite Clearance

This report discloses the recommendations as stated in the original inspection report. The report states which items were repaired and the costs to cure. Certification by the inspector of all statements and any additional standard disclosures are also included in this report. The report must be signed by the inspector that did the repairs or performed a re inspection following the repairs.

The broker/processor should review both the original pest inspection report and the completion prior to submitting it to the lender to be familiar with the requirements. If additional documentation is needed, the broker/processor should request it immediately instead of waiting for the underwriter's review, which will take time.

WOOD DESTROYING PESTS AND ORGANISMS INSPECTION REPORT

Building No.	Street	City	Zip	Date of Inspection 8/31/2009	Number of Pages 6

Report # :

Registration # :

Escrow # :

☐ CORRECTED REPORT

Ordered by	Property Owner and/or Party of Interest:	Report sent to:

COMPLETE REPORT ☒   LIMITED REPORT ☐   SUPPLEMENTAL REPORT ☐   REINSPECTION REPORT ☐

GENERAL DESCRIPTION:

Single Family, Single Story House, Frame and Stucco, Furnished and Occupied, Attached Garage

Inspection Tag Posted: Garage

Other Tags Posted: Fumigation Tag 6/23/05

An inspection has been made of the structure(s) shown on the diagram in accordance with the Structural Pest Control Act. Detached porches, detached steps, detached decks and any other structures not on the diagram were not inspected.

Subterranean Termites ☒   Drywood Termites ☒   Fungus / Dryrot ☒   Other Findings ☒   Further Inspection ☐

If any of the above boxes are checked, it indicates that there were visible problems in accessible areas. Read the report for details on checked

Diagram Not To Scale

** See our AAA rating on bbb.org
** See our Testimonials on aimhighexterminators.com

OVERVIEW:

* Escrow Fee $65.00
* Fumigation $1,395.00
* Subterranean Termite Treatment $400.00
* Repairs $765.00
* Repairs Painting $125.00
  Grand: $2,750.00

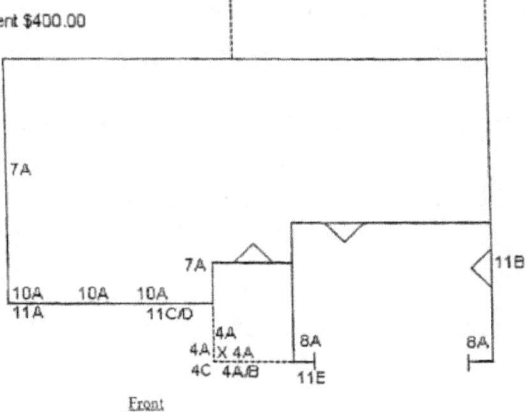

Front

Inspected By: _____   State License No. _____   Signature: _____

You are entitled to obtain copies of all reports and completion notices on this property reported to the Structural Pest Control Board during the preceding two years. To obtain copies contact: Structural Pest Control Board, 1418 Howe Avenue, Suite 18, Sacramento, California, 95825-3204.
NOTE: Questions or problems concerning the above report should be directed to the manager of the company. Unresolved questions or problems with services performed may be directed to the Structural Pest Control Board at (916) 561-8708, (800) 737-8188 or www.pestboard.ca.gov.   43M-41 (Rev. 10/01)

Figure 34: Termite Inspection Report
Page 1 of 6

Exterminators Inc.

Page 2 of inspection report

Address of Property Inspected		City	State	Zip
	8/31/2009			
Stamp No	Date of Inspection	Co. Report No.	Escrow No.	

WHAT IS A WOOD DESTROYING PEST & ORGANISM INSPECTION REPORT? READ THIS DOCUMENT. IT EXPLAINS THE SCOPE AND LIMITATIONS OF A STRUCTURAL PEST CONTROL INSPECTION AND A WOOD DESTROYING PEST & ORGANISM INSPECTION REPORT.

A Wood Destroying Pest & Organism Inspection Report contains findings as to the presence or absence of evidence of wood destroying pests and organisms in visible and accessible areas and contains recommendations for correcting any infestations or infections found. The contents of Wood Destroying Pest & Organism Inspection Reports are governed by the Structural Pest Control Act and regulations.

Some structures do not comply with building code requirements or may have structural, plumbing, electrical, mechanical, heating, air conditioning or other defects that do not pertain to wood destroying organisms. A Wood Destroying Pest & Organism Inspection Report does not contain information on such defects, if any, as they are not within the scope of the licenses of either this company, or it's employees.

The Structural Pest Control Act requires inspection of only those areas which are visible and accessible at the time of inspection. Some areas of the structure are not accessible to inspection, such as the interior of hollow walls, spaces between floors, areas concealed by carpeting, appliances, furniture or cabinets. Infestations or infections may be active in these areas without visible and accessible evidence. If you desire information about areas that were not inspected, a further inspection may be performed at an additional cost. Carpets, furniture or appliances are not moved and windows are not opened during a routine inspection.

The exterior Surface of the roof was not inspected. If you want the water tightness of the roof determined, you should contact a roofing contractor who is licensed by the Contractor's State License Board.

This company does not certify or guarantee against any leakage, such as (but not limited to) plumbing, appliances, walls, doors, windows, any type of seepage, roof or deck coverings. This company renders no guarantee, whatsoever, against any infection, infestation or any other adverse condition which may exist in such areas or may become visibly evident in such area after this date. Upon request, further inspection of these areas would be performed at an additional charge.

In the event damage or infestation described herein is later found to extend further than anticipated, our bid will not include such repairs. OWNER SHOULD BE AWARE OF THIS CLOSED BID WHEN CONTRACTING WITH OTHERS OR UNDERTAKING THE WORK HIMSELF/HERSELF.

If requested by the person ordering this report, a re-inspection of the structure will be performed. Such requests must be within four (4) months of the date of this inspection. Every re-inspection fee amount shall not exceed the original inspection fee.

Wall paper, stain, or interior painting are excluded from our contract. New wood exposed to the weather will be prime painted, only upon request at an additional expense.

All pesticides and fungicides must be applied by a state certified applicator (sec. 8555 Business and Professions Code Division 3) and in accordance with the manufacturer's label requirements.

This company will reinspect repairs done by others within four months of the original inspection. A charge, if any, can be no greater than the original inspection fee for each reinspection. The reinspection must be done within ten (10) working days of request. The reinspection is a visual inspection and if inspection of concealed areas is desired, inspection of work in progress will be necessary. Any guarantees must be received from parties performing repairs.

"NOTICE: Reports on this structure prepared by various registered companies should list the same findings (i.e. termite infestations, termite damage, fungus damage, etc.). However, recommendations to correct these findings may vary from company to company. You have a right to seek a second opinion from another company."

This Wood Destroying Pest & Organisms Report **DOES NOT INCLUDE MOLD** or any mold like conditions. No reference will be made to mold or mold-like conditions. Mold is not a Wood Destroying Organism and is outside the scope of this report as defined by the Structural Pest Control Act. If you wish your property to be inspected for mold or mold like conditions, please contact the appropriate mold professional.

Figure 34: Termite Report
Page 2 of 6

Exterminators Inc.

Address of Property Inspected		City	State	Zip
	8/31/2009			
Stamp No	Date of Inspection	Co. Report No.	Escrow No.	

WHAT IS A WOOD DESTROYING PEST & ORGANISM INSPECTION REPORT? READ THIS DOCUMENT. IT EXPLAINS THE SCOPE AND LIMITATIONS OF A STRUCTURAL PEST CONTROL INSPECTION AND A WOOD DESTROYING PEST & ORGANISM INSPECTION REPORT.

A Wood Destroying Pest & Organism Inspection Report contains findings as to the presence or absence of evidence of wood destroying pests and organisms in visible and accessible areas and contains recommendations for correcting any infestations or infections found. The contents of Wood Destroying Pest & Organism Inspection Reports are governed by the Structural Pest Control Act and regulations.

Some structures do not comply with building code requirements or may have structural, plumbing, electrical, mechanical, heating, air conditioning or other defects that do not pertain to wood destroying organisms. A Wood Destroying Pest & Organism Inspection Report does not contain information on such defects, if any, as they are not within the scope of the licenses of either this company, or it's employees.

The Structural Pest Control Act requires inspection of only those areas which are visible and accessible at the time of inspection. Some areas of the structure are not accessible to inspection, such as the interior of hollow walls, spaces between floors, areas concealed by carpeting, appliances, furniture or cabinets. Infestations or infections may be active in these areas without visible and accessible evidence. If you desire information about areas that were not inspected, a further inspection may be performed at an additional cost. Carpets, furniture or appliances are not moved and windows are not opened during a routine inspection.

The exterior Surface of the roof was not inspected.   If you want the water tightness of the roof determined, you should contact a roofing contractor who is licensed by the Contractor's State License Board.

This company does not certify or guarantee against any leakage, such as (but not limited to) plumbing, appliances, walls, doors, windows, any type of seepage, roof or deck coverings. This company renders no guarantee, whatsoever, against any infection, infestation or any other adverse condition which may exist in such areas or may become visibly evident in such area after this date. Upon request, further inspection of these areas would be performed at an additional charge.

In the event damage or infestation described herein is later found to extend further than anticipated, our bid will not include such repairs.   OWNER SHOULD BE AWARE OF THIS CLOSED BID WHEN CONTRACTING WITH OTHERS OR UNDERTAKING THE WORK HIMSELF/HERSELF.

If requested by the person ordering this report, a re-inspection of the structure will be performed. Such requests must be within four (4) months of the date of this inspection. Every re-inspection fee amount shall not exceed the original inspection fee.

Wall paper, stain, or interior painting are excluded from our contract. New wood exposed to the weather will be prime painted, only upon request at an additional expense.

All pesticides and fungicides must be applied by a state certified applicator (sec. 8555 Business and Professions Code Division 3) and in accordance with the manufacturer's label requirements.

This company will reinspect repairs done by others within four months of the original inspection. A charge, if any, can be no greater than the original inspection fee for each reinspection. The reinspection must be done within ten (10) working days of request. The reinspection is a visual inspection and if inspection of concealed areas is desired, inspection of work in progress will be necessary. Any guarantees must be received from parties performing repairs.

"NOTICE: Reports on this structure prepared by various registered companies should list the same findings (i.e. termite infestations, termite damage, fungus damage, etc.). However, recommendations to correct these findings may vary from company to company. You have a right to seek a second opinion from another company."

This Wood Destroying Pest & Organisms Report **DOES NOT INCLUDE MOLD** or any mold like conditions. No reference will be made to mold or mold-like conditions. Mold is not a Wood Destroying Organism and is outside the scope of this report as defined by the Structural Pest Control Act. If you wish your property to be inspected for mold or mold like conditions, please contact the appropriate mold professional.

Figure 34: Termite Report
Page 3 of 6

Exterminators Inc.

Page 2 of inspection report

Address of Property Inspected		City	State	Zip
	8/31/2009			
Stamp No	Date of Inspection	Co. Report No.	•	Escrow No

WHAT IS A WOOD DESTROYING PEST & ORGANISM INSPECTION REPORT? READ THIS DOCUMENT. IT EXPLAINS THE SCOPE AND LIMITATIONS OF A STRUCTURAL PEST CONTROL INSPECTION AND A WOOD DESTROYING PEST & ORGANISM INSPECTION REPORT.

A Wood Destroying Pest & Organism Inspection Report contains findings as to the presence or absence of evidence of wood destroying pests and organisms in visible and accessible areas and contains recommendations for correcting any infestations or infections found. The contents of Wood Destroying Pest & Organism Inspection Reports are governed by the Structural Pest Control Act and regulations.

Some structures do not comply with building code requirements or may have structural, plumbing, electrical, mechanical, heating, air conditioning or other defects that do not pertain to wood destroying organisms. A Wood Destroying Pest & Organism Inspection Report does not contain information on such defects, if any, as they are not within the scope of the licenses of either this company, or it's employees.

The Structural Pest Control Act requires inspection of only those areas which are visible and accessible at the time of inspection. Some areas of the structure are not accessible to inspection, such as the interior of hollow walls, spaces between floors, areas concealed by carpeting, appliances, furniture or cabinets. Infestations or infections may be active in these areas without visible and accessible evidence. If you desire information about areas that were not inspected, a further inspection may be performed at an additional cost. Carpets, furniture or appliances are not moved and windows are not opened during a routine inspection.

The exterior Surface of the roof was not inspected. If you want the water tightness of the roof determined, you should contact a roofing contractor who is licensed by the Contractor's State License Board.

This company does not certify or guarantee against any leakage, such as (but not limited to) plumbing, appliances, walls, doors, windows, any type of seepage, roof or deck coverings. This company renders no guarantee, whatsoever, against any infection, infestation or any other adverse condition which may exist in such areas or may become visibly evident in such area after this date. Upon request, further inspection of these areas would be performed at an additional charge.

In the event damage or infestation described herein is later found to extend further than anticipated, our bid will not include such repairs. OWNER SHOULD BE AWARE OF THIS CLOSED BID WHEN CONTRACTING WITH OTHERS OR UNDERTAKING THE WORK HIMSELF/HERSELF.

If requested by the person ordering this report, a re-inspection of the structure will be performed. Such requests must be within four (4) months of the date of this inspection. Every re-inspection fee amount shall not exceed the original inspection fee.

Wall paper, stain, or interior painting are excluded from our contract. New wood exposed to the weather will be prime painted, only upon request at an additional expense.

All pesticides and fungicides must be applied by a state certified applicator (sec. 8555 Business and Professions Code Division 3) and in accordance with the manufacturer's label requirements.

This company will reinspect repairs done by others within four months of the original inspection. A charge, if any, can be no greater than the original inspection fee for each reinspection. The reinspection must be done within ten (10) working days of request. The reinspection is a visual inspection and if inspection of concealed areas is desired, inspection of work in progress will be necessary. Any guarantees must be received from parties performing repairs.

"NOTICE: Reports on this structure prepared by various registered companies should list the same findings (i.e. termite infestations, termite damage, fungus damage, etc.). However, recommendations to correct these findings may vary from company to company. You have a right to seek a second opinion from another company."

This Wood Destroying Pest & Organisms Report **DOES NOT INCLUDE MOLD** or any mold like conditions. No reference will be made to mold or mold-like conditions. Mold is not a Wood Destroying Organism and is outside the scope of this report as defined by the Structural Pest Control Act. If you wish your property to be inspected for mold or mold like conditions, please contact the appropriate mold professional.

Figure 34: Termite Report
Page 4 of 6

Exterminators Inc.

Page 5 of 6 of Standard Inspection Report

Address of Property Inspected			City	State	Zip
	8/31/2009				
Stamp No.	Date of Inspection	Co. Report No.		Escrow No.	

11 OTHER - EXTERIOR:

11A - FINDING - Fungus damage wood noted at EAVE FASCIA.

RECOMMENDATION - Remove fungus damaged wood member(s) and patch or replace with new material. SECTION 1

11B - FINDING - Fungus damage wood noted at GARAGE SIDE DOOR.

RECOMMENDATION - Remove fungus damaged wood member(s) and patch or replace with new material. SECTION 1

11C - FINDING - Evidence of Drywood Termite Infestation noted at RAFTER.

RECOMMENDATION - Fumigate the entire structure for the control of drywood termites. Remove or cover drywood termite fecal pellets in accessible areas. Owner/agent to prepare for fumigation as per list of instructions to be furnished by this company. The structure must be vacated until released for re-entry by the licensed fumigator.
The following fumigant will be used:
  A. VIKANE- active ingredient;Sulfuryl Flouride
  B. CHLOROPICRIN- active ingredient;Chloropicrin
Aim High Exterminators will warranty the fumigation for Two years. SECTION 1

11D - FINDING - Evidence of drywood termites and damage noted at the RAFTER.

RECOMMENDATION - Repair the drywood termite damaged wood member(s) noted in the above. SECTION 1

11E - FINDING - Earth wood contact and faulty grade levels noted at foundation in subarea.

RECOMMENDATION - Re-grade the soil level to break the earth wood contact. SECTION 2

The company will re-inspect repairs done by others within four months of the original inspection. A charge, if any, can be no greater than the original inspection fee for each re-inspection. The re-inspection must be done within ten (10) working days of request. The re-inspection is a visual inspection and if inspection of concealed areas is desired, inspection of work in progress will be necessary. Any guarantees must be received from parties performing repairs"
SPECIAL NOTE: After completion of above item(s), the seller or agent may need to contact a qualified person to repair roof or roof coverings that may be damaged during replacement process.

"Thank you for selecting our company to perform a structural pest control inspection on your property. "This Wood Destroying Pests & Organisms Report DOES NOT INCLUDE MOLD or any mold like conditions. No reference will be made to mold or mold like condition. Mold is not a Wood Destroying Organism and is outside the scope of this report as defined by the Structural Pest Control Act. If you wish your property to be inspected for mold or mold like conditions, please contact the appropriate mold professional." Our inspectors have determined that your
property will benefit from the safe application of a chemical commonly used for structural pest control. In accordance with the laws and regulations of the State of California, we are required to provide you and your occupants with the following information prior to any application of chemicals to such property. Please take a few moments to read and become familiar with the content.

State Law requires that you be given the following information:

Figure 34: Termite Report
Page 5 of 6

Exterminators Inc.

Address of Property Inspected			City	State	Zip
	8/31/2009				
Stamp No	Date of Inspection	Co. Report No.		Escrow No.	

"**CAUTION - PESTICIDES ARE TOXIC CHEMICALS.** Structural Pest Control Operators are licensed and regulated by the Structural Pest control Board, and apply pesticides which are registered and approved for use by the California Department of Food and Agriculture and the United States Environmental Protection Agency. Registration is granted when the state finds that based on scientific evidence, there are no appreciable risks weighted by the benefits. The degree of risk depends on the degree of exposure, so exposure should be minimized."

"If within 24 hours following application, you experience symptoms similar to common seasonal illness comparable to the flu, contact your physician or poison control center and your pest control operator immediately." AimHigh Exterminators Inc. -877-246-4488

For further information contact any of the following:
County Poison Control Center - 1-800-662-9886
County Health Departments:
Los Angeles...213-240-8203
Ventura County...805-652-5914
Santa Barbara County...805-681-4200
County Agricultural Commissioners:
Los Angeles... 213-240-8203
Ventura County...805-933-3165
Santa Barbara...805-681-5600
Structural Pest Control Board - 916-561-8704
2005 Evergreen St Ste 1500 Sacramento Ca 95815-3831

Figure 34: Termite Report
Page 6 of 6

STANDARD NOTICE OF WORK COMPLETED AND NOT COMPLETED

NOTICE - All recommendations may not have been completed - See below - Recommendations not completed.

This form is prescribed by the Structural Pest Control Board.

Building No.	Street	City	Zip	Date of Completion
				10/12/2009

Exterminators Inc.

Report #:

Registration #:

Escrow #:

Ordered By:	Property Owner and/or Party of Interest:	Completion Sent To:

The following recommendations on the above designated property, as outlined in Wood Destroying Pests and Organisms Inspection Report No. ___125051___, dated ___8/31/2009___, have been and/or have not been completed.

Recommendations completed by this firm that are in accordance with the Structural Pest Control Board's Rules and Regulations:

ITEMS 04A & 10A (SUBTERRANEAN TERMITE TREATMENT)
ITEMS 04B, 04C, 11A, 11B & 11D (REPAIRS)
ITEMS 07A, 08A & 11C (FUMIGATION FOR DRYWOOD TERMITES - TENT)

Recommendations completed by this firm that are considered secondary and substandard measures under Section 1992 of the Structural Pest Control Board's Rules and Regulations including person requesting secondary measure.

Cost of work completed:		
	Cost:	$ 2,560.00
	Inspection Fee:	$ 65.00
	Other:	$ 0.00
	Total:	$ 2,625.00

Recommendations not completed by this firm:
ITEMS 09A & 11E (SECTION 2)

Estimated Cost: _____

Remarks:
This is to certify that the property described herein is now free of evidence of active infestations or infections in the visible and accessible areas.

Signature _____

You are entitled to obtain copies of all reports and completion notices on this property reported to the Board during the preceding two year upon payment of a search fee to: Structural Pest Control Board, 1418 Howe Ave., Ste. 18, Sacramento, California, 95825-3204.

NOTE: Questions or problems concerning the above report should be directed to the manager of this company. Unresolved questions or problems with services performed may be directed to the Structural Pest Control Board at (916) 561-8708. (800) 737-8188 or www.pestboard.ca.gov.

43M-44 (Rev. 10/01)

Figure 35: Standard Notice of Work completed and Not Completed/Termite Clearance

CHAPTER 13
APPRAISAL

HOME VALUATION CODE OF CONDUCT (HVCC)

The **HOME VALUATION CODE OF CONDUCT/HVCC** was implemented as part of the Dodd-Frank Act on May 1, 2009, to establish standards for solicitation, selection, compensation, and to avoid conflicts of interest by appraisers. Appraisals have historically been chosen by the loan agent/broker. Beginning May 1, 2009, appraisals must be ordered through the lender according to HVCC guidelines. The requirement to order through the lender was repealed by Congress in 2010 for RESPA and FRB requirements, but not for FNMA or FHLMC. Most lenders still require the appraisal be ordered through the lender's chosen appraisal management company.

HVCC was created to establish standards for solicitation, selection, compensation, and conflicts of interest by appraisers. HVCC also helps eliminate abuses by those who were elevating property values beyond a realistic value for personal gain. This practice by unscrupulous brokers and appraisers caused consumers to lose equity and property value, which ultimately caused many to owe more than the property was worth.

The appraisal is ordered through the lender. Appraisers are no longer chosen by the mortgage broker; this change was made to prevent outside influence on the appraiser's decisions and evaluations. It is crucial that appraisals can be trusted, as the lender bases its determination of creditworthiness on the appraiser's statements.

The Mortgage Disclosure Improvement Act (MDIA) stipulates that the appraisal cannot be ordered until the disclosures have been delivered to the borrower by the lender unless the broker is paying for the appraisal. Delivery may be made electronically, and the borrower must confirm receipt to allow the order of the appraisal to be paid by the borrower. If the borrower does not respond to the electronic delivery, the appraisal may not be ordered for seven (7) business days from the date it was sent to the borrower.

The borrower is allowed the opportunity to review the closing costs prior to becoming financially committed for services required as part of the loan process except for the cost of the credit report.

This requires that all appraisals be ordered through the lender, who will hire the appraiser from an appraisal management company (AMC), which in turn orders the appraisal from an independent appraiser. This eliminates any conflict of interest by removing the appraiser from the party requesting it. This in turn eliminates any influence by the broker and allows the appraiser the ability to determine the value without any undue influence.

The appraiser will need the following for access - the property address and the borrower's name and phone number. The appraiser will ask the type of loan, and a copy of the prelim and the purchase contract may also be required. The appraiser will evaluate a fair value, and if they are unable to evaluate the property as needed, they will let the processor or loan agent know before completing the report. In this situation, the loan agent will determine whether the appraiser should complete the appraisal, or the processor could provide additional information to the appraiser to establish a higher value.

If the appraised value is less than the sales price, there are three possible outcomes. Depending on the type of loan, the amount may be reduced, the borrower may not be able to receive cash-out, or, in case of a purchase, the buyer may choose to cancel the transaction. Generally, contracts to purchase property have an appraisal clause that allows the buyer to cancel the contract if the appraised value is less than the purchase price.

HVCC cannot change the normal fluctuations in property values that occur periodically due to changes in the economy.

PURPOSE AND FUNCTION OF AN APPRAISAL

The **PURPOSE AND FUNCTION OF AN APPRAISAL** is to estimate the value of a given property on the day of the evaluation. A real estate appraiser may be asked or required to provide an appraisal report that performs or serves several purposes.

Function is the intended use of the appraisal. The appraisal serves the function of providing the information as required. The following are the most common reasons that a property owner may want to know the value of their property.

Appraisals are often prepared in real estate practice to determine the value for the following uses:

- **Sell** at a good/fair price.
- **Buy** at a good/fair price.
- **Refinance**
- **Tax purposes**
- **Potential improvements**
- **Development**
- **Insurance replacement value**
- **Condemnation action,** such as through eminent domain
- **Distribution or disposal,** such as in a court action of probate or divorce

The **PURPOSE** of an appraisal is the reason that the appraisal is being done. What is the homeowner looking for? Do they want a high value to establish a good sales price, or are they looking for a lower value to reduce property taxes? What is the party ordering the appraisal looking for? The appraiser must determine the purpose of the appraisal in order to collect the correct data and develop the process of calculating the value.

Mortgage brokers are dealing with parties who want to know the value of their property to either refinance, obtain a new loan, or to verify the value is equal to the price if they plan to purchase the property.

The **DEFINITION OF AN APPRAISAL** is a written report providing the determination of the value of a specified parcel of real estate on a given date. A licensed, certified, and impartial appraiser prepares the appraisal. An appraised value is good for the date that the value was determined because values change on a regular basis.

COMPONENTS OF AN APPRAISAL

The **COMPONENTS OF AN APPRAISAL** are the various areas of information that make up the total report and influence the appraiser's opinion in determining the value of a property.

PRICE AND VALUE are affected by any number of influences, and these can change the value of a property at any moment in time. The sale of a comparable property in the subject property's neighborhood could increase the value of the subject if it sold for more than the market price of the subject property; likewise, it could decrease the value by selling for less. Social and political changes affect the value, such as an increase in interest rates by the Fed, which would likely cause property values to decrease. Recessions decrease property values because there are fewer buyers in the market.

PRICE is the amount that a buyer pays for a property. The market price is established as the amount actually paid when escrow closes. The logic is that a property owner can ask any price they choose, but until a buyer offers an amount, the appraiser establishes value, and the lender agrees to loan the requested amount, the actual market price is not determined. The market price is the amount that a ready, willing, and able buyer will pay a ready, willing, and able seller under any circumstances.

VALUE is what a particular item or thing is worth.

MARKET VALUE is the value that the property will generate when there is a ready, willing, and able buyer and a ready, willing, and able seller when available on the market for a reasonable amount of time. The buyer is ready to buy, willing to buy, and able to pay the amount agreed upon, and the seller is ready to sell, willing to sell, and able to accept. If there is no agreement as to the value between the buyer and seller, the value is not what the market will bear. Both parties must be aware of the property's uses, advantages, and defects. Neither party can be under an inordinate amount of pressure or undue influence.

UTILITY VALUE is a subjective value based on the use or utility that the property's use has to an individual purchaser. This aspect of property value generally applies to a property that is not the usual property or one that has unusual amenities. A one-bedroom home is an example of a property that would be valued based on its utility because the average home buyer would not want a one-bedroom home. Only a particular homebuyer would want a one-bedroom home which will affect the property's utility value.

There are FOUR ESSENTIAL ELEMENTS OF VALUE that must be considered when appraising real property are as follows:

- **Demand:** There must be a demand or buyers that are buying. The more people that are in the market to buy a home, the more valuable the property becomes.
- **Scarcity or Supply:** The more unusual or the more amenities a property has, the scarcer the property is and therefore more desirable, increasing the value of the property.
- **Utility or Use:** There must be a practical use for the property. The more a property suits the needs of the buying public, the more valuable the property will be.
- **Transferability or Marketability:** If the owner of a property is unable to transfer ownership easily, the value of the property will decrease. The cleaner the title, the higher the value.

Location! Location! Location! Environmental and physical aspects outside of the property also influence the value of real property. This is the mantra of the real estate industry.

SOCIAL IDEALS, LIFESTYLES, AND CUSTOMS all influence a neighborhood through changes that occur as parties move into a neighborhood, make changes to their homes, or move out of the neighborhood.

ECONOMIC INFLUENCES affect the value of real property as inflationary and recessionary economic periods go in and out. The established or older neighborhoods will experience the greatest fluctuation in values.

During an inflationary period, new homes and developments are built and established. Even though all properties increase during these economic times, they will not increase as quickly as when they were new because the new homes and developments are in greater demand for those who can afford them. The established neighborhoods become available to the lower income range of potential home buyers. When the inflationary period ends, the older established neighborhoods will have undergone a change from higher income owners to a lower income range of home owners.

GOVERNMENT AND POLITICAL REGULATIONS always have an effect and influence on property in a variety of ways. Local zoning laws are the most obvious and frequent influence on neighborhoods. A change in a neighborhood's zoning may be as drastic as converting a neighborhood, or portion of one, from residential to commercial. The adjacent neighborhood will also be affected, although not as drastically. The change to an adjacent neighborhood may be positive if the re-zoned neighborhood's values increase. This could happen with the addition of upscale shopping to a formerly residential neighborhood. Similarly, the values may be decreased if a residential neighborhood begins to become an industrialized area.

PRINCIPLES OF VALUE that an appraiser will consider when inspecting a property in preparation to determine the values are as follows:

1. HIGHEST AND BEST USE is the starting point for an appraisal. This term refers to the best use for a particular piece of property that will generate the highest value. The highest and best use is not necessarily the current use of the property.

    Example 1: A single-family residence in a neighborhood zoned for residential use.

    Example 2: A single-family residence in a commercial neighborhood would not be the highest and best use for that particular piece of property.

The use must be feasible, legal, and the use of the adjacent property must be taken into consideration.

2. SUBSTITUTION is an important principle when appraising real property. Substitution is the basis for the sales comparison approach and is used for all three approaches to appraisal. A property that is similar to the subject property in desirability, size, room count, and location is used to determine the value or price of the subject. The comparable property must have closed escrow within a reasonable amount of time prior to the comparison in order to have established a usable market value. When the subject is an income-producing property, the comparables must be income-producing in establishing the value and the rental income.

    When identical properties are for sale simultaneously, the property with the lower price will sell first.

3. **SUPPLY AND DEMAND** refers to the number of properties of a certain type that are available for purchase in a certain area, and the demand or desire for that type of property. Demand is determined by the number of potential buyers who want a particular property type. The number of properties in relation to the number of potential buyers constitutes the supply.

When a greater number of properties are available on the market, there is a large supply. If there are not as many buyers as there are available properties, the result is that the values will decrease, which creates a *buyer's market*. The buyers have the favorable position in this market.

Conversely, when there are fewer available properties for sale than there are potential buyers, the values will increase as the buyers will be bidding to be able to purchase a property. This creates *a seller's market,* and the sellers are in a favorable position.

4. **CONTRIBUTION** is a principle concerned with the value that any particular item or amenity adds to a property. An extra bathroom, a fireplace, or swimming pools are all examples of amenities that will increase the value of a property over comparable properties that do not have those amenities.

5. **INCREASING RETURNS** are improvements that add more value to the property than the improvement cost.
   Example: Sam renovated his kitchen with new cabinets, counter-tops, flooring and appliances. The total cost was $30,000. The improvement is an increasing return because the overall value of his property increased by $45,000, which is $15,000 more than the cost of the investment.

6. **DECREASING RETURNS** are improvements that cost more than the value that will be gained in the overall property value. Decreasing returns are items or improvements that are generally made for the enjoyment of the property owner for long term use and occupancy.
   Example: Sam installed a swimming pool in his yard. The costs of the improvements are $45,000. The overall value of the property has increased by $15,000 because of the addition of the swimming pool. The overall increased property value is $30,000 less than the cost of the improvement.

> **NOTE**
>
> *The greater the demand, the more valuable the property. The greater the supply, the less valuable the property will be.*

7. **CONFORMITY** occurs when a reasonable degree of economic and social similarity exists in an area, creating the maximum value for the properties within the neighborhood. When the socioeconomic make-up is similar, the residents have a comfort level, and the stability of the area is established because the properties are rarely sold.

   Conformity also exists when there is uniformity in architectural style and similar properties. This is a desirable attribute of a neighborhood; however, an overly conforming neighborhood can become mundane and boring, resulting in decreasing values.

8. **PROGRESSION** is when a property of lesser value because of size, quality, or lack of amenities, becomes more valuable as the surrounding properties increase in value through improvements. The subject property is said to be "under-improved" for the neighborhood.

   Progression can occur as the property owners begin to improve properties in a neighborhood, increasing the overall value of the area. Homeowners who do not improve their properties benefit from the improvements made by other owners by virtue of being in a neighborhood of **increasing values**. The under-improved properties increase in value solely because of being surrounded by improved properties.

9. **REGRESSION** occurs when a property of greater value is devalued because of its proximity to properties of lesser size, quality, or amenities. Such a property is said to be "overbuilt" for the neighborhood. This usually occurs when one owner improves their property beyond the other properties in the neighborhood.

   Regression can also occur when the neighboring properties become rundown through lack of maintenance. This may occur when a neighborhood becomes predominantly non-owner-occupied or consists largely of rental properties, which generally show less pride of ownership. The improved property decreases in value because it is in a neighborhood of **decreasing value**.

10. **LIFE-CYCLES** are typical neighborhood changes involving progression and regression. These changes occur in most areas, especially low- to- mid range housing, but it affects all neighborhoods to some extent. A neighborhood begins as new housing, whether as a subdivision or development, or as individual homes built over a period of time. The new homes are typically owner-occupied, and display pride in ownership. After a period of time, the houses begin to show wear.

Some of the property owners may experience an increase in income and choose to move up to another neighborhood. They may choose to rent the property once they have moved on. A rented property typically is not maintained as well as it would be if owner-occupied, which means that the property will experience deferred maintenance and lose value. If the previous owners choose to sell the now devalued property, it may sell to one who cannot afford a newer home and may be unable to afford the maintenance that an older home often requires. The neighborhood is on a downward trend in values, or a period of regression.

Eventually, the neighborhood may begin to attract potential homeowners who are looking for homes that need renovation or "fixer-uppers" with the intention of flipping them and making a profit through speculation. The properties may also be purchased by potential homeowners who cannot afford more and who view such a neighborhood as a way to attain home ownership. Once one property owner begins to fix a property in an otherwise run-down neighborhood, many of the surrounding homeowners will begin to repair theirs. Progression has begun and the neighborhood is now in a period of increasing values.

A typical life cycle of a neighborhood will generally be over a period of 20 to 50 years. Progression and regression do not usually occur quickly but happen over a number of years.

11. **SPECULATION** creates anticipation as a part of the process of progression and regression. The anticipation of making a profit by investing in real property has been a driving force in the real estate industry since the beginning. Many people make a living by investing in real property.

Some of the ways of investing in real property in anticipation of making a profit include:

- **Fixing** or improving a property for re-sale to gain profit.
- **Speculation** is the practice of buying properties on the assumption that values will increase, with the intention of selling at a later date and making a profit.
- **Development** construction or renovation to sell for profit.
- **Rental** leasing a property to generate long-term income.

APPRAISAL PROCESS

The **APPRAISAL PROCESS** is made up of several steps and processes. The appraiser must determine the purpose of the appraisal in order to collect the correct data and develop the correct process of calculating the value.

The appraiser will need the property address and the borrower's name, phone number, and email. The appraiser will ask the type of loan, a copy if the prelim and the purchase contract may also be required. The appraiser must determine a fair value, but having an idea of what is needed will be helpful and they will do their best to accommodate.

If the appraiser is unable to evaluate the property as needed, they may let the mortgage broker/processor or loan agent know prior to completing the report. Under these circumstances, the loan agent will determine whether the appraiser should complete the appraisal with the established value, or the processor may be able to provide additional information to the appraiser to establish a higher value. Depending on the loan being obtained, the amount may be reduced, the borrower may not be able to receive cash-out, or, in the case of a purchase, the buyer may choose to cancel the transaction if the appraised value is less than the sales price. Contracts to purchase property generally have an appraisal contingency allowing the buyer to cancel the contract if the appraised value is less than the purchase price.

Depending on how busy the appraiser is, the report should be completed within three to four days of the physical inspection, or approximately one week from the date the appraisal is ordered.

The SALES COMPARISON (COMP) is the most commonly used method of establishing a value. The sales comparison approach is a method of using comparable properties, referred to as Comps, as discussed previously. The appraiser locates properties in the subject property's area that are as similar to the subject as is possible. The appraiser looks for properties that are similar in size, style, condition, room count, and amenities.

Three comps are the norm unless the property is a high-dollar property, or the comps are not similar enough to the subject. It is preferred that the comps "bracket the subject," meaning the at least one comp should have greater square footage and at least one should have lesser square footage. This principle of bracketing carries through to all of the amenities being compared, including the sales price of all of the comps.

All of the comps must have closed escrow although an appraiser may use sales not yet closed. The true value is not established until the sale is closed. Any number of issues can cause a real estate sale to fall through, especially if the buyer determines that the value is not equal to the price, or the seller determines that the purchase price is too low. Occasionally an appraiser will use a sale that has not yet closed escrow because it helps establish the property value. The lender will usually require that comps close escrow prior allowing the subject to close escrow.

COST APPROACH is a method of determining the value by establishing the cost to build the subject improvements new. The cost approach works well for newer properties; however, it can be difficult and inaccurate on older properties. This method is best used to appraise new or unusual properties that do not have available comps. An example of an unusual property where the cost approach may be employed would be a church or a post office.

The upper end of the value is reached by using the cost approach because it uses the value of new materials and current construction costs. The formula used to determine value by using the cost approach is:

Cost to Build New
– Accrued Depreciation (based on age and condition of the structure)
<u>+ Land Value</u>
= Value

REPRODUCTION COST as a method of the "cost to build new" that establishes the replication of the building exactly as it stands based on current construction costs and current costs of materials using the same quality of workmanship. This establishes the costs of building an exact replica.

ACCRUED DEPRECIATION is the amount that the building has depreciated, or declined, in value because of the aging of the materials and wear and tear to the structure.

LAND VALUE determines the value of the land if it were vacant with no improvements. The value of land can be determined by establishing comparable vacant lots in the subject property's neighborhood. Land value is determined on all appraisals.

REPLACEMENT COST NEW is a method of using the cost approach that is more practical for older buildings. It may not always make sense to use the reproduction cost method to appraise an older building that was built with outdated methods and materials. To appraise the value of a house such as a 1900 Victorian using the reproduction method would not create a fair value because of the reproduction cost of items such as stained-glass windows and detailed moulding.

Replacement cost new allows for the cost of building an equivalent replacement of the subject instead of replicating the property exactly. The replacement cost new method determines the value of a property that serves the same function and utility as the subject but uses current materials and methods.

FIVE METHODS OF DETERMINING COST of the building materials and the construction cost are used whether using the replacement or reproduction method to determine value by use of the cost approach.

- **Quantity survey** is the most accurate method of determining the cost of replacing a building. The costs of the materials and labor are determined using a book that provides a breakdown of the materials (and often costs) to build various styles of houses. The books allow for items such as the amount of stucco required to build a Spanish-style home of a designated square footage. Appraisers refer to these handbooks as a means of determining the quantity of the required building supplies.

They are then able to determine the cost to build by multiplying the cost of material by the square footage of the house. One of the most commonly used books is the Marshall and Swift Manual.

- **Unit Cost-in-Place** is the second most accurate method which establishes the costs to rebuild by adding the various units, once installed by each of the various contractors. An example is the total cost the dry-wall contractor will charge for the job, including materials and labor. This method will provide the complete cost for each unit separately and totaled for the complete project.

- **Square Footage** is a common and quick method of determining value, based on the construction cost per square foot of the completed building. Marshall and Swift and the other available handbooks provide the amount of materials per square foot based on the structure's style, and the appraiser can then determine the cost per square foot based on current costs. Building contractors will quite often provide a bid to build based on the square footage method, as they are familiar with the costs at any given date in time. This method is often used for single-family residences.

The formula for square footage is: **Length x Width= Square Footage**

- **Cubic Footage** is similar to the square foot method and is commonly used for large industrial buildings, such as factories or warehouses, where the value is not based on the length and width alone, but also the height. The formula for cubic footage is:

Length x Width x Height = Cubic Footage

- **The Index Method** is not a fully accurate method of determining the cost of construction but may work well for properties that are not old. The appraiser can determine the cost of the subject when it was built, then multiply the total cost by the percentage of change in the cost from the time of construction to the current market.

NOTE

To determine the size of a triangle, the total square footage must then be divided by two.

Example: Appraiser Jones is determining the value of a property that was built 5 years ago. At that time, the building cost for the quality of construction was $250 per square foot. He knows that the current cost for similar quality construction is $350 per square foot.

$350-$250 =$100
$100/$250=40%

The cost of construction has increased by 40% since the subject property was built. The factor, or index, is 40%.

$375,000	Cost to build property 5 years ago.
x 40%	Index% Costs Increase
(=) + $150,000	Increase in $
= $525,000	Cost to build new today

SALES COMPARISON APPROACH or the MARKET DATA APPROACH is the method used for residential appraisals for lenders or mortgage loans. The principle of this method is to locate properties that are similar in location, size, amenities, condition, and quality. Comparison is made to the similar properties by adjusting value of the changes to a comp to make the comp an identical property to the subject.

Example: Comp 1 has a swimming pool, but the subject does not. The value of Comp 1 will be reduced by $15,000 to make it the equivalent to the subject.

DEPRECIATION OR PHYSICAL DEPRECIATION of the properties and the amenities must be considered when determining the value. A roof generally has an estimated life of 20 years. If the roof is 15 years old, the value of the property will be reduced to depreciate or accommodate for the wear of that component of the property. A new roof would not be depreciated because there is minimal wear or usage to the component. Depreciation applies to all aspects of a structure and other improvements, such as fencing.

NOTE

Land is never depreciated. Values may change with the economy; however, the land itself is never considered in the depreciation factors.

FUNCTIONAL OBSOLESCENCE refers to the functionality of a structure that is functional or works, but it is obsolete according to current standards. Older homes may have floor plans that were common when built but would no longer be acceptable. Small or no closet space is another form of functional obsolescence. Functional obsolescence can be cured or corrected.

> *Example: Simi Valley, northwest of Los Angeles, was a large ranch in the early 1900s. During that time there were small, one-bedroom houses built for the ranch hands that would come from their homes in Los Angeles or other places to work on the ranch for a couple of weeks at a time then go home. The ranch hands lived in these houses only during the week when they were at work. The houses typically have a floor plan that allows access to the only bathroom through the bedroom. This was an acceptable floor plan for ranch hands who lived there on a temporary basis.*
>
> *As the ranch was parceled out and sold, these houses were sold and many still exist today. The bathroom is functional; however, the floor plan is obsolete or not an acceptable floor plan in today's market.*

EXTERNAL OBSOLESCENCE refers to things outside the property that will render a property obsolete or not up to current standards and expectations. **External obsolescence is not curable**. These are issues that the property owner has no control over. Some examples of external obsolescence are as follows:

- Zoning
- Neighborhood change
- Airport creation
- Freeway expansion
- Street re-routing

Computation of the value will be discussed in the following section. There are several websites that can be used to obtain an estimated value of a property as a guideline while waiting for an appraisal to be prepared. One such site is *www.zillow.com.*

RECONCILIATION AND REPORT PREPARATION

REPORT PREPARATION will generate a report of approximately fifteen pages, with the most pertinent information on the first three to four pages. The real estate professional should review the appraisal when completed to be certain the property is acceptable. If there are any issues with the property, the appraiser's comments should be reviewed to be certain the issues have been properly explained and also to be competent to discuss the property with the client, whether that is the buyer or seller. Many transactions have been declined or cancelled because the property was unacceptable. See Figure 36, Residential Appraisal Report.

An appraisal is good for six months, at which time a new appraisal must be provided. Once an appraisal is four months old, a re-certification of value will be required from the appraiser. This is a one-page document, generally in the form of a letter stating that the value is still valid.

SUBJECT: The subject address must match the complete address on the prelim. The prelim will have the correct address. Request a correction from the appraiser if there are any discrepancies.

LEGAL DESCRIPTION and the **ASSESSOR'S PARCEL NUMBER** must be compared to the plat map in the prelim. Different numbers may indicate fraud, and any errors must be corrected.

BORROWER must match the name of the primary borrower on the loan application or the buyer of the property.

CURRENT OWNER must match the name of the borrower for a refinance or the seller for a purchase transaction.

OCCUPANT must match the "occupancy status" of the purchase contract or the loan application. If the loan is being done as an owner-occupied, the borrower's name must be in this space. If it states another person's name or states "tenant," the issue must be addressed to establish the accurate occupancy and prevent fraud.

NOTE

The words road, street, avenue, etc., must match the prelim exactly, and are important to ascertain that the subject is the correct property.

THE PROPERTY RIGHTS APPRAISED indicate the type of ownership. Most property is owned as **"fee simple,"** which is the term used indicating full ownership with no contingencies on that ownership. **Leasehold** indicates that someone other than the borrower owns the land, and the borrower owns only the improvements or house and pays rent on the land the house is on.

PROJECT TYPE will most commonly be an SFR, PUD, or condo. If the property is a PUD or condo, the name of the project will be included.

SALES PRICE will indicate the purchase price for a sales transaction. If the loan is a refi, the last date of transfer may be indicated in this space, or it may be left blank.

If the sales date for a refi is indicated and it has sold less than a year prior to the current closing date, the lender will use **the lesser of the purchase price or the current appraised value**. If this is an issue, the closing can be scheduled to be after the one-year anniversary date of the purchase.

LENDER/CLIENT must be the name of the broker/company. If the borrower has an appraisal that was prepared for another mortgage company, the appraiser can change the name to the current brokerage, providing the borrower has paid for the appraisal. The borrower may pay for the appraisal at this point to release any obligation by the former broker, in which case the broker will release the appraisal to the new broker.

NEIGHBORHOOD: Location, etc., the preferred responses will appear in the first or the middle columns starting with the property being "urban" or "suburban." When items are marked in the third column, "rural," the appraiser should address these at the bottom of this page in the "COMMENT" section or in detail in the addendum, which will be found on pages 3, 4, or 5 in most appraisals.

A **RURAL PROPERTY** indicates to the lender that comparable properties will not be nearby, the subject property may be zoned as agricultural, and the marketing time will probably be longer than for an urban property.

MARKETING TIME is the biggest issue to a lender if it is "over 6 months." This will indicate to the lender that if the property goes into default, there may be additional losses due to extended marketing time or that it will take approximately 6 months or more to sell the property if the lender has to foreclose.

PREDOMINANT OCCUPANCY indicates whether the value of the property will continue as it would with a predominantly owner-occupied neighborhood or will decrease as it would with non-owner-occupied neighborhood.

SINGLE-FAMILY HOUSING should bracket the value of the subject property in dollar amounts representing recent sales within the neighborhood. The main concern would be that if the value of the subject were greater than the rest of the neighborhood, the subject would not be easily sold at its highest value. If the subject is worth less than most of the other properties in the neighborhood, it indicates to the lender that there is much room for improvement or that the subject is being sold below value. This places the buyer and their lender in a strong position and the house could be sold quickly if necessary.

PRESENT LAND USE AND **LAND USE CHANGE** are also indicators of future value. If the appraiser indicates that the present use of land is likely to continue, values are likely to remain the same or increase with the economy. Land use change indicates that there may be dramatic changes. The changes may occur in many different ways, but the appraiser must clarify, or the appraisal/subject property may be unacceptable. Some changes occurring may be from single- family to multi-family, or condos and PUDS (acceptable); residential to commercial (unacceptable); or agricultural to residential (acceptable). Some of the possible changes may also indicate a change in zoning affecting the value in use.

NEIGHBORHOOD AND MARKET CONDITIONS contain appraiser's notes that should be read for any comments affecting the marketability of the subject property. The appraiser should explain any adverse comments. Negative comments can cause the loan to be declined due to unacceptable property.

PUD: Project information for PUDs applies to both PUDs and condos. The information should be checked against what is on the prelim. The name of the project is at the top of the page. The number of units is stated in this section. It can be difficult to find a lender willing to finance a complex of less than 10 units. Complexes of less than four units are financed by a small number of lenders.

SITE: Zoning is of the utmost importance to the use and future of the property. The zoning for a residential property must be "residential." The designation will vary in different communities.

Examples of typical zoning designations are:
- *R1- residential, single family*
- *R2- residential, up to two units*
- *R3- residential, up to three units*
- *R4- residential, up to four units*
- *MR- multiple family*
- *C1- small commercial*
- *C2- large commercial*

These are commonly used zoning designations, but it is wise to verify the local classifications as they will vary.

"LEGAL" means that it is zoned according to the current use. For residential use, an "R" zoning will apply, and the number of units allowed for that lot is indicated by the number following the "R." For example, an SFR with an R-1 zoning complies because it is one unit. An SFR in an R-4 zone is still in compliance although it is one unit in an area zoned for four residential units. An SFR in a C-1 zoning is not in compliance or is considered "Not Legal."

LEGAL NONCONFORMING is also referred to as "grandfathered use" and indicates that the subject does not conform, such as a 2-unit property located in an area that is zoned R1 or one unit per lot. Grandfathered use indicates that the subject was built and in use prior to the current zoning. A lender will require the Building and Planning Department of the local area to provide a "rebuild letter" stating that the property can be rebuilt for its current use if damaged by natural causes. These are not always obtainable and will require contacting the local Department of Building and Development. The local governing agency may merely fax a copy of the building codes with the pertinent information.

HIGHEST & BEST USE, as improved, should be marked "present use." If not, look for related comments at the end of this section. Highest & best use means the best purpose or usage of the property, which is not always its current use.

PUBLIC UTILITIES indicates whether the property has utilities provided by the local government or if the property is self-contained by using a septic tank, well, or a generator. Septic tanks may require a septic cert (certification) from a licensed company unless the tank is less than five years old, which will generally require proof in the form of a receipt for the installation of a new septic tank. A well for water may require a cert from a qualified/licensed company and may require a perc (percolation) test.

A FEDERAL EMERGENCY MANAGEMENT AGENCY (FEMA) Special Flood Hazard Area will require flood insurance if the appraiser has marked this "Yes." A Flood Cert will be obtained from FEMA if there is financing involved in the transaction.

FEMA ZONE indicates if there is a need for flood insurance. Zones "C" and "B" will generally not require flood insurance. The lender will run a flood cert to verify the appraiser's findings. A flood zone which is classified "A" will generally require flood insurance.

DESCRIPTION OF IMPROVEMENTS: A general description does just that. It is good to review this section as well as the comments immediately following it. The age of the subject will be found in the first column. Legally, free-standing appliances that are not built-in are personal property, and the sales price on a purchase transaction can be reduced by the estimated value of the item. In a purchase transaction, this is done at the lender's discretion.

COMMENTS: Additional features, condition of the improvements etc., and adverse environmental conditions should always be read thoroughly for consideration of any negative information, which may indicate that the subject is unacceptable property.

COST APPROACH: This section looks at the replacement cost of the subject if it had to be rebuilt. The value that the improvements, or structures, add to the value of the land is a consideration. Depending on the area and the property, the value of the land may be too excessive for the structure. This is especially true for properties with acreage in rural areas.

SALES COMPARISON ANALYSIS: Lists the main amenities and features taken into consideration when evaluating the value of any given property.

This section will provide the attributes of the subject property along with additional properties that sold recently and used to compare, thereby establishing a fair market value. Three properties are generally used as comparables (comps), but additional comps may be requested based on several issues, such as sale dates of the comps and how similar the properties are. The following guidelines are used to determine the similarities in properties. The comps should be:

- Within a ten-block radius of the subject.
- COE (close of escrow) date of the comp should be within six months of the appraisal date.
- Line adjustments should not exceed 8% of the value of the property.
- Total line adjustments, or the net adjustments, should not exceed 17% of the value of the property.

See Page 2 of Figure 36, Residential Appraisal Report for the following calculations to determine adjustments and similarities:

> **Example:** *Comparable No. 2, Sales Price is $295,000. Comp is 0.35 miles from the subject property. In this case, the distance is acceptable because it is in the neighborhood. See the location map in the appraisal.*
>
> *The comp is in inferior condition to the subject, so the appraiser increased the value of the comp by $20,000 to equalize the value to match the subject more closely.*

> $20,000 *Line adjustment*
> ÷$295,000 *Property value*
> = .0677 *or 7% of property value*

This is an acceptable line adjustment. The net adjustment is $20,000, which is less than 10% and there is no need to be concerned.

> *The total of all adjustments is:*
> $20,000 *Line adjustment*
> + 3,000 *Line adjustment*
> =$23,000 *Gross line adjustment*
> ÷ $295,000 *Property value*
> = 7.797% *of property value*

The maximum acceptable gross adjustment is 15%. This is an acceptable gross adjustment.

In situations where the adjustments are excessive, the appraiser may offer explanations or provide additional comps to verify that the chosen properties are acceptable for the area. "Typical for the area" is one of the most important issues for the lender, especially in terms of resale. The lender is always concerned about the ability to sell the property quickly in the event of foreclosure.

COMMENTS ON SALES COMPARISONS immediately follows the comps and should be reviewed for any adverse comments that may affect the value of the property and the ability to obtain a loan for the property.

INDICATED VALUE BY SALES COMPARISON APPROACH will be the last item in this section. This figure represents the total of the figures used to make the properties of equal value. The appraiser totals each column for an adjusted value of the individual comps. This figure represents the value of the property once the adjustments make it identical to the subject. The figures are reviewed from a subjective point of view and reconciled to determine the value of the subject property. The figures are not averaged.

RECONCILIATION will provide the date of the appraisal or the date of determination of the value; the property's value as determined by the appraiser on that date, the appraiser's signature and their state certification/license number.

The pages immediately following the comps will contain various comments the appraiser may wish to make concerning the property and the decisions made in reaching the value.

Also included in this area will be a statement regarding the chain of title and whether the subject has been listed for sale or sold within the last 12 months. If the loan is a refi and the appraiser states the property is currently listed or has been listed for sale in the last 12-month period, a listing cancellation and a letter of explanation will be required. If the property has been purchased within the last 12- month period and the loan is a refinance, the property value will be the lesser of the purchase price or the appraised value.

NOTE

The comps are always adjusted to match the subject, and the figures are reconciled rather than averaged.

If the loan is a cash-out refi and the property has been listed for sale recently, it is an indication that the borrower is taking money out of the property's equity to purchase another home. This is often done with the intent of moving to the new home and renting the subject, which is being refinanced as an owner-occupied property. This may be an indication of fraud, and the real estate professional must not be a party to fraud. The photos of the subject should be examined closely at this point to see if there are any telling indicators such as a "For Sale" sign on the property. To avoid fraud, the loan application and appraisal must be honest and accurate.

THE SKETCH ADDENDUM: This page is a diagram of the subject property's floor plan. The floor plan should be checked for obsolescence. This means that the floor plan may be functional but is obsolete or no longer used. The most frequently seen form of functional obsolescence would be a floor plan requiring that a bedroom or a bathroom is accessed through another room. These issues usually only exist in older homes.

SITE PLAN ADDENDUM: This is a copy of the plat map and should be compared to the one in the prelim. The appraiser takes the map directly from the prelim and may occasionally request a copy when the appraisal is ordered.

LOCATION MAP ADDENDUM: The location map is an area street map that shows the location of the subject property and the comparable properties. Comparing the distance between the subject property and the comps may be helpful if there are any issues.

PHOTOGRAPH ADDENDUM: Photos for the front, back, and street scene are required for the subject property. Occasionally the appraiser will provide additional photos if the property is exceptional or if the additional photos will validate decisions made on the value. Photos will also be provided for the front of each comp.

The appraiser is liable for anything disclosed or intentionally omitted from the appraisal. They will work to explain any problems, but they are obligated by law to disclose any problems or issues of which they are aware. They cannot make changes without good cause or justification. A more thorough explanation will generally suffice.

REVIEWING THE APPRAISAL

The MLO should REVIEW THE APPRAISAL as soon as it is received to become familiar with the main items that will be of concern to the lender. This is approximately a fifteen-page document, with the most pertinent information on the first three to four pages. The MLO should review the appraisal to be certain the subject property will be acceptable to the lender. If there are any issues, the MLO should review the appraiser's comments to be certain they have been properly explained.

Many loans are declined because the subject property is unacceptable. Occasionally the appraiser may make unnecessary comments that will cause the lender concern. If the comments are truly unnecessary, the appraiser may be willing correct the comments or issues if the change can be substantiated. The appraisal may provide a correction or supplement to the appraisal if requested by the lender/underwriter.

As mentioned earlier, an appraisal is good for six months, after that a new appraisal must be provided. When an appraisal is four months old, a re-certification of value will be required from the appraiser; this is typically a one-page document in the form of a letter stating that the value is still valid.

COMPARATIVE MARKET ANALYSIS (CMA)

COMPARATIVE MARKET ANALYSIS (CMA) is a report that shows the properties that are comparable to the subject property. The report merely shows the price of currently marketed properties in the same area as the subject property. The purpose of the CMA is to help determine the range of prices that the subject property may bring if placed on the market within a reasonable period of time from the sale of the comparable properties.

A Comparative Market Analysis is a report that can be prepared by a real estate agent for their selling clients to aid in determining a fair price at which to list the property.

NOTE

The CMA is not an appraisal and should not be presented as one.

Uniform Residential Appraisal Report

File # 9-510

The purpose of this summary appraisal report is to provide the lender/client with an accurate, and adequately supported, opinion of the market value of the subject property.

Property Address		City VENTURA	State CA Zip Code 93003
Borrower		Owner of Public Record	County VENTURA
Legal Description REF: 053MR 001 tr 1975 LOT			
Assessor's Parcel # 136-0-1		Tax Year 2008	R.E. Taxes $ 2,058.08
Neighborhood Name PACE II		Map Reference 492 E4	Census Tract 0015.0
Occupant ☒ Owner ☐ Tenant ☐ Vacant	Special Assessments $	☐ PUD HOA $	☐ per year ☐ per month
Property Rights Appraised ☒ Fee Simple ☐ Leasehold ☐ Other (describe)			
Assignment Type ☐ Purchase Transaction ☒ Refinance Transaction ☐ Other (describe)			
Lender/Client MORTGAGE	Address	E. MAIN STREET	

Is the subject property currently offered for sale or has it been offered for sale in the twelve months prior to the effective date of this appraisal? ☐ Yes ☒ No

Report data source(s) used, offering price(s), and date(s) VENTURA MLS/OWNER

I ☐ did ☒ did not analyze the contract for sale for the subject purchase transaction. Explain the results of the analysis of the contract for sale or why the analysis was not performed. REFINANCE

Contract Price $ N/A   Date of Contract N/A   Is the property seller the owner of public record? ☐ Yes ☐ No Data Source(s)

Is there any financial assistance (loan charges, sale concessions, gift or downpayment assistance, etc.) to be paid by any party on behalf of the borrower? ☐ Yes ☐ No

If Yes, report the total dollar amount and describe the items to be paid

Note: Race and the racial composition of the neighborhood are not appraisal factors.

Neighborhood Characteristics				One-Unit Housing Trends				One-Unit Housing		Present Land Use %	
Location	Urban	☒ Suburban	☐ Rural	Property Values	Increasing	☐ Stable	☒ Declining	PRICE	AGE	One-Unit	95 %
Built-Up	☒ Over 75%	☐ 25-75%	☐ Under 25%	Demand/Supply	☐ Shortage	☒ In Balance	☐ Over Supply	$ (000)	(yrs)	2-4 Unit	%
Growth	☐ Rapid	☒ Stable	☐ Slow	Marketing Time	☐ Under 3 mths	☒ 3-6 mths	☐ Over 6 mths	275 Low	NEW	Multi-Family	%
Neighborhood Boundaries TELEPHONE ROAD TO THE NORTH, 101 FRWY TO THE WEST AND								450 High	65	Commercial	5 %
SOUTH AND MONTGOMERY AVENUE TO THE EAST.								350 Pred.	45	Other	%

Neighborhood Description SUBJECT IS LOCATED IN THE CENTRAL SECTION OF THE CITY OF VENTURA. SCHOOLS, SHOPPING CENTERS AND PUBLIC TRANSPORTATION ARE WITHIN 1 MILE OF THE SUBJECT. THE NEIGHBORHOOD CONSISTS OF PREDOMINANTLY ONE STORY DETACHED SFRS BUILT IN THE 1950'S-1980'S ALL GENERALLY UNDER 2,000 S/F ON LOTS UNDER 9,000 S/F

Market Conditions (including support for the above conclusions) THE AREA CONTINUES TO BE ON A DECLINING TREND SINCE THE BEGINNING OF 2006. DECLINE IS IN PART TO THE SECONDARY MARKET COLLAPSE IN 2007 AND AN OVER-SUPPLY OF LISTINGS AND OVERALL ECONOMIC SLUMP. CURRENTLY A 2-2.5% DECLINE PER MONTH IN THE AREA. MK. TIME 3-6 MOS. IF PRICED COMPETITIVELY

Dimensions SEE ATTACHED PLAT MAP	Area 6,200 SQ/FT	Shape REGULAR	View RESIDENTIAL
Specific Zoning Classification R16 RESIDENTIAL		Zoning Description SINGLE FAMILY RESIDENCE	

Zoning Compliance ☒ Legal ☐ Legal Nonconforming (Grandfathered Use) ☐ No Zoning ☐ Illegal (describe)

Is the highest and best use of subject property as improved (or as proposed per plans and specifications) the present use? ☒ Yes ☐ No If No, describe

Utilities	Public	Other (describe)		Public	Other (describe)	Off-site Improvements - Type	Public	Private
Electricity	☒		Water	☒		Street ASPHALT	☒	
Gas	☒		Sanitary Sewer	☒		Alley NONE	☐	☐

FEMA Special Flood Hazard Area ☐ Yes ☒ No FEMA Flood Zone ZONE C FEMA Map # 060419 0010 C FEMA Map Date 08/19/1987

Are the utilities and off-site improvements typical for the market area? ☒ Yes ☐ No If No, describe

Are there any adverse site conditions or external factors (easements, encroachments, environmental conditions, land uses, etc.)? ☐ Yes ☒ No If Yes, describe

General Description		Foundation		Exterior Description	materials/condition	Interior	materials/condition
Units ☒ One ☐ One with Accessory Unit		☒ Concrete Slab ☐ Crawl Space		Foundation Walls	CONCRETE/AVG	Floors	CPT/TILE-AVG/GD
# of Stories ONE		☐ Full Basement ☐ Partial Basement		Exterior Walls	STUCCO-AVG	Walls	DRYWALL-AVG
Type ☒ Det. ☐ Att. ☐ S-Det./End Unit		Basement Area N/A sq.ft.		Roof Surface	COMP-AVG	Trim/Finish	WOOD-PAINT-AVG
☒ Existing ☐ Proposed ☐ Under Const		Basement Finish N/A %		Gutters & Downspouts	METAL/AVG	Bath Floor	VINYL-AVG
Design (Style) 1-STORY/CONV		☐ Outside Entry/Exit ☐ Sump Pump		Window Type	METAL-AVG	Bath Wainscot	FIBERGLASS-AVG
Year Built 1971		Evidence of ☐ Infestation		Storm Sash/Insulated	NO/YES	Car Storage	☐ None
Effective Age (Yrs) 20		☐ Dampness ☐ Settlement		Screens	YES-AVG	☒ Driveway # of Cars 2
Attic ☐ None		Heating ☒ FWA ☐ HWBB ☐ Radiant	Amenities	☐ Woodstove(s) #	Driveway Surface ASPHALT
☐ Drop Stair ☐ Stairs		☐ Other Fuel GAS		☐ Fireplace(s) #	☒ Fence WOOD	☒ Garage # of Cars 2
☐ Floor ☐ Scuttle		Cooling ☐ Central Air Conditioning		☒ Patio/Deck CONC	☒ Porch COVERE	☐ Carport # of Cars
☐ Finished ☐ Heated		☐ Individual ☐ Other		☐ Pool	☐ Other	☒ Att. ☐ Det. ☐ Built-in

Appliances ☐ Refrigerator ☒ Range/Oven ☒ Dishwasher ☒ Disposal ☐ Microwave ☐ Washer/Dryer ☐ Other (describe)

Finished area above grade contains: 4 Rooms 2 Bedrooms 1 Bath(s) 895 Square Feet of Gross Living Area Above Grade

Additional features (special energy efficient items, etc.) NONE NOTED

Describe the condition of the property (including needed repairs, deterioration, renovations, remodeling, etc.) NO FUNCTIONAL OR EXTERNAL OBSOLESCENCES NOTED. SUBJECT IS IN OVERALL AVG/GOOD CONDITION WITH AVERAGE CONDITION LEVELS. UPGRADES INCLUDE BUILT-IN POOL AREA, MIRRORED CLOSET DOORS, CEILING FANS, TILE FLOORING AND WELL MANICURED GROUNDS. SUBJECT HAS BEEN WELL MAINTAINED. PLEASE SEE PHOTOS

Are there any physical deficiencies or adverse conditions that affect the livability, soundness, or structural integrity of the property? ☐ Yes ☒ No If Yes, describe

Does the property generally conform to the neighborhood (functional utility, style, condition, use, construction, etc.)? ☒ Yes ☐ No If No, describe

Figure 36: Residential Appraisal Report
Page 1 of 12

Uniform Residential Appraisal Report

File # 9-510

There are 1 comparable properties currently offered for sale in the subject neighborhood ranging in price from $ 349,000 to $ 349,000

There are 6 comparable sales in the subject neighborhood within the past twelve months ranging in sale price from $ 285,000 to $ 331,000

FEATURE	SUBJECT	COMPARABLE SALE # 1		COMPARABLE SALE # 2		COMPARABLE SALE # 3	
Address	VENTURA	VENTURA		VENTURA, CA 93003		VENTURA, CA 93003	
Proximity to Subject		0.20 miles		0.35 miles		0.19 miles	
Sale Price	$ N/A	$ 331,000		$ 295,000		$ 408,000	
Sale Price/Gross Liv. Area	$ sq.ft.	$ 318.27 sq.ft		$ 341.44 sq.ft.		$ 297.16 sq.ft	
Data Source(s)		VENTURA MLS/NDCDATA		VENTURA MLS/NDCDATA		VENTURA MLS/NDCDATA	
Verification Source(s)		DOC #180605		DOC #154510		DOC #141377	
VALUE ADJUSTMENTS	DESCRIPTION	DESCRIPTION	+(-) $ Adjustment	DESCRIPTION	+(-) $ Adjustment	DESCRIPTION	+(-) $ Adjustment
Sales or Financing		NOT MADE		NOT MADE		NOT MADE	
Concessions		PUBLIC		PUBLIC		PUBLIC	
Date of Sale/Time		12/17/2008		10/17/2008		09/18/2008	-41,000
Location	AVERAGE	AVERAGE		AVERAGE		AVERAGE	
Leasehold/Fee Simple	FEE SIMPLE	FEE SIMPLE		FEE SIMPLE		FEE SIMPLE	
Site	6,200 SQ/FT	7,040 SQ/FT		7,200 SQ/FT		6,210 SQ/FT	
View	RESIDENTIAL	RESIDENTIAL		RESIDENTIAL		RESIDENTIAL	
Design (Style)	1-STORY/CONV	1 STORY CONV		1-STORY/CONV		1 STORY/CONV	
Quality of Construction	AVERAGE	AVERAGE		AVERAGE		AVERAGE	
Actual Age	38	57		57		38	
Condition	AVG/GOOD	AVG/GOOD		AVERAGE	+20,000	AVG/GOOD	
Above Grade	Total Bdrms Baths	Total Bdrms Baths	-10,000	Total Bdrms Baths		Total Bdrms Baths	-10,000
Room Count	4 2 1	5 3 1		4 2 1		5 3 2	-10,000
Gross Living Area	895 sq.ft	1,040 sq.ft	-5,800	864 sq.ft	0	1,373 sq.ft	-19,100
Basement & Finished	N/A	N/A		NONE		NONE	
Rooms Below Grade	N/A	N/A		N/A		N/A	
Functional Utility	AVERAGE	AVERAGE		AVERAGE		AVERAGE	
Heating/Cooling	FWA/NONE	WALL/NONE	+3,000	WALL/NONE	+3,000	FWA/NONE	
Energy Efficient Items	AVERAGE	AVERAGE		TYP-AGE&AREA		TYP-AGE&AREA	
Garage/Carport	2 CAR GAR	2 CAR GAR		2 CAR GARAGE		2 CAR GARAGE	
Porch/Patio/Deck	PORCH/PATIO	PORCH/PATIO		PORCH/PATIO		PORCH/PATIO	
POOL/FENCE	POOL	FENCE	+10,000	POOL		FENCE	+10,000
EXPOSURE TIME	N/A	29 DOM		8 DOM		201 DOM	
Net Adjustment (Total)		[ ] + [X] -	$ 2,800	[X] + [ ] -	$ 23,000	[ ] + [X] -	$ 70,100
Adjusted Sale Price		Net Adj. 0.8 %		Net Adj. 7.8 %		Net Adj. 17.2 %	
of Comparables		Gross Adj. 8.7 %	$ 328,200	Gross Adj. 7.8 %	$ 318,000	Gross Adj. 22.1 %	$ 337,900

I [X] did [ ] did not research the sale or transfer history of the subject property and comparable sales. If not, explain

My research [X] did [ ] did not reveal any prior sales or transfers of the subject property for the three years prior to the effective date of this appraisal.

Data Source(s) NDC DATA

My research [X] did [ ] did not reveal any prior sales or transfers of the comparable sales for the year prior to the date of sale of the comparable sale.

Data Source(s) NDC DATA

Report the results of the research and analysis of the prior sale or transfer history of the subject property and comparable sales (report additional prior sales on page 3)

ITEM	SUBJECT	COMPARABLE SALE #1	COMPARABLE SALE #2	COMPARABLE SALE #3
Date of Prior Sale/Transfer	07/06/2008	NO PRIOR TRANSFERS	08/11/2008	NO PRIOR TRANSFERS
Price of Prior Sale/Transfer	DEED TRANSFER ONLY	WITHIN 12 MONTHS	$340,000	WITHIN 12 MONTHS
Data Source(s)	NDC DATA	NDCDATA	NDCDATA	NDCDATA
Effective Date of Data Source(s)	01/05/2009	01/05/2009	01/05/2009	01/05/2009

Analysis of prior sale or transfer history of the subject property and comparable sales SUBJECT TRANSFERRED AS NOTED ABOVE. THIS IS A DEED TRANSFER ONLY. COMP 2 WAS BANK OWNED AND TRANSFERRED AS NOTED ABOVE. NO OTHER TRANSFERS WITHIN 12 MONTHS PER NDC DATA.

Summary of Sales Comparison Approach S/F ADJUSTMENTS WERE GIVEN AT $40 S/F OVER 100 S/F OF DIFFERENCE. NO SITE ADJUSTMENTS WARRANTED DUE TO SIMILAR LOT UTILITY AMONG COMPS. BOTH BEDROOMS AND BATHS WERE ADJUSTED AT $10,000 PER DIFFERENCE. DUE TO A LACK OF SALES IN THE IMMEDIATE TRACT, THE APPRAISER HAD TO GO TO COMPETING TRACTS TO FIND SIMILAR COMPS. THIS IS TYPICAL FOR THE AREA. POOLS WERE ADJUSTED AT $10,000 PER DIFFERENCE. COMP #2 WAS A BANK REO AND IN INFERIOR CONDITION AND CONSIDERED A FIXER UPPER. COMP #5 WAS ALSO ADJUSTED FOR INFERIOR CONDITION AND IS CURRENTLY A VACANT SHORT SALE PROPERTY. THIS PROPERTY HAD DEFERRED MAINTENANCE UPON INSPECTION AS WELL. COMP #3 IS THE LAST RECENT SALE FROM THE SUBJECT'S IMMEDIATE TRACT AND WAS ADJUSTED 10% FOR DECLINING MARKET TRENDS. NET AND GROSS ADJUSTMENTS MAY EXCEED 15-25% IN SOME CASES. THIS IS TYPICAL FOR THE AREA.

Indicated Value by Sales Comparison Approach $ 320,000

Indicated Value by: Sales Comparison Approach $ 320,000 Cost Approach (if developed) $ 316,316 Income Approach (if developed) $

FINAL VALUE WAS DERIVED THROUGH THE DEVELOPMENT OF THE MARKET APPROACH DUE TO AN ABUNDANCE OF SALES IN THE AREA AND MARKET APPROACH REFLECT ACTIONS OF BUYERS AND SELLERS. COST APPROACH WAS WEAKENED DUE TO ACCRUED DEPRECIATION.

This appraisal is made [X] "as is", [ ] subject to completion per plans and specifications on the basis of a hypothetical condition that the improvements have been completed, [ ] subject to the following repairs or alterations on the basis of a hypothetical condition that the repairs or alterations have been completed, or [ ] subject to the following required inspection based on the extraordinary assumption that the condition or deficiency does not require alteration or repair

Based on a complete visual inspection of the interior and exterior areas of the subject property, defined scope of work, statement of assumptions and limiting conditions, and appraiser's certification, my (our) opinion of the market value, as defined, of the real property that is the subject of this report is $ 320,000 , as of 01/13/2009 , which is the date of inspection and the effective date of this appraisal.

Figure 36: Residential Appraisal Report

Page 2 of 12

Uniform Residential Appraisal Report

File # 9-510

SOURCE OF MARKET VALUE DEFINITION: THE MARKET VALUE DEFINITION IS CONSISTENT WITH REGULATIONS PUBLISHED BY FEDERAL REGULATORY AGENCIES PURSUANT TO TITLE X1 OF THE FINANCIAL INSTITUTIONS REFORM, RECOVERY AND ENFORCEMENT ACT (FIRREA) OF 1989.

CONCESSIONS: CONCESSIONS WERE NOT LISTED IN THE REPORT DUE TO A LACK OF MLS INFORMATION AND/OR LACK OF RESPONSE FROM THE AGENTS INVOLVED IN THE TRANSACTIONS. TYPICAL CONCESSIONS ARE 1-3% OF SALES PRICE AND DO NOT HAVE A NEGATIVE IMPACT ON VALUE AT THE PRESENT TIME. NO APPARENT CREATIVE FINANCING NOTED IN THE COMPS.

MARKET CONDITIONS: REO SALES AND SHORT SALES HAVE INCREASED IN THE SUBJECT'S MARKET. ALTHOUGH ARMS LENGTH TRANSACTIONS ARE STILL THE BEST INDICATORS OF MARKET VALUE, IN SOME CASES REO SALES ARE THE BEST INDICATORS OF VALUE IF PRICED ACCORDING TO MARKET WITH NORMAL EXPOSURE TIME. VALUES IN THE AREA HAVE BEEN AFFECTED BY THE INFLUX OF THESE TYPE OF SALES AND THEREFORE THEY ARE CONSIDERED TO BE GOOD MARKET INDICATORS. LIST TO SELL RATIO'S RANGE FROM 5%-10% DEPENDING ON ACTUAL LISTING PRICE VERSES PROPERTY CHARACTERISTICS.

COST APPROACH TO VALUE (not required by Fannie Mae)

Provide adequate information for the lender/client to replicate the below cost figures and calculations.

Support for the opinion of site value (summary of comparable land sales or other methods for estimating site value) THE ESTIMATED SITE VALUE WAS EXTRACTED DUE TO A LACK OF VACANT LAND SALES IN THE AREA.

ESTIMATED ☐ REPRODUCTION OR ☒ REPLACEMENT COST NEW	OPINION OF SITE VALUE			=$	210,000
Source of cost data MARSHALL & SWIFT COST HANDBOOK	DWELLING	895 Sq.Ft. @ $	99.05	=$	86,650
Quality rating from cost service 3.0 Effective date of cost data 12/08		N/A Sq.Ft. @ $		=$	
Comments on Cost Approach (gross living area calculations, depreciation, etc.)	POOL			=$	50,000
THE APPRAISER'S DIRECT MEASUREMENTS INDICATE SLIGHTLY	Garage/Carport	495 Sq.Ft. @ $	26.57	=$	13,152
MORE LIVING AREA THAN IS INDICATED IN THE BUILDER'S	Total Estimate of Cost-New			=$	151,802
ESTIMATES. THE ESTIMATED REMAINING ECONOMIC LIFE OF THE	Less	Physical	Functional	External	
SUBJECT PROPERTY IS APPROX. 55 YRS. AND WAS DETERMINED	Depreciation	40,486	30,000		=$	70,486)
BY THE AGE/LIFE METHOD.	Depreciated Cost of Improvements			=$	81,316
	"As-Is" Value of Site Improvements			=$	25,000
Estimated Remaining Economic Life (HUD and VA only) 55 Years	INDICATED VALUE BY COST APPROACH			=$	316,316

INCOME APPROACH TO VALUE (not required by Fannie Mae)

Estimated Monthly Market Rent $ N/A X Gross Rent Multiplier N/A = $	Indicated Value by Income Approach

Summary of Income Approach (including support for market rent and GRM)

PROJECT INFORMATION FOR PUDs (if applicable)

Is the developer/builder in control of the Homeowners' Association (HOA)? ☐ Yes ☐ No Unit type(s) ☐ Detached ☐ Attached

Provide the following information for PUDs ONLY if the developer/builder is in control of the HOA and the subject property is an attached dwelling unit.

Legal Name of Project

Total number of phases	Total number of units N/A	Total number of units sold
Total number of units rented	Total number of units for sale N/A	Data source(s)

Was the project created by the conversion of existing building(s) into a PUD? ☐ Yes ☐ No If Yes, date of conversion.

Does the project contain any multi-dwelling units? ☐ Yes ☐ No Data Source

Are the units, common elements, and recreation facilities complete? ☐ Yes ☐ No If No, describe the status of completion.

Are the common elements leased to or by the Homeowners' Association? ☐ Yes ☐ No If Yes, describe the rental terms and options.

Describe common elements and recreational facilities. N/A

Figure 36: Residential Appraisal Report
Page 3 of 12

Uniform Residential Appraisal Report   File # 9-510

This report form is designed to report an appraisal of a one-unit property or a one-unit property with an accessory unit; including a unit in a planned unit development (PUD). This report form is not designed to report an appraisal of a manufactured home or a unit in a condominium or cooperative project.

This appraisal report is subject to the following scope of work, intended use, intended user, definition of market value, statement of assumptions and limiting conditions, and certifications. Modifications, additions, or deletions to the intended use, intended user, definition of market value, or assumptions and limiting conditions are not permitted. The appraiser may expand the scope of work to include any additional research or analysis necessary based on the complexity of this appraisal assignment. Modifications or deletions to the certifications are also not permitted. However, additional certifications that do not constitute material alterations to this appraisal report, such as those required by law or those related to the appraiser's continuing education or membership in an appraisal organization, are permitted.

SCOPE OF WORK: The scope of work for this appraisal is defined by the complexity of this appraisal assignment and the reporting requirements of this appraisal report form, including the following definition of market value, statement of assumptions and limiting conditions, and certifications. The appraiser must, at a minimum: (1) perform a complete visual inspection of the interior and exterior areas of the subject property, (2) inspect the neighborhood, (3) inspect each of the comparable sales from at least the street, (4) research, verify, and analyze data from reliable public and/or private sources, and (5) report his or her analysis, opinions, and conclusions in this appraisal report.

INTENDED USE: The intended use of this appraisal report is for the lender/client to evaluate the property that is the subject of this appraisal for a mortgage finance transaction.

INTENDED USER: The intended user of this appraisal report is the lender/client.

DEFINITION OF MARKET VALUE: The most probable price which a property should bring in a competitive and open market under all conditions requisite to a fair sale, the buyer and seller, each acting prudently, knowledgeably and assuming the price is not affected by undue stimulus. Implicit in this definition is the consummation of a sale as of a specified date and the passing of title from seller to buyer under conditions whereby: (1) buyer and seller are typically motivated; (2) both parties are well informed or well advised, and each acting in what he or she considers his or her own best interest; (3) a reasonable time is allowed for exposure in the open market; (4) payment is made in terms of cash in U. S. dollars or in terms of financial arrangements comparable thereto; and (5) the price represents the normal consideration for the property sold unaffected by special or creative financing or sales concessions* granted by anyone associated with the sale.

*Adjustments to the comparables must be made for special or creative financing or sales concessions. No adjustments are necessary for those costs which are normally paid by sellers as a result of tradition or law in a market area; these costs are readily identifiable since the seller pays these costs in virtually all sales transactions. Special or creative financing adjustments can be made to the comparable property by comparisons to financing terms offered by a third party institutional lender that is not already involved in the property or transaction. Any adjustment should not be calculated on a mechanical dollar for dollar cost of the financing or concession but the dollar amount of any adjustment should approximate the market's reaction to the financing or concessions based on the appraiser's judgment.

STATEMENT OF ASSUMPTIONS AND LIMITING CONDITIONS: The appraiser's certification in this report is subject to the following assumptions and limiting conditions:

1. The appraiser will not be responsible for matters of a legal nature that affect either the property being appraised or the title to it, except for information that he or she became aware of during the research involved in performing this appraisal. The appraiser assumes that the title is good and marketable and will not render any opinions about the title.

2. The appraiser has provided a sketch in this appraisal report to show the approximate dimensions of the improvements. The sketch is included only to assist the reader in visualizing the property and understanding the appraiser's determination of its size.

3. The appraiser has examined the available flood maps that are provided by the Federal Emergency Management Agency (or other data sources) and has noted in this appraisal report whether any portion of the subject site is located in an identified Special Flood Hazard Area. Because the appraiser is not a surveyor, he or she makes no guarantees, express or implied, regarding this determination.

4. The appraiser will not give testimony or appear in court because he or she made an appraisal of the property in question, unless specific arrangements to do so have been made beforehand, or as otherwise required by law.

5. The appraiser has noted in this appraisal report any adverse conditions (such as needed repairs, deterioration, the presence of hazardous wastes, toxic substances, etc.) observed during the inspection of the subject property or that he or she became aware of during the research involved in performing the appraisal. Unless otherwise stated in this appraisal report, the appraiser has no knowledge of any hidden or unapparent physical deficiencies or adverse conditions of the property (such as, but not limited to, needed repairs, deterioration, the presence of hazardous wastes, toxic substances, adverse environmental conditions, etc.) that would make the property less valuable, and has assumed that there are no such conditions and makes no guarantees or warranties, express or implied. The appraiser will not be responsible for any such conditions that do exist or for any engineering or testing that might be required to discover whether such conditions exist. Because the appraiser is not an expert in the field of environmental hazards, this appraisal report must not be considered as an environmental assessment of the property.

6. The appraiser has based his or her appraisal report and valuation conclusion for an appraisal that is subject to satisfactory completion, repairs, or alterations on the assumption that the completion, repairs, or alterations of the subject property will be performed in a professional manner.

Figure 36: Residential Appraisal Report
Page 4 of 12

Uniform Residential Appraisal Report
File # 9-510

21. The lender/client may disclose or distribute this appraisal report to: the borrower; another lender at the request of the borrower; the mortgagee or its successors and assigns; mortgage insurers; government sponsored enterprises; other secondary market participants; data collection or reporting services; professional appraisal organizations; any department, agency, or instrumentality of the United States; and any state, the District of Columbia, or other jurisdictions; without having to obtain the appraiser's or supervisory appraiser's (if applicable) consent. Such consent must be obtained before this appraisal report may be disclosed or distributed to any other party (including, but not limited to, the public through advertising, public relations, news, sales, or other media).

22. I am aware that any disclosure or distribution of this appraisal report by me or the lender/client may be subject to certain laws and regulations. Further, I am also subject to the provisions of the Uniform Standards of Professional Appraisal Practice that pertain to disclosure or distribution by me.

23. The borrower, another lender at the request of the borrower, the mortgagee or its successors and assigns, mortgage insurers, government sponsored enterprises, and other secondary market participants may rely on this appraisal report as part of any mortgage finance transaction that involves any one or more of these parties.

24. If this appraisal report was transmitted as an "electronic record" containing my "electronic signature," as those terms are defined in applicable federal and/or state laws (excluding audio and video recordings), or a facsimile transmission of this appraisal report containing a copy or representation of my signature, the appraisal report shall be as effective, enforceable and valid as if a paper version of this appraisal report were delivered containing my original hand written signature.

25. Any intentional or negligent misrepresentation(s) contained in this appraisal report may result in civil liability and/or criminal penalties including, but not limited to, fine or imprisonment or both under the provisions of Title 18, United States Code, Section 1001, et seq., or similar state laws.

SUPERVISORY APPRAISER'S CERTIFICATION: The Supervisory Appraiser certifies and agrees that:

1. I directly supervised the appraiser for this appraisal assignment, have read the appraisal report, and agree with the appraiser's analysis, opinions, statements, conclusions, and the appraiser's certification.

2. I accept full responsibility for the contents of this appraisal report including, but not limited to, the appraiser's analysis, opinions, statements, conclusions, and the appraiser's certification.

3. The appraiser identified in this appraisal report is either a sub-contractor or an employee of the supervisory appraiser (or the appraisal firm), is qualified to perform this appraisal, and is acceptable to perform this appraisal under the applicable state law.

4. This appraisal report complies with the Uniform Standards of Professional Appraisal Practice that were adopted and promulgated by the Appraisal Standards Board of The Appraisal Foundation and that were in place at the time this appraisal report was prepared.

5. If this appraisal report was transmitted as an "electronic record" containing my "electronic signature," as those terms are defined in applicable federal and/or state laws (excluding audio and video recordings), or a facsimile transmission of this appraisal report containing a copy or representation of my signature, the appraisal report shall be as effective, enforceable and valid as if a paper version of this appraisal report were delivered containing my original hand written signature.

APPRAISER CARRIE A. AUSTIN	SUPERVISORY APPRAISER (ONLY IF REQUIRED)
Signature	Signature
Name CARRIE A. AUSTIN	Name
Company Name CHANNEL ISLANDS APPRAISALS	Company Name
Company Address	Company Address
Telephone Number 805-383-6003	Telephone Number
Email Address	Email Address
Date of Signature and Report January 15, 2009	Date of Signature
Effective Date of Appraisal 01/13/2009	State Certification #
State Certification # AR0	or State License #
or State License #	State
or Other (describe) State #	Expiration Date of Certification or License
State CA	
Expiration Date of Certification or License 2/5/2010	SUBJECT PROPERTY
ADDRESS OF PROPERTY APPRAISED	☐ Did not inspect subject property
	☐ Did inspect exterior of subject property from street
VENTURA, CA 93003	Date of Inspection
APPRAISED VALUE OF SUBJECT PROPERTY $ 320,000	☐ Did inspect interior and exterior of subject property
LENDER/CLIENT	Date of Inspection
Name SHELLY NORTH	
Company Name 101 MORTGAGE	COMPARABLE SALES
Company Address MAIN STREET	
93001	☐ Did not inspect exterior of comparable sales from street
Email Address	☐ Did inspect exterior of comparable sales from street
	Date of Inspection

Figure 36: Residential Appraisal Report
Page 5 of 12

Uniform Residential Appraisal Report

File # 9-510

FEATURE	SUBJECT	COMPARABLE SALE # 4		COMPARABLE SALE # 5		COMPARABLE SALE # 6	
Address							
	VENTURA	VENTURA, CA 93003		VENTURA			
Proximity to Subject		0.37 miles		0.22 miles			
Sale Price	$ N/A	$ 359,000		$ 349,000		$	
Sale Price/Gross Liv. Area	$ sq.ft	$ 260.14 sq.ft		$ 248.58 sq.ft		$ sq.ft	
Data Source(s)		MLS/NDCDATA		VENTURA MLS/NDCDATA			
Verification Source(s)		SALE PENDING		ACTIVE LISTING			
VALUE ADJUSTMENTS	DESCRIPTION	DESCRIPTION	+ (-) $ Adjustment	DESCRIPTION	+ (-) $ Adjustment	DESCRIPTION	+ (-) $ Adjustment
Sales or Financing		PENDING -3%	-10,800	LISTING -5%	-35,000		
Concessions		N/A		N/A			
Date of Sale/Time		12/30/2008		04/09/2008			
Location	AVERAGE	AVERAGE		AVERAGE			
Leasehold/Fee Simple	FEE SIMPLE	FEE SIMPLE		FEE SIMPLE			
Site	6,200 SQ/FT	6,390 SQ/FT		8,546 SQ/FT	-5,000		
View	RESIDENTIAL	RESIDENTIAL		RESIDENTIAL			
Design (Style)	1-STORY/CONV	1-STORY/CONV		1 STORY CONV			
Quality of Construction	AVERAGE	AVERAGE		AVERAGE			
Actual Age	38	43		55			
Condition	AVG/GOOD	AVG/GOOD		AVERAGE	+20,000		
Above Grade	Total / Bdrms / Baths	Total / Bdrms / Baths	-10,000	Total / Bdrms / Baths		Total / Bdrms / Baths	
Room Count	4 / 2 / 1	5 / 3 / 2	-10,000	4 / 2 / 1			
Gross Living Area	895 sq.ft	1,380 sq.ft	-19,400	1,404 sq.ft	-20,400	sq.ft	0
Basement & Finished	N/A	NONE		N/A			
Rooms Below Grade	N/A	N/A		N/A			
Functional Utility	AVERAGE	AVERAGE		AVERAGE			
Heating/Cooling	FWA/NONE	FWA/NONE		WALL/NONE	+3,000		
Energy Efficient Items	AVERAGE	AVERAGE		AVERAGE			
Garage/Carport	2 CAR GAR	2 CAR GARAGE		2 CAR GAR			
Porch/Patio/Deck	PORCH/PATIO	PORCH/PATIO		PORCH/PATIO			
POOL/FENCE	POOL	FENCE	+10,000	FENCE	+10,000		
EXPOSURE TIME	N/A	45 DOM		290 DOM			
Net Adjustment (Total)		☐ + ☒ - $	40,200	☐ + ☒ - $	27,400	☐ + ☐ - $	
Adjusted Sale Price		Net 11.2 %		Net 7.9 %		Net %	
of Comparables		Gross 16.8 % $	318,800	Gross 26.8 % $	321,600	Gross % $	

Report the results of the research and analysis of the prior sale or transfer history of the subject property and comparable sales (report additional prior sales on page 3).

ITEM	SUBJECT	COMPARABLE SALE # 4	COMPARABLE SALE # 5	COMPARABLE SALE # 6
Date of Prior Sale/Transfer	07/06/2006	08/11/2008	NO PRIOR TRANSFERS	
Price of Prior Sale/Transfer	DEED TRANSFER ONLY	$33,925	WITHIN 12 MONTHS	
Data Source(s)	NDC DATA	NDCDATA	NDC DATA	
Effective Date of Data Source(s)	01/05/2009	01/05/2009	01/05/2009	

Analysis of prior sale or transfer history of the subject property and comparable sales   COMP #4 IS BANK OWNED AND TRANSFERRED AS NOTED ABOVE
THIS IS THE ONLY TRANSFER WITHIN 12 MONTHS.

Analysis/Comments   ALL COMPS CONSIDERED ARE THE BEST INDICATORS OF VALUE AND SUPPORT THE APPRAISED VALUE GIVEN.

Figure 36: Residential Appraisal Report
Page 6 of 12

Location Map

Borrower/Client			
Property Address			
City VENTURA	County VENTURA	State CA	Zip Code 93003
Lender MORTGAGE			

Figure 36: Residential Appraisal Report
Page 7 of 12

Plat Map

Business/Client				
Property Address				
City	County VENTURA	State CA	Zip Code 93003	
Lender				

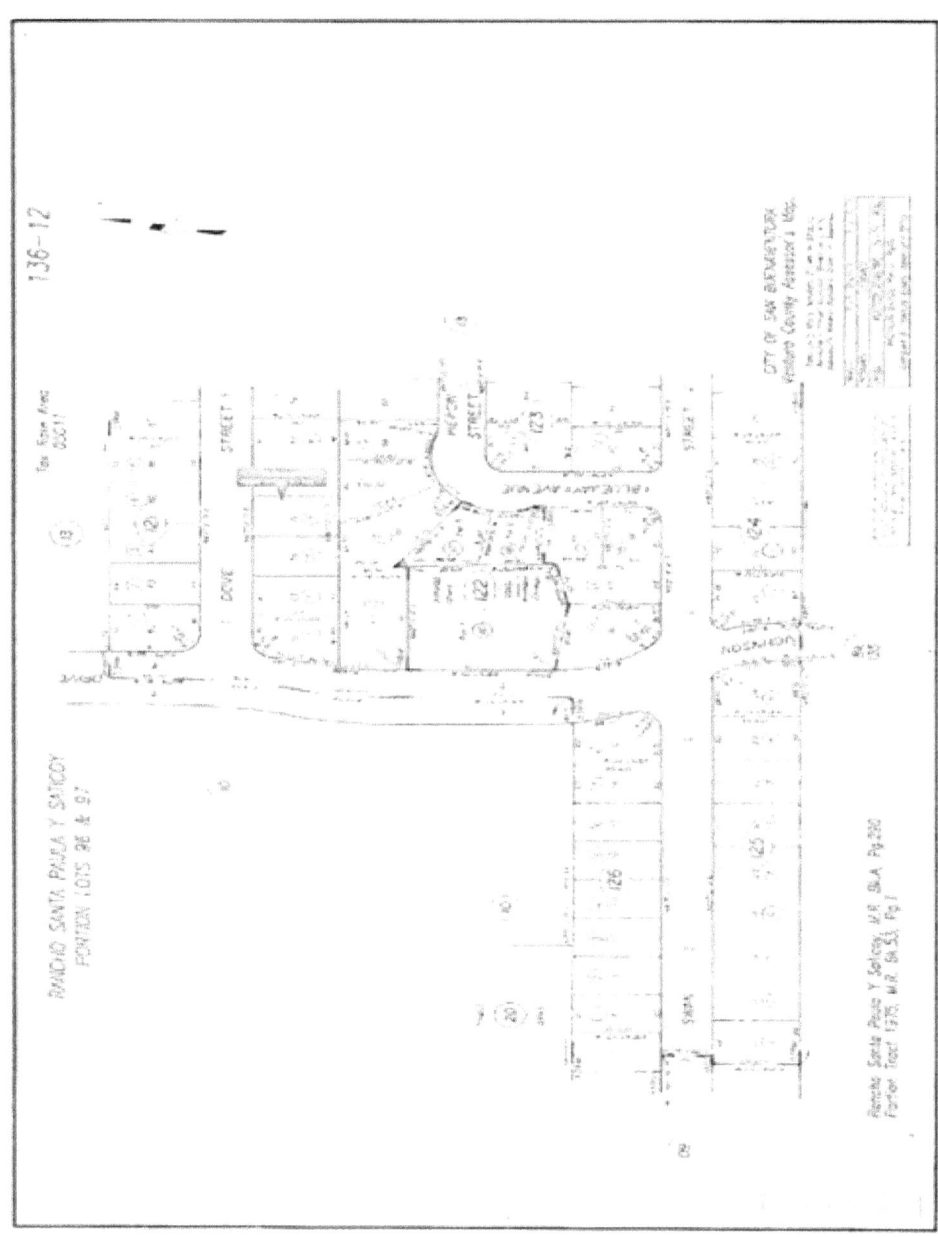

Figure 36: Residential Appraisal Report
Page 8 of 12

Subject Photo Page

Subject Front

Sales Price	N/A
Gross Living Area	895
Total Rooms	4
Total Bedrooms	2
Total Bathrooms	1
Location	AVERAGE
View	RESIDENTIAL
Site	6,200 SQ FT
Quality	AVERAGE
Age	38

Subject Rear

Subject Street

Figure 36: Residential Appraisal Report
Page 9 of 12

Comparable Photo Page

Borrower/Client			
Property Address			
City VENTURA	County VENTURA	State CA	Zip Code 93003
Lender			

Comparable 1

Prox. to Subject	0.20 miles
Sale Price	331,000
Gross Living Area	1,040
Total Rooms	5
Total Bedrooms	3
Total Bathrooms	1
Location	AVERAGE
View	RESIDENTIAL
Site	7,040 SQ/FT
Quality	AVERAGE
Age	57

Comparable 2

Prox. to Subject	0.35 miles
Sale Price	295,000
Gross Living Area	864
Total Rooms	4
Total Bedrooms	2
Total Bathrooms	1
Location	AVERAGE
View	RESIDENTIAL
Site	7,200 SQ/FT
Quality	AVERAGE
Age	57

Comparable 3

Prox. to Subject	0.19 miles
Sale Price	408,000
Gross Living Area	1,373
Total Rooms	5
Total Bedrooms	3
Total Bathrooms	2
Location	AVERAGE
View	RESIDENTIAL
Site	6,210 SQ/FT
Quality	AVERAGE
Age	38

Figure 36: Residential Appraisal Report
Page 10 of 12

Comparable Photo Page

Borrower/Client			
Property Address			
City VENTURA	County VENTURA	State CA	Zip Code 93003
Lender			

Comparable 4

Prox. to Subject	0.37 miles
Sale Price	359,000
Gross Living Area	1,380
Total Rooms	5
Total Bedrooms	3
Total Bathrooms	2
Location	AVERAGE
View	RESIDENTIAL
Site	6,390 SQ/FT
Quality	AVERAGE
Age	43

Comparable 5

Prox. to Subject	0.22 miles
Sale Price	349,000
Gross Living Area	1,404
Total Rooms	4
Total Bedrooms	2
Total Bathrooms	1
Location	AVERAGE
View	RESIDENTIAL
Site	8,546 SQ/FT
Quality	AVERAGE
Age	55

Comparable 6

Prox. to Subject	
Sale Price	
Gross Living Area	
Total Rooms	
Total Bedrooms	
Total Bathrooms	
Location	
View	
Site	
Quality	
Age	

Figure 36: Residential Appraisal Report
Page 11 of 12

Building Sketch (Page - 1)

AREA CALCULATIONS SUMMARY				LIVING AREA BREAKDOWN		
Code	Description	Size	Net Totals	Breakdown		Subtotals
GLA1	First Floor	894.50	894.50	First Floor		
GAR	Garage	495.00	495.00		23.0 x 37.5	862.50
					2.0 x 16.0	32.00
	TOTAL LIVABLE	(rounded)	895	2 Calculations Total (rounded)		895

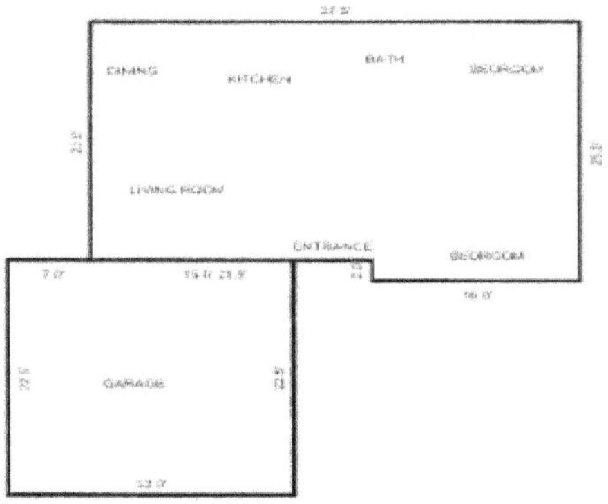

Figure 36: Residential Appraisal Report
Page 12 of 12

INCOME CAPITALIZATION

INCOME CAPITALIZATION is used to determine the value of income producing properties. An appraiser will provide the usual sale comps as well as comps that are rental properties.

CAPITALIZATION OF NET INCOME is a method of determining the value of a property based on the income the property is producing or is capable of producing. This method is also used as a method to determine the potential income. The real estate professional must know the formula whether specializing in commercial properties or assisting the occasional purchaser of residential properties.

The following process uses four steps to determine the net operating income (NOI). Gross income or before tax income is always used. The figures used can be either monthly or annual.

- Estimate the adjusted gross income (AGI) as though the property were fully occupied.
- Determine effective gross income (EGI) by subtracting allowances for uncollected rents and vacancies.
- Deduct allowable expenses.
- Net operating income (NOI) is determined by:

> **Potential Gross Income**
> **-Vacancy & Income Loss**
> **=Effective Gross Income (EGI)**
> <u>**-Expenses**</u>
> **=Net Operating Income (NOI)**

> *Example: An apartment building with ten units:*
> *$ 15,000 Potential Monthly income ($1,500 x 10)*
> *$4,500 three units @ $1,500/month vacancy – EGI*
> <u>*$6,000*</u> *Maintenance, utilities, mortgage, tax, insurance*
> *= $4,500 NOI*

IRV FORMULA is then used to calculate the capitalization from the NOI. **Income, rate, and value** are used in a basic algebraic calculation to determine a rate, which will then be used to determine the value of a subject property, based on a comparable and similar income producing property.

There are three figures in the formula and as long as there are two parts of the formula, the third part can be calculated. There must be at least two parts of the formula that are known. The required parts of the formula are:

- NOI or Net Operating Income = **I**
- Capitalization Rate (Cap) or Rate =**R**
- Value of the property = **V**

The following equation is used for calculating:

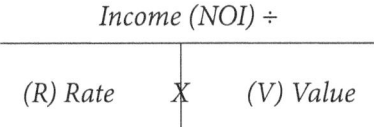

The T formation above includes 3 elements (NOI, R, V). The figure on top (NOI)Income will be divided by the known figure, either the (R)Rate or (V)Value, to calculate the 3rd missing element. To determine the income (NOI), the (R) and (V) are multiplied together.

When working with this formula, it is important to remember that you must have two of the figures to generate the third figure. In other words, to calculate the value of a property, one must know the cap rate and the income; to calculate income, one must know the value and the rate; to calculate the cap rate, one must know the income and the value.

Another way of showing the equation is:
Income ÷ Rate =
Value Income ÷ Value
= Rate
Rate x Value =
Income

Example: Joe is considering the purchase of a house for rental purposes. He needs to find out what the rent should be to determine the value of the property.

A house that is rented in the neighborhood recently sold for $200,000. The house is currently rented for $1,500. This can be calculated as monthly or annually. The cap rate will appear as a considerably different figure if calculated monthly.

$$
\begin{array}{ll}
\$1,500 & \textit{Monthly Income} \\
\underline{\ x\ 12\ } & \textit{Months per Year} \\
= \$18,000 & \textit{Annual Income} \\
\div \$200,000 & \textit{Value} \\
= .09\ or\ 9\% & \textit{Rate or Cap Rate}
\end{array}
$$

$$
\frac{\$18,000 = Income}{9\% = Cap\ Rate \quad | \quad \$200,000 = Value}
$$

This has provided a percentage of the property value that represents income. Now the value of the property being purchased can be calculated or the amount of income that should be charged on the new rental property.

Joe has determined that the subject property can demand a monthly rental income of $1,600 per month. The seller has the property listed for sale at a price of $250,000.

$$
\begin{array}{ll}
\$1,600 & \textit{Monthly Rental Income} \\
\underline{\ X\ 12\ } & \textit{Months per Year} \\
= \$19,200 & \textit{Annual} \\
\textit{Income}\ X\ 9\% & \textit{Cap Rate} \\
= \$331,776 & \textit{Value}
\end{array}
$$

This would be a particularly good investment. The cap rate should not exceed 12%. The higher the cap rate, the higher the risk and therefore, the lesser the value. The quality of the income is related to the financial responsibility of the tenant. A good building that attracts professional tenants in an upscale neighborhood indicates the financial responsibility of the potential tenants, whereas a lesser- quality building in a neighborhood of lower income residents will be a higher risk due to decreased financial stability resulting in financial irresponsibility. The average cap rate is around 8 to 9%, based on annual income.

NOTE

If the cap rate increases, but the income does not change, the property value will decrease.

It does not matter whether the calculations are done on monthly or annual income, but it is best to be consistent. When the same figures in the previous example are prepared using the monthly income, the following cap rate is generated:

$1,500   *Monthly Rental Income*
÷$200,000   *Value*
= .007 or .7%   *Cap Rate*

GROSS RENT MULTIPLIER is the same as the capitalization of net income with the exception of not using the net operating income but using the gross income. The gross rent multiplier is the same as the cap rate.

FACTORS TO VALUE

FACTORS TO VALUE include some of the following terms:

ASSEMBLAGE is the combining of two or more properties to create one large lot or parcel of land. The new larger parcel may prove to be significant enough to create an assembled value that is greater than the total value of the separate parcels if left as separate parcels.

> *Example: Sam purchased three small parcels of vacant land for $30,000 each for a total value of $90,000. The purpose of purchasing all three was to assemble them into one large lot for building one large structure. Once the individual parcels underwent assemblage and were recorded with the county recorder's office, the value of the new larger parcel is $120,000.*

PLOTTAGE OR PLOTTAGE INCREMENT refers to the increase in the value of the parcels which were assembled into one parcel.

ACTION OF THE SUN can be an important factor for a retail business in as much as the sun will fade any display items in the store's windows, especially if the store is located on the north side of the street. The sun will also increase the temperature of the building and any pedestrians outside.

The most desirable location for a retail store is a southeast corner because it has the least exposure to the sun and the morning sun is less harsh than the afternoon sun.

The sun may also be a consideration for residential properties in different climates. Houses in colder climates would prefer to face south and west to get the benefit of the sun's warmth in the winter months. Houses in the southern and warmer climates may prefer to face north and east to receive less sun to the living areas during the summer months.

FRONTAGE is the amount of land that is on the street. This is a lineal measurement from one lot line along the street to the opposite lot line. Building sites have minimum frontage requirements to allow for access to a property. Some areas may require that there be at least enough frontage to allow for a driveway giving access to a property.

FRONT FOOT is related to frontage and refers to the measurement of the property on the street. This is most often used in retail or commercial property evaluations. Retail and commercial structures are assigned a higher value when there is a greater frontage or front feet on the street. A retail business, in particular, is more valuable with a greater amount of space along the sidewalk, which is essentially built-in advertising.

Front footage is not used in residential property other than meeting building codes for access to the property.

The **LAND RESIDUAL METHOD** is a way to determine the value of land when there are no comps of vacant land available in the subject property's neighborhood. In order to determine the value of the land, the appraiser must know the value of the entire property with a structure and the value of the structure alone.

> *Example: Appraiser Smith needs to prepare an appraisal for a vacant lot. There are no recent sales of vacant land in the vicinity. Appraiser Smith uses a nearby comp with a recent sales price or value of $225,000. He is able to establish the cost new of the structure at $150,000. By subtracting the value of the structure form the total value of the property, Appraiser Smith can determine the value of the lot:*

$225,000	*Total Property Value*
-$150,000	*Value of the Structure*
= $75,000	*Lot Value*

LICENSING OF APPRAISERS

The Uniform Standards of Professional Appraisal Practice (USPAP) is the ethical and performance standards for the appraisal profession in the United States. USPAP was adopted by Congress in 1989, and encompasses standards for all types of appraisal services, including real estate, personal property, business, and mass appraisal. Compliance is mandatory for state-licensed and state-certified appraisers involved in federally related real estate transactions.

To be a real property appraiser in the United States, appraisers must take the 15- hour national USPAP Course, or its equivalent. Furthermore, real property appraisers must take the 7-Hour National USPAP Update Course, or its equivalent, once every two calendar years.

Bureau of Real estate Appraisers (BREA)

In 1989, Title XI of the federal Financial Institutions Reform, Recovery and Enforcement Act (FIRREA) was passed by Congress, requiring all states to license real estate appraisers who appraise real property in federally related transactions

In response to the federal mandate, the Real Estate Appraisers' Licensing and Certification Law was enacted by the California Legislature in 1990. The law instructed the Bureau of Real estate Appraisers (BREA) in licensing real estate appraisers in the state of California and implementing national ethical and professional standards and qualifications that conform with the mandate.

BREA entails two primary functions - appraiser licensing/AMC registration and enforcement.

The Licensing Unit ensures that applicants for appraisal licenses meet minimum requirements for education, experience, and examination that conform with federal mandates and ensure that only qualified persons are licensed to perform appraisals in federally related real estate loan transactions.

NOTE

USPAP is updated every two years so that appraisers have the information they need to deliver impartial and rational opinions of value.

NOTE

Effective January 1, 2010, California law mandated the registration of Appraisal Management Companies (AMC) with the BREA.

The Enforcement Unit investigates complaints of violations of USPAP and makes sure that licensees observe all applicable laws and regulations.

Summary of License Levels

There are four levels of real estate appraiser licensing:

- **AT - Trainee License.** 150 hours, covering specific modules including the 15-hour National USPAP Course (or its equivalent as determined by the Appraiser Qualifications Board (AQB). Trainee applicants must also complete an approved Supervisory/ Trainee Appraisers course prior to obtaining a Trainee Appraiser license. All initial applicants must complete an approved state and federal laws course prior to obtaining a license; *No experience required*; *Scope of practice* is any property which the supervising appraiser is permitted to appraise.

- **AL - Residential License.** 150 hours, covering specific modules including the 15-hour National USPAP Course (or its equivalent as determined by the AQB). All initial applicants must complete an approved California state and federal laws course prior to obtaining a license; *Experience Requirements* would be 2,000 hours and encompassing no less than 12 months of acceptable appraisal experience; *Scope of practice* would be any non-complex 1-4 family property with a transaction value up to $1 million and non- residential property with a transaction value up to $250,000.

- **AR - Certified Residential License.** Two hundred hours, covering specific modules, including the 15-hour National USPAP Course **and** meeting the criteria of one of the options listed in the next table labeled "College Level Education Options for Certified Residential." All initial applicants must complete an approved California state and federal laws course prior to obtaining a license; *Experience Requirements* would be 2,500 hours and encompassing no less than 2.5 years (30 months) of acceptable appraisal experience; *Scope of practice* would be any 1-4 family property without regard to transaction value or complexity and non-residential property with a transaction value up to $250,000.

- **AG - Certified General License.** Three hundred hours, covering specific modules, including the 15-hour National USPAP Course; and a bachelor's degree or higher from an accredited college or university. All initial applicants must complete an approved California state and federal laws course prior to obtaining a license; *Experience Requirements* would be 3,000 hours and encompassing no less than 2.5 years (30 months) of acceptable appraisal experience, of which 1,500 hours must be non-residential; *Scope of practice* would be ALL real estate without regard to transaction value or complexity.

Changes in Real Property Appraiser Qualifications Criteria

On February 1, 2018, the Appraisal Qualifications Board (AQB) of the Appraisal Foundation adopted changes to the Real Property Appraiser Qualification Criteria that became effective on May 1, 2018. California is adopting the changes to education criteria as of May 1, 2018. Additional information may be found in the Department of Consumer Affairs/Bureau of Real Estate Appraisers.

Qualifying College Level Education

College education requirements are a fundamental component of these changes. Applicants for a residential license no longer need to complete any college-level education. Applicants for a Certified Residential license now have six (6) options to meet the education requirements. Please review the Summary of Each License Level and College Level Education Options for Certified Residential tables for details.

These requirements became effective for individuals seeking the real property appraiser credential after May 1, 2018. The requirements also apply to existing real property appraisers seeking to upgrade a license. Appraisers wishing to upgrade their license will have to meet the new criteria.

Supervisory and Trainee

- Both the Trainee Appraiser and Supervisory Appraiser are required to complete an AQB approved Supervisory/Trainee Appraisers course. The Trainee Appraiser must complete the course prior to obtaining a Trainee Appraiser License, and the Supervisory Appraiser must complete the course prior to supervising a Trainee Appraiser. Existing credential holders can use this course regarding the roles and responsibilities of the Supervisor and Trainee Appraiser for continuing education.

- Supervisory and Trainee affiliations established prior to January 1, 2015, are "grandfathered" and the courses are not required; however, BREA highly recommends both Supervisory Appraiser and Trainee/Applicant search appraisal course providers for classes regarding the roles and responsibilities of the Supervisor and Trainee.

- A Supervisory Appraiser shall be state-certified and must be in "good standing" in the area in which the Trainee Appraiser practices for a period of at least three (3) years. Supervisory Appraisers shall not have been subject to any disciplinary action within any jurisdiction within the last three (3) years that affects the Supervisory Appraiser's legal eligibility to engage in appraisal practice. A Supervisory Appraiser subject to disciplinary action would be considered to be in "good standing" three (3) years after successful completion/termination of the sanction imposed against the appraiser.

- A Supervisory Appraiser may not supervise more than three (3) Trainee Appraisers at one time. However, a Trainee Appraiser is permitted to have any number of Supervisory Appraisers.

Source: Department of Consumer Affairs/Bureau of Real estate Appraisers.

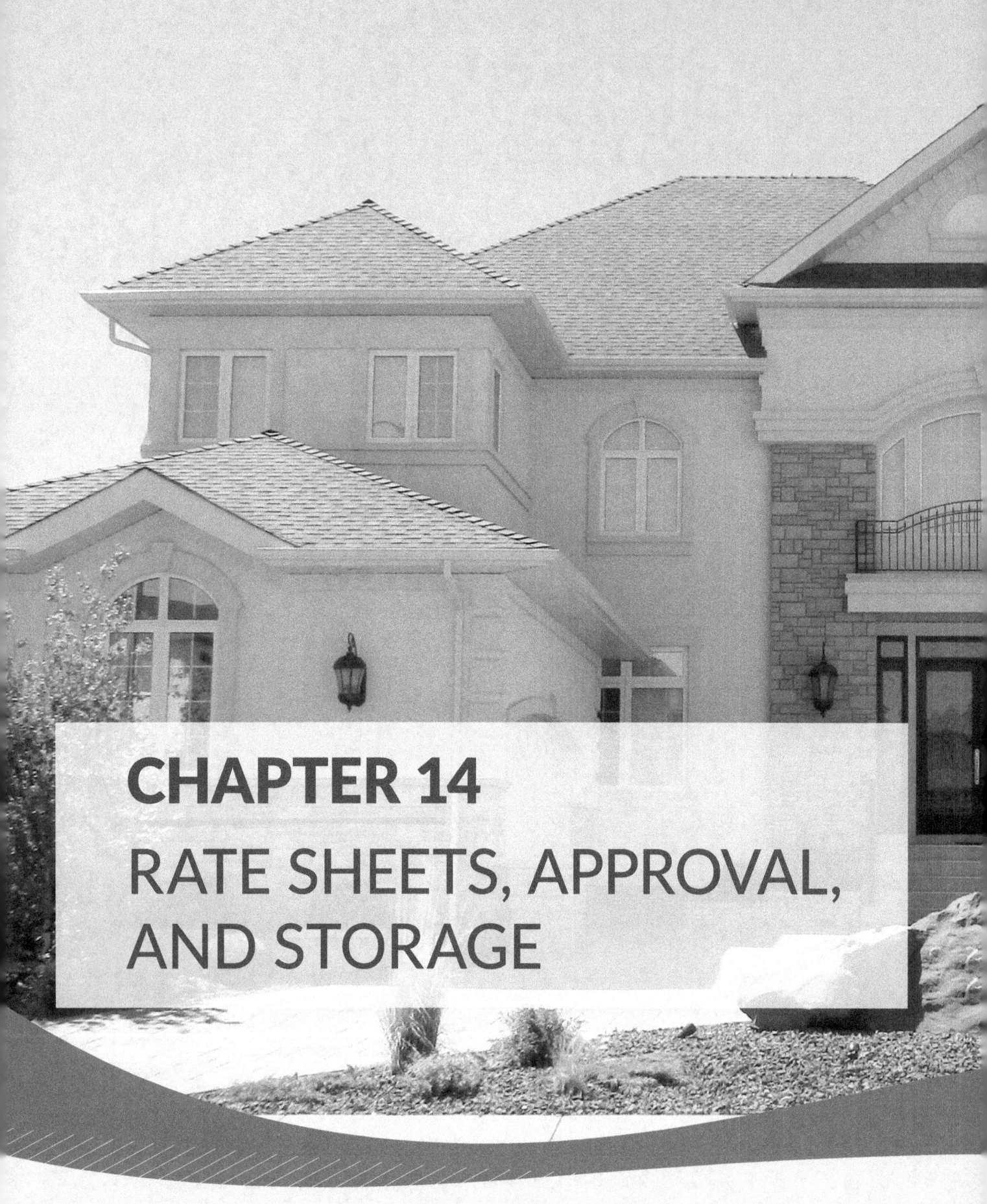

CHAPTER 14
RATE SHEETS, APPROVAL, AND STORAGE

RATE SHEETS

The broker/loan agent uses rate sheets to select a loan program, interest rate, and lender's costs according to the borrower's needs and wishes. The loan officer should provide the processor with the loan information, or a copy of the rate sheet used. The broker/processor/loan officer must be able to read a rate sheet and be able to check the selected program and rate sheet for guidelines. They must then be able to confirm that the loan file fits into the chosen program. See Figure 37, Rate Sheet.

Add-ons and Adjustments are any additional fees the lender is charging for special circumstances. In Figure 37 to the right of the loan programs, there is a section titled "Price Adjustments (add to pts)." This section lists the reasons for an additional charge and tells whether the charge is added to the fee or points (in this case), or to the rate. This is also referred to as pricing. Adjustable loans may also include an add-on to the margin. The add-ons and adjustments are fees charged to the borrower for any variations to their loan request. The broker/ processor/loan officer must check for any adjustments that may apply to the loan file.

Some commonly used Add-ons and Adjustments include:
- Cash-out
- >80% LTV
- Credit score
- Impounds
- Non-owner-occupied (n/o/o)

Admin Fee: $845 for Purchase & Refis; $495 for FHA/VA streamlines, $295 for Hud Repos, Redraw Fee $150, Tax Service Fee $80, Flood Cert Fee $12 (1st), MERS Fee $6.95; Wire Fee $50
Loan amount < $50,000 add 1 point (Min loan amt $30K)

will not fund a loan that is within the Federal Section 32 or any other State/County/City High Cost Calculation.

"All rates and programs are subject to change without notice. This information is intended for mortgage professionals only and is not an advertisement to extend consumer credit as defined by REGZ."

Max Financing available on conforming conventional products in AZ, CA, NV, & FL is 90% LTV.

All files must be received in the branch within 10 calendar days of the lock.

15 day lock terms require SPM underwriting approval, otherwise loans will be locked on a 30 day term.

Page 1

MARKET WATCH

Economic Calendar:	Indexes:		Lock Information:
Mon: Construction Spending, ISM Index	1 Yr Treas.	0.4700	Rate lock cut-off at 4:00 p.m. Pacific
Tues: Factory Orders, Pending Home Sales, Auto & Truck Sales	6 mo. LIBOR	0.4256	30 Day Lock Price: Add .125 to 15 Day
Weds: Challenger Job Cuts, ADP Employment Report, ISM Services,	11th Dist. COFI	2.0940	45 Day Lock Price: Add .20 to 30 Day
Crude Inventories	1 Yr Libor	0.9603	15 Day lock expiration: 1/20
Thurs: Initial Claims, Continuing Claims	1 mo. LIBOR	0.2322	30 Day lock expiration: 2/4
Fri: Avg WorkWk, Hrly Earnings, Nonfarm Payrolls, Unemp Rate	MTA Index	0.4808	"Subject to worst case pricing upon lock expiration."

CONVENTIONAL CONFORMING FIXED RATE

CONFORMING FIXED RATE MORTGAGES

30yr/20yr FRM		High Balance		15yr/10yr FRM	
RATE	15 Day	RATE	15 Day	RATE	15 Day
4.375	2.186	4.375	3.286	4.000	1.698
4.500	1.736	4.500	2.836	4.125	1.348
4.625	1.316	4.625	2.416	4.250	-0.032
4.750	0.296	4.750	1.396	4.375	-0.932
4.875	-0.684	4.875	0.416	4.500	-1.352
5.000	-1.134	5.000	-0.034	4.625	-1.652
5.125	-1.514	5.125	-0.414	4.750	-2.402
5.250	-2.264	5.250	-1.164	4.875	-3.102
5.375	-3.064	5.375	-1.964	5.000	-3.302
5.500	3.444	5.500	2.844	5.125	-3.652
5.625	-3.694	5.625	-2.594	5.250	-3.652

Price Adjustments (add to pts):
2-4 Unit Properties: add 1.0
Condo w/ LTV > 75%: add .75
Loans < $110K: add .125
Loans < $50K: add 1.000
No impounds: add .25
30yr Buydown T303: add 2.375
LPMI - see page 2
Investment Property Adj. (max 80%):
<=75%: add 1.75
75.01-80%: add 3.00
Conforming High Balance FNMA only (no LP)
All Cash Out high bal transactions (T300J09 & T301J09); additional adj. of 1.0 to the price
T301J09 (15 Year High Balance): add 1 point to the standard 15 year price

Hybrid MI (HPMI): add 1.0 (not avail. on High Balance Transactions, 3-4 Units, 2/1 Buydowns, and Non-owner transactions). Minimum fico: 720

Max rebate 3.0 after adds!!

The following RISK-BASED adjustments apply to ALL programs except for 10 & 15 year terms.

Agency FICO/LTV Grid

	<= 60%	60.01-70%	70.01-75%	75.01-80%	80.01-85%	85.01-90%	90.01-95%
740+	-0.25	0.00	0.00	0.00	0.00	0.00	0.00
720-739	-0.25	0.00	0.00	0.25	0.00	0.00	0.00
700-719	-0.25	0.50	0.50	0.75	0.50	0.50	0.50
680-699	0.00	0.50	1.00	1.50	1.00	0.75	0.75
660-679	0.00	1.00	2.00	2.50	2.25	1.75	n/a
640-659	0.50	1.25	2.50	3.00	2.75	2.25	n/a
620-639	0.50	1.50	3.00	3.00	3.00	2.75	n/a

The following are RISK-BASED adjustments that apply to all programs:

Agency Cash-Out Refi FICO/LTV Grid

	<= 60%	60.01-75%	75.01-80%	80.01-85%
740+	0.00	0.250	0.500	n/a
720-739	0.00	0.625	0.75	n/a
700-719	0.00	0.625	0.75	n/a
680-699	0.00	0.75	1.375	n/a
660-679	0.25	0.75	1.50	n/a
640-659	0.25	1.25	2.25	n/a
620-639	0.25	1.25	2.75	n/a

The following are RISK-BASED adjustments that apply to all programs:

Mortgages with Subordinate Financing:

LTV Range	CLTV Range	FICO Range	
		Fico < 720	Fico >= 720
65.01-75%	90.01-95%	0.50	0.25
75.01-95%	75.01-95%	0.50	0.50

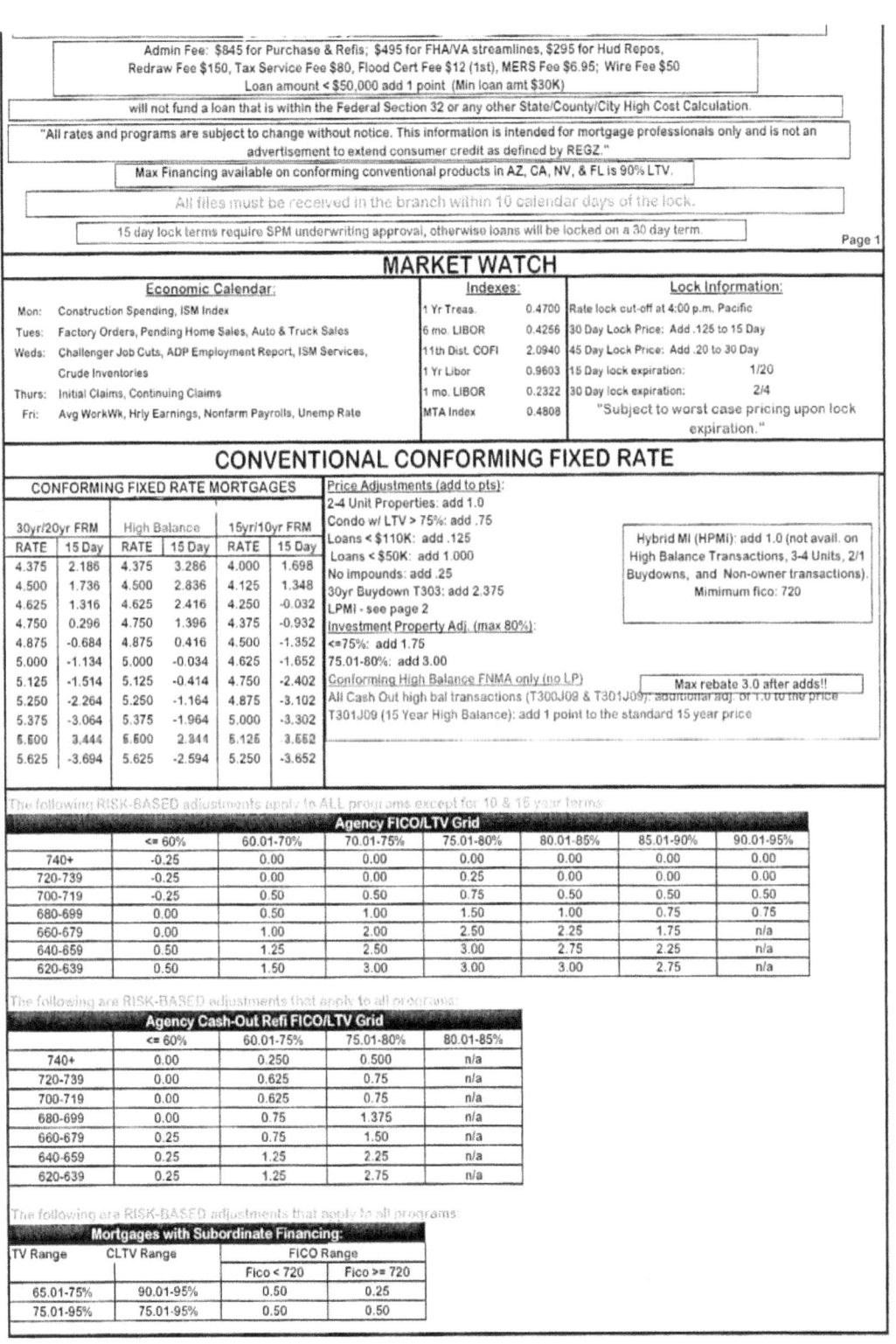

Figure 37: Rate Sheet

Example 1: From the rate sheet, add-ons are added to the points

5.00%	-1.134%	*Interest Rate with a Rebate*
	.75%	*Condo <75%*
	.125%	*30 Day Lock*
	.75%	*Cash-Out, credit score 725, 80% LTV*
5.00%	=.491%	*Total cost or points for 5% rate*

Example2: Add-ons to the interest rate (Not from shown rate sheet)

	5.25%	*Interest rate*
	.375%	*Cost for a 15-day lock*
	+.25%	*Cost add-on for 90% LTV*
+.625%	**=.625%**	**Total add-on to the rate**
=5.875%		**Interest rate**

Example 3: Add-on to margin (Not from shown rate sheet) 4.25% interest rate

	2.00%	*Margin*
	.50%	*Credit score <725*
	+.75%	*30-day lock*
+1.25%	**=1.25%**	**Total add-on to margin**
=3.25%		**Total margin**

The add-ons may apply to the interest rate, the fees, or the margin for an adjustable-rate loan.

RATE SHEET ITEMS

TYPICAL ITEMS on a rate sheet are as follows:
PROGRAMS CF-30 is a commonly used designation of a loan program identifying a conforming 30-year fixed-rate loan program. Every lender provides a name to identify the individual loan programs. In this example, "C" indicates conforming, "F" indicates fixed, and 30 discloses the number of years, or term, of the loan. A jumbo fixed loan program may be indicated with the use of JF-. This is a common use of loan identification.

RATE is the amount of the interest rate or note rate. Interest rate is the percentage of the loan balance that the borrower pays the lender for the use of their money. This is the means of generating income for the mortgage bank.

15 DAY AND 30 DAY shows the amount the lender will charge for the given note rate for the term of the requested lock or how long they are being asked to hold the chosen interest rate. This is also known as the lock period.

On this particular day, the broker can lock the interest rate of 4.75% for 15 days and the lender will pay the borrower .296% of the loan amount. If 30 days are needed to complete this loan transaction, the file will be locked at the same rate for that period and the lender will charge the borrower .50% of the loan amount. The lender's fee will be placed on the good faith estimate or the MLDS, page 1, item #801, Lender's Loan Origination Fee.

The loan is locked to guarantee the chosen interest rate, but it can only be locked for a pre-determined period of time. When the broker locks a loan with the lender, they lock that interest rate and loan amount with their investor on the secondary mortgage market. The broker needs to make every effort to close that loan within the lock period.

If the loan does not close within the lock period, the lender will allow the broker to re-lock the loan at the current Interest rate or the previously locked rate, whichever is higher. If the rate only needs to be extended for a few days, the lender has the option to extend the rate for no additional charge or to charge a small fee, such as .25%, to extend the rate.

The lender will allow a few extra days on their lock with the investor to deliver the closed loan file prior to their lock expiring. For example, the broker locked the loan at 5.25% for 15 days. The lender then locks the loan for 20 days with the investor. The lender must deliver the closed loan file to the investor within the lock period and if they do not ship the file by that date, they will be charged a late fee called a pair-off fee by the investor. When the broker locks their single file with the lender, the lender does not just lock in the loan amount of a single loan with the broker but commits to deliver of a large block of loans. The lender will commit to deliver loan files equal to a set dollar amount, such as $2,000,000. If the broker does not deliver the loan file as promised, the lender will replace that file with another to meet the total dollar amount.

HEDGING is a practice of lenders when they determine that interest rates are likely to go down and they do not lock or make a commitment with their investor. The lender is betting that the rate will go down and by taking the broker's lock at a higher interest rate and when the investor's rate is reduced, they will make their commitment and will increase their profit. Investors charge a fee or offer a rebate in the same way that lenders do. Lenders will add in a fee for their own profit on top of the investor's fees. By hedging, the lender is able to increase their profits as long as the rates do go down. If rates increase, the lender will lose their profit margin.

When opening a new loan file that has not been processed, and the loan agent has quoted the borrower 0% fee to the lender to obtain the rate they want, a 30-day or 45- day lock may be needed. The lender will charge the borrower an add-on, or fee, to the loan amount to obtain that interest rate by closing the loan within the next 30 days. Any add-ons or adjustments should be discussed with the loan agent, as the borrower is their client, and the borrower must be notified of any changes to the quoted fees or costs.

FLOATING THE LOAN OR RATE occurs if it has been decided that the loan will not be locked until a later date. There are times when it may be best not to lock the loan but wait until the loan has been submitted. It could even be beneficial to wait until the loan is ready for loan docs in order to get the shortest lock period and therefore, the smallest charge from the lender. This is a decision that has to be made by the broker/loan agent and the borrower.

REBATE PRICING occurs when the lender offers a higher interest rate and offers the borrower money back to take that higher rate. On the same rate sheet, if the chosen interest rate is 5.0% and the lock period is **15 days,** the lender is going to give a **rebate,** which is always displayed with a **minus sign (-) or in parentheses ( )**. In this case, the rebate pricing is **1.134% of the loan amount shown on the rate sheet as -1.134.** In other words, the lender is going to give the broker or borrower 1.875% of the loan amount for taking a higher interest rate.

This rebate is generally used to offset the borrower's costs or compensation to the broker/loan agent. Using rebate pricing will help to qualify a borrower who is short on funds for closing costs.

YIELD-SPREAD PREMIUM (YSP) is similar to a rebate in that the lender pays the broker or MLO a percentage of the loan amount for increasing the lender's yield or profit on the loan by selling the borrower at a higher interest rate.

SERVICING RELEASE PREMIUM (SRP) is an amount paid to the broker/ MLO for releasing the servicing rights to the loan to the lender. This practice is generally used when doing table funding or when the broker is acting in the capacity of a correspondent lender.

Brokers and loan agents should be careful with the wording when advertising such a loan program or quoting this to a borrower. The loan should be advertised as no-cost to the borrower. The borrower is in essence paying for the costs of the loan by paying the higher interest rate. The APR disclosure is extremely important when advertising and providing a no-cost loan because it will clearly show the APR, demonstrating that the loan costs will be noticeably higher that the note rate. The broker/loan officer must be clear about the form of payment of the closing costs.

The MLDS/GFE(LE) will disclose the interest rate being charged, all of the costs involved in obtaining the loan, and the rebate that is paid for those costs.

ADVERTISING by a broker must always include the APR if any of the following items or wording is used in the advertisement whether print or verbal advertising is used:
- Terms: loan program in type or number of monthly payments/years
- Payment amount
- Interest rate
- Down payment
- LTV

In other words, any figures or calculations provided in an advertisement will trigger or require the disclosure of the APR based on those terms.

BASIS POINT (bp) SYSTEM is used by a few lenders to show pricing on the rate sheet instead of the usual percentage. The basis points will appear as 100 for par or 0 Cost. Any figure more than 100 indicates a rebate. In other words, 100.25 indicates a .25% rebate.

> **NOTE**
>
> *Rebates and YSPs must be disclosed to the borrower prior to ordering loan documents or, at the latest, before locking the loan/rate. SRPs do not need to be disclosed as it is not considered a type of rebate.*

> **NOTE**
>
> *"No-Points" loans are loans that use the rebate to pay the costs of the loan. There is no such thing as a no-cost or no-point loan. Nobody is going to work for free, including the broker.*

A figure less than 100 is a cost to the borrower. For example, 99.75 indicates a .25% cost. This system is more commonly used on the secondary mortgage market, but some lenders use it for their rate sheet pricing.

Mortgage rates are most often adjusted by 1/8th of a percent; in decimals this is shown as .125. The broker/processor/loan officer should be familiar with following figures that are the conversions to from fractions to decimals, which are always used for mortgage rates:

.125	=	1/8
.25	=	¼
.375	=	3/8
.50	=	1/2
.625	=	5/8
.75	=	¾
.875	=	7/8
1.00	=	100

Converting figures from decimals to percentages requires moving the decimal point two places to the right and adding the % mark.
    Example: .08 = 8%

PARAMETERS are the same as guidelines and this area includes allowable issues according to the loan program such as LTV requirements and the maximum LTVs for issues such as a non-owner-occupied property. Some lenders may also require a minimum FICO Score required for qualifying. Anything that makes the file a greater risk will usually require the additional fees or add-ons to be charged.

EXPANDED CRITERIA on a rate sheet provides loan programs that exceed normal guidelines but are still A-paper. The rates and fees are generally higher than for the regular loan programs but will accommodate loans such as those with a high LTV that must be done as a stated-income loan. Brokers/processors and loan agents should check for expanded loan programs before resorting to a sub-prime loan program.

FEES showing on most rate sheets are the lender's charges for providing a loan. These generally include the following and will vary with lender:

- **Admin fee** - $845.
- **Tax service** - $80.
- **Wire** - $50.
- **Underwriting** -$275.
- **Document (Doc) prep** - $150.
- **Flood cert** - $12.
- **Redraw fee** if the lender has to redraw the loan docs - $150.
- **Piggyback** refers to both a first and a second TD that are being processed and will close escrow with the same lender at the same time or concurrently but with different lenders.

When a second TD is being done independently, it is referred to as a **STANDALONE**. Most lenders will have a variation in fees for a second TD according to its piggyback, or standalone policy.

When preparing the original loan (LE) estimate, the rate sheet should be checked for these fees if the lender is known. The fees will vary with lenders, but in most situations these fees may be used if unknown. If there is a conflict between the information given to the borrower and the rate sheet, it should be discussed with the borrower prior to submission, and a new MLDS/GFE(LE) must be provided, especially if the fees differ more by than .125% from the original MLDS/GFE(LE). A copy of the current rate sheet, on which the LE was based, should be included in the file as a confirmation of the rate and fees.

PREPARING THE LE ACCURATELY IS CRITICAL, AS ERRORS MAY COST PENALTIES.

SUBMISSION TO THE LENDER

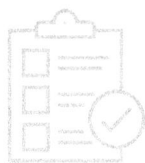

SUBMISSION SHEETS are provided by each lender and can be obtained online or by fax if requested. It will save time to prepare a separate file for the most often used lenders and retain a copy of their submission sheet and other pertinent information. The submission sheet asks for information in the form of a synopsis of the loan. Usually when the lender receives a loan package, a clerical employee will enter the provided information into a computer, therefore, the form should be completed as accurately, completely, and neatly as possible.

The form asks the borrower's name, subject property address, and type of loan: refinance, purchase, cash-out, conventional, first or second TD, as well as the broker's fees. Some lenders will require the file to be in a stacking order to their specifications, which is usually provided on the submission sheet if it is not in compliance with FNMA.

The **FILE COVER SHEET** will show the amount charged by the appraiser, the credit reporting agency, and any other amounts, such as courier fees that have already been paid, or is due from the borrower. These fees can be adjusted at the time of locking the rate and ordering loan docs, but it should be as close as possible at this point. A few lenders will require this form to be delivered to them prior to submission as a pre-registration of the loan.

Compare the name to the spelling in the prelim if the loan is a refinance. For a purchase, compare the name with the escrow instructions or call the escrow officer for updated information. If escrow has not received the documentation from the borrower, the broker/loan agent may contact the borrower for exact spelling of the name and the vesting information. The broker/processor should check the address on the prelim and the appraisal for comparison and accuracy.

Every piece of information on the 1003 and 1008 must be double-checked for changes, such as the information received on the verifications, name, address, and appraised value of the property. Once the information has been thoroughly checked, print out the final 1003 and 1008, and compile the entire package in the standard stacking order or in the lender's requested stacking order.

This is the original loan file which is usually held in the broker's office. Occasionally, the original file will be required to be submitted to the lender. It used to be common practice to deliver the original file to the lender; however, most lenders now accept and even require that loans be submitted online or paperless. Most lenders have an upload on their website so that the portion of the loan file that is on the broker's LOS can be transferred directly to the lender for submission.

NOTE

Many lenders will draw loan docs using the information on the submission sheet, so everything should be thorough and accurate.

NOTE

The preliminary title report is considered the most accurate source of recorded property information, as it reflects documents that are recorded with the county recorder's office.

This is followed by uploading the broker's file with all of the supporting documentation such as the credit report, income and asset documentation, escrow, prelim, etc., or they should provide an email address specifically for Submitting the loan file.

Some lenders may still require a hard copy to be submitted. Hard copies are usually a copy package, not the original, but the broker/processor should verify prior to submission. Some brokers are not online, and they will need the lender to provide a hard copy, whether it is the original or a copy.

COVER LETTERS are not necessary but should be written and included in the package if there are any unusual circumstances that need to be explained. Addressing the issues in the loan file upfront will help move the file through the system to be properly handled. Pointing out and addressing negative information as well as the positive aspects of the loan file will aid the underwriter in making an appropriate decision.

APPROVAL AND CONDITIONS

UNDERWRITING a loan file usually takes 24 to 48 hours. At that point, the approval is forwarded to the broker's office with any necessary conditions that must be completed prior to closing (PTC) or funding (PTF) the loan. Some of the conditions may be required to be met prior to drawing up loan documents (PTD).

Any conditions marked "S" **are suspense** items and must be submitted to and approved by the underwriter (UW) before the loan will be approved. A suspended loan file is neither approved nor declined. The UW needs this additional information/documentation to determine the creditworthiness of the file.

PTD (Prior-to-Docs) conditions must be approved by the UW before loan documents can be ordered and before a loan can be locked for the shortest period offered by the lender, such as 10 or 15 days. It is a common requirement by lenders that the PTD conditions should be forwarded to the lender at the same time. Examples of conditions that are typically PTDs are:
- Appraisal
- Credit report
- Current and complete income documentation
- Current and complete asset documentation

- Escrow instructions
- Prelim
- Upfront disclosures
- Any missing items necessary to verify the statements of the 1003 or the borrower's creditworthiness.

PTF (Prior-to-Funding) or **PTC (Prior-to-Closing)** must be provided to, and approved by, the lender before the loan can fund and close escrow.

Most lenders assign a number to their conditions and often group them according to the priority, which makes it easier to track by the lender and by the broker/ processor. Underwriters prefer receiving all conditions at once, at least for a particular group, such as PTDs. As the conditions are assembled, each one should be marked in the lower right corner with the corresponding lender's number from the approval sheet.

When the compiled conditions are ready to submit for UW approval, a copy must be retained for the broker's file and the originals sent to the lender. If the conditions are submitted to the underwriter through the lender's website or online, the broker/processor will retain the originals unless requested specifically by the lender. When submitting a hard copy of the conditions, the approval, with all submitted conditions high-lighted, should be included on top of the conditions to the lender. This will assist the lender to quickly identify the proper loan file. Each condition should be dated on the broker/processor's approval sheet with the date that the conditions were submitted to the lender. If any conditions are lost or misplaced, the broker/processor will have a record of the date the originals were sent as well as a copy. The broker/processor should never send conditions to the lender without identifying the loan file associated with the conditions. The lender will set unidentifiable conditions aside. All conditions should be submitted at once, to avoid frustration for the underwriter. Develop a good working relationship and establish the fact that you underline submit clean and complete packages.

> **NOTE**
>
> *Making the lender's job easier will move the loan file through the system faster and more easily.*

If the broker/processor feels the UW is being unfair or is mistaken about any conditions or aspects of the loan file, a phone call or email to the UW/lender is advisable. If the broker/processor is unsure of a requested condition or is unable to provide one exactly as requested, a call to the UW explaining the problem can generally result in a viable solution or alternative documentation.

There are usually other ways of satisfying a condition if the requested way is not possible. Many times, the broker/processor can verbally verify an item or issue and can provide a letter stating the findings and certifying the accuracy of the statement. This would be done in a letter called a processor's cert (certification).

The broker/processor should always be creative and be open with the underwriter about the circumstances and work to find an alternative when necessary.

CONDITIONS that are commonly required may be as follows:
- **Most recent paystub**- This is a common condition and is usually a PTC. Reminding the borrower to provide the most recent paystub prior to going to escrow when signing loan docs can ensure the best resolution. Most borrowers will be capable of uploading, emailing, or faxing a condition to the broker's office as needed.
- **Appraisal prepared by a lender-approved appraiser** is always a PTD condition.

Appraisals are no longer submitted with the initial submission because they are now ordered through the lender after the loan is submitted. If there are time constraints and the approval is needed quickly, check with the lender to determine if the file will be underwritten without the appraisal.

> **NOTE**
>
> *Some lenders will not allow the processor to talk to the UW, but the lender's processor or the loan rep can help with any questions or disputes. Underwriters will return calls to the broker/processor when necessary. The rep is usually the most helpful because they are paid a commission only and do not want to lose a loan, especially when the problem can be easily remedied. Underwriters will rarely speak to a loan agent and will never speak to the borrower or the real estate agent. The borrower and real estate agent must never be provided the UW's direct line or email address. The broker/processor is the contact with the lender.*

There are times when the broker/processor may not want the appraisal ordered until the loan has been approved. This may be the case if there is a possibility that the borrower may not qualify or has limited funds with which to pay the appraiser. Most lenders will allow this request, but it should be clarified and agreed to prior to submission.

- **Verification of sufficient funds to close** – a PTD condition. If the VODs and bank statements that were submitted do not reflect sufficient funds to close, it is possible to verify additional funds in a variety of ways. A lender will not draw loan documents without verification that the borrower is capable of closing the loan.

One way to assist the borrower with closing costs is to increase the interest rate to cover a portion of the closing costs with the rebate. The UW may need to review the file to verify that the borrower can qualify for the higher interest rate.

The loan agent should have a discussion with the borrower to let them know the additional amount required and advise them to deposit the required amount into their accounts. They will need proof of that deposit, so they must get a deposit receipt from the bank. The lender will require proof of the source of these funds, such as an additional paystub, a gift from an immediate relative, the sale of an asset, such as a car or a collectible, or cash on hand/ mattress money.

- **Verify sufficient income or reduce debt ratio**. If the borrower's debt ratio is borderline or is in excess of the lender's guidelines to qualify, the underwriter may require that they verify additional income or pay off debt to qualify.

Most A-paper lenders will only allow installment debt to be paid for qualifying purposes. Sub-prime lenders will generally allow revolving debt to be paid off for qualifying purposes.

There are situations when the borrower is receiving a pay raise soon or has additional income not previously disclosed, such as a bonus or a second job. A pay raise will need to be verified with a paystub prior to COE. Any additional income must be verified with proof of a 2-year history of that income.

Cancelled checks may be obtained to verify income for private jobs or bonuses.

Unclaimed income, such as tips for a waiter/waitress are often verified with twenty-four months of bank statements. The underwriter averages the deposits shown on the bank statements and they are averaged to provide a 24-month average income figure. Not all lenders will allow this method, so the processor should ask the underwriter what income is acceptable and what documentation will be needed for any unusual income.

For verification that debt obligations are less than the credit report, the borrower may provide current credit card statements verifying a lower payment. If a borrower has an installment debt that is too much to be paid in full, they may be able to pay down the balance to a 10-month remaining balance. If they are able to do this, the payment will not be included in the debt ratio.

Any time a debt must be paid, it must always be done through escrow to be verifiable. When the funds are paid to escrow, escrow will in turn pay that debt directly to the creditor at COE.

Reducing the loan amount to an amount that the borrower will qualify for, reducing the interest rate, or changing the loan program to one with a lower start rate, such as an ARM, may also solve the problem.

- **Final corrected 1003 and LE signed by borrower and loan agent – PTF/PTC condition.** The broker/processor will be required to complete a final 1003, 1008, loan estimate, and final closing disclosure with the most accurate closing costs, interest rate, and loan amount possible on every loan package.

The underwriter may provide a marked-up copy of the 1003 showing the figures that they want on the final 1003. Not all underwriters will provide this information, in which case the processor should be certain that all information is as accurate as possible. Income, assets, and liabilities information should all be updated along with any corrections or changes to the borrower's name or the subject property address.

- **Appraisal corrections or supplements to the appraisal,** which may include additional comps will be PTF conditions.

> **NOTE**
>
> *The final decision is made by the borrower with the broker/loan agent's advice. The broker/processor is crucial to the loan agent and the borrower in determining and suggesting the viable possibilities for each loan and as the contact with the lender.*

The broker/processor will need to address a potentially wide array of conditions, as every loan package and every borrower is different, and every borrower will bring different circumstances to the loan process. The previous conditions are among the most common. The examples provide possible alternatives or documentation that will satisfy the condition.

DOCS AND FUNDING

Docs can be ordered once all suspense and PTD conditions have been signed off (approved) by the UW; the loan rate must be locked before loan docs can be ordered.

The method of LOCKING THE RATE will vary with each lender. Most lenders require the lock be done online on the lender's website. Others use the submission form with the lock section completed, re-signed, and re-dated. Brokers who are not computerized may be able to initially lock the loan verbally, before a lock and doc form is faxed to them for verification, signing, and returning to the lender.

Double-checking the rate sheet for add-ons is important and should be confirmed with the loan agent and borrower. The loan agent always makes the final decision to determine the rate along with the borrower. The broker/processor may, on the loan agent's instructions, lock the loan and order docs. The lender should provide a written lock confirmation, which should be retained in the loan file in case there is a discrepancy on the loan docs. If there are any questions about the correct rate or fees, the lender should be contacted prior to finalizing the doc order.

LOAN DOCS ARE ORDERED after locking the rate and having all PTD conditions signed off will constitute doc ordering with many lenders. Some lenders will email or call the broker/processor to say they are ready for the doc request. The doc request form is to be completed either online on the lender's website or signed and emailed or faxed to the lender.

Other lenders use the original submission form and by re-signing, the broker/ processor verify the rate, loan amount, and fees. A doc drawer may call the broker/processor to confirm fees before drawing the docs. This is done over the phone. Until the lender calls to confirm fees, the docs will not be drawn. Keep in mind that each lender will have their own system and process. They will walk the broker/processor through their process, and it is acceptable to call and ask when unsure.

It is good practice to call to confirm that docs have been ordered and to ask the turnaround time or when escrow can expect to receive them. These actions and requests should always be recorded on the conversation log for reference. If the time has passed without a response, the broker/ processor should follow up with a phone call or email to confirm the docs are being prepared.

The broker/processor should call the escrow officer to give them a heads-up that docs are being drawn and tell them when they may expect them to be delivered so they are prepared to schedule the clients. The loan agent should notify the borrowers, so they are prepared to be available for signing when escrow is ready.

The escrow officer will contact the borrowers and schedule them to sign docs as soon as possible. Ideally, they should be returned to the lender by overnight mail on the same day is at all possible. Escrow does not schedule any appointments for doc signing until they actually have the docs in their office.

FedEx delivers by 10:30am every weekday and on Saturday if requested, and the escrow will begin scheduling the signing as quickly as possible. The broker/processor should give escrow the best way to contact the borrower, and have the borrower prepared to be available. During a signing with escrow, if the borrower has questions that the escrow officer cannot answer, they may call the loan agent or broker/processor for assistance. Some loan agents try to attend doc signing to be available for questions. If the loan agent is not available, the broker/processor will need to be on hand for questions and assistance.

DOCUMENTS SENT TO ESCROW by the broker to be signed, along with loan docs, will almost always be a PTF condition requiring changes or corrections to the 1008 and 1003, and signatures from the borrowers.

Some of the documents that the broker will need to send to escrow to be signed and forwarded to the lender are:

- Corrected 1003 and 1008
- Final loan estimate (LE) for signature by the borrowers. It is required by law to have a copy of the final MLDS that has been signed by the borrower in all closed loan packages.
- Original LE if the borrowers did not sign.
- Loan agent must sign the final 1003, Page 3, and Page 2 of the LE. The processor should always request that escrow returns a copy of any forms for signatures to the broker with the original going to the lender.

- Page 2 of the IRS 1040s re-signed by all borrowers.
- Letter of explanation

The broker/processor must check the conditions for any other forms that require the borrower's signature. The loan agent or broker should always, whenever possible, attend the doc signing. Most questions from borrowers are about the loan and closing. By being there, the loan agent/broker can answer them and help the loan and escrow close. Sales agents/brokers really appreciate this. It is worth remembering that almost everyone in a real estate transaction is on commission.

The broker/processor may choose to prepare a demand to include the broker's fees and any other outstanding costs that the broker is responsible for, such as credit report, appraisal, and courier fees. The demand should clearly state any amounts owed to others, such as the credit reporting agency or the appraiser and to whom it is owed. The demand should request that any amounts due to others be paid directly to them, or that the checks be prepared in the name of the proper entity. This will avoid any conflict with the trust account laws, as it will prevent any commingling of funds. It is not a necessary or required form but may be advisable under certain circumstances, such as when there are additional fees due to a service provider.

If the hard copies are being sent to escrow, it is helpful to the escrow officer to highlight the places where a signature is required or to flag it. There are sticky flags available that say, "sign here." This package can be sent to escrow by courier, or it can be faxed or emailed. Request that the escrow officer send the originals to the lender with the loan docs and return a copy to the broker's office for the broker's file.

NOTE

Copies of these signed forms are required to be in the closed broker files along with the entire loan file. The broker/processor must always retain a copy of the unsigned set as they were delivered to escrow, along with the request for a copy. If escrow does not return a copy, the requests can be verified, and the broker is protected.

FUNDING

The escrow officer will try to return the loan documents to the lender the same day they were received. Lenders generally try to review the docs the day they are received unless they are extremely busy. Lenders will often require that docs be returned to them 48 hours prior to funding to allow sufficient time to verify proper signing and sign-off all conditions.

If there are any missing conditions, the funder will prepare a "missing conditions" list. Depending on the importance of the condition and the relationship between the lender and broker, they may pre-fund that same day for funding the next day, trusting that escrow and broker will provide acceptable conditions.

PRE-FUNDING is a process the lender is required to follow whereby they notify their bank in writing (fax) with the request for funds to be wired the next day. This allows the bank time to prepare the needed amount of cash to be withdrawn from the lender's account and prepare the wires. The following morning, the lender's bank wires the requested funds to the appropriate escrow company's accounts. Verification that funds have been wired is usually received around 1:00 p.m. A lender may, under special circumstances, allow a same day funding, meaning that they did not notify their bank a day ahead. When this happens, there will be an additional charge in the range of $20-$50. This additional fee may be charged to the broker.

The lender can "pull funds," or request that escrow return their funds if conditions have not been met or when conditions are received, and they are unacceptable.

Funding conditions are important and must be submitted prior to the close of escrow. Lenders used to allow favors to brokers by funding a loan based on the broker's promise to forward any missing conditions immediately. Unfortunately, this practice was abused and is now rarely allowed. In an emergency, and when the broker and lender have a good relationship, it may be allowed.

FOLLOW THE PRE-FUNDING CLOSELY. MAKE YOURSELF AVAILABLE. TO CONFIRM FUNDING AND KEEP ALL PARTIES INFORMED. BOTH OF YOU WILL SLEEP BETTER THAT NIGHT.

RECORDING & CLOSING

On **THE DAY OF FUNDING**, escrow prepares all the deeds and real estate-related documentation to be recorded with the county recorder's office. At 8:00 a.m. the following morning, the recorder's office accepts filings from the title companies ahead of all others. The purpose is to be certain that no liens are filed ahead of the new trust deeds. If there are liens filed against the property that did not show on the prelim, escrow is obligated to notify the lender, who may then choose to pull funds. An example of a lien that would cause this kind of concern and action is a tax lien or a mechanic's lien.

Escrow will receive notice from the county recorder's office when the documents have been recorded and will be given a recording number for verification. This notice is usually received midday. The escrow officer will contact the broker when funds are released, and checks are available. The loan agent is generally responsible for informing the borrower that the escrow has closed for a refi transaction, while a real estate agent does this for a purchase. If the loan agent is not available, the broker/processor may be required to notify the borrower at the request of the agent, or if the borrower or realtor calls for closing confirmation.

Escrow will provide the final closing disclosure to the broker and to the borrower. This form is the breakdown of total costs and expenses paid through escrow with the loan proceeds. This form must be retained in the loan file on the top right side, along with a copy of the check from escrow to the broker and to any vendors, such as the appraiser.

TRUST ACCOUNT

Brokers are required by the state, whether licensed under the Department of Real Estate or the Department of Financial Protection and Innovation, to maintain a trust account to hold and disburse the borrower's funds. This is to prevent the broker from commingling those funds with their own.

The demand should request separate checks to any entity other than the broker. This would typically be for the credit report fee and any courier fees. Escrow rarely does this. Some brokers will not accept a single check that includes their funds as well as payment for other fees. Retaining the demand in the file will verify to any auditors that the request was made and escrow failed to accommodate. It would be at the auditor's discretion to accept this.

This is an issue to be decided by the broker. Any funds collected early in the process will have been deposited into the broker's trust account (if the check was made out to the broker), with a copy of the check placed in the file.

With the introduction of the HVCC and the current billing process used by the credit reporting agencies, there are few times when the broker is actually handling the borrower's Funds. The broker usually pays for the credit report before the loan closes, which means the broker is reimbursed at close of escrow for a fee already paid on behalf of the borrower. Alternatively, the broker can charge the borrower up front for the credit report.

Most brokers now collect credit card information from the borrower to pay for the appraisal once the three-day waiting period has passed, per the MDIC. This also eliminates the need for separate checks or billing at close of escrow.

The broker must maintain trust account records on a monthly basis. These records are retained for three years for the DRE, five years for RESPA, and seven years for Fair Lending. The same guidelines also apply to loan files.

STORING LOAN FILES

All documentation sent to the lender (right side of file package) must be retained. On top of this documentation should be all closing documentation to include from the top:
- Copy of check paid to broker from escrow.
- Final closing disclosure.
- Copy of any funds paid to other vendors, such as the appraiser or credit- reporting agency.
- Copies of final signed 1003, 1008, LE, and any other documents signed at escrow.

For storage purposes, only the conversation log and any tracking sheets or broker forms that record the loan process should be retained on the left side of the folder. All other documentation on the left-hand side of the file should be removed and destroyed because it was not sent to the lender or used in qualifying the borrower. **Any documentation that was not used in the approval of the loan or sent to the lender should be removed from the file and disposed of by shredding or returning to the borrower.**

In the event of an audit, any documentation in the file may be forwarded to the lender at the auditor's discretion, whether it was previously submitted or not.

A copy of the appraisal with original photos, if available, should be forwarded to the borrower along with a letter of thanks from the broker. Each broker handles this differently. Close out the file on the loan log and file the package.

Any loan applications that were declined or canceled for any reason must be retained by the broker of record for four years from the date of decline or cancellation.

The left side of the file should be cleaned out as is done with a closed loan.

Within 72 hours of decline or cancelation, a statement of credit denial must be completed and mailed to the borrower, even if the loan was canceled at their request. A copy must be placed on the top right-hand side of the loan file.

If the reason for denial was a credit issue, the credit reporting agency's address must be disclosed on the form for the borrower's information. RESPA laws provide borrowers with the right to dispute any erroneous reports to the credit bureaus. The primary borrower must be given a copy of the adverse action/statement of credit denial; however, all borrowers must receive a copy when the denial was based on a credit report.

The file is complete. It is always important to remember that the borrower is the client and is paying the bill. The broker must always work in the best interest of the client and respect the position of the all others involved. The laws are written to protect all parties, especially the borrower, who is the least knowledgeable of the process, and has the most to lose. This should be a win-win transaction for all involved.

CHAPTER 15
CLOSING AND TITLE COMPANIES

CLOSING AGENTS/COMPANIES

CLOSING COMPANIES are unbiased, neutral third parties to a real estate transaction. Their role is to be a neutral entity that will manage the funds, deeds, and other items of value involved in the transaction to ensure proper distribution and the fair and equitable closing or execution of the transaction.

As a neutral third party, the closing company performs the following duties:

- **Holds the original contract** to track and ensure that the terms of the contract are met.
- **Prepares the escrow instructions** as a summary of the contract.
- **Holds the buyer's deposit funds**.
- **Holds the seller's deed**.
- **Prepares both an estimated closing disclosure and a final closing disclosure** to provide estimated and final closing costs for both the buyer and seller.
- **Collects the various items** to meet the terms, such as the pest inspection report, and distributes to the necessary parties, such as the lender.
- **Obtains required information,** such as the pay-off demand from the seller's lender, to ensure the payment of debts owed by the seller.
- **Reviews the preliminary title report (prelim)** to search for undisclosed liens or debts and to ensure they carry over to the buyer.
- **Notifies the buyer and the seller** of any issues found on the prelim, such as encroachments or easements.
- **Receives loan documents** from the lender, reviews, and has the borrower sign. This is typically done in the presence of the broker so that they can assist the borrower. The broker then notarizes the documents.
- **Prepares the deeds and arranges for Recording** with the county recorder's office.
- **Distributes funds** accordingly and closes escrow or finalizes the transaction.
- **Disperses and refunds** to the appropriate party.

Closing companies must be licensed as a corporation under the Department of Financial Protection and Innovation (DFPI) in California. Licensing will vary in different states.

The Financial Code contains the laws that govern closing companies. The exceptions to the licensing of a closing company are as follow:
- **Title insurance companies**
- **Attorneys**
- **Banks, and savings and loans**
- **Real estate brokers**
- **Mortgage brokers**

In instances when a real estate broker owns a closing company that functions as a real estate office or mortgage brokerage, the following rules and regulations apply:
- **Licensing** can be in the name of the broker of record only, not an associate licensee.
- **Duties such as clerical** jobs may be delegated to employees of the broker under the broker's supervision.
- **The broker must be a party** to the transaction in some way, such as listing agent or buyer's agent, or mortgage broker. A broker cannot perform escrows for other brokerages without full licensing.
- **Closing Agent/Escrow** can only be incidental to the main operation of the real estate business.
- **Advertising** of closing services can only be a part of their regular business.
- **Cannot use a DBA (doing business as)** or fictitious business name using the words "escrow" or "title."
- **Escrow funds** must be retained in a trust account separate from other brokerage funds and available for audit.

The **CLOSING OFFICER** acts as a dual agent to both the buyer and seller during the transaction. Once escrow closes, the closing officer becomes a single agent for each party separately while they finish the remaining details of the transaction. The closing agent/officer is the person within the closing company that will handle the individual transactions. The closing company and its officers are bonded with a $25,000 surety bond. A surety company insures, through bonds, people who handle funds and other items of value on behalf of others.

The closing officer must remain impartial to the parties to the transaction in order to retain their neutrality.

OPENING ESCROW for a purchase transaction will require:
- Purchase agreement and joint escrow instructions.
- Property address.
- Buyer's name and vesting, if known.
- Loan amount.
- Buyer's current mailing address, phone numbers, and Social Security numbers.
- Estimated closing date.

The closing agent will provide the buyer with a form requesting a ten-year address history, along with former names and names of spouses, if applicable. The purpose of this form is to help positively identify the true owner of the property should questions of ownership arise. The buyer should complete this form and return it to escrow as soon as possible.

Valid delivery of instructions must be provided to all parties to a real estate transaction. *Figure 38: Escrow Instructions*

The closing officer will also require:
- Seller's name, address, and contact information.
- Demand for pay-off from the existing lender.
- Accurate information from the seller for the lender's name, address if available, and the account number.

THE BUYERS CHOOSE THE CLOSING COMPANY for a purchase transaction.

Federal RESPA Law states that the choice of title companies is the buyer's. If the seller or their agent selects the title, the seller and their agent may be held liable for three times the buyer's title fees. RESPA also requires that when a real estate licensee is asked for a referral for a service provider, such as title, the real estate professional must provide a list of no less than five names of individuals or companies from which the client may select.

Once the offer to purchase is accepted, the real estate agent will open the **purchase transaction escrow** on behalf of the client. The buyer's realtor will provide the loan officer or mortgage broker the name of the title, closing company, or closing agent, along with contact information. The mortgage broker will contact the closing agent to request the instructions, fully executed purchase contract, and a copy of the receipt for deposit. In this case, the receipt for deposit is a copy of the actual receipt that the closer gave the buyer for their deposit; it is not a copy of the purchase offer.

REFINANCE TRANSACTIONS by mortgage brokers are opened by the mortgage broker and the same *RESPA* rules apply. The broker must provide the borrower with a list of no less than five referrals or use any other title or escrow company or closing agent that the borrower chooses. The closing officer will need the borrower's personal information, as well as the payoff information to acquire a demand from the current lender, if applicable. Any mortgage payoff will be verified by the closer, and all other debts being paid through the loan or closing will be verified with the borrower's most recent statements, which they will bring when they sign loan docs. If statements are not provided, the balances shown on the credit report will be used. An approximate payoff amount and information should be given to the closing agent when opening the loan.

The closing agent can accept only written documents that have been signed by all parties to the transaction. Oral instructions must not be followed; the only exception to this would be a request to amend the instructions, which will generate written documentation that will be signed by all parties prior to being accepted as a part of the transaction. Any discrepancy must be directed to the real estate agents for clarification. The closing agent is not responsible for explaining terms of the contract or interceding in disputes and should never become an arbitrator in a transaction dispute.

Interpleader action is a legal action brought by the closing agent to resolve a disagreement between the parties to the transaction. The courts will determine any disputes and clarify the terms as the law allows. Material facts of the transaction should be disclosed to the parties as soon as they are known; however, the closing agent should not offer an opinion as to the benefit or harm the material fact may cause the parties to the transaction. The pest inspection is an example of material information that is pertinent to the transaction as a report of material facts.

The pest inspection is provided to the closing agent by the pest inspection company. The closer will ensure that all concerned parties—the buyer, seller, agent, and lenders—receive a copy. The closer will then oversee the distribution of funds for any required work, as well as the payment of the report and any recommended repairs. It is not the closer's responsibility to give their opinion regarding any reported issues.

Similarly, it is unethical and not the job of the closer to pass a determination on the quality of the loan being obtained against the property.

NOTE

The closing agent/closer must remain neutral.

XYZ Escrow Company

LOAN ESCROW INSTRUCTIONS
(Institutional Lender)

To: XYZ Escrow Company

Date: **January 27, 2009**

File No.: 11-23456

Re: 508 West College Avenue   Los Angeles, California

Funds and/or Documents: Borrower has applied for a new Conventional loan in the amount of $277,000.00 with   Mortgage and will cause   "Escrow Holder") to be handed funds and/or documents required to close the above referenced escrow pursuant to Lender's Instructions. Borrower's signature on loan documents shall constitute Borrower's approval of the terms and conditions contained therein.

Showing title vested in: Samuel A. Smith and Sally A. Smith Husband and Wife as Joint Tenants

Proceeds: Borrower directs Escrow Holder to deliver the proceeds in the manner set forth in the Borrower Information Request form.

Escrow General Provisions: The parties acknowledge receipt of the Escrow General Provisions which are incorporated herein by reference.

BORROWER:

_____   _____

Samuel A. Smith   Sally A. Smith

Please indicate your forwarding address and phone number:

_____

_____

_____

Home Phone: _____

Cell Phone: _____

Work Phone: _____

We certify this to be a true and correct copy of the original.

Figure 38: Escrow Instructions

The **RESPONSIBILITIES** of each party to the transaction must be met to attain a successful escrow. The closer keeps a checklist of all duties that must be met to successfully complete the escrow. Certain portions of the closer's checklist will be the same on every file; however, every transaction is different and must be treated as such by ensuring that all details are addressed.

THE CLOSING AGENT'S RESPONSIBILITIES and transaction checklist will have the following basic needs plus others that are peculiar to the individual transaction:

_____Date of contract.

_____Date of opening escrow.

_____Scheduled closing date and time.

_____Order title report.

_____Buyer/Borrower (refi) info: full name and correct spelling, contact info, address.

_____Vesting for new title/deed.

_____Seller Info: full name and spelling, contact info, address.

_____Property address.

_____Purchase price.

_____Terms of contract.

_____Loan contingency, amount, and approval date.

_____Deposit amount and receipt.

_____Appraisal contingency and approval date.

_____All cash offer.

_____Pest inspection report and distribution.

_____Other reports: home inspection, mold test, and geological report.

_____Items remaining with property.

_____Passive or active removal of contingencies.

_____Additional conditions or terms.

_____Names and contact info for buyer's agent.

_____Names and contact info for seller's agent.

_____Prepare deeds: grant deed, quitclaim deed.

_____Seller to sign deed and documents.

_____Buyer to sign loan documents.

_____Record deed/mortgage.

_____Disperse funds.

_____Close file.

_____Calculate pro-rations such as taxes and rents.

The **SELLER'S RESPONSIBILITIES** consist of the following:

- Execute deed.
- Lease agreements if property is rented.
- Contact info for tenants if property is rented.
- Amount and proof of tenant's security deposit credited to buyer.
- Lender's info for mortgage payoff.
- HOA and Condo or PUD info and CC&Rs.
- Lien releases for mechanic's liens and any other debts showing on prelim.
- Subordination agreement if carrying second TD.
- Note for second TD.
- Pay for:
  - Reports and inspections as required per the terms of the contract.
  - Share of escrow fees.
  - Termite report, repairs, clearance.
  - Beneficiary statement.
  - Property taxes to close of escrow.
  - Maintain property in the condition determined by the terms of the contract.
  - All closing fees in a VA transaction.
  - Notary fees for seller's documentation.

The **BUYER'S RESPONSIBILITIES** consist of:

- Complete identification form.
- Sign escrow instructions.
- Deposit funds into escrow.
- Apply for loan.
- Order appraisal.
- Obtain homeowner's insurance.
- Review prelim.
- Review pest inspection report.
- Perform final walk-through inspection.
- Sign loan documents.
- Provide required closing costs in form of a cashier's check.

RECORD KEEPING

RECORD KEEPING must be efficient and accurate. All pertinent information—financial or otherwise—must be recorded immediately. Recording financial information is the highest priority. The closer is responsible for accurate record keeping regarding all financial elements of the transaction.

FEDERAL Closing Disclosure (CD) is a detailed disclosure of estimated closing costs that must be provided to the parties to the transaction. At the close of escrow, the *final CD* will provide the final accounting of all funds dispersed, per the terms of the contract, including the commissions paid the real estate agents and mortgage brokers. The CD must be as clear and concise as possible. Clarification of expenditures should include not only the amount but should clearly spell out the recipient of all funds. For example, the *CD* should not say: Real estate commissions, $12,000. The proper disclosure of disbursement of funds should show: RE Commissions ABC Realty, $6,000 and Joe's Realty, $6,000.

PRORATIONS are calculations of items that will be carried over to the Buyer whether as a cost or as an expense. These are called Date Items as they are calculated based on the Closing Date. Such items include Rent and Property Taxes. The Closing Agent must calculate the items based on the date the item was due and the date the Escrow will Close. Property Taxes are prorated according to the date of Closing. The Seller owes taxes up to the Close of Escrow and the Buyer will owe taxes from the day Escrow closes.

Unless otherwise agreed to in the contract for a date item, the seller is responsible up to the date that escrow closes and the buyer is responsible from that day onward. The closing agent will determine the date that escrow will close, then determine which party will be debited or credited for the item.

PROPERTY TAXES CALCULATIONS are based on the fiscal tax year, which is July 1 through the following June 30 in most states. If the escrow closes on June 30, the seller owes the entire previous year's property taxes, and the buyer will owe for the entire year following the close of escrow.

When counting calendar days, one cannot merely subtract the number 15 from 30 to arrive at 15. The 15th is also included for a total of 16 days. Escrow uses 364 days in a year and 30 days in a month unless instructed to do otherwise by the parties to the transaction.

Example: John is in escrow for the sale of his home. Escrow is scheduled to close on May 15. John has already paid his property taxes of $3,000 for the year.

The closing agent will calculate that buyer Linda must reimburse John the taxes that he has already paid for the period of the tax year that she will own the property, which is from May 15 through June 30. Remember that the buyer is responsible for the day of closing. Buyer Linda will owe John for 16 days in May and 30 days in June for a total of 46 days.

$3,000	*Annual Property Taxes*
÷ 364	*Days in Escrow year*
= $8.24	*Daily tax amount*
x 46	*Days owned by Linda*
=$379.12	*Property Taxes owed by Linda*

Buyer Linda will be charged $379.12 at close of escrow, which will be credited to John as reimbursement for property taxes he has already paid. If John had not paid his property taxes, the total amount of $3,000 would have been calculated by determining John's share:

364	*Days in the year*
− 46	*Days Linda owes*
= 318	*Days John owes*
x $8.24	*Daily tax amount*
= $2,620.32	*Taxes John owes*

*The closing agent would collect these amounts and forward the total property taxes collected to the county tax collector. The closer builds into the buyer's estimated closing costs a "pad" or "cushion," usually for a dollar amount of $300 to $500. This cushion is used to cover any miscalculations caused by escrow closing on a day different from the day that the estimates were based upon. **NOTE: This "cushion" is not allowable on the LE.***

RENT CALCULATIONS are calculated the same way, except that a 30-day base is used for calculations.

Example 1: John's property is rented, and he collected $1,000 rent on May 1. When Escrow closes on May 15, he will owe Linda rent from the 15th through the 30th.

$1,000	*Month rent collected*
÷ 30	*Days in an escrow month of 30 days not actual 31 days in May*
= $33.33	*Daily rent*
x 16	*Days owned by Linda*
= $533.33	*John owes Linda*

Example 2: John has not collected the rent on the first. Linda will collect the rent after the close of escrow. Linda will be charged the amount of rent that is owed to John for the period that John owned the property.

$1,000	*Month rent collected*
÷ 30	*Days in an Escrow month of 30 days not actual 31 days in May*
= $33.33	*Daily rent*
X 14	*Days owned by John*
=$466.62	*Linda owes John*

LENDER'S INSTRUCTIONS TO CLOSER

The **LENDER'S INSTRUCTIONS TO CLOSER** is part of the loan documents. They inform the closer of the terms of the loan and the lender's requirements. The lender's instructions provide the terms of the loan being obtained by the buyer/borrower, whether it is a purchase or refinance transaction. The costs accrued as a part of the loan are included in the instructions, including any rebate or premium that is paid back to the broker or borrower by the lender when obtaining a loan with a higher interest rate. The rebate can be credited towards the borrower's non-recurring closing costs or can be used to pay the mortgage broker or loan officer their commission or supplement the commission.

REBATES are used as a way to offset non-recurring closing costs including paying the loan agent. Lenders will only allow the rebate or seller paid closing costs to pay for a percentage of the loan amount usually not to exceed three percent. Some lenders will allow up to 6% of the loan amount to be paid by rebate or seller-paid closing costs. The lender will not allow any outside contribution to the buyer's closing costs to be applied to any fees other than non-recurring closing costs. Non-recurring costs are fees charged to the buyer/borrower for this transaction only. Typical non-recurring closing costs include:

- Appraisal fee
- Credit report
- Loan processing fee
- Mortgage broker or loan commission
- Lender's fees
- Underwriting
- Flood cert
- Tax service fee
- Doc drawing
- Wire transfer
- Escrow fees
- Notary fees
- Recording fee

The recurring fees that CANNOT be paid by outside contribution are:

- Interest
- Taxes
- Insurance

These items will be paid repeatedly and are not fees resulting from this loan transaction.

A person other than the borrower may sign loan docs if they have a properly prepared specific power of attorney. An attorney must have prepared the power of attorney for this particular transaction. A general power of attorney is rarely accepted.

CLOSING A REAL ESTATE TRANSACTION

CLOSING a real estate transaction involves several different duties or actions. The closer will receive the loan documents including the lender's instructions from the lender.

Once they have prepared the deeds and mortgage documents and all other pieces of documentation that will be included in the transaction, the closer will arrange meetings with the buyer and seller to sign the necessary items. The buyer or borrower for a refinance transaction will sign loan documents except in the case of a purchase transaction that will be all cash. The buyer is instructed on the amount of cash they need to close the transaction. The seller will sign the grant deed.

DRY FUNDING is the term used to describe the way escrows are closed in certain States. In a dry-funding state, the ink has had time to dry by the time escrow closes. In other words, several days pass from the time that the buyer/borrower signs the documents until it funds and escrow closes.

In a dry-funding state, the closer returns the loan documents to the lender and allows the lender 2- to 3- days to review the documents and to confirm that the buyer has brought their funds to the closer. The lender wires funds to the closer which constitutes funding. The closer prepares all the documentation to go to the county recorder's office to be recorded the day after funding, at which time the transaction closes.

WET FUNDING is a term used to describe the closing of a transaction when the ink has not had time to dry before the closing and the ownership transfers. Many states use the wet funding method, in which the parties to the transaction meet in one place, such as the office of the closer or attorney. All parties sign the required documentation, including deeds and loan documents. The funds change hands, and the transfer of ownership takes place. The buyer is handed the keys at this meeting, closing the transaction.

The borrower of an owner-occupied transaction still has a three-day right of rescission. If the borrower chooses to rescind, the funds are returned, and everything reverts to its original condition.

RESPA requires that the CD be given to the borrower at least one business day prior to the close of escrow. This requirement is fulfilled through the normal course of business with a dry-funding, but it is especially important that this be done in a wet- funding because the transaction closes at the signing/ meeting. Closing cannot occur until one business day after the borrower has received the CD, even if that occurs after the signing/meeting.

This is called a **complete escrow** because all conditions and contingencies have been met and the escrow is ready to close.

The day after funding, the title company representative is at the county recorder's office when it opens for business to record all of the documentation, such as deeds, prior to any other recordings that may affect the property, such as a mechanic's lien. The county recorder's office will time and date stamp all documentation. Depending on how busy the county recorder's office is, it may take into the afternoon to confirm the recording of the deeds. Escrow cannot close and ownership does not legally transfer until the county recorder's office has confirmed that the documentation has been recorded.

At this point the escrow is classified as a PERFECT ESCROW as it is now completed and closed.

DEEDS PREPARED BY TITLE

A GRANT DEED is a deed that is used to transfer, or grant, interest from the current property owner to others. This may be a new owner, as in a purchase transaction, or may involve granting a lien interest to a new lender, as in a refinance transaction. A grant deed must be prepared by the escrow officer and signed with loan documents. A new **grant deed** is prepared for all real estate transactions, even for a refinance transaction that will not change ownership but will change the lien holder's interest. The **grant deed** will include the information for a new owner of a purchase transaction and confirm the lien holder or lender for either a purchase or refinance transactions.

QUITCLAIM DEEDS are used to remove a party's interest in property ownership. The party signing the quitclaim deed is quitting any claim that they may have to the property. For example, a party could release their interest in another's property by quit claiming an easement. With a purchase transaction an escrow officer will prepare a **quitclaim deed** if the buyer is married, and the spouse will not be on the title or will not claim ownership of the property.

An officer will prepare a **quitclaim deed** if the buyer is married, and the spouse will not be on the title or will not claim ownership of the property. The non-buying spouse will sign the **quitclaim deed** when the buying spouse signs their loan documents. Some states are community property states, which means that any property purchased during marriage is owned by both spouses as community property.

A **lender** cannot provide a loan using real property as security unless all owners are on the loan. If a lender does provide such financing and the party that is on the loan dies, the loan is uncollectable from the remaining co-owners. A **quitclaim deed** eliminates the lending issue.

A **quitclaim deed** also relieves a purchasing spouse's obligation to the non-purchasing spouse. One spouse may choose to invest money in a property to be held separately from the spouse. A **quitclaim deed** will ensure that the property belongs to the investing spouse. When a couple divorces, one spouse will "quitclaim" their interest in the marital property. When divorcing, the releasing spouse needs to be aware that this does not release them from any loan obligations that they were a party to when financing the property.

Escrow may prepare a **quitclaim deed** for the current owner of a refinance transaction that is forfeiting ownership rights or any claim to the property. The purpose of the quit deed is to legally relinquish ownership of, or claim to, the property. The escrow officer should be notified as soon as the possibility is known.

TITLE SEARCH

A TITLE SEARCH is a search performed by the title insurance company to provide the **preliminary title report (prelim)**. The prelim provides a complete report of all information that is recorded with the county recorder's office against the subject property. The documents and terms will vary in different areas; however, the basic information is the same. See Figure 39, Preliminary Title Report.

The closing agent orders the PRELIM (Preliminary Title Report) and forwards it to the broker/ lender, along with instructions within a few days. When the prelim is received, the buyer, seller, and their agents should each review the contents of the prelim.

The BUYER and their agent want to ascertain that there are no items that will affect their interest in the property, such as when a neighbor's fence is over the property line and infringing on the subject property by several feet.

The SELLER and their agent need to review the prelim to be certain that there are no liens against the property that have previously been paid in full or are erroneous. It is common for previous mortgages to not be released or reconveyed once paid in full. Most refinance transactions performed through escrow have been removed because escrow provides the reconveyance deed to the lender to be paid and records the document at close of escrow. Occasionally, a reconveyance deed may be overlooked. In most cases, however, a lien that was not released was a private money loan in which the party who loaned funds was not aware of reconveyance deeds and did re-convey their interest back to the borrower once paid in full.

Another common error on a prelim occurs when a party owes child support. In many states, a district attorney will try to collect unpaid child support by filing a blanket claim against any property owned by everybody in the state with the same name as the perpetrator and will file the claim in every county of the state. This may be effective but will obviously result in a large number of erroneous claims. If the seller claims that they are not the person in question, the title company will contact the DA's office that filed the lien, and once the seller's Social Security number is compared against the perpetrator's, the lien will be released.

The **prelim** will be checked for seller's or borrower's name, vesting, property tax amount owed, the accurate and complete property address, and the legal description. If any of these items are incorrect, they must be corrected in other documentation, such as the escrow instructions or the appraisal if necessary.

The name and vesting of the current owner is usually found on the first page, with the address found on the **"note"** page at the end of the report. The property tax figures are found approximately three pages into the prelim.

FLAG POLICY is a shortened form of a prelim used for second trust deeds and VA refinance transactions and is less expensive. It is assumed that there has been little or no activity against the title if a flag policy is used.

NOTE

The prelim is assumed to be accurate, as this information is the same as what is recorded with the county recorder's office.

The **PROPERTY TAX** amount appears in the prelim as item #1 and shows the amount of taxes to be paid on the subject property. The tax amount is divided by two to determine the bi-annual payments for a refinance transaction. A monthly tax amount for qualifying purposes is derived by dividing the taxes by six (6 months).

The amount of property taxes for a purchase transaction will be different, as a new tax amount will be determined by the county tax assessor based on the purchase price of the property.

If there is an additional name appearing in the prelim as a current owner that is not a party to the transaction, the escrow officer will need to:

- **Add that person to the transaction** for a purchase by amending the contract or instructions. All owners must agree to and sign the purchase offer for the contract to be valid.
- **Complete a loan application** for a refinance transaction.
- **Prepare a quitclaim deed** for a refinance transaction.

The **prelim** will disclose any additional liens to be paid, including mechanic's liens, judgments, and mortgages; delinquent taxes; easements; and encumbrances.

Delinquent taxes must be brought current through escrow. In the case of a refinance transaction, the amount will be collected through the loan proceeds. The escrow officer will prepare the estimated *CD* to disclose to the borrower and the lender whether there will be sufficient loan proceeds to pay any delinquent taxes. A letter of explanation will be required from the borrower for any delinquent taxes or for any liens not disclosed.

ENCUMBRANCES will include such items as utilities crossing the property or roads and driveways crossing the property. A private road (easement) that is owned by a property owner but used by someone else to access their own property will require a *road maintenance agreement*. Request this document immediately from the property owner. Alternatively, escrow can order the document from the title officer. These items will not affect the loan, but the title company will insure against damage and loss due to these encumbrances.

A ROAD MAINTENANCE AGREEMENT is an agreement between property owners to share the responsibility of maintaining a shared road or driveway that crosses more than one property. The situation will occur when there are several adjoining properties and only one property has direct access to a main road or a public access. The buyer and the lender should review the document to confirm that the subject property does not have excessive responsibility or liability to the other property owners or adjoining properties.

TRUSTS OR CORPORATIONS are acceptable and common forms of property ownership. Few lenders will fund into a trust or a corporation because they are not individuals, and taking legal action, such as foreclosure, against them would be difficult for the lender. Lenders will require the owners to quitclaim from the trust or corporation to the individuals prior to funding. Once the loan has been funded and recorded, the owners/borrowers can, and usually do, grant deed ownership back into the trust. There are some lenders that will fund into a trust, but it is usually easier for the borrower, if they are willing, to change ownership. Some title companies will not insure a funding to a trust, so this must also be confirmed early in the process.

LOW INCOME ASSISTANCE PROGRAMS are sponsored by municipalities for the purpose of helping families buy homes. This i s generally done by assisting contractors with loans or other incentives to complete housing projects and new subdivisions. In exchange for help from the local government, the builder reserves a set number of homes for special assistance programs, usually in the form of municipal or county bonds which create the funds to loan the down payment. This agreement stays with the land and the entire project and will control the maximum value for resale purposes. This agreement becomes an attachment of sorts and is called **inclusionary zoning.**

TITLE INSURANCE

TITLE INSURANCE is insurance for the homeowners' protection against current and prior claims against the title or ownership of the property. The **title company** provides insurance on the property's title or guarantees that everything recorded with the county recorder's office is accurate and that all those on title or claiming a right to the property actually have that right. An information form is sent to the buyer prior to the close of escrow requesting complete information for the buyer covering a 10-year period.

This must be completed and returned to escrow prior to closing, as this assists the title company in verifying the rightful owner of the property. They also insure the rights of those who have a right to use the property, such as utility companies that have access across the property and all other easements.

When escrow is ready to close, the title company will provide a **title insurance policy** for both the seller and the buyer. The **seller's policy** insures against items occurring during their tenure as the owner of the property.

This also insures that the party that sold the property is the actual owner of the property and had the right to transfer title and receive the funds derived from the sale.

The **buyer's title insurance policy** insures that they have purchased a property free of any undisclosed encumbrances, liens, and that has good and sellable title.

TITLE INSURANCE COMPANIES are regulated by the various state insurance commissioners or other governing agencies. As insurance companies, they are regulated as such and are required to meet laws, rules, and regulations as required by the *insurance commissioner,* including retaining a title insurance surplus fund to guarantee the ability to pay any claims and to fulfill any needs of the insured. A title insurance policy and company are available to correct issues that may arise, such as:

- **Party claims ownership** that was not granted
- **Unpaid mechanic's liens**
- **Unpaid property taxes** by a previous owner

These are examples of issues that may arise in the future. The title company researches and reviews county records and documentation, including the closer's files to determine the legitimacy of any claim. Claims are either released by proving them invalid or correcting. Payment for items such as an overlooked mechanic's lien that was legally recorded is paid by either the title insurance or the escrow company if they were at fault. The property owner will not be liable for the debt.

Historically, the record of ownership and claims against a property were kept in a permanent record with the county recorder's office. Prior to the introduction of title insurance, a purchaser of real property wanted to know that they were purchasing a property with a good, marketable title, meaning that they wanted to know that they would be the legitimate owners of the property. In order to ensure this, a search of the history of the title needed to be performed. This was performed in several different ways and varied in different areas of the country. The following are some of the methods used for determining the chain of title. Some are still in use in some states.

The history of a property and its owners is known as the chain of title. The abstract of title provides the data, and the title insurance guarantees it.

ABSTRACT OF TITLE is a report that contains all recorded history of a specified property. The abstract of title is similar to reading a book, giving all the details from the time the property was recorded. The report is usually quite thick as the record will show all owners, transfers, liens, and building permits that may go back as far as the 1700s. An abstract company prepares the report or gathers the records. An attorney reviews the records and provides a lawyer's opinion of title, commenting on the apparent marketability of title.

This method provides a clear picture, and the buyer can be confident of the marketability of the title as is unlikely that anything is hidden. It should be noted, however, that fraud by a previous owner or person with an interest may not be as easily identifiable and there is no insurance or guarantee.

CERTIFICATE OF TITLE began to be used by abstract companies as a result of the records that they had accumulated. The filing systems had become so complete and accurate that abstract companies were able to research the history of the title and prepare a certificate of title without the need for an attorney's opinion. The abstract company certifies that the title is marketable. This certification also makes the abstract company liable for errors.

GUARANTEE OF TITLE was the result of the research and compilation of the records held by abstract companies. Abstract companies began to guarantee the title, functioning in much the same way as a title insurance company.

XYZ Title Company

Order Number: 11-23456

Title Officer:
Phone: (866)
Fax No.: (866)
E-Mail:

Escrow Officer:
Phone:
Fax No.:
E-Mail:

E-Mail Loan Documents to:
Borrower: Samuel A. Smith
Property: Sally A. Smith

PRELIMINARY REPORT

In response to the above referenced application for a policy of title insurance, this company hereby reports that it is prepared to issue, or cause to be issued, as of the date hereof, a Policy or Policies of Title Insurance describing the land and the estate or interest therein hereinafter set forth, insuring against loss which may be sustained by reason of any defect, lien or encumbrance not shown or referred to as an Exception below or not excluded from coverage pursuant to the printed Schedules, Conditions and Stipulations of said Policy forms.

The printed Exceptions and Exclusions from the coverage and Limitations on Covered Risks of said policy or policies are set forth in Exhibit A attached. *The policy to be issued may contain an arbitration clause. When the Amount of Insurance is less than that set forth in the arbitration clause, all arbitrable matters shall be arbitrated at the option of either the Company or the Insured as the exclusive remedy of the parties.* Limitations on Covered Risks applicable to the CLTA and ALTA Homeowner's Policies of Title Insurance which establish a Deductible Amount and a Maximum Dollar Limit of Liability for certain coverages are also set forth in Exhibit A. Copies of the policy forms should be read. They are available from the office which issued this report.

Please read the exceptions shown or referred to below and the exceptions and exclusions set forth in Exhibit A of this report carefully. The exceptions and exclusions are meant to provide you with notice of matters which are not covered under the terms of the title insurance policy and should be carefully considered.

It is important to note that this preliminary report is not a written representation as to the condition of title and may not list all liens, defects, and encumbrances affecting title to the land.

This report (and any supplements or amendments hereto) is issued solely for the purpose of facilitating the issuance of a policy of title insurance and no liability is assumed hereby. If it is desired that liability be assumed prior to the issuance of a policy of title insurance, a Binder or Commitment should be requested.

Figure 39: Preliminary Title Report
Page 1 of 7

Dated as of December 30, 2008 at 7:30 A.M.

The form of Policy of title insurance contemplated by this report is:

ALTA Loan Policy 1056.06 (6-17-06)

A specific request should be made if another form or additional coverage is desired.

Title to said estate or interest at the date hereof is vested in:

Samuel A. Smith and Sally A. Smith Husband and Wife as Joint Tenants :

The estate or interest in the land hereinafter described or referred to covered by this Report is:

A fee.

The Land referred to herein is described as follows:

(See attached Legal Description)

At the date hereof exceptions to coverage in addition to the printed Exceptions and Exclusions in said policy form would be as follows:

1. General and special taxes and assessments for the fiscal year 2009-2010, a lien not yet due (payable.

2. General and special taxes and assessments for the fiscal year 2008-2009.

First Installment:	$1,063.91, PAID
Penalty:	$0.00
Second Installment:	$1,063.91, PAYABLE
Penalty:	$0.00
Tax Rate Area:	05011
A. P. No.:	136-0-

3. The lien of supplemental taxes, if any, assessed pursuant to Chapter 3.5 commencing with Section 75 of the California Revenue and Taxation Code.

Figure 39: Preliminary Title Report
Page 2 of 7

4.   Covenants, conditions, restrictions and easements in the document recorded September 05, 1969 as Instrument No. 47251 in Book 3544, Page 480 of Official Records, but deleting any covenant, condition, or restriction indicating a preference, limitation or discrimination based on race, color, religion, sex, sexual orientation, marital status, ancestry, disability, handicap, familial status, national origin or source of income (as defined in California Government Code §12955(p)), to the extent such covenants, conditions or restrictions violate 42 U.S.C. §3604(c) or California Government Code §12955. Lawful restrictions under state and federal law on the age of occupants in senior housing or housing for older persons shall not be construed as restrictions based on familial status.

5.   An easement shown or dedicated on the Map as referred to in the legal description

       For: public utilities and incidental purposes.

6.   An easement for overhead and/or underground electrical supply systems, communication systems and incidental purposes, recorded October 21, 1969 as Book 3567, Page 332 of Official Records.
       In Favor of: Pacific Telephone and Telegraph Company
       Affects: The Southerly 6 feet and Easterly 2 feet of said land

7.   An easement for overhead and/or underground electrical supply systems, communication systems and incidental purposes, recorded as Book 3582, Page 559 of Official Records.
       In Favor of: Southern California Edison Company
       Affects: The Southerly 6 feet and Easterly 2 feet of said land

8.   Covenants, conditions, restrictions and easements in the document recorded as Book 3806, Page 783 of Official Records, but deleting any covenant, condition, or restriction indicating a preference, limitation or discrimination based on race, color, religion, sex, sexual orientation, marital status, ancestry, disability, handicap, familial status, national origin or source of income (as defined in California Government Code §12955(p)), to the extent such covenants, conditions or restrictions violate 42 U.S.C. §3604(c) or California Government Code §12955. Lawful restrictions under state and federal law on the age of occupants in senior housing or housing for older persons shall not be construed as restrictions based on familial status.

9.   A Deed of Trust to secure an original indebtedness of $179,500.00 recorded July 06, 2006 as Instrument No. 06-   Official Records.
       Dated: June 22, 2006
       Trustor: **Samuel A. Smith and Sally A. Smith**

       Trustee: Fidelity National Title Company
       Beneficiary: Mortgage Electronic Registration Systems, Inc., as nominee for
       Lender: First Magnus Financial Corporation, an Arizona Corporation

10.   A declaration of homestead executed by   recorded January 23, 2007 as Instrument No. 07-   of Official Records.

Figure 39: Preliminary Title Report.
Page 3 of 7

Order Number: 11-23456
Page Number: 4

INFORMATIONAL NOTES

Note: The policy to be issued may contain an arbitration clause. When the Amount of Insurance is less than the certain dollar amount set forth in any applicable arbitration clause, all arbitrable matters shall be arbitrated at the option of either the Company or the Insured as the exclusive remedy of the parties. If you desire to review the terms of the policy, including any arbitration clause that may be included, contact the office that issued this Commitment or Report to obtain a sample of the policy jacket for the policy that is to be issued in connection with your transaction.

The map attached, if any, may or may not be a survey of the land depicted hereon. First American expressly disclaims any liability for loss or damage which may result from reliance on this map except to the extent coverage for such loss or damage is expressly provided by the terms and provisions of the title insurance policy, if any, to which this map is attached.

1.   This report is preparatory to the issuance of an ALTA Loan Policy. We have no knowledge of any fact which would preclude the issuance of the policy with CLTA endorsement forms 100 and 116 and if applicable, 115 and 116.2 attached.

     When issued, the CLTA endorsement form 116 or 116.2, if applicable will reference a(n) Single Family Residence known as 508 West College Avenue Los Angeles, California

2.   According to the public records, there has been no conveyance of the land within a period of twenty-four months prior to the date of this report, except as follows:

     None

Figure 39: Preliminary Title Report.
Page 4 of 7

WIRE INSTRUCTIONS
for

XYZ Title
Company

ABA 122
Credit to
Account No. 300

Reference Escrow Order Number 11-23456   and Escrow Officer.

Please wire the day before recording. Also, notify the Escrow Officer of your intent to wi

Funds for other loans being insured by *XYZ Title Company*   must not be combin
into one wire or funds may be returned.

Figure 39: Preliminary Title Report.
Page 5 of 7

Order Number: 11-23456
Page Number: 6

LEGAL DESCRIPTION

Real property in the City of Los Angeles County of Los Angeles State of California, described as follows:

LOT 7 . TRACT NO. 19 AS PER MAP RECORDED IN BOOK 53, PAGES 1 THROUGH 5 OF MAPS, IN THE OFFICE OF THE COUNTY RECORDER OF VENTURA COUNTY STATE OF CALIFORNIA.

APN: 136-0-

Figure 39: Preliminary Title Report.
Page 6 of 7

Chapter 15

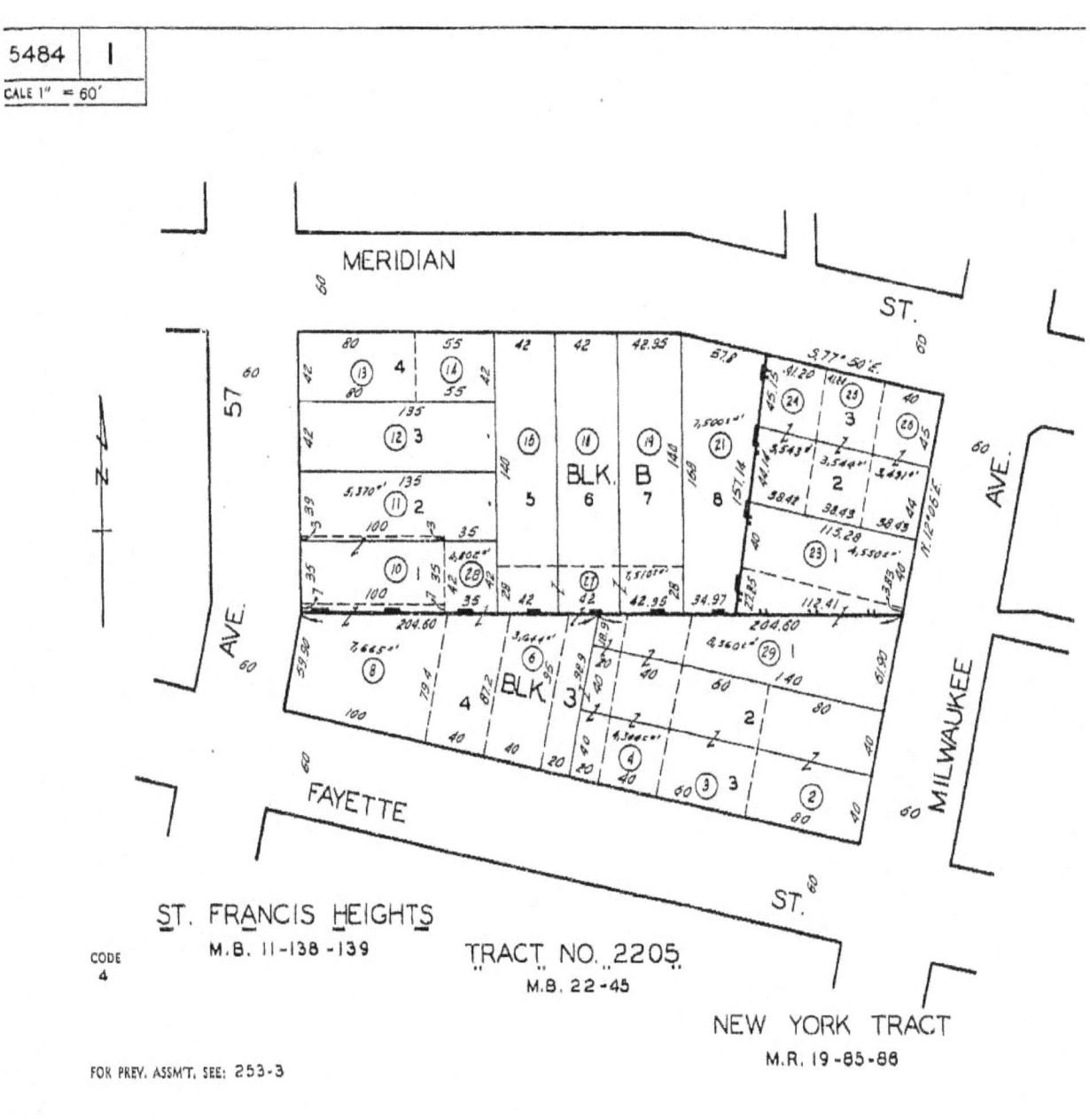

Figure 39: Preliminary Title Report
Page 7 of 7

15-27

TITLE INSURANCE was the ultimate step in the process of verifying and guaranteeing that title to a property was marketable. Several attorneys in Chicago, Illinois, created the first title insurance company and worked closely with abstract companies that continued to research the records. Title companies have assumed the role of abstract companies in most parts of the country.

The OWNER'S TITLE POLICY is the standard policy of title insurance. The policy assumes that the purchaser of real property has had the opportunity to inspect the property and reasonably determine the proper use and condition of it, as well as the apparent ownership. The owner's policy insures the property owner against:

- Matters of record
- Forgery and fraud
- Lack of capacity
- Improper delivery
- Legal description
- Encumbrances

AMERICAN LAND TITLE ASSOCIATION (ALTA) is an extended insurance coverage policy. This policy is most often used for the benefit of the lender and is rarely used when there is no mortgage against the property. The ALTA allows the lender to inspect the property; however, that is rarely possible as the lender is probably some distance from the property. The assumption of property inspection was implemented as part of the insurance process during a time when mortgages were commonly obtained through local banks, which conducted property inspections. Because this changed so dramatically from the mid-to late twentieth century, the lender will now require the extended policy, as it insures the following:

- Unrecorded easements.
- Unrecorded liens.
- Mining claims.
- Water rights.
- Rights or claims of persons in possession.
- Reservations.
- Survey claims.
- Forgeries occurring after the issuance of the policy.
- Removal of a structure for lack of building permits or violation.

The ALTA policy will not cover any title defects that are known to the buyer of real property at the time of the purchase.

Neither the owner's policy nor the ALTA will insure against zoning changes or any affect that a zoning change has on real property.

Fees charged for a title Insurance policy must be posted and available to the public and will be charged as one fee. The cost of a title insurance policy can be negotiated as part of the purchase offer; however, the buyer usually pays for the ALTA policy, as it benefits them and is required by their lender. The payment or the owner's policy is commonly negotiated between buyer and seller. The manner in which this negotiation is handled varies in different communities.

NOTE

It is illegal for a title company to pay a referral fee to any party in exchange for business or for the purpose of generating business in the future.

www.ingramcontent.com/pod-product-compliance
Lightning Source LLC
Chambersburg PA
CBHW081527120626
46550CB00009B/2636

* 9 7 8 1 9 6 7 3 0 0 0 5 1 *